WITHDRAWN

DATE DUE

APR 14 '89	NOV 25 '96		
APR 23 '91	APR 27 '97		
JUN 8 '92	NOV 21 '97		
JUL 12 '94	MAR 11 2002		
DEC 10 '95			
Jan3			
FEB 27 '96			

Handbook
of Learning and
Cognitive Processes

Volume 3

Approaches to
Human Learning and Motivation

Handbook
of Learning and
Cognitive Processes

Volume 3

Approaches to
Human Learning
and Motivation

EDITED BY

W. K. ESTES

Rockefeller University

LAWRENCE ERLBAUM ASSOCIATES, PUBLISHERS
1976   Hillsdale, New Jersey

DISTRIBUTED BY THE HALSTED PRESS DIVISION OF

JOHN WILEY & SONS

New York   Toronto   London   Sydney

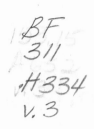

Copyright © 1976 by Lawrence Erlbaum Associates, Inc.
All rights reserved. No part of this book may be reproduced in
any form, by photostat, microform, retrieval system, or any other
means, without the prior written permission of the publisher.

Lawrence Erlbaum Associates, Inc., Publishers
62 Maria Drive
Hillsdale, New Jersey 07642

Distributed solely by Halsted Press Division
John Wiley & Sons, Inc., New York

Library of Congress Cataloging in Publication Data
Main entry under title:

Approaches to human learning and motivation.

  (Handbook of learning and cognitive processes;
v.3)
  Includes bibliographical references and indexes.
  1. Learning, Psychology of —Addresses, essays,
lectures. 2. Motivation in education—Addresses,
essays, lectures. I. Estes, William Kaye.
BF311.H334 vol. 3 [LB1055]   153.1'5'08s
ISBN 0-470-15121-8 [153.1'5]   76-15010
Printed in the United States of America

Contents

Foreword

This volume is the third in a series that spans the principal areas of research in learning and cognitive processes. Our plan is to provide an organized picture of the state of the field that will be up to date with regard to theoretical and technical developments for purposes of investigators and students of cognitive psychology and yet sufficiently self-contained to be readable for anyone with a reasonable scientific background, regardless of his acquaintance with the technical vocabulary of particular specialties. Our first emphasis has been to present the major concepts, theories, and methods with which one should be familiar in order to be able to follow the progress of research, or to participate in research in any of the various facets of cognitive psychology. In addition, each of the authors has taken on the responsibility of giving attention wherever possible to the orienting attitudes and long-term goals that tend to shape the overall course of research and of bringing out both points of potential practical application of findings and implications with respect to interactions with other disciplines.

In Volume 1, we presented an overview of the field and introduced principal theoretical and methodological issues that persistently recur in the expanded treatment of specific research areas which comprise the later volumes. The areas traditionally associated with conditioning, learning theory, and the basic psychology of human learning are treated in Volumes 2 and 3. The last three volumes will range over presently active lines of research having to do with human cognitive processes: Volume 4, attention, memory storage and retrieval; Volumes 5 and 6, information processing, reading, semantic memory, and problem solving. The organization by volumes is necessarily somewhat arbitrary, but so far as possible, the lines of demarcation have been drawn with respect to theory rather than tradition. Thus, for example, developmental approaches and practical applications are represented by chapters or sections in several volumes rather than being collected as units.

The overall plan of the handbook has been presented more fully in the foreword and introduction to Volume 1.

W. K. ESTES

Introduction to Volume 3

W. K. Estes

The lines of classification dividing this volume from the one that precedes and the one that follows in the Handbook series are somewhat arbitrary, but nonetheless reflect at least an element of rationality. Overall, the sequence from Volume 2 through Volume 6 exhibits a trend from treatments of learning and motivation to treatments of memory, from concern with the adjustment of the whole organism in its environment to concern with progressively more abstract aspects of cognitive organization and function. In this volume, we shall deal primarily with conditions of acquisition, retention, and forgetting, and the manner in which acquired information and motivation combine to determine performance.

The organization of Volume 3 can be understood in terms of four principal categories. The first category deals with general problems of methodology, the second and third with basic concepts arising from research on human learning and performance, and the fourth with applications:

1. In Chapters 1 and 2, Postman treats the methods basic to research in adult human learning, retention, and transfer, Rohwer the methods and research designs bearing on the study of individual differences in both age and ability.

2. In Chapters 3–5, Ross and Ross, Medin, and Myers, respectively, review conditioning, discrimination, and probability learning. In each case, consideration of traditional approaches is combined with emphasis on cognitive interpretations.

3. In Chapters 6–8, Nelson, Nuttin, and Weiner treat respectively reinforcement and its basis in memory, reinforcement in relation to motivation and goal-directed activities, and cognitive aspects of motivation.

4. In Chapter 9, Buchwald discusses the bearing of research and theory on human problems, with primary reference to psychopathology.

METHODOLOGY

By methodology we refer not to expertise in wiring up memory drums, but rather to ways of solving the problems of controlling experimental comparisons and interpreting data that are necessary to move from empirical exploration toward general principles, from limited facts toward theory.

Advances in theory depend on advances in methods, and in the area of human learning and memory, these have been so extensive during the past ten years that we have found it necessary to treat them in separate chapters in Volumes 3 and 4 of the Handbook. The consideration of methodology in the present volume is oriented around the distinction between learning and memory, the problems of experimentally distinguishing and measuring logically separable aspects of these processes, and the special problems attendant on research involving individual or developmental differences as major variables.

As Postman makes clear in Chapter 1 of this volume, learning and memory can be operationally distinguished in terms of the researcher's primary focus on the increment to performance added by a training trial in the former case as compared to the change in performance occurring over an interval between trials in the latter case. As I have indicated elsewhere (Volume 1, Chapter 1), I think that the distinction goes deeper, the term *learning* referring primarily to the organism's adjustment to a given set of circumstances as a consequence of experience, and *memory* to a more abstract conception of the changes in the organism's state of information as a consequence either of experience or time.

In any event, there is no doubt but that the point of emphasis in the literature of cognitive psychology, broadly defined, has shifted from learning toward memory in recent years. A consequence, or concomitant, of this shift has been the revival of the concept of *memory trace,* which has largely taken over the overworked role of *association* or *connection* as a basic conceptual unit. The consequences are far reaching, for the principal focus of research strategy has naturally, if not inevitably, shifted from that of characterizing the changes in strengths of associations or connections during acquisition and retention to that of identifying and analyzing the stages of encoding, maintenance, and retrieval of information from memory traces. Here we encounter a mine field of new methodological problems and traps. As Postman brings out clearly, there is no obvious or easy way of experimentally separating the processes of encoding, maintainance, and retrieval since all are implicated in every situation in which we can measure acquisition or retention of information. Perhaps the most direct approach is to look for variables having effects specific to one stage. This strategy is one of the most popular in the current literature, but it carries no guarantee of success, and, as Postman shows, the most obvious approaches do not withstand critical analysis.

Some of the methodological problems are perplexing enough that even the best-qualified investigators may find themselves unable to reach agreement concerning the direction in which we might find solutions. Take the currently much-studied problem of determining whether information stored in memory spontaneously decays as a function of time. Following a meticulous examination of the research literature, Postman finds a lack of any firm empirical support for a conception of decay, and consequently argues that it is not feasible to attempt to build models for memory which include such an assumption. But in Volume 4 we will find that Wickelgren is engaged in building just such a model and believes both that the approach is feasible and that the model is testable. Which is right?

I think that on consideration of this and other examples, the student may conclude that the truth lies, not between, but perhaps in a sense above these two lines of argument. Just as one cannot test significance of group differences in experimental data without assuming that the assumptions of a statistical model (such as the analysis of variance model) are satisfied, one cannot test hypotheses concerning decay of information except by presupposing the validity of the assumptions of a model for memory in which the hypothesis is embedded. But if one cannot validate the model without knowing whether the hypothesis is true and cannot test the hypothesis without presupposing the model, how does one make progress?

I think that in practice one proceeds by a stepwise procedure. First, one gains some support for the model and the degree to which predictions are sensitive to perturbations of particular assumptions, just as one may gain some information as to applicability of an analysis of variance model by looking at frequency distributions of measures and conducting sampling studies. Then one interprets a new experiment involving the test of a specific hypothesis within the framework of the model. If the result seems enlightening, one then reevaluates both the model and the state of knowledge concerning the phenomena at issue with the new result added, and adjusts the model if necessary.

When the time comes to evaluate another hypothesis, one embeds the test procedure, not in the original model, but in the model as reassessed and possibly revised in the light of the intervening experience. A major implication of this analysis is that one cannot expect anything theoretically significant to come from the one-shot attempts to test hypotheses, whether they have to do with decay from memory storage or any other hypothetical process. Progress comes only from continuing interplay of theory and experiment.

A methodological development that has been a long time in coming is the appearance of some sign of integration of research on individual and age differences into the general psychology of learning and memory. The lack of such integration has long been mourned by critics (for example, Melton, 1967), but a major break in the cross-sectional bias of investigators of learning was slow to appear. Now that developmental research is becoming fashionable, there is need for criticism to be directed equally cogently at the way in which it is accomplished. As indicated by Medin and Cole (Volume 1, Chapter 4), it does not suffice just to look at differences between individuals or differences in ages. What is required is a theoretically oriented research strategy, sketched by Medin and Cole, and followed up in the present volume by Rohwer (Chapter 2) with detailed illustrations of some major recurring problems of interpretation and types of research tactics that have been evolving to deal with them.

CONCEPTIONS OF LEARNING AND MEMORY

The distinction between the concepts of human learning as treated in this volume and human memory as treated in Volumes 4 and 5 corresponds to a substantial shift in both methods and concepts during the past decade. Until the early 1960s the overall organization of the field of human learning had not changed greatly over that laid down by Thorndike and the "functionalists," for example, Carr, McGeoch, and Woodworth during the first few decades of this century (Hilgard, 1948; Hilgard & Bower, 1966). This organization was crystallized in the first highly influential textbook on human learning (McGeoch, 1942).

The entire conceptual structure was shaped by the overriding view of learning as improvement in task performance—that is, progress, measured by speed or reduction of errors, toward meeting some criterion of success, whether the task was acquisition of a motor skill, the learning of a maze pathway, the mastery of a list of verbal items, or the memorization of poetry. As a natural consequence, conditions of efficiency had first priority in research. Textbooks for twenty years following that of McGeoch had much the same chapter headings, with major attention to spaced versus distributed practice, whole versus part learning, factors in proactive and retroactive inhibition. Retention and transfer were conceived largely in terms of the central problem for education—the prediction of the ways in which training will carry over to new situations. Theory was strictly cross sectional with regard to age and developmental levels, with individual differences being vaguely consigned to variation in capacities or differences in knowledge and skill arising from variation in opportunities to learn. The discipline was relatively encapsulated, having little interaction with other lines of research and theory in or out of psychology.

Following a decade of almost explosive transition, associated with the impacts of inputs from linguistics, communication theory, mathematical models, and the rise of computer-based information-processing systems, the study of human learning and memory presents a drastic change both with respect to surface appearance and deeper organization. The approach to human learning by way of an extension of principles of animal learning to human behavior has given way to a broader view of human learning as one aspect of the actively developing field of cognitive psychology. The major emphasis tends increasingly to be centered on the question of what is learned rather than on how performance changes, on how information is transformed and organized in memory rather than on the conditions of retention of lists of items. The currently flourishing lines of research on short-term memory, coding processes, semantic memory, and other aspects of information processing will be the subject of detailed treatment in later volumes of this Handbook.

CLASSICAL CONCEPTS AND CONTINUITY

It would be a mistake, however, to be completely carried away with enthusiasm for new methods and models. The relevance of learning and cognitive psychology to practical affairs still depends to an important extent on the body of methodology and knowledge that has accumulated in the tradition of Thorndike and the functional psychologists. The current emphasis on man as an information processing system has been salutory, but a by-product of this change in frame of reference is a tendency to lose sight of the relationship between cognition and action, the role of intellectual functioning in the total economy of the organism. In this present volume, the relationships of memory and cognition to motivation and behavioral adjustment are a primary focus of attention.

Although there is a shift of emphasis from animals to man between Volumes 2 and 3 of the Handbook, there is also substantial concern for continuity. Students of animal learning have heard to the point of tedium that we do research on animal learning, for the most part, in order to better understand human behavior. That aim is certainly worthy, but it is not enough to have research on animal learning pursued as a self-contained specialty with occasional speculative applications of the results to everyday human problems. We need, rather, hard evidence regarding the extent to which ideas emerging from animal research enter into research and theory at the human level. Several of the authors in this volume are among those who have thought most deeply about this problem and thus are in a position to assess the extent to which research at the two phylogenetic levels has begun to mesh and yield progress toward a common body of theory.

Human learning as treated in this volume represents a mixture of old and new concepts. Such terms as conditioning, extinction, and reinforcement are no longer the most fashionable in dealing with human learning, but, nonetheless, they refer to mechanisms and processes that have had a great deal of study in a variety of contexts. They provide points of continuity between animal and human learning and, within the latter, between biological and social frames of reference. Although these terms have had long histories of association with certain rather stereotyped experimental paradigms, the concepts they represent manifest considerable vitality and adaptability to new intellectual circumstances. Thus, in this volume, Ross and Ross (Chapter 3) give major attention to changing views of conditioning that bring out interactions with other aspects of cognitive functioning. Again Medin (Chapter 4) and Nelson (Chapter 6) emphasize continuity between animal and man with regard to mechanisms of reinforcement and discrimination, although at the same time offering reinterpretations of both in terms of contemporary concepts of memory and information processing.

The continuing use of familiar terms sometimes tends to mask changes in concepts. Consider, for example, *reinforcement,* still a workhouse in the experimental literature at the human as well as animal level, although out of favor among theoretical writers. The once dominant conception of reinforcement in terms of the essentially automatic and mechanical strengthening or stamping in of associations by satisfying aftereffects has all but faded from the scene. Currently we see convergence on a conception of the human learner acquiring information regarding relationships between choices and outcomes, then in choice situations scanning available alternatives, generating expectations on the basis of memory for previous experiences, and selecting actions in accord with expectations.

Since its initial popularization by Tolman (1932, 1938), the concept of expectation, or *expectancy* has seemed to offer promise as an antidote to overly mechanical views of reinforcement. But the concept has lacked specificity, and even in the more formal elaborations (for example, Seligman & Johnston, 1973), it has not been clear how an expectation on the part of a learner differs from a memory with respect to the previous outcome of a choice situation. Some clarification has finally begun to emerge from the researches of Nuttin (1953) and related, more recent work (Estes, 1972). Whereas memory for an aftereffect involves only the storage and retrieval of information regarding the relation between a specific alternative and a rewarding or punishing outcome, an expectation includes also information bearing on the likelihood that the same relationship will obtain in the future in either the same or similar contexts.

The principal theoretical advance from the somewhat speculative proposals of Tolman to the literature of the past decade is that we have begun to recognize the futility of debating the alternative merits of broad systematic approaches, as, for example, reinforcement versus expectancy theory. To interpret specific phenomena and to predict behavior in specific types of situations, we need to know not only the type of process responsible but the details. Just how is information regarding outcomes of past choices organized in memory? Just how is information retrieved and brought to bear on response selection in new situations? A picture of how we stand with regard to these important specifics is developed by Nelson in Chapter 6 of this volume.

Nearly as ubiquitous as reinforcement in the past literature of learning and behavior theory has been the concept of discrimination. Here again there has been a major restructuring of the dominant theoretical viewpoint. Discrimination, as it appears either in or out of the laboratory, is inherently more complex than simple conditioning or motor learning. Consequently, it was natural for the emphasis in earlier theoretical work to be upon analysis, with special attention to the possibilities of reducing discrimination to simpler concepts of reinforcement and extinction. The idea that discrimination might be conceived solely in those terms was explored vigorously in the classic works of Hull (1945) and Spence (1937), and even the literature on human learning up to about 1960 was organized to a major extent in terms of the extension of the conditioning-extinction model to various types of verbal learning of both children and adults. Medin's chapter in this volume portrays the transition from the conditioning model to the currently more influential view of discrimination as a multistage process in which selective attention plays as important a role as presumably more basic processes of association.

A great part of human learning outside of the laboratory involves adjusting to environmental uncertainties, hence the long-standing research interest in probability learning. Here again we have witnessed during the past few years a major shift in emphasis. Much of the research on probability learning that followed upon the pioneering studies of Humphreys (1939) was cast within the framework of conditioning and reinforcement theory. A substantial amount of work carried out within this frame of reference led to a body of theory that accounted quite well for some details of acquisition and permitted an account of the frequently observed phenomenon of probability matching (Estes, 1964), but it gradually became clear that the capabilities of adult human learners for coping with the intricacies of probabilistic event schedules could not be encompassed in terms of the concepts of conditioning, at least as we now understand them. More recent work has branched off in two principal directions. In one of these the emphasis has been on decision processes (Lee, 1971), in the other on processes of information storage and retrieval (Estes, 1976). Myers, in this volume (Chapter 5), traces these developments and shows how they relate to newer lines of research on higher order structure in sequence learning.

COGNITION AND MOTIVATION

Progress in bringing cognitive psychology to bear on problems of human adjustment requires not only increasingly sophisticated concepts and theories of memory, but also commensurate advances in our understanding of motivation and choice. The substantial imbalance that has characterized the research literature meets some corrective influences in the approach of Nuttin (Chapter 7). With his conception of open and closed tasks, Nuttin has begun to show how the sometimes apparently capricious effects of various rewarding and punishing events on human learning can be understood in terms of relations between the learner's task and his motivational system. In a similar vein, Weiner in Chapter 8 reviews the contribution of several lines of investigation, including those associated with expectancy and attribution theory, that bear on the ways in which cognition and motivation jointly influence human performance.

APPLICATIONS OF LEARNING THEORY

Over the past half century there have been two main areas of application of learning theory to practical problems. The first, historically, is education, with a substantial literature running from the pioneering work of Thorndike (1913) to the recent studies of Atkinson (1972, 1974) and Suppes (1974). Applications to education will be found to be a recurring motif in the presentations of many of the Handbook authors, beginning with Medin and Cole and Hunt and Lansman in Volume 1, and will receive more concentrated attention in later volumes.

The second area is psychotherapy, first brought within the province of cognitive psychology by Dollard and Miller's (1950) integration of the approaches of psychoanalysis and learning theory and more recently cultivated via approaches oriented around conditioning, behavior modification, and social learning theory (Kanfer & Phillips, 1970; Krasner & Ullman, 1965). Of these two main types of applications, the second fits the more naturally into this volume and is the subject of Buchwald's article on learning theory and psychopathology (Chapter 9).

It should be noted that only one aspect of psychopathology receives extensive treatment in this volume—namely, research explicitly aimed at the development and evaluation of therapeutic methods. A great deal of additional research has been motivated at least in part by concern for the possibilities of deepening our understanding of behavior problems at a more theoretical level and for possibilities of long-term contributions to the theories and concepts underlying therapeutic methods. These motifs involve too wide a range of ideas and methods to be brought together within a single chapter, but they will be found to enter importantly into the orientations and research strategies presented in many chapters of this Handbook.

REFERENCES

Atkinson, R. C. Ingredients for a theory of instruction. *American Psychologist,* 1972, **27,** 921–932. Republished in M. C. Wittrock (Ed.), *Changing education: Alternatives from educational research.* Englewood Cliffs, New Jersey: Prentice-Hall, 1973.

Atkinson, R. C. Teaching children to read using a computer. *American Psychologist,* 1974, **29,** 169–178.

Dollard, J., & Miller, N. E. *Personality and psychotherapy.* New York: McGraw-Hill, 1950.

Estes, W. K. Probability learning. In A. W. Melton (Ed.), *Categories of human learning.* New York: Academic Press, 1964. Pp. 89–128.

Estes, W. K. Reinforcement in human behavior. *American Scientist,* 1972, **60,** 723–729.

Estes, W. K. The cognitive side of probability learning. *Psychological Review,* 1976, **83,** 37–64.

Hilgard, E. R. *Theories of learning.* New York: Appleton-Century-Crofts, 1948.

Hilgard, E. R., & Bower, G. H. *Theories of learning.* (3rd ed.) New York: Appleton-Century-Crofts, 1966.

Hull, C. L. The discrimination of stimulus configurations and the hypothesis of afferent neural interactions. *Psychological Review,* 1945, **52,** 133–142.

Humphreys, L. G. Acquisition and extinction of verbal expectations in situations analogous to conditioning. *Journal of Experimental Psychology,* 1939, **25,** 294–301.

Kanfer, F. H., & Phillips, S. *Learning foundations of behavior therapy.* New York: John Wiley & Sons, 1970.

Krasner, L., & Ullman, L. P. *Research in behavior modification.* New York: Holt, Rinehart, & Winston, 1965.

Lee, W. *Decision theory and human behavior.* New York: John Wiley & Sons, 1971.

McGeoch, J. A. *The psychology of human learning.* New York: Longmans, Green, 1942.

Melton, A. W. Individual differences and theoretical process variables. In R. M. Gagné (Ed.), *Learning and individual differences.* Columbus, Ohio: Merrill, 1967. Pp. 238–252.

Nuttin, J. *Tâche, réussite, et éche.* Louvain, Belgium: Publications Universitaires, 1953.

Seligman, M. E. P., & Johnston, J. C. A cognitive theory of avoidance learning. In F. J. McGuigan & D. B. Lumsden (Eds.), *Contemporary approaches to conditioning and learning.* New York: John Wiley & Sons, 1973.

Spence, K. W. The differential response in animals to stimuli varying within a single dimension. *Psychological Review,* 1937, **44,** 430–444.

Suppes, P. The place of theory in educational research. *Educational Researcher,* 1974, **3,** 3–10.

Thorndike, E. L. *The psychology of learning. Educational psychology.* Vol. 2. New York: Teachers College, 1913.

Tolman, E. C. *Purposive behavior in animals and men.* New York: Appleton-Century-Crofts, 1932.

Tolman, E. C. The determiners of behavior at a choice point. *Psychological Review,* 1938, **45,** 1–45.

1

Methodology of Human Learning

Leo Postman

University of California, Berkeley

One of the fields conventionally listed in taxonomies of psychological research is "human learning and memory." This designation implies the existence of separate but related domains of inquiry—acquisition or learning on the one hand and retention or memory on the other. Since the two are invariably linked, both in theory and in experimental practice, why do the separate labels continue to be retained? The primary reason is that one cannot avoid making a distinction between learning and memory on abstract theoretical grounds. The distinction has also remained pragmatically useful in the classification of experimental procedures and the organization of empirical findings. No operations, however, have been devised that permit fully independent measurements of the two processes. Hence, the methodologies and the explanatory concepts of the domains of learning and memory have always been inextricably interwoven; they have become increasingly so in recent years. In order to focus on the problems considered in this chapter it is useful to begin with a brief discussion of the rationale of the distinction between learning and memory.

I. THE DISTINCTION BETWEEN LEARNING AND MEMORY

A. Acquisition and Retention

A differentiation between acquisition and retention, or an equivalent distinction, appears to be logically required. As Mc Geoch (1942) put it succinctly a long time ago, "An act must be fixated before it can be retained [p. 4]." More recently, Melton (1963) made the same point in more precise terms. Our basic experimental observations are changes in performance from Trial n to Trial $n + 1$. Whenever such changes occur, they must be taken to be the result of three theoretically separable but functionally confounded events, namely (a) trace formation, (b) trace storage, and (c) trace utilization. (The concept of trace is used here as an hypothetical construct, with no specific physiological connotations, to refer to the representation of input events in the nervous system.) When one speaks of encoding, storage, and retrieval, the postulated sequence of events is, of course, exactly the same.

Within this descriptive framework we can consider the difference between acquisition and retention in three different ways:

1. If one equates trace formation with acquisition, and storage and trace utilization with retention, it follows logically that acquisition must precede retention.

2. One can make an essentially arbitrary operational distinction between studies of learning and of memory in terms of the independent variables to which changes in performance are related. This is the conventional definition articulated by Melton. Changes from Trial n to Trial $n + 1$ are taken to index learning "when the variable of interest is the ordinal number of Trial n." On the other hand, the changes are used to assess retention "when the variable of interest is the interval, and the events during the interval, between Trial n and Trial $n + 1$" (Melton, 1963, p. 3).

3. Given this conventional definition, one can inquire into the relationship between measures of learning and of retention. When that is done, it becomes readily apparent that independent measurement of the logically separable processes is not possible.

Inferences about trace formation must of necessity be based on observations of trace utilization. We cannot know that learning has occurred except by measuring retention after some arbitrarily chosen interval. We typically chart the progress of learning by repeatedly administering tests of retention after a constant interval. The learning curve rises over trials not only because new traces are formed but also because there is an increasing number of traces that persist between input and output. This state of affairs has, of course, been recognized for a long time. To quote McGeoch (1942) again, "A curve of learning represents a progressively greater balance in favor of retention, so that it is, in part a retention curve [p. 4]." On the assumption that a single input is always sufficient for trace formation, one can carry the argument further and equate learning with increased resistance to forgetting (Murdock, 1974, p. 12).

If tests of learning are inevitably measurements of retention, it is equally true that an evaluation of retention scores on Trial $n + 1$ requires an independent assessment of the degree of learning that existed at the end of

Trial n. Unless one can specify the condition of the system at the end of Trial n, there is no way of drawing inferences about the effects of the events that presumably occur during the period of storage and at the time of retrieval. The pragmatic resolution of this dilemma again must take the form of an arbitrary convention. Degree of learning at the end of Trial n is defined in terms of performance on an immediate test of retention, and losses after longer intervals are then referred to this baseline. What is required, then, is the determination of a difference between an immediate and a delayed test if appropriate conclusions are to be drawn about processes subsequent to trace formation. While the logic of measurement is straightforward, we shall see that it has proved quite difficult in practice to implement it by procedures that are free of bias.

B.   Analysis of Trace Utilization

The definitions of learning changes and of retention changes proposed by Melton include the implicit assumption that the characteristics of the material and the nature of the subject's task remain constant between Trial n and Trial $n + 1$. Systematic manipulation of the latter variables between trials constitute the defining operations of a study of transfer, that is, "the availability and utilization of the memorial products of Trial n in a 'different' situation" (Melton, 1963, p. 3). This criterion for delimiting the domain of transfer studies requires further examination in the light of current experimental practice. Much of the work on memory today is concerned not only with the examination of progressive changes in storage but also with the composition of the memory trace (see Tulving & Bower, 1974) and the conditions determining access to memorial representations. The investigation of these problems usually involves the deliberate introduction of changes in the characteristics of the task between Trial n and Trial $n + 1$, for example, between input and output. A variety of probing procedures can be used to obtain information about the composition of the trace; the targets of such probes are not only attributes of the to-be-remembered (TBR) units themselves but also such features of the input events as modality of presentation, frequency and recency of occurrence of individual items, and so on. One may also attempt to infer the composition of the memory trace from the types of cues, for example, semantic and acoustic ones, that are effective in retrieval. This approach is based on the assumption that only those cues can be effective whose informational content overlaps with that of the trace (Tulving & Bower, 1974; Tulving & Thomson, 1973). Manipulation of the conditions of cuing has also been the preferred method for studying the processes by which memory traces become accessible. When apparently forgotten items are recovered in the presence of appropriate cues (for example, the names of the categories of which the TBR items are instances), it can be concluded that these items were temporarily inaccessible rather than unavailable (Tulving & Pearlstone, 1966).

There is a clear continuity, then, between the defining operations of studies of transfer, on the one hand, and the procedures used to investigate the composition of the memory trace and the conditions of access to the trace, on the other. This continuity of methods exists because systematic manipulation of the conditions of testing is required for the evaluation of hypotheses about the contents of storage or about potentially effective modes of retrieval. Transfer designs have, of course, been used traditionally to answer questions about "what has been learned." Classical examples in the area of animal learning are the latent learning paradigm and the factorial designs for separating the effects on acquisition and performance of such variables as stimulus intensity and drive level (see Kimble, 1961, pp. 118 ff.). In research on verbal learning, transfer procedures have been the primary vehicle for identifying the nature of the functional stimulus, for example, in the acquisition of serial lists (Bewley, 1972; Young, 1968), and for assessing stimulus-component selection (Richardson, 1971, 1972). The methods discussed earlier, which are explicitly directed toward the assessment of the contents and the accessibility of the memory trace, are based on the same logic. The continuity of methods should not be obscured by the fact that in experiments on transfer the emphasis is often on the acquisition of the test task; the observed transfer effects can be understood only to the extent that the products of past learning and their mode of interaction with the requirements of the test task can be specified.

II. DIFFERENTIATION OF STAGES

As has been noted, it is possible to distinguish among measurements of learning, retention, and transfer on the basis of somewhat arbitrary but pragmatically useful operations. At the same time, it must be recognized that there are no well articulated rules of inference for relating observed experimental effects to one or the other of the theoretically separable stages of encoding, storage, and retrieval. In a recent discussion of the problem of analytic separation of stages, Murdock (1974) emphasized the fact that these processes are sequential and concluded that they should therefore be assumed to be interdependent. He went on to point out that, as a consequence, any variable that influences encoding may affect storage and retrieval as well; similarly, conditions that influence storage may also affect retrieval. Presumably the effects of retrieval variables are unique to that stage. The assumption of interdependence of successive stages is not logically required; it is in principle possible for sequential processes to be independent. However that may be, any attempt at analytic separation must begin with the identification of variables and operations that are assumed to be specific to a given stage. Once that is done, the next step is to resolve the ambiguities entailed by the sequential nature of the hypothetical processes. Many such attempts have been made, but the rules of inference seem to be getting less, rather than more, consistent.

A. Retrieval

Let us begin with what appears on the surface to be the simplest case, namely the identification of effects that are localized in the retrieval stage.

1. Analysis of Cuing Effects

At one time, manipulation of the conditions of cuing during recall appeared to be a rather straightforward method for studying the characteristics of the retrieval process. With subjects treated alike up to the point of the retention test, any differences in performance related to the cueing procedure implicate the retrieval process. The distinction between availability and accessibility of stored information (Tulving & Pearlstone, 1966) is based on this logic. When the inclusion of some cues (namely items from within the list) on tests of free recall proved ineffective or even detrimental, however, conclusions about the characteristics of storage as well as retrieval were drawn from the results. Slamecka (1968, 1969, 1972) argued for the principle of independent trace storage, with interitem relations influencing only the retrieval plan. Other investigators (Roediger, 1973; Rundus, 1973) saw the results as supporting an hierarchical model of the organization of higher-order units and assumed that items presented as cues become a source of output interference. The merits of these arguments need not concern us here. These studies are cited simply as an illustration of the explanatory burden that has been placed on the results of cuing studies.

This burden is increasing. As we noted earlier, the successive administration of different retrieval cues has been proposed as a method for determining the elements of the trace of a previously presented item (Tulving & Bower, 1974; Tulving & Watkins, 1975). The essential steps in the application of the method are as follows. Suppose that an associative cue (X) and a rhyming cue (Y) are used to probe the trace. These cues are administered to different subgroups of subjects in each of the two possible orders $(X_1 Y_2$ and $X_2 Y_1)$. For each subgroup, the raw probability of recall in the presence of a given cue is a measure of the gross valence (that is, effectiveness) of that cue. Since cues may overlap in informational content, it is also necessary to assess the effectiveness of each cue when such redundancy is taken into account. The measures used for this purpose are the proportions of cases in which a cue proves effective after a failure to recall to the other one ($X_2\bar{Y}_1$ and $\bar{X}_1Y_2$). The latter indices are the reduced valences of the two cues. These estimates are taken to be free of any contaminating effects of the preceding test, on the assumption that the administration of an ineffective cue leaves the trace intact. From a set of the observed values (specifically, the gross valences of the first cues and the reduced valences of the second cues) a matrix is finally derived that represents the informational structure of the trace in terms of the probabilities of recall and nonrecall to the nonoverlapping components of cues X and Y.

Within the framework of this analysis, the trace thus becomes an hypothetical construct the characteristics of which are to be ascertained on the basis of multiple cue-response relations. This approach represents a fundamental change in the rationale for the manipulation of recall cues. The focus has shifted away from the conditions of access to stored representations and is now on the informational content of the trace. Since that content is mapped in terms of the probabilities of recall to different cues, immediate access to the trace in the presence of an appropriate cue appears to be implicitly assumed. It will be necessary to clarify the inferential rules. Is it possible to study both the properties of the retrieval process per se and the composition of the trace by the same operations?

2. Recall versus Recognition

When a variable influences recall but not recognition, investigators often infer that the locus of the experimental effect is in the retrieval rather than the encoding or storage phase. The reason is, of course, that according to dual-process theory (Kintsch, 1970) the retrieval process is bypassed on a test of recognition. For example, after presenting successive items separated by a period of distractor activity, Bjork and Whitten (1974) observed long-term recency effects in recall but not in recognition. They concluded that, given the validity of the dual-process postulate, the serial position effects reflected retrieval rather than storage processes (Bjork & Whitten, 1974, p. 186). The complementary argument is that the presence of equivalent effects in recall and in recognition removes retrieval effects from consideration. Thus, after observing a buildup of proactive inhibition (PI) on successive recognition tests in a Brown–Peterson situation, Petrusic and Dillon (1972) argued that PI has its origin at encoding or storage rather than retrieval. The argument can be turned around, however, and equivalent effects on the two types of tests can be taken as evidence against the assumptions of dual-process theory. Gorfein and Jacobson (1972) advanced exactly this argument, again on the basis of the similarity of the PI functions for short-term recall and recognition. One must certainly agree with Murdock's (1974, p. 264) point that the usefulness of the comparison between recall and recognition for purposes of identifying retrieval effects depends on the assumptions of the theoretical model one chooses to adopt. If one holds the view that recognition involves retrieval (Tulving & Thomson, 1971), the comparison obviously cannot serve this purpose.

Apart from a priori theoretical considerations, the analytic value of comparisons between recall and recognition is often vitiated by large differences in the level of performance. Such differences were present, for example, in the results of Bjork and Whitten, and Petrusic and Dillon, cited above. Many other examples could be given. Even when there are technically no ceiling effects, the two sets of measures in such cases differ greatly in sensitivity, and comparisons are necessarily made between different samples of items.

At the present time, there appears to be little consensus on the rules of inference for the identification of retrieval effects. One recurrent difficulty is that positive and negative findings are not interpreted in a consistent manner. Thus, facilitation of recall by cuing is readily explained in terms of increased trace accessibility. A lack of facilitation, on the other hand, leads to speculations about the characteristics of storage. When an experimental variable has a differential effect on recall and recognition, the operation of a retrieval effect is readily invoked. By contrast, when an experimental treatment is effective but does not interact with the type of test, one can (*a*) attribute the effect, by default, to events in the encoding or the storage phase, or (*b*) question the assumption that the retrieval process is bypassed in recognition. Specific examples of such divergent interpretations have been given above. Since performance in any given task inevitably reflects the cumulative influence of the entire sequence of hypothetical events, it is not surprising that the isolation of retrieval effects per se is proving to be extremely difficult. The problems are compounded when attempts are made to localize the source of differences in performance in the encoding or the storage phase.

B. Storage

The variables conventionally manipulated in investigations of storage processes are the length of the retention interval and the activities filling the interval. Two major sources of uncertainty have made it difficult to draw the desired inferences from the results of these manipulations. First, assessment of the effects of the passage of time per se, which would provide information bearing uniquely on the characteristics of storage, are vitiated by intractable problems of experimental control. Second, when forgetting is related to the nature of the interpolated activity, the question inevitably arises of whether the observed effects reflect storage or retrieval processes.

1. Retention after Sleep

In spite of recurrent attempts, no satisfactory operations have been developed for testing the hypothesis that information in store decays as a function of time. The problem cannot really be dismissed as trivial on the ground that time cannot be a causative factor but only provides a framework for the description of events (Mc Geoch, 1932). The identification of a functional relation that is strictly time-dependent would greatly narrow the range of explanatory possibilities. The basic operational difficulty is, of course, that rehearsal cannot be controlled if the interval is unfilled; if the interval is filled, delay and interpolated activity are confounded. A classical procedure designed to overcome this difficulty is the comparison of retention after periods of sleep and wakefulness (Jenkins & Dallenbach, 1924; Lovatt & Warr, 1968; Van Ormer, 1932). The most extensive and systematic investigations were carried out by Ekstrand (1972). The logic of the manipulation is, of course, that the amounts retained should be the same after periods of sleep and of wakefulness, if the length of the retention interval were the critical variable. The superiority of retention after sleep is by now a well-established fact, but it is far from clear that the experimental arrangements used in these studies fully control rehearsal and other interpolated activities. For example, since the onset of sleep is not immediate, there may well be more rehearsal at the beginning of a sleep interval (when the TBR material is fully accessible) than during the corresponding period of wakeful activity. The finding that recall declines as the introduction of a period of sleep is delayed (see Ekstrand, 1972, pp. 75 ff.) is understandable on this basis and does not necessarily imply that sleep favors consolidation.

In the most recent studies, interest has focused increasingly on the role of sleep in consolidation, and in particular on the effects of different stages of sleep on retention. One significant finding was that retention loss was greater after the second than after the first four hours of sleep (Ekstrand, 1972, pp. 72–75; Yaroush, Sullivan, & Ekstrand, 1971). Since Stage-IV sleep occurs primarily in the first half of the night and rapid eye movement (REM) sleep in the second half, the implication is that the former facilitates consolidation whereas the latter inhibits it. It must be noted, however, that time of original learning and time of test are necessarily confounded variables in these experiments, occurring either early or late during the night. Differences in the amount of rehearsal at the beginning of the retention interval again cannot be ruled out. Results reported by Hockey, Davies, and Gray (1972) indicate that temporal locus per se may have important effects on performance. These investigators found that original learning was higher and retention losses were greater in the morning than during the night, regardless of whether the subjects were awake or asleep during the retention interval. The critical finding here is the difference in original learning; given that difference, the retention measures are difficult to evaluate since the samples of items are not strictly comparable. Retention was measured by free recall, and the differences on the immediate test were largely limited to the last few positions. If these items were excluded from consideration, it is doubtful that appreciable differences in retention would remain. However that may be, in view of the confoundings inherent in the experimental designs and the limited control over the subjects' activities, no strong conclusions about storage processes can be drawn from the results of these studies.

2. Decay from the Short-Term Store?

While the possibility of uncontrolled rehearsal in the sleep experiments cannot be ruled out, it is not now known whether and to what extent this factor contributes to the observed differences in retention. When we turn to tests of the decay hypothesis in short-term memory, however, the critical importance of uncontrolled rehearsal is readily documented. What appeared to be a very promising new procedure for assessing the effects of the sheer passage of time on short-term retention was introduced by Reitman (1971). The interval between item presentation and test was filled with an exacting tone-detection task that fully occupied the subject's attention and thus should have served to eliminate rehearsal. The criterion initially used for determining whether rehearsal was, in fact, prevented was the equivalence of signal-detection performance during memory trials and during control trials on which no TBR items were presented to the subjects. In Reitman's original experiment this criterion was satisfied. Since there was no forgetting over a 15-sec interval under this arrangement, the results appeared to constitute strong evidence against the decay hypothesis. These findings were confirmed and extended by Shiffrin (1973). A short time later, however, Reitman (1974) published the results of additional experiments in which the validity of the original criterion for establishing the presence or absence of rehearsal was carefully evaluated. She developed a series of measures that would be sensitive to different rehearsal strategies, such as tradeoffs between detection and processing of the TBR words over trials, and momentary shifts from one activity to the other during a single trial. According to these more sensitive criteria, only a small percentage of the subjects strictly adhered to instructions and avoided rehearsal when told to do so. These subjects showed a substantial retention loss over a 15-sec interval. Forgetting increased when the detection task required the processing of verbal inputs, specifically discrimination between similar syllables. Reitman concluded, therefore, that both decay and displacement interference contribute to short-term forgetting.

In the meantime, Reitman's earlier conclusion that information in the short-term store does not decay even when rehearsal is avoided had already been challenged on the ground that the signal-detection task is not sufficiently demanding to prevent recycling of the material, and evidence was presented that the interpolation of other nonverbal distractors produces substantial amounts of forgetting (Watkins, Watkins, Craik, & Mazuryk, 1973). Any finding showing an absence of decay can be questioned by postulating undetected covert rehearsal. By the same token, however, any evidence for decay can be questioned equally well by postulating covert activities that become a source of interference. In fact, it is quite likely that subjects performing a tone-shadowing or pursuit rotor task (as in the study just cited) engage in a variety of implicit verbalizations. The possibility that such verbal activity can interfere with the retention of TBR words certainly cannot be ruled out. It appears that the question of whether forgetting is caused by decay as well as interference is not likely to be settled experimentally in the foreseeable future. The decision depends on too many assumptions about unobservable implicit events.

3. Storage Interference

The ambiguity of the distinction between storage and retrieval effects has been a major source of difficulty in the theoretical interpretation of the phenomena of retroactive and proactive inhibition (RI and PI). At what locus or loci do the interference processes responsible for retroaction and proaction come into play? Many years of experimental effort have failed to produce a decisive answer to this question. Although a dual-locus interpretation of RI has been generally accepted for a long time, the theoretical emphasis has continued to seesaw between storage and retrieval processes. As for PI, it was traditionally viewed as a pure case of retrieval interference, but in recent years the possibility that proactive losses may reflect an encoding deficit has been receiving increasing attention. Since our primary concern here is with storage interference, this discussion will be limited to the measurement and interpretation of RI.

a. *Historical developments.* When Müller and Pilzecker (1900) discovered RI, they attributed the detrimental effects of interpolated learning (IL) to a disruption of the consolidation of the original trace. As the conditions of RI were explored in detail, the theory was discarded, primarily because (a) it predicted incorrectly that RI should decrease progressively with the length of the interval between original learning (OL) and IL, and (b) it failed to provide a satisfactory explanation of the powerful effects of intertask similarity on RI (see McGeoch, 1942, pp. 485–488). The theory of reproductive inhibition advocated by McGeoch gained wide acceptance precisely because it was able to give a systematic account of the relations between interlist similarity and RI. Thus, *AB–AD* (identical stimuli and different responses) became the reference paradigm, and RI was viewed as a special case of negative transfer and as attributable entirely to the competition between incompatible responses to identical or similar stimuli. Storage interference had no place in this explanatory scheme; old associations were assumed to remain intact during the acquisition of new ones (the independence hypothesis). There was little direct evidence for the hypothesized process of competition since overt intrusions at recall are few and far between; the manifestations of competition were assumed to remain largely covert. This position became untenable when Melton and Irwin (1940) discovered a nonmonotonic relationship between overt intrusions and RI. As is well known, this led to the formulation of a two-factor theory according to which both unlearning of the original associations during IL and competition at recall contribute to RI. The processes responsible for RI were thus given a dual locus: interference was assumed to be operative during both storage and retrieval. With the introduction of the modified modified free-recall (MMFR) test (Barnes & Underwood, 1959), it has become possible to assess the relative importance of the two factors in producing RI. On such a test, the subject is instructed to reproduce both the first-list and the second-list response to each stimulus in either order; the test is typically unpaced, and identification of the list membership of the responses is not required at the time of recall. Under these conditions, the effects of response competition should be largely eliminated. Nevertheless, the amount of RI under the MMFR procedure is comparable to that observed on tests requiring recall of the first list only. The apparent implication is that unlearning carries far greater weight in producing retroactive decrements than does response competition.

The potential importance of retrieval processes was given renewed emphasis when the concept of generalized competition (Newton & Wickens, 1956) was introduced and later elaborated into an hypothesis of response suppression (Postman, Stark, & Fraser, 1968). The gist of that hypothesis is that suppression of the repertoire of first-list responses is a major determinant of retroactive losses in recall. Suppression is brought about through the operation of a response-selector mechanism during IL. Having restricted himself to the responses from the interpolated list, the subject has difficulty in shifting back to the first-list repertoire. Suppression is a reversible process, and the interference attributable to it is, therefore, transitory. There is by now reliable evidence for spontaneous recovery of first-list associations, at least over relatively short retention intervals (Forrester, 1970; Kammann & Melton, 1967; Martin & Mackay, 1970; Postman, Stark, & Fraser, 1968; Postman, Stark, & Henschel, 1969; Shulman & Martin, 1970). While rises in first-list retention may certainly reflect factors other than the dissipation of response suppression, they cannot be reconciled with a process of destructive storage interference.

The possibility of item-specific unlearning is not denied by the hypothesis of response suppression; whether and to what extent response suppression and associative unlearning come into play under a given treatment is a problem for experimental analysis. The evidence for and against the hypothesis has been reviewed elsewhere (Postman & Underwood, 1973), and most of it need not concern us here. What is of immediate interest is the nature of the evidence that has emerged from some of the relevant studies regarding the relative importance of storage interference and retrieval interference under conditions of negative transfer.

b. Retroactive interference in recognition and recall. Consider the *AB–AD* paradigm and assume for the moment that response losses reflect reversible retrieval failures owing to the operation of a suppression mechanism. (This is not a necessary assumption since response losses may be attributed to the unlearning of contextual associations; see McGovern, 1964.) Associative losses, on the other hand, are a consequence of unlearning or storage interference. A first approach to the analytic separation of the retrieval and storage components is a comparison of the amounts of RI observed on tests of recall and of associative matching under comparable conditions of transfer. The logic is that successful recall depends on both response retrieval and the integrity of specific associations; correct performance on the matching test requires only the latter. To the extent that the scales of measurement are comparable (which should not necessarily be taken for granted), the measures of associative matching provide an independent estimate of the amount of associative loss that contributes to the retroactive decrements in recall. Apart from the problem of scaling, methodological difficulties arise in the implementation of appropriate experimental procedures for carrying out the desired comparison.

In the majority of the relevant experiments, subjects were originally trained on both the *AB* and the *AD* list by the recall method, and associative losses were then assessed by means of a matching test. Typically, a small amount of associative loss is found, usually of the order of one item or so, relative to a control condition (for example, Delprato, 1971; Garskof, 1968; Garskof & Sandak, 1964; Greenberg & Wickens, 1972; Sandak & Garskof, 1967). Such results are difficult to interpret because a change in the method of testing is introduced between acquisition and the test of retention. This arrangement introduces two potential sources of bias:

1. Attainment of a recall criterion may represent overlearning with respect to the requirement of the matching test. If so, the amount of associative loss may be underestimated.

2. Subjects trained under a recall procedure are likely to continue recalling the responses during the matching test and to decide among the alternatives presented to them by means of a retrieval check (see Mandler, 1972). Failure to recall a response may lead to the false rejection of the corresponding target. Thus, response loss can lead to a degradation of performance on the matching test. This would serve to inflate the apparent amount of RI.

An alternative procedure is to measure performance by recognition both during acquisition and on the test of retention. When that is done, the amounts of retroaction under the *AB–AD* paradigm are again small relative to those typically found on tests of recall (Anderson & Watts, 1971; Petrich, 1974; Postman & Stark, 1969; Sanders, Whitaker, & Cofer, 1974). The difference between the *AD* and the control treatment sometimes reaches statistical significance, and sometimes does not. Although the biases mentioned earlier are eliminated, another interpretative problem remains: what is originally stored under conditions of recognition learning may differ systematically from what is acquired during recall training (see Carey & Lockhart, 1973; Loftus, 1971; Tversky, 1973). It is uncertain, therefore, how valid an estimate of the associative component of recall is obtained on a matching test.

The analytic problems are obviously considerable. Nevertheless, all the available evidence suggests that associative unlearning under the *AB–AD* paradigm develops very slowly. This conclusion is strengthened by the finding that no RI is found on a recognition test when *AB* and *AD* pairs are presented once (Bower & Bostrom, 1968; Underwood & Brown, 1975). Under this arrangement, degree of OL is low, and the associations should be maximally susceptible to interference. Taken together, the results obtained on recognition tests make it reasonable to conclude that storage interference is secondary to retrieval failure in producing retroactive losses in recall. The null hypothesis—that associative unlearning never occurs—has not been at issue. The fact that there is clear evidence for RI on multiple-choice recognition tests under the *AB–ABr* (original stimuli and responses re-paired) paradigm indicates that associative unlearning is likely to develop under conditions of heavy and persistent interference (see Postman & Stark, 1969).

c. Retrieval failure and RI.   The trend toward considering retrieval failure as the primary determinant of retroactive inhibition is also apparent in Martin's (1971a, 1972, 1973) theoretical analysis of the underlying processes of interference. The guiding theoretical assumption is that the encoding of a nominal stimulus, that is, the set of features or attributes sampled, varies over time. A simple example of such encoding variability is the selection of different letters of a trigram as functional cues (see Martin, 1968). Which features are sampled depends in large measure on the characteristics of the response. Since the analysis proceeds from the assumption that two responses cannot be simultaneously attached to the same stimulus, the substitution of D for B in the $AB–AD$ paradigm requires the sampling of a new set of features. A feature-sampling bias is thus established in the transfer phase, and this bias is carried over to the test of first-list recall. Retroactive losses occur because the subject fails to sample those features of the stimuli that are required for retrieval of the first-list responses. The associations established during the acquisition of the successive lists are assumed to remain independent and intact. The possibility of storage interference is not considered. A related analysis by Greeno, James, and Da Polito (1971), which also emphasizes the detrimental effects of the persistence of inappropriate encodings, attributes RI to the suppression or degradation during IL of the original retrieval plan.

Finally, the results of experiments on RI in free recall have served to reinforce the emphasis on retrieval processes. Retroactive losses under conditions of free-recall learning are heavy and set in rapidly (for example, Postman & Keppel, 1967; Tulving & Thornton, 1959). More important, in the case of categorized lists at least, categorical cuing serves to eliminate RI (Tulving & Psotka, 1971). That is, RI is produced by a reversible failure of access to higher-order units. The general implications of such results are worthy of emphasis. For historical reasons, the development of interference theory has been closely tied to the paradigm of associative learning. As a consequence, postulated mechanisms of interference have been equally closely tied to the operations used to measure associative recall. Martin's formulation, which centers on the analysis of nominally identical stimuli during successive stages of learning, reflects this state of affairs. The same may be said about concepts such as unlearning, which lose precision when specific cues to specific responses cannot be identified. Hence, it is important to consider findings obtained outside the traditional paradigms of associative learning in speculating about the generality of such processes as similarity-dependent storage interference. The data on free recall are only one case in point. Studies of retroaction in verbal discrimination learning have yielded functional relations that differ in important respects from those observed with associative tasks, implicating a breakdown of frequency discrimination as the basic determinant of RI (Underwood & Freund, 1970; Underwood, Shaughnessy, & Zimmerman, 1972). As was suggested elsewhere (Postman, in press, a), it may not be possible at this time to formulate general laws of interference that apply to all types of learning tasks and retention tests. There are clear indications that the effective mechanisms of interference vary in important ways with the nature of the encoded information and the requirements of the retention test. Thus, any conclusions that the existing evidence permits concerning the relative contributions of storage interference and retrieval failure to RI probably have limited generality.

4. Decay and Storage Interference as Hypothetical Constructs

In light of the lack of firm empirical support for decay, and the weakness of the evidence for storage interference, the question arises of how appropriate it is to pursue the development of a general theory of memory based on these hypothetical constructs. The "single-trace fragility theory of memory dynamics" proposed by Wickelgren (1974) does just that. The theory postulates two mechanisms that produce decay of the memory trace: (a) similarity-dependent storage interference, and (b) an interference-free time-decay process. It is further assumed that memory traces have "two partially coupled dynamic properties," namely strength and fragility. Strength is reflected in the level of recall and recognition, whereas fragility determines the susceptibility of the trace to time decay but not to interference. Both strength and fragility are assumed to decline over time.

Since the central constructs do not rest on a broad empirical base but on the contrary have resisted direct verification, it is not surprising that rather implausible ad hoc assumptions have to be added to reconcile the theory with relevant facts. The evaluation of the evidence for similarity-dependent storage interference is a case in point. According to the theory, associative unlearning should be found whenever an *AB–AD* paradigm (same stimuli and unrelated responses) is compared with an *AB–CD* paradigm (unrelated stimuli and unrelated responses). The results of multiple-trial experiments give some limited, although far from unequivocal, support to this expectation. As noted, however, no differences between the two conditions of interpolation are found when successive pairs are presented within the same list and retention is tested by recognition. This result was first reported by Bower and Bostrom (1968) for letter–digit pairs. In an attempt to explain these results, Wickelgren argued that (a) encoding was semantic in the multiple-trial experiments but phonetic in the short-term experiments, and (b) the difference in stimulus similarity between the *AD* and *CD* treatments was, therefore, greater in the former than in the latter case. The argument was ad hoc in the first place and is rendered highly implausible by the results of Underwood and Brown (1975), who used lists of paired words and again failed to obtain any evidence of RI. Even more damaging is the finding of Bruce and Weaver (1973) that short-term recall of minimally learned paired associates shows retroactive facilitation rather than inhibition under the *AB–AD* paradigm.

Since fragility determines the susceptibility of the trace to decay but not to interference, the theory must predict that, over a given retention interval, RI should be independent of the length of the interval between OL and IL (the temporal point of interpolation). Much of the available evidence does not agree with this prediction; in several recent studies RI was found to increase as IL moved closer to the test of recall (Abra, 1969; Howe, 1969; Postman, Stark, & Henschel, 1969). Since retrieval failure may influence RI in recall, Wickelgren (1974) investigated the effect of the temporal point of interpolation on RI in recognition, with original and interpolated pairs presented once each. As might have been expected on the basis of earlier findings, the level of RI was minimal (significant at the .05 level by one-tailed test). Recognition performance was poorest when the delay between pairs was longest, but not significantly so.[1] Such evidence is singularly unconvincing. The same is true for other empirical findings cited in support of the theory. For example, the function relating recency judgments to the length of the delay interval is viewed as providing a direct measurement of trace fragility. This interpretation ignores the findings which cast serious doubt on the possibility that temporal discriminations can be based on a unidimensional characteristic of the trace, such as strength or fragility (Anderson & Bower, 1972, pp. 100 ff.; Hintzman & Block, 1971). There appear to be no consistent rules for drawing inferences about storage as distinct from retrieval processes. Thus, retrograde amnesia is described as reversible retrieval failure but, by virtue of its temporal selectivity, is assumed to reflect trace fragility. By the same token, spontaneous recovery from RI should be related to trace fragility since the reversible retention losses are also temporally selective, occurring for the first, but not for the second, list. According to the theory, however, fragility does not determine susceptibility to interference.

Wickelgren's latest theory has been considered in some detail because it illustrates the risk of retaining as hypothetical constructs processes that fail to gain clear empirical support when subjected to experimental tests. The interpretative problems that come to light in such direct tests will inevitably recur in the evaluation of deductions from the formal model. Thus, formalization does not remove the difficulty of separating decay from interference, nor can it do away with the logical and empirical objections to trace strength as the common determinant of success in recognition and recall (see Anderson & Bower, 1972; Underwood, 1969).

---

[1] A second experiment yielded similar effects, but the results cannot be evaluated since no measures of performance were reported.

5. The Difficulty of Testing Hypotheses about Storage Processes

In general, it has proved extremely difficult to devise experimental arrangements that permit unequivocal conclusions about storage processes per se. Serious problems of control and of inference continue to complicate attempts to separate decay from storage interference and retrieval failure on the one hand, and to distinguish between the latter two on the other. Empirical support for the operation of a consolidation process in the acquisition of verbal materials has been unimpressive. No firm conclusions have emerged from the studies of the effects of sleep on retention. An even less promising approach is the manipulation of conditions of interference for purposes of demonstrating consolidation. This approach was taken in a recent series of experiments by Landauer (1974).

In Landauer's experiments, the lists of paired associates presented to the subjects consisted of (a) critical pairs, (b) interpolated noncritical pairs the stimulus terms of which were similar to those of the critical items, and (c) interpolated noncritical pairs, the stimulus terms of which were dissimilar to those of the critical items. The basic independent variable was the order of presentation of the two types of interpolated items. The closer the point of interpolation of the interfering similar items, the poorer was the retention of the critical pairs. These results show only that there are differences in retroactive interference related to the structure of the interpolated series. The reasons for these differences are difficult to gauge, especially since no measures of retention for noncritical items are reported. It is worth noting, however, that the operations in these experiments closely resemble those used in studies of the isolation effect (see Wallace, 1965). That is, a critical pair followed by a sequence of dissimilar items is isolated in the series. An isolated pair occupying one of the initial positions in the list can be rehearsed easily because it is followed by items that are distinct from it. Continuing rehearsal is obviously more difficult when the critical pairs and the items that follow it are highly confusable. Such an interpretation is in no way contradicted by Landauer's (1974) finding that the order of presentation had no effect when noncritical items preceded the critical ones. His comparison between retroactive and proactive effects was quite inappropriate since the serial position of the critical items was a confounded variable, that is, retroaction for items in the initial positions was compared with proaction for items in the terminal positions. Differential rehearsal is again implicated by the fact that retention of the terminal items was considerably lower than that of the initial ones. Landauer (1974) is right when he says that, "Clearly something important goes on with respect to the long-term storage of a paired-associate during the time when the rest of the list is presented, and as a function of the nature and order of the rest of the list [p. 52]." From this conclusion there is, however, a rather wide inferential leap to the postulation of a consolidation process in a nontrivial sense, that is, a process which is not reducible to such factors as item differentiation and selective rehearsal.

C. Encoding

It is a reasonable guess that "encoding" is the theoretical term with the highest frequency of usage in contemporary discussions of verbal learning and memory. There is universal agreement that verbal inputs undergo selective processing, transformations, and elaborations as they are stored in memory. Since a nominal stimulus may be processed in many different ways, the concept of encoding has a variety of distinct connotations. For example, Bower (1972b) has distinguished among four types of encoding: (a) selection of components out of a complex pattern, (b) rewriting of the input into another format, (c) componential description of the input item in terms of a list of attributes or features, and (d) elaboration by additions to the nominal input. It is apparent that the appropriate methods for manipulating and assessing the characteristics of encoding will depend on the type of selective processing or transformation that is under study.

In view of the pervasiveness of the concept, it would be impossible to develop an exhaustive classification of the experimental procedures that are directed toward the analysis of encoding processes. Certain major classes of operations can be identified, however:

1. An attempt is made to ensure the use of a particular mode of encoding by means of instructions, for example by requesting subjects to generate interacting images during the acquisition of noun pairs.

2. With a view to gaining direct control over the encoding process, the subject is required to perform an orienting task, for example, to make judgments about selected characteristics of the TBR units. An orienting task carried out under conditions of incidental learning is assumed to be the primary determinant of the subject's encoding activities.

3. The context in which the learning materials are presented is manipulated so as to bias a particular encoding of the TBR items. A typical arrangement is the presentation of homographs in different sentence contexts.

4. The subject is provided with encoding devices during the presentation of the learning materials. For example, the stimulus and response members of paired associates are embedded in sentences on one or more of the learning trials.

5. Item properties, such as concreteness and meaningfulness, are varied, on the assumption that these properties influence encoding in predictable ways. Thus, concreteness is assumed to favor imaginal encoding, and encoding variability is expected to vary inversely with meaningfulness.

6. An hypothesis is formulated about the specific modes of encoding involved in the acquisition of a given type of task, and the conditions of learning are then varied in order to verify this hypothesis. Tests of the frequency theory of verbal discrimination learning exemplify this approach.

The procedures listed above are examples of experimental manipulations designed to influence the subject's encoding or to modify the effectiveness of such activities. We now turn to methods that are used to assess the characteristics of the encodings established during acquisition. There is no sharp dividing line between these two classes of operations, but in the procedures listed next the primary purpose is not to influence the way in which the material is processed but rather to ascertain what encodings have occurred:

1. Subjects are interrogated about the encoding devices they used during acquisition, for example, about the "natural language mediators" (NLMs) employed to link the stimulus and the response members of paired associates.

2. To determine whether componential selection has occurred, recall in the presence of a component is tested following the acquisition of compound-response associations.

3. In order to ascertain the nature of the functional stimulus controlling the responses during the acquisition of a particular task, transfer tests are administered which are sensitive to the effectiveness of the inferred functional stimuli. Similarly, transfer tests are used to probe for the existence of higher-order units developed during acquisition. This line of attack on the identification of the functional stimulus has been prominent in recent analyses of serial learning.

4. The degree to which there is interference between successive TBR units is used as a basis for inferring the dimensions of encoding that were activated during the processing of these units. The specific reference here is to the procedure advocated by Wickens (1970, 1972) of using release from PI as the criterion for the presence of a dimension of encoding.

5. As seen earlier, the effectiveness of different retrieval cues is taken to provide information about what was encoded. This method derives its rationale from the principle of encoding specificity (Tulving & Thomson, 1973), according to which the only cues that can be effective in retrieval are those with respect to which the TBR unit was encoded during input.

6. In order to determine whether a particular feature or attribute of the stimulus event was encoded, attribute-specific tests can be devised. Thus,

as noted earlier, one may probe for information about such attributes of the event as frequency of occurrence, recency, modality of presentation, spatial location, etc.

Some of the methods listed here were recently discussed by Tulving and Bower (1974) with respect to their usefulness in providing information about the composition of the memory trace. The focus in the sections that follow is on methodological problems that arise in the application of these techniques.

1. Instructions

The use of instructions to influence encoding is predicated on the assumption that the manner in which the input material is processed is under the subject's control. While this assumption is, on the face of it, reasonable, there are some obvious sources of difficulty. First, in view of the uncertain validity of introspective reports, it is usually hard to know what the mode of processing is in the absence of instructions; consequently, there is no determinate baseline against which instructional effects can be evaluated. If the instructions have little or no influence on performance, one possible reason is that the mode of attack recommended in the instructions is spontaneously adopted by a substantial number of subjects who are left to their own devices. Second, the degree of the subjects' compliance with the instructions is often difficult to assess. The validity of reports obtained in postexperimental inquiries is particularly questionable when subjects are asked to indicate whether or not they carried out the experimenter's instructions. Quite apart from the problem of candor, subjects may often be unable to reconstruct the nature of their activities with any degree of precision. Shifts in the mode of processing may not be remembered or may, indeed, remain undetected. The encoding habits that the subject brings to the experimental situation are highly overlearned, and he need not necessarily be aware of the degree to which such habits were activated.

The existence of these problems is, of course, generally recognized and has led to caution in the interpretation of instructional effects. Unfortunately, some investigators have not been entirely able to resist the temptation of engaging in circular reasoning and have used the experimental outcome as a criterion for deciding whether or not subjects had complied with the instructions. The complexities inherent in the analysis of the effects of instructions on encoding are illustrated by a group of experiments performed by Paivio and his associates. These experiments were concerned with the role of verbal and imaginal strategies in the acquisition of noun pairs varying in degree of concreteness.

a. *Imaginal and verbal sets.*   According to the two-process theory proposed by Paivio (1971), both imaginal and verbal mediators may serve to facilitate paired-associate learning. The relative effectiveness of the two types of mediators is expected to depend on the concreteness of the words of which the pairs are composed. Images are aroused much less readily by abstract than by concrete words, whereas verbal mediators are elicited with equal ease by the two types of items (Yuille & Paivio, 1967). It follows that, relative to a control condition in which mediation is minimized, a set to use images should facilitate performance much more for concrete (C–C) than abstract (A–A) pairs. By contrast, a set to use verbal mediators should produce equivalent amounts of facilitation for the two kinds of items. Further expectations flow from the assumption that with suitable materials imaginal mediators are more effective than verbal ones. For C–C pairs, learning should, therefore, be faster under the imaginal than the verbal set, whereas a difference in the opposite direction should be obtained for A–A pairs.[2] In short, an interaction of concreteness with mediational set is predicted. This interaction proved, as Paivio aptly put it, elusive; its pursuit and eventual capture make an interesting case history.

In three successive experiments, verbal and imaginal sets were found to produce equivalent amounts of facilitation (relative to a rote-repetition control treatment) in the acquisition of concrete and of abstract pairs (Paivio & Yuille, 1967, 1969; Yuille & Paivio, 1968). The measures of performance showed no hint of a difference between the two instructional treatments. There were also clear indications from the subjects' reports that the choice of mediators was determined not only by the instructions but also by the concreteness value of the items. Thus, other things being equal, subjects used imaginal mediators more often for C–C than for A–A pairs. There was no question, however, about the effectiveness of the instructions in changing the relative frequency of the two types of mediators. This pattern of results led Paivio (1971) to the hypothesis that the expected interaction failed to materialize because of ". . . the difficulty of establishing strong and persistent sets to use mediating devices that are incongruent with the associative processes most readily aroused by the nouns themselves [p. 366]." This explanation is puzzling, if not circular, since the instructions apparently had a substantial effect on the choice of mediators. Some reversion to natural habits of encoding might attenuate the interaction but could not account for the null results.

In any event, the next step was to force subjects to produce the required mediators overtly, by drawing the images and writing down the verbal elaborations (Paivio & Foth, 1970). The predicted interaction was finally

[2] While all possible stimulus–response combinations of concrete and abstract words were considered in some of these experiments, the present discussion will be confined to the results obtained with C–C and A–A pairs.

obtained. Subjects found it much more difficult to draw pictures representing the images generated for abstract pairs than to write down mediating
phrases for such pairs, and there were corresponding differences in recall.
Verbal and imaginal mediators for concrete pairs could be produced with
equal ease, but the latter resulted in better recall. The experimental arrangements differed drastically, of course, from those in an ordinary learning situation, and it is far from clear what conclusions can be drawn from the
results. As Paivio and Foth (1970) showed, the interaction disappeared
when the requirement of overt production of the mediators was removed. In
one subsidiary experiment with abstract pairs, the effect of overt production was directly evaluated. When images had to be drawn and sentences
had to be written down, recall was again higher under the verbal than under
the imaginal condition. When the mediators did not have to be recorded,
however, there was a difference—and not a very much smaller one, at
that—in the opposite direction! When all is said and done, the experiments
may have demonstrated nothing more than interference from an intractable
task, namely to draw a concrete image of an abstract relation. Under
normal circumstances, there may be sufficient continuity and overlap between imaging and verbal elaboration that deliberate attempts to engage in
one or the other strategy have only slight effects on acquisition, or at best
transitory ones.

There are other data in the voluminous literature on imagery that bear on
the role of verbal and imaginal sets. Some findings may be viewed as giving
some support to Paivio's position whereas others are clearly at variance
with it. Perhaps not surprisingly, the experimental results are far from
consistent. This is not the place to review them. We chose to discuss this
group of experiments entirely for the purpose of illustrating the methodological and interpretative uncertainties in the study of instructional sets.

b. Rehearsal sets. Of course, instructional manipulations do not
necessarily or always produce ambiguous or inconsistent results. A great
deal depends on the nature of the evidence that can be adduced to determine
whether or not the instructions had functionally important effects on the
subjects' encoding activities. In particular, it is important that the strategies
suggested to the subjects have distinctive consequences other than sheer
variations in the level of performance. The greater the internal consistency
of the behavioral effects, the stronger becomes the inference that the instructional manipulations were indeed effective. For example, Elmes and
Bjork (1975) presented persuasive evidence that subjects can be induced by
instructions to engage either in maintenance rehearsal or constructive rehearsal of a string of words. Maintenance or "primary" rehearsal consists
of cyclic repetition of the items, of the type one uses in trying to remember a
new telephone number. Constructive or "secondary" rehearsal involves

the establishment of mediating relations among the members of the string. Prior evidence had indicated that retention was lower after primary than after secondary rehearsal (for example, Craik & Watkins, 1973; Woodward, Bjork, & Jongeward, 1973). Elmes and Bjork found the expected difference in retention when they manipulated the type of rehearsal by means of instructions. In addition, they were able to identify several characteristics of the subjects' recall performance that provided collateral evidence for the success of the instructional manipulation: intrusions were primarily acoustic after primary rehearsal, and semantic after secondary rehearsal; output order was more closely correlated with input order in the former than in the latter case; clustering by input string was higher after secondary than after primary processing. This internal evidence for the effectiveness of the instructional manipulation is quite convincing.

So far so good. Unfortunately, certain predictions (which need not be of concern here) regarding the influence of the type of rehearsal on the spacing effect in free recall were not borne out in the experiment. In attempting to account for these results, Elmes and Bjork proceeded to retreat from the originally postulated sharp distinction between primary and secondary rehearsal. They suggested that some "obligatory" secondary or semantic processing accompanies primary rehearsal but that such secondary encoding is relatively unstable. This suggestion may well be correct since modes of processing are not likely to fall into dichotomous categories. It is fair to ask, however, whether this question would have been raised if the predicted relations between type of processing and spacing had been observed. Instructional effects can easily be reinterpreted in light of the experimental outcomes, and therein lies the basic weakness of this class of manipulations, in practice if not in principle.

2. Orienting Tasks

Historically, the use of orienting tasks has its origin in studies concerned with the effects of an instructional manipulation, namely experiments comparing intentional and incidental learning. Operationally, intentional and incidental learning are distinguished by the nature of the instructions given to the subject. The intentional learner is informed that his retention will be tested, whereas the incidental learner is not. (An essential minimal check on the success of the manipulation is a postexperimental inquiry designed to screen out incidental subjects who expected a test of retention. For some reason this necessary step has been neglected in many recent investigations of incidental learning.) An orienting task is used to expose the incidental subject to the learning materials; if one wishes to determine the effects of instructions per se, this task must also be performed by the intentional subject.

a. *Conditions of effectiveness.*   It was recognized early that the differences in retention between intentional and incidental learners, depend critically on the nature of the orienting task. The suggestion was made, therefore, that one may conceive of a continuum of orienting tasks ranging from those maximally antagonistic to learning to those maximally favorable to learning (Postman, 1964, p. 188). Thus, intent per se has no effect on learning. The intentional subject surpasses the incidental one only to the extent that the responses required by the orienting task are less favorable to acquisition than those activated by explicit instructions to learn. How favorable a particular orienting task is depends on the materials and on the method by which retention is tested. The nature of the materials is important because it determines what has to be learned and hence the relative usefulness of different orienting tasks. For example, when the TBR items are nonsense syllables, response integration is an essential component of acquisition; with such materials, repeated overt pronunciation of the items is a highly effective orienting task which leads to equally high levels of recall under intentional and incidental conditions (Mechanic, 1964). With meaningful materials, on the other hand, orienting tasks that require discrimination of word characteristics such as frequency of occurrence (Postman, Adams, & Bohm, 1956) or associative responses to the TBR words (Plenderleith & Postman, 1957; Postman & Adams, 1956; Silverstein, 1964) yield relatively small or negligible differences between intentional and incidental learners.

For a given type of material, it is possible to determine to what extent the orienting task is a source of interference by comparing intentional learners who do and who do not perform the task. When such comparisons are made, the interaction of the nature of the orienting task with item properties becomes apparent. Thus, producing an association to each individual item significantly depresses recall of nonsense syllables but not of adjectives (Postman &Adams, 1956). It appears likely that associative responding to nonsense items reduces the amount of time spent in response integration to the point where recall suffers; on the other hand, associative elaboration is a strategy that is entirely appropriate when the learning materials are familiar words. Intentional learners may or may not be disposed to choose that particular strategy spontaneously, but they can readily adopt it without suffering a loss in efficiency.

It is important to understand that an orienting task can be a source of interference. This fact is easy to demonstrate under conditions of intentional learning, where the addition of an orienting task is often detrimental to performance. The orienting task may be expected to depress performance when (a) the subject's attention is expressly directed to features of the TBR items that are irrelevant to subsequent recall or recognition, (b) the responses required by the task function as an inhibitory interpolated activity, and (c) these same responses are later used as retrieval cues and prove ineffective or conducive to error. In the case of incidental learning, orienting tasks cannot be directly classified as facilitative or interfering because of the lack of baseline information about the level of performance in the absence of either instructions to learn or an orienting task. Most of the incidental learning outside the laboratory occurs precisely under these conditions. With respect to such a baseline the conditions of interference should be the same as those postulated above. It is a mistake to consider an orienting task simply as a device for inducing the subject to process each individual TBR item in a particular way; it is also an activity that can have retroactive effects and can increase the probability of confusion errors.

   b. *Conditions of testing.*   How effective an orienting task is relative to instructions to learn depends on the conditions of testing. Several studies, in which a variety of orienting tasks was used, agree in showing substantial superiority of intentional over incidental learners in recall but not in recognition (Dornbush & Winnick, 1967; Eagle & Leiter, 1964; Estes & Da Polito, 1967; Postman, Adams, & Phillips, 1955). The most extensive analysis of this interaction of the conditions of training and testing was offered by Estes and Da Polito. The materials in their experiment were paired associates, with nonsense syllables as stimuli and digits as responses. The orienting task given to the incidental learners was to abstract the principle according to which syllables were paired with digits. After two presentations of the list, subjects received either two recall tests followed by a recognition test, or two recognition tests followed by a recall test. On the initial tests, intentional subjects recalled more than did the incidental subjects, whereas there was no difference in recognition scores. A prior recognition test enhanced recall for incidental but not for intentional learners; a prior recall test did not affect the level of recognition for intentional learners but led to some impairment of recognition for incidental learners. Estes and Da Polito suggested that information storage sufficient for recognition occurred to an equal extent under both conditions of learning. Intentional learners had an advantage in recall because they were more likely to engage in active rehearsal of the responses, which facilitated subsequent retrieval. The recall scores of the incidental learners rose after a test of recognition because such a test provided an opportunity for response rehearsal; the impairment on the final test of recognition is attributable to the establishment of incorrect associations during unsuccessful attempts at recall.

   The study of Estes and Da Polito (1967) has been described in some detail because it has important methodological and theoretical implications that are often overlooked in later research on incidental learning discussed below. The primary conclusion from this experiment is that the instructional treatment influenced the availability of items for retrieval rather than the nature of the stored information. Variations in recall associated with different orienting tasks may well occur, at least in part, for the same reason. It is a potentially serious error, therefore, to relate the effectiveness of orienting tasks entirely to the manner in which individual TBR items are encoded. Admittedly, it is extremely difficult to differentiate between the effects of an experimental manipulation on encoding and on retrieval. Comparisons of recall and recognition, and systematic analyses of the interaction between the two types of tests, represent at least a first step toward this objective.

The studies discussed thus far show that the effectiveness of a given orienting task depends on both the nature of the material and the conditions of testing. Attention also has been called to the fact that an orienting task cannot be regarded simply as a means of controlling the encoding of individual items, primarily for two reasons: (a) the nature of the orienting task may influence not only the encodings of individual items but also such "secondary" activities as displaced rehearsal; (b) the responses required by the orienting task occur immediately after the presentation of the TBR items, and as such may become a source of retroactive interference and also serve as either facilitative or inhibitory cues for retrieval. Against this background some recent studies of the effects of different orienting tasks on incidental learning are now considered. The formal designs are continuous with those of the earlier experiments, but there has been a heavily emphasized change in the theoretical thrust of the investigations. The basic objective of these new studies is to exhibit the overriding importance of the mode of encoding for subsequent retention. Methodologically, this objective is reflected in the classification of orienting tasks according to the types or levels of encoding they are assumed to foster.

c. *Semantic versus nonsemantic tasks.*   The experiments of Jenkins and his associates (Hyde, 1973; Hyde & Jenkins, 1969, 1973; Johnston & Jenkins, 1971; Till, Diehl, & Jenkins, 1975; Till & Jenkins, 1973; Walsh & Jenkins, 1973) center on the contrast between semantic and nonsemantic orienting tasks. Semantic tasks presumably lead the subject to process the meaning of the TBR word; during the performance of a nonsemantic task the subject is assumed to attend to attributes of the word other than its meaning. The assignment of tasks to these dichotomous classes was made on intuitive grounds. The semantic task used most often consisted of rating the words as to their pleasantness or unpleasantness; other rating dimensions included frequency of usage, importance of the word, and the position of the word on an active–passive scale. On one occasion, a nonrating procedure was employed, viz., requiring the subject to generate a word that could be appropriately paired with the target item. The nonsemantic tasks were quite heterogenous but may be roughly grouped into three classes: (*a*) orthographic, (*b*) acoustic, and (*c*) syntactic. A listing of the specific procedures falling into each of these categories follows: (*a*) checking for the presence of certain letters, estimating or counting the numbers of such letters, estimating the number of syllables; (*b*) identifying the speakers who recorded a list of TBR words by their voices, generating rhymes of the target words; (*c*) categorizing words according to part of speech, judging the appropriateness of a word for a simple sentence frame. In some cases at least, the validity of the semantic–nonsemantic classification is open to question. It is not self-evident that one has to engage in extensive semantic processing in order to judge the frequency of occurrence of a word, nor is it obvious that one can entirely ignore meaning when making decisions about parts of speech.

The major finding in these experiments is that semantic tasks lead to higher recall than nonsemantic ones. This difference is found for both intentional and incidental learners. For the most part, instructions to learn have little effect, even when the orienting tasks are nonsemantic. On the face of it, such instructions do not lead subjects to go beyond the processing activities involved in the orienting task. However that may be, the general conclusion that attention to semantic features is favorable to the recall of meaningful words is likely to prove correct, but complex methodological and interpretative problems remain to be resolved before this effect is adequately understood.

First, it is essential to make sure that the difference between semantic and nonsemantic tasks is not confounded with other factors that are likely to influence recall. One potentially important source of confounding is that the semantic tasks typically call for subjective ratings of the items on a single dimension, whereas most of the nonsemantic tasks require discriminative judgments specific to a single item. In rating a series of words on the same dimension the subject is very likely to make comparisons among the items for purposes of establishing a subjective scale.[3] Such comparisons—what Jacoby (1974) called "looking back" through the list—entail displaced rehearsal and bring related items into functional contiguity with each other. Thus, a subjective rating task should enhance clustering of associatively related items as well as the level of recall. Both results have been obtained in the experiments of the Jenkins group. The potential importance of the rating process per se is underscored by the results of a recent study by Eagle and Mulliken (1974, Experiment II). These investigators found that rating the pleasantness of words and rating the pleasantness of the sounds of the words without regard to meaning produced highly similar levels of recall and of recognition under both intentional and incidental conditions.

[3] This point was called to my attention by Dr. John J. Shaughnessy. I also want to thank Dr. Shaughnessy for his helpful comments on this chapter.

To the extent that semantic and nonsemantic tasks entail different amounts of displaced rehearsal, the variations in recall cannot be simply related to item-specific encoding. The question of whether the two types of tasks create different amounts of interference also warrants serious consideration. It has been emphasized that an orienting task is not just a device for activating a certain type of processing; it is also an event interpolated after exposure to the TBR item and as such can become a source of interference. The amount of interference can be expected to be a function of the difficulty of the orienting task, where difficulty refers essentially to the amount of information reduction required of the subject. When this definition of difficulty is used, retroactive losses in short-term retention are found to vary directly with difficulty (Posner & Konnick, 1966; Posner & Rossman, 1965). In performing the nonsemantic tasks the subjects have to make decisions that could be objectively right or wrong rather than subjective judgments. Thus, it becomes reasonable to say that a greater amount of information has to be reduced in the nonsemantic than the semantic tasks, and in that sense the former are more difficult than the latter and are more likely to interfere with the processing and storage of the TBR items.

Walsh and Jenkins (1973) discounted the possibility that the difficulty of the orienting task can have a systematic effect on recall, primarily on the ground that the addition of a nonsemantic to a semantic task did not produce a significant decline in performance. Two comments on this conclusion are in order. First, the differences between single-task and dual-task conditions were always in the expected direction. In the assessment of these effects, exclusive reliance was placed on multiple comparisons among individual groups receiving different combinations of tasks; the appropriate contrasts between combined single-task and dual-task treatments were not evaluated. Thus, the empirical facts are in doubt. Second, whatever the significance of these particular results, one could not seriously entertain the proposition that recall will remain unchanged no matter how many orienting tasks are imposed on the subject, provided one of them is semantic. The products of semantic processing cannot be assumed to have unlimited resistance to interference from other activities. To isolate the effects of the mode of processing per se, it is necessary to compare tasks that can reasonably be assumed to be equal in difficulty and interfering potential (see Treisman & Tuxworth, 1974).

d. *Item-specific encoding.*   The variations in orienting tasks considered thus far were designed to encourage particular types of processing by directing the subject's attention to selected attributes or dimensions of the materials. The next step in the evolution of the method was the use of orienting tasks that prescribe a specific encoding for each individual item.

Such item-specific orienting tasks were employed in a recent series of experiments by Craik and Tulving (1975). These investigators took their point of departure from the concept of depth of processing formulated by Craik and Lockhart (1972). According to this view, the processing of a stimulus evolves through a series of stages which can be graded along a continuum of depth, from sensory analysis and pattern recognition to semantic–cognitive elaboration. The depth to which analysis proceeds determines subsequent retention. The purpose of the experiments of Craik and Tulving was to verify the postulated relationship between depth of processing and retention.

The independent index of depth adopted initially was processing time, on the assumption that the deeper the level of analysis the more time is required to attain it. The nature of the orienting task was varied to control the level of processing. For this purpose, an ingenious new procedure was introduced: before a word was shown, the subject was asked a question about it which he answered after the presentation of the item. Three kinds of questions were asked, requiring decisions about physical, phonemic, and semantic characteristics of the words, respectively. These decisions were assumed to depend, in the order listed, on increasingly deeper levels of processing. Typical queries were whether the word was (a) printed in capital letters, (b) rhymed with a sample word, or (c) was a member of a specified taxonomic category or would fit into a given sentence frame. Usually the three types of queries occurred with equal frequency during the presentation of a list, with half of the questions of each type requiring a "yes," and the other half a "no," answer. It is important to note that each of the phonemic and semantic queries was unique, that is, rhymes and categories (or sentence frames) were not used more than once, whereas the question about case remained the same.

The results showed consistently that both decision latencies and performance on tests of recognition and recall increased monotonically as the questions moved from the structural to the phonemic and then to the semantic level. These trends were obtained under both incidental and intentional conditions, although instructions to learn did serve to enhance the amount retained. Thus, the expected correlation between processing time (the independent index of depth) and retention was observed. A check experiment made it clear, however, that level of retention was not critically tied to processing time; thus, the latter was discarded as an index of depth. Furthermore, a difficulty was created for the original conceptualization by the finding that "yes" responses led to better retention than "no" responses, especially at the deeper levels. Positive and negative decisions presumably required the same level of processing. Further analysis of this relationship led the authors to the conclusion that the encoding was richer or more elaborate when the TBR word was congruent rather than incongruent with the question (see Schulman, 1974). Thus, richness or "spread" of encoding may be more important for subsequent retention than sheer depth.

An important question that remained was whether and to what extent the variations in retention were attributable to interitem similarity, that is, the distinctiveness of the encoding operations. This issue is of critical importance since the queries about case were all identical whereas those at the other two levels were unique; as Craik and Tulving (1975) note, however, the encoding operations for successive rhyme decisions may reasonably be regarded as more similar than those for category decisions. For purposes of assessing the influence of this factor, the relative frequency (set size) of the three types of queries was varied systematically, with the total number of queries held constant. The results showed that recognition improved substantially as set size was reduced for rhyming items, such that performance was equal after a small number of rhyming queries and a large number of categorical queries. Set size had no effect on the retention of categorical items (which was near ceiling) and of case items. The authors concluded that isolation effects may contribute to the difference in retention but cannot provide a full explanation of the findings.

This conclusion warrants further examination. Consider the rhyming and the categorical queries. Since it was possible to find an adjustment of set sizes that entirely eliminated differences in retention between these two classes of items, it is no longer possible to argue that the durability of the traces of *individual items* is significantly influenced by the nature of the encoding operation. (In this connection, also note a reference to as yet unpublished data showing that differences in cued recall were likewise minimized or eliminated when identical questions were used for several words.) The only necessary inference is that the two classes of items differ in susceptibility to intralist interference. This difference bears primarily on the similarity relations within the two classes. Note, for example, that the query and the target are highly similar for rhymes but not for categories. In any event, susceptibility to interitem interference has no direct implications for the depth of encoding of individual words.

There remains the finding that set size did not influence retention following case judgments. Retention of this particular class of items remained low, however, even under intentional conditions at a slow rate of presentation. It appears, therefore, that the structural judgment is a source of interference. Moreover, it is difficult to see in what sense a judgment of case can be taken to reflect an encoding of the word, no matter how shallow, since the discrimination can be based on the perception of a single letter. This is not the place to speculate about the reasons why an interpolated case judgment is so detrimental to retention. One may wonder, however, whether the results would have remained the same, under intentional conditions at least, if unmixed rather than mixed lists had been used. The intentional learner may well give priority (see Underwood, 1964a, pp. 67 ff.) to items for which a potentially useful retrieval cue, such as a rhyme or a category name, is supplied.

The experiments of Craik and Tulving deserve careful and detailed examination because they represent the most systematic and analytic attempt made thus far to bring encoding under direct control by means of orienting tasks. The results illustrate well both the power and the limitations of this class of manipulations. Large differences in retention were produced, many of which had been predicted on theoretical grounds. At the same time, the total pattern of results appears to give considerable support to the conclusion that orienting tasks influence retention in a variety of ways, not just by activating a particular type of encoding. There is clear evidence for significant effects of intralist similarity related to the nature of the task. The procedures used in these experiments bring to the fore the fact that components of the orienting task can function as important retrieval cues, and there is strong circumstantial evidence that some tasks are highly effective sources of interference. It is difficult indeed to manipulate encoding *qua* encoding, even under conditions of incidental learning, without involving other processes that are important for retention.

3. Forced Encoding

The orienting tasks developed by Craik and Tulving are directly continuous with manipulations of the verbal context at the time of presentation for purposes of controlling the encoding of the TBR words. Investigators using the latter procedure have been interested primarily in influencing the specific semantic interpretation of the items.

a. Biasing the interpretation of ambiguous words. How sensitive is the encoding process to variations in context? In seeking an answer to this question, investigators have relied heavily on the use of homographs— words that are spelled alike but have different and unrelated meanings. A widely cited study by Light and Carter-Sobell (1970) showed that recognition was significantly higher when the context during training and test remained the same than when it was changed so as to suggest a different meaning of the homograph. Recognition was less severely impaired when the context was changed but the original meaning of the homograph was preserved, or when the context was deleted altogether at the time of test. These trends conformed to expectations (see also Marcel & Steel, 1973). The results of a study by Hunt and Ellis (1974) have, however, served to blur the picture. Comparing the effects of several contextual variations within the same design, these investigators found, among other things, that changes in context that did, and changes that did not, preserve the original meaning of the homograph yielded essentially equivalent levels of recognition. Furthermore, deletion of context led to better performance than any condition of contextual change. The most recent relevant finding is that the effect of contextual change on the recognition of homographs is eliminated altogether under conditions of forced choice (Pellegrino & Salzberg, 1975). It should also be noted that contextual change appears to have no effect on the amount of improvement in recognition produced by repetition of the TBR homographs (Davis, Lockhart, & Thomson, 1972).

Homographs have also been used widely in investigations of the spacing effect in free recall to test the hypothesis that the advantage of distributed over massed repetition is attributable to greater variability of encoding. The use of homographs presumably makes it possible to control the encoding of the critical words, and the spacing effect should be eliminated when the sequence of encodings is the same for massed and distributed items. Furthermore, the level of recall should be higher when the interpretation of the homograph changes between repetitions than when it remains the same. The results of numerous studies based on this logic have yielded widely divergent results (for a brief summary see Postman, 1975, p. 317).

Apart from the troublesome inconsistencies in experimental findings, the use of homographs is probably not a promising technique for the analysis of context-dependent encoding processes. The basic shortcoming of this method lies in the use of materials that are not representative of the large majority of words. The distinguishing characteristic of homographs is that the alternative meanings of such words are not related. Thus, whatever the outcome of the experiments, the results cannot be generalized to words that have different but related meanings. Furthermore, the existence of separate and distinct meanings makes it easy for a subject to adopt a strategy that nullifies the intent of the experimental manipulation. Once a subject realizes that the targets and distractors on a recognition test are homographs, he should in many, if not most, cases be able to generate the alternative meaning and thus gain access to the trace of the original presentation regardless of the change in context. The possibility that subjects engage in such additional processing has been recognized (Light & Carter-Sobell, 1970; Pellegrino & Salzberg, 1975). The point worth emphasizing is that the use of homographs probably maximizes the subject's ability to ignore the test context in sampling the semantic features of the TBR item. The likelihood that subjects adopt the strategy of ignoring context undoubtedly varies from one experimental arrangement to the next. The variability of the empirical findings can be understood on this basis, as well as the absence of a context effect in forced-choice recognition. In the latter case, the requirement to make a decision on each item presumably encourages additional processing (Pellegrino & Salzberg, 1975).

b. Elaboration.   Contextual manipulations such as those discussed in the last section are expected to influence the encoding of individual TBR words. Procedures designed to bring the process of associative mediation or elaboration under direct experimental control are now considered. One widely used method consists of presenting paired associates embedded in sentences or phrases; the subject is informed that the use of these mnemonic aids will facilitate the acquisition of the paired-associate task. The objective is to engage the same types of encoding processes as are activated by instructions to the subjects to generate their own verbal mediators. Prescribing the specific mnemonics for each pair makes it possible to vary the nature of the mediators systematically.

The problems of interpretation are similar to those encountered in the analysis of instructional effects: the control baseline remains indeterminate, and the degree of compliance on the part of the subject is difficult to ascertain. For what they are worth, responses to postexperimental inquiries indicate that subjects are sometimes disposed to ignore the prescribed mnemonics in favor of constructions of their own (for example, Kulhavy, 1970). When subjects do appear to attend to the supplied encodings, two other important questions come to the fore. First, are the devices provided by the experimenter as effective as those the subject could have generated by himself? If not, why not? Second, can the presented encodings become a source of interference if they come into conflict with the subject's idiosyncratic ones? These questions concern rather elusive subjective events, and the answers may reasonably be expected to vary from one experimental situation to the next. Thus, it is not surprising that investigations of the effects of supplied mnemonics have yielded inconsistent results.

Supplied mnemonics should be especially beneficial to children who have not as yet developed mediational skills of their own. This expectation was fully borne out in a series of investigations by Rohwer and his associates (Rohwer, 1966; Rohwer & Levin, 1968; Rohwer & Lynch, 1966, 1967; Rohwer, Lynch, Levin, & Suzuki, 1967; Rohwer, Shuell, & Levin, 1967; Suzuki & Rohwer, 1968). The learning materials were paired nouns. Facilitation was greater when a verb rather than a preposition was used as a connective; conjunctions were entirely ineffective. (Potential artifacts, such as variations in semantic constraint and intralist similarity, were ruled out.) Normal sentences improved performance whereas anomalous ones did not. Presentation of the mnemonic during study (rather than at the time of test) was a necessary condition of facilitation. Thus, systematic effects of semantic structure on the encoding and storage of the TBR words could be inferred. The picture is unfortunately clouded, however, by several failures to replicate the basic finding that sentence embedding enhances learning (Davidson, Schwenn, & Adams, 1970; Levin, 1970; Levin & Horvitz, 1971; Levin, Horvitz, & Kaplan, 1971; Yuille & Pritchard, 1969).

There is no clear reason for the discrepant results. Levin and his colleagues suggested that the modality of presentation may be a critical factor: in their experiments, facilitation occurred when the presentation of the embedding sentences was aural, but not when it was visual as well as aural. They speculated that visual presentation fosters the establishment of competing responses that interfere with the recall of the TBR words. This explanation is hardly tenable, however, in view of the fact that in all but one of the successful experiments cited above the subjects saw the sentences. The phenomenon is apparently a labile one, and the exact conditions on which facilitation depends remain to be identified.

With adult subjects, the results are even more erratic. A variety of experimenter-supplied mnemonics has been used, ranging from one-step mediators to sentential elaboration. In some studies, the expected facilitation relative to a control treatment was observed (Bower & Winzenz, 1970; Duffy, 1971; Epstein, Rock, & Zuckerman, 1960; Schwartz, 1971). In other studies, the operation was ineffective (Bower, 1972a; Dallett, 1964; Kulhavy, 1970; Pelton, 1969). Finally, Duffy and Montague (1971) found that supplied sentence mnemonics significantly lowered learning performance, apparently because they interfered with the use of more effective idiosyncratic encodings. This interpretation is consistent with the results of several investigations in which subject-generated mnemonics proved significantly more beneficial than equivalent ones supplied by the experimenter (Bobrow & Bower, 1969; Bower & Winzenz, 1970; Pelton, 1969; Schwartz, 1971). The question then arises of whether subject-generated linkages are more effective because they are idiosyncratic or because they are generated rather than provided externally.

Idiosyncratic mediators might be superior because they are highly available to the subject. After finding that prior familiarization failed to change the relative effectiveness of mediators, Bobrow and Bower (1969) advanced the hypothesis that generated encodings foster a deeper understanding of the verbal sequences than do supplied ones and thereby aid retention. The fact that semantic orienting tasks produce better incidental learning than nonsemantic ones appeared to give at least some indirect support to this contention. The argument is far from conclusive, however, as long as an appreciable proportion of supplied mediators differs from those the subject would have generated on his own. Subsequently, Schwartz and Walsh (1974) showed that under conditions ensuring the identity of generated and supplied mediators the differences in retention were eliminated. One has to agree with their conclusion that the importance of mediator origin per se remains to be demonstrated.

On the face of it, the procedure of supplying mediators to a subject learning a list of paired associates appears to be a straightforward technique for assessing the relative efficiency of different modes of encoding. In practice, the results have often proved variable and inconsistent. The source of the difficulty seems to be that the subject is given a hybrid task, namely, to learn the paired associates as such and also to establish the embedding sentences or phrases as retrieval cues to the response terms. These two tasks may conflict to varying degrees, depending on the subject's preexperimental dispositions and the magnitude of the memory load imposed by the addition of prescribed verbal contexts. Consequently, both the potential usefulness of specific mediators and the extent of the subjects' compliance with the instructions may be expected to vary widely. If one is interested in demonstrating that sentential contexts are facilitative, the most direct procedure is to ask the subjects to learn the sentences and then to test for retention of the constituent terms.

4. Item Properties and Encoding

Inferences about encoding processes become necessarily indirect when item properties such as frequency, meaningfulness, or concreteness are manipulated. Certain assumptions are made about correlations between specific item properties and modes of processing; on the basis of these assumptions, predictions then are made about the effects of these properties on acquisition and retention. This approach has a long and continuous history in the study of verbal learning. The logic has remained the same, although the characteristics of processing related to item properties have changed concomitantly with theoretical developments. The relevant literature is far too voluminous and complex to permit a systematic discussion of the methodological problems in this line of research. Therefore, only a few selected points that bear on the usefulness and the limitations of experimental analyses based on the manipulation of item properties are considered.

a. Isolation of variables.   An obvious problem is that the item property nominally manipulated may not be the functionally effective one. This difficulty is unavoidable because verbal units can be classified and scaled in many ways, and there is a complex pattern of intercorrelations among the various scaled properties (e.g., Frincke, 1968; Paivio, 1968). One may then attempt to isolate the contribution of a particular variable by holding other variables constant statistically, that is, by determining the partial correlation between the variable of interest and measures of learning. One well-known analysis of this type was carried out by Underwood and Schulz (1960) to separate out the effects on response learning of trigram frequency and pronunciability. They found that the apparent positive relationship between frequency and learning was attributable entirely to the correlated variable of pronunciability (Underwood & Schulz, 1960, pp. 188ff.). Partial correlations were also used to support the contention that word meaningfulness has no residual effect on learning when the imagery value of nouns is controlled (Paivio, 1967; Paivio & Olver, 1964).

An alternative approach is to construct lists of items in which one attribute is held constant at some arbitrary value and the other attribute is allowed to vary. The direction and magnitude of the effects of each separate variable can then be assessed and compared. This method of holding a correlated variable constant experimentally rather than statistically has been used to contrast the influence of such attributes as word frequency and meaningfulness (Modigliani & Saltz, 1969; Saltz, 1967; Saltz & Modigliani, 1967), and imagery value and meaningfulness (Smythe & Paivio, 1968; Paivio, Smythe, & Yuille, 1968). The former studies yielded a complex pattern of results: on the stimulus side, increases in frequency retarded learning, whereas increases in meaningfulness had a facilitative effect; on the response side, increases in the values of both variables improved acquisition, but only if the other variable was held constant at a high level. In the latter studies, imagery value proved to be a potent positive factor, whereas the influence of meaningfulness, if any, intended to be negative.

One basic difficulty inherent in such designs stems from the constraints on item sampling imposed by the existence of a correlation between the relevant attributes. Thus, nouns that have high frequency and low meaningfulness are rare, and items meeting both these criteria are likely to have special properties. Probably as a consequence of these constraints, the m values compared in Saltz's experiment were all relatively high, whereas the frequency values varied over a very wide range. In the experiment of Paivio *et al.* (1968), the limitations on item sampling were apparently such that the independent assessment of the effects of meaningfulness was based on lists composed almost entirely of abstract words of relatively low frequency. Hence, the results do not permit any sweeping generalizations about the effects of meaningfulness on learning unless the gratuitous assumption is made that meaningfulness interacts with neither concreteness nor word frequency. (As mentioned above, an interaction of meaningfulness with frequency, in fact, has been reported, even over a restricted range of relatively high m values.) In short, artificial constraints on item sampling make it difficult to assess the role of a single attribute in learning, with correlated attributes held constant.

There is never any assurance, of course, that all confounding variables have been considered when the effects of a particular item property are evaluated. The variable of imagery–concreteness again provides a useful illustration. Considerable experimental evidence has been marshaled to demonstrate that neither word frequency nor meaningfulness can account for the positive effects of this variable on learning. In light of some recent findings it becomes necessary to consider the influence of other item characteristics that appear to be systematically related to imagery–concreteness. Thus, Kintsch (1972) has shown that speed of learning varies directly with imagery value and inversely with lexical complexity when these two factors are manipulated orthogonally. Since abstractness and complexity are correlated, it is likely that the influence of imagery value per se has been consistently overestimated. Galbraith and Underwood (1973) have reported that abstract words have higher subjective frequency and are perceived as occurring in a greater variety of contexts than concrete ones. There may be other correlates of concreteness that remain to be identified. The existence of possible confounding factors is, of course, not peculiar to the dimension of imagery–concreteness. It becomes a matter of special concern, however, when item scaling serves as the primary operational base for a comprehensive theory of verbal processes.

b. *Meaningfulness.* The manipulation of item properties yields essentially correlational data, from which inferences are drawn about characteristics of the learning process. The validity of such inferences can often be checked by independent experimental operations. Consider, for example, the empirical finding that variations in response meaningfulness produce substantially larger effects on speed of paired-associate learning than do corresponding variations in stimulus meaningfulness (for example, Cieutat, Stockwell, & Noble, 1958). One explanation of this fact is that response meaningfulness influences both the response-learning and the associative stages of acquisition, whereas stimulus meaningfulness influences only the latter (Underwood & Schulz, 1960). This interpretation led to several predictions that could be checked experimentally: (*a*) prior response familiarization should facilitate subsequent paired-associate learning by shortening the duration of the response-learning stage (Underwood, Runquist, & Schulz, 1959); (*b*) response familiarization should be more beneficial than stimulus familiarization, especially when the critical items are unfamiliar and require integration (for example, Schulz & Martin, 1964; Underwood & Schulz, 1960); (*c*) The positive effects of response familiarization should be reduced or eliminated when performance on the test task is measured by recognition so that response recall is no longer required (Kuiken & Schulz, 1968; Saltz & Felton, 1968). With the exception of the experiment by Saltz and Felton, all the studies cited yielded results in accord with the predictions. There are other data that complicate the picture, especially with respect to the effects of familiarization when the critical items are familiar words. This matter will not be pursued here. The important point is that within the framework of two-stage theory there has been a productive interplay of correlational measurement and analytic experimentation in the exploration of the relationship between meaningfulness and learning.

It has proved more difficult to obtain independent experimental support for the interpretation of the effects of stimulus meaningfulness in terms of encoding variability. Martin (1968) advanced the hypothesis that, at least for nonintegrated stimuli, encoding variability is inversely related to meaningfulness. Since progress in associative learning depends on the stability of stimulus encoding, speed of paired-associate acquisition should be related directly to stimulus meaningfulness. The opposite relation should obtain for transfer learning when a new response has to be attached to an old stimulus (AB–AD, AB–ABr). Establishment of the new association is assumed to require recoding of the stimulus, which should be easier when meaningfulness is low rather than high. Tests of these predictions have yielded inconsistent results (Martin, 1968; Martin & Carey, 1971; Postman & Stark, 1971; Weaver, McCann, & Wehr, 1970). Perhaps more important, the proposition that differences in encoding variability are responsible for the effects of stimulus meaningfulness on acquisition and transfer has not been translated into experimental tests that go beyond the correlation of item properties with performance.

   c. *Imagery–concreteness.*   When one comes to the scaled attributes of imagery value and concreteness, one finds that the effects of these attributes on learning and retention are explained in terms of the differential involvement of two independent (although partially interconnected) systems of information processing, namely, the imagery system and the verbal system (Paivio, 1971, 1975). The former is assumed to be most effective for spatial organization, and the latter for sequential organization. The most important converging operation for validating this inference has been the instructional manipulation of the subject's encoding activities. Some of the difficult problems of interpretation posed by the results of such studies have already been discussed. The hypothesis that the two systems are differentially specialized for spatial and for sequential organization has also been tested experimentally. On the assumption that the development of referential imagery is a time-dependent process, interest has centered on the interaction of rate of presentation, type of task (sequential versus nonsequential), and item properties (Paivio & Csapo, 1969, 1971). For verbal items, the results were far from impressive. For example, in the earlier experiment, the differences between concrete and abstract words in free recall and recognition (nonsequential tasks) showed only minimal increases when the presentation rate was decreased by a factor of more than two. The pattern is more clearly consistent with theoretical expectations when pictures and abstract words are compared. The interpretation hinges on the validity of the assumption that under a fast rate of presentation subjects do not have time to label the pictures (they may have labeled at least some of the stimuli). Furthermore, it is far from certain that the only critical difference between pictures and words as input stimuli lies in the relative availability of verbal and imaginal codes. Finally, in other experiments retention of sequential order was found to be better after pictorial than after verbal presentation (Nelson, Brooks, & Borden, 1973; Snodgrass & Antone, 1974; for a discussion of these findings, see Paivio, 1975).

The differentiation between a verbal and an imagery system of information processing appears to derive its basic support from the correlations between item properties and performance and has only weak independent support. Hence, the theoretical superstructure rests on a tenuous foundation. The inferential gap between correlational data and the postulation of entire systems of representation is not easily bridged. The study of item properties is most likely to yield theoretically useful results when the interpretation centers on circumscribed subprocesses of learning that are amenable to independent manipulation.

5. Discriminative Coding

The procedures discussed thus far focus on attributes that are, in Underwood's (1969) terms, task dependent. Semantic or associative attributes are clearly of this type. Another approach has been used successfully in the exploration of the role of task-independent attributes. Such attributes are assumed to be encoded regardless of task content and serve primarily to discriminate one memory from another. To demonstrate the functional value of a discriminative attribute, it is necessary to create test situations in which it can be used effectively. Thus, Underwood has been able to marshal considerable evidence that the frequency attribute becomes salient on tests of recognition (e.g., Underwood, 1972a, 1974). The development of the frequency theory of verbal discrimination learning (Ekstrand, Wallace, & Underwood, 1966) shows how the hypothesized function of a specific attribute can be progressively validated by means of converging operations. The gist of the theory is, of course, that under the arrangements of the verbal discrimination task greater subjective frequency accrues to the correct than to the incorrect items. It follows that any operation that serves to enhance the frequency differential between the members of a pair should increase speed of acquisition; any operation that serves to reduce the frequency differential should have the opposite effect. A large number of such operations have been devised, for example, prior familiarization with right or wrong items, and intralist repetition of the two types of items. The theory also entails specific predictions about the course of transfer, retroaction, and proaction, on the assumption that performance should become degraded as the frequency discrimination becomes increasingly difficult. Many of the predictions have been confirmed. The relevant evidence was reviewed recently (Eckert & Kanak, 1974), and it will not be considered further here, nor will the question of what processes other than frequency discrimination might contribute to the mastery of this task be examined. The main point of interest here is methodological. The procedures used to test the frequency theory illustrate well the value of converging operations in establishing the functional significance of a particular dimension of encoding.

6. Assessment of the Characteristics of Encoding

In this section I comment very briefly on some of the methods that are used to determine the nature of the subject's encoding activities during the acquisition of a particular task. A common feature of these methods is that the assessment occurs after the end of practice; in a broad sense, they may, therefore, be regarded as transfer procedures, regardless of whether the experimental arrangements would be conventionally classified under this heading. As transfer procedures, the methods of assessing encoding are likely to share common interpretative problems. Questions that inevitably arise are: (a) to what extent performance on the critical test task is determined by the characteristics of that task itself rather than by the products of prior learning; and (b) to what extent test performance reflects prior encoding activities directly as distinct from the subject's ability to transform what he has learned so as to meet the requirements of a new task.

a. *Subjects' responses to postexperimental inquiries.* This method of ascertaining how items were encoded during acquisition is used widely, especially in studies of natural language mediators and imagery (for a review see Montague, 1972). The difficulties that arise in the interpretation of the subjects' reports are obvious and generally recognized. One never knows whether the reported mediators occurred to the subject at the time of test or were actually used in learning. Even if the subject did think about the mediators in the course of learning, it is uncertain whether the mediators actually influenced acquisition in a significant way or were, as Underwood (1972b, p. 17) put it, epiphenomenal. This uncertainty remains when the subjects are required to report mediators during the learning trials. Furthermore, the latter procedure drastically changes the nature of the subject's task and permits no conclusions about what happens without such intervention. Finally, it should be noted that the scaling of items with respect to the frequency of mediator elicitation has proved an indifferent predictor of learning (Montague & Kiess, 1968).

b. *Component selection.* Tests for cue selection represent one of the basic methods for distinguishing between nominal and functional stimuli. After a response has been learned to a compound, individual components of the compound, or combinations of components, are presented as cues to determine which of them had become functional stimuli during acquisition. The logic of the procedure is straightforward, but serious problems of measurement and interpretation arise when it is implemented in experimental practice. These problems were discussed extensively in a review by Richardson (1971), and it will be sufficient for present purposes to enumerate the major points emphasized by him:

1. On the test of transfer, the probability of recall in the presence of a given component is a measure of cue effectiveness but does not in itself index the degree of cue selection. The basic reason is, of course, that cue effectiveness reflects not only selection but also the difficulty of forming an association between the component and the response. Thus, when a compound consists of trigrams surrounded by colors, the latter may be more effective cues, even in the absence of differential selection, because they lead to more rapid learning. Consequently, degree of selection must be defined in terms of the difference between cue effectiveness and component-response difficulty.

2. Average differences in cue selection may be observed either because a majority of subjects responds to one cue and the remainder to another, or because most subjects distribute their responses unevenly between the two cues. Thus, the consistency of cue selection must be considered in the interpretation of transfer results. Consistency may be relatively low for a group, but high for individual subjects.

3. Selection, if it occurs, may be more or less efficient. Efficiency refers to the probability that only one component is selected as the functional cue. Efficiency is obviously an important parameter of selection, but its assessment requires that the same subjects be tested with different components, with all the attendant problems of repeated measurement.

4. When a component is effective, it often remains uncertain whether the correct response was mediated by another component.

These problems of measurement and interpretation are not in principle insurmountable, although some of them have proved difficult to resolve. It remains uncertain, for example, what an appropriate basis is for distinguishing between mediated and nonmediated responses to a component. One possibility is to impose the dual criterion that the component elicit the correct response and that the subject be unable to recall other components of the compound (Postman & Greenbloom, 1967). Application of this rule probably leads to an underestimation of the amount of cue selection. The assumption that associations between components develop in the course of learning has itself been questioned (Martin, 1971b; Wichawut & Martin, 1970) but the evidence on this point is far from conclusive (see Postman & Underwood, 1973). The most serious limitation of existing data is the frequent failure to take account of the factor of component-response difficulty; in such cases, variations in cue effectiveness are demonstrated, but the degree of cue selection cannot be specified.

Transfer tests at the end of learning indicate which components of a compound were selected and thus provide information about the factors influencing selection, for example, the meaningfulness or the spatial position of the component. Such data tell us little, however, about the ways in which stimulus selection influences the process of acquisition. The analysis of the latter problem brings to the fore the relationship between efficiency of learning and the opportunities for selection of discriminative cues afforded by the structure of the stimulus set. Runquist (1973, 1975) has presented persuasive evidence that, with fractionable stimuli, the nonredundant elements available for selection form the basis for the establishment of a discriminative code, a code that serves to reduce cue confusion and thus to alleviate intralist interference. The operation of this code is better described as " . . . a rule for generating particular codes than the learning of a separate code for each stimulus" (Runquist, 1975, p. 147). The ease with which the discriminative code is established depends not so much on the sheer amount of element redundancy (for example, letter duplication) as on the regularity of the positions of both discriminative and redundant elements. Runquist's experiments are important because they focus systematically on the functional consequences of cue selection for acquisition. In this area of inquiry, there may have been too much emphasis on the measurement of selection per se, at the expense of analytic investigations of the role of selection in the development of associations and the reduction of interference.

c. Identification of the functional stimulus. A test for componential selection is a special case of the transfer procedures directed toward the identification of functional stimuli. The distinguishing characteristic of componential tests is that the alternative cues are limited to components of the nominal compound. In other cases, the range of potential cues is not similarly restricted; the search for the functional stimulus in serial learning is a case in point. As is well known, there is some experimental support for each of the major hypotheses about the nature of the effective stimulus in serial learning—item-to-item chaining, association to serial position, and a dual-process principle combining the two (for a review of the literature see Bewley, 1972). Furthermore, individuals apparently vary considerably in their preferences for these and other more complex cues (Posnansky, 1972). Thus, the search has proved inconclusive. The history of this problem brings out clearly the basic limitations of transfer tests for assessing prior encoding activities.

First, the inherent characteristics of the transfer test have been shown to have a decisive influence on the conclusions that are drawn about the products of serial learning. Thus, when double-function paired-associate lists are used as the transfer task, the evidence for associations between adjacent items is typically weak (see Young, 1968). In a double-function list, individual items serve as both stimuli and responses, just as they presumably do in serial learning. The acquisition of such a list is extremely difficult, apparently because of the heavy interference between forward and backward associations; under these circumstances, differential transfer effects of prior learning are likely to be minimal. By contrast, when Crowder (1968) measured transfer between serial and continuous paired-associate lists, he obtained clear evidence for sequential chaining.

Second, transfer performance depends to a significant degree on whether or not the subject attempts to make use of the previously acquired serial information, and not necessarily on the manner in which that information was originally encoded. Thus, positive transfer from serial to paired-associate learning is facilitated when subjects are informed about the relationship between successive lists, that is, when they know that the TBR pairs are composed of adjacent members of the serial list (e.g., Postman & Stark, 1967). If the strategy of relying on serial dependencies is inefficent for the acquisition of the paired associates, the instructed subjects fall behind the uninstructed ones (Lesgold & Bower, 1970). Characteristics of transfer performance do not permit any firm conclusions, therefore, about the process of serial learning per se. This reservation also applies to recent attempts to document the role of organizational factors in serial learning by measures of output order and clustering obtained on subsequent tests of free recall (Martin & Noreen, 1974).

d. Release from PI. Wickens (1970, 1972) and numerous other investigators following his lead have used release from PI as the criterion for inferring the functional effectiveness of a dimension of encoding. The basic experimental procedure consists of the presentation of a series of TBR strings, each of which is followed by a test of retention. When the class of materials remains the same, performance typically declines over the successive tests, that is, there is a buildup of PI. Release from PI is said to occur when a change in an item attribute (for example, the introduction of a new conceptual category) leads to improved retention. That attribute then qualifies as a dimension of encoding. A large number of dimensions, both semantic and nonsemantic, has been identified in this manner. The critical link in the chain of inference is the assumption that the reduction in interference reflects a change in encoding. This assumption has now been called into question by the finding that the degree of release from PI remains unchanged when a shift in item classification is first induced at the time of test rather than during input (Gardiner, Craik, & Birtwistle, 1972). The implication is, of course, that the buildup and reduction of interference reflect changes in the effectiveness of retrieval cues. Important questions have also been raised about the validity of the inference that all the dimensions for which release from PI is observed are simultaneously encoded during the presentation of a word. The various attributes are not necessarily independent; more important, to the extent that the experimental arrangements serve to prime the encoding of successive items along the critical dimension, the total number of attributes encoded simultaneously is likely to be substantially overestimated (Underwood, 1972b). Thus, it is far from clear that the list of attributes found to be effective in release experiments adds up to a description of the dimensions of word encoding.

   e. *Retrieval cuing.*   Having alluded earlier to the problems of inference that arise when retrieval cuing is used to ascertain how an input event was encoded, I now wish to call attention to two additional points. First, when the effectiveness of an extralist output cue serves as the criterion for deciding whether or not a given type of information was encoded and stored, there is an important difference between the conclusions that can be drawn from positive and from negative outcomes. If the cue is effective, it is possible to infer that the informational content of the cue and the trace overlapped. If the cue is ineffective, however, the opposite inference—that the relevant information had not been encoded and stored—is hazardous. A cue may be ineffective for other reasons: recognizing the cue as new, the subject may not attempt to retrieve the TBR word, terminate his search prematurely, or adopt a high criterion in deciding on the correctness of a potential response. Evidence for the operation of such factors has come to light in recent investigations of the principle of encoding specificity proposed by Tulving and Thomson (1973), in which the effectiveness of extralist cues is used to assess the nature of the information in the episodic trace (e.g., Murphy & Wallace, 1974; Pellegrino & Salzberg, 1975; Postman, in press, b; Santa & Lamwers, 1974).

   Second, the use of successive retrieval cues for purposes of mapping the content of the memory trace (Tulving & Bower, 1974; Tulving & Watkins, 1975) confronts us squarely with the problem of delimiting the circumstances under which the subject's response dispositions are not changed as a result of successive testing operations. On logical grounds, it is doubtful whether such circumstances can ever be identified with confidence. As Woodworth (1938) put it a long time ago, ''We cannot observe the state of a memory trace without letting it act and so strengthening or perhaps distorting it and altering its subsequent history [p. 90].'' It is now being argued that the administration of an ineffective cue leaves the trace intact; only the presentation of a cue that leads to successful recall might result in a recoding of the trace (Tulving & Watkins, 1975, p. 266). It is far from clear that this assumption is justified, especially in the context of experiments in which the subject is exposed to more than one item. The difficulty is that a failure of recall cannot be taken to imply the absence of any response involving TBR units. The correct item may be retrieved and erroneously rejected, or, more likely, another word from the input list may be retrieved either covertly or overtly. The traces of TBR items that are thus incorrectly processed certainly may be altered; when these traces become targets, performance would then be systematically influenced. In short, it is difficult ever to rule out the possibility that prior tests, even if they are unsuccessful, will bias the outcome of subsequent tests.

f. Attribute-specific tests. Such tests are designed either to assess the retention of specific attributes of input events or to examine the functional role of attributes in mediating retrieval, or discriminations among memories. The latter approach, exemplified by investigations of recognition and verbal discrimination learning within the framework of frequency theory, has already been considered. Studies exploring the range of encoded attributes have yielded evidence of retention for a variety of input features, including spatial location (Schulman, 1973; Zechmeister & McKillip, 1972), sense modality, and within-modality variations (Hintzman, Block, & Inskeep, 1972; Light, Stansbury, Rubin, & Linde, 1973). Since subjects retain some information about such features without being instructed to do so, the question arises of whether the encoding of nonsemantic attributes is automatic. The evidence bearing on this question is as yet sparse, but several experiments have shown that instructions to attend to the mode of input can serve to depress retention of the TBR words (Bray & Batchelder, 1972; Light & Berger, 1974; Madigan & Doherty, 1972; Schulman, 1973). Thus, the processing of physical attributes functions as a subsidiary task that can interfere with the encoding of semantic features. If registration of the mode of input were obligatory and automatic, reallocation of attention would not be required and retention of the TBR words would not be affected (see Light & Berger, 1974).

While the intentional learning of surface features can be an interfering activity, the incidental retention of such features can, under some circumstances, facilitate the retention of the TBR items. Thus, Kolers (1973) found that sentences were recognized better when they were originally presented in an unfamiliar rather than a familiar typography. He concluded that recognition was aided by memory for the operations performed during the original exposure to the materials. The unfamiliar typography favored subsequent recognition because it required more complex operations at the time of encoding. Kolers' argument is a potentially important one because it suggests that current theories may place undue emphasis on depth or quality of processing as determinants of retention. Quite apart from depth, the memorability of the encoding operations themselves may be of critical importance.

III. MEASUREMENT OF RETENTION

Some persistent methodological problems in the measurement of retention are considered in this final section. These problems arise whenever one wishes to evaluate the effects on retention of variables other than degree of original learning. Since there is a strong positive relationship between degree of learning and retention, the influence of other variables cannot be assessed unless degree of learning is controlled.

A. Control of Degree of Learning

The consequences of failing to control degree of learning and the procedures that can be used to minimize the resulting bias in the measurement of retention have been discussed in detail by Underwood (1954, 1964b, 1966) and need be summarized only briefly here. The need for careful control procedures stems from the fact that degree of learning at the end of practice is likely to vary whenever there are differences in speed of learning, owing to either task or subject characteristics. Such will obviously be the case when the number of learning trials is held constant. Attainment of a common criterion does not eliminate the problem: the steeper the curve of acquisition, the more will be learned on the criterial trial; furthermore, the magnitude of the criterion fall is inversely related to speed of learning. Consequently, higher retention scores are to be expected when acquisition is fast than when it is slow. Direct comparisons of declines from the criterial level, therefore, yield inflated estimates of differences in retention.

1. Immediate and Delayed Tests of Retention

One apparently simple device for taking account of differences in degree of learning is the administration of a test of retention immediately after attainment of a fixed criterion. The immediate retention scores then provide baseline measures for evaluating retention losses after longer intervals. While it has often proved useful, this procedure is subject to an important limitation. If an independent variable, such as meaningfulness or concreteness, produces a substantial separation between the groups tested immediately, subsequent differences in the same direction are difficult to interpret because the slope of the forgetting function may depend on the terminal level of acquisition. Under such circumstances, one can conclude with confidence that the independent variable influences retention only if the direction of the difference observed immediately is reversed after an interval of time (see Underwood, 1966, pp. 550–552). Furthermore, if a high criterion of acquisition is used, the immediate test is likely to be insensitive to variations in the degree of overlearning for individual items.

2. Equalizing Expected Retention Scores

An alternative procedure is to adjust the number of practice trials under different experimental treatments so that projections of the learning curves to a trial following the last one yield the same, or nearly the same, values. These projected values are the expected retention scores. The projections are made on the basis of the pooled data of the subjects in a given condition by means of a successive probability analysis; that is, the function is determined relating the probability of recall on Trial $n + 1$ to the number of correct responses given during Trials 1 through n. When projections derived from the group data are applied to the protocols of individual subjects, high correlations are typically found between predicted and observed values. After a retention interval, differences between expected and obtained scores index the amount of forgetting.

It is known that this method of measuring retention loss is not entirely free of bias. The most serious shortcoming of the successive probability analysis is its insensitivity to increments in the strength of individual items produced by overlearning. (In that respect, the limitations are the same as for immediate tests.) In the interest of obtaining valid projections, it is advisable, therefore, to choose levels of learning that minimize the number of items that reach asymptotic strength; furthermore, comparisons of retention scores may be restricted to items that remain below asymptote.

3. Is Retention Invariant When Degree of Learning Is Controlled?

When degree of learning is controlled, however imperfectly, by the methods described above, differences in retention expected on theoretical grounds have failed to materialize with depressing regularity. A few examples will suffice to illustrate this well-known fact. Contrary to predictions, retention is not better for: (a) familiar than unfamiliar letter sequences (Underwood & Keppel, 1963); (b) words of high than low meaningfulness (Ekstrand & Underwood, 1965); (c) lists with high than with low interstimulus similarity (Joinson & Runquist, 1968); (d) pairs of high than low imagery value (Postman & Burns, 1973). A much longer list of references could be offered in support of the proposition that amount of retention is very likely to be invariant when degree of learning is controlled. There are occasional exceptions, of course, that prevent this theoretically uninteresting proposition from being accepted. Note, for example, the recent demonstration by Barrett and Ekstrand (1975) that the presence of a rule structure specifying the relationship between stimulus categories and response categories significantly retards forgetting. Again, other instances could be cited, but the variables that do appear to influence the rate of forgetting remain to be tied together conceptually.

B. Persistence of Methodological Errors in the Measurement of Retention

It is necessary to point out that indeterminate or biased estimates of degree of learning continue to be used in studies of both short-term and long-term retention. Other closely related sources of bias are also often overlooked. Some of the most common interpretative problems are briefly illustrated here.

1. Asymptotic Item Strength

Degree of learning cannot be assessed whenever the level of acquisition, as measured by the probability of immediate recall, is at asymptote. The resulting indeterminacy of retention measures poses an especially acute problem in studies of short-term memory, in which the probability of immediate recall is likely to be at or near 100%. To give just one example, differences in forgetting for visually and aurally presented items in the Brown–Peterson situation cannot be evaluated appropriately when immediate recall is perfect under both conditions (for example, Scarborough, 1972). One possible solution to the problem of asymptotic performance is to increase the difficulty of the task so that the level of immediate recall is well below ceiling (Nowaczyk, Shaughnessy, & Zimmerman, 1974). This line of attack necessarily involves a change in the characteristics of the TBR materials, for example, the length of the word strings presented on each trial. Nevertheless, such a procedure may be useful when there are no reasons to suppose that the necessary changes in materials systematically influence the phenomenon under study. The buildup of PI considered by Nowaczyk et al. (1974) is a case in point.

2. Unequal Levels of Acquisition

Attempts continue to be made to compare rates of forgetting for materials learned to quite different levels in a fixed number of trials. This approach has been taken in several recent investigations of the effects of imagery value on retention (Begg & Robertson, 1973; Butter, 1970; Butter & Palermo, 1970; Paivio & Csapo, as reported by Paivio, in press; Yuille, 1971). Expressing delayed recall as a percentage of the number correct attained in original learning does not help. There is no reason to assume that an easy and a difficult item which were given correctly at least once during acquisition were learned to an equal degree. Hence, the percentages are taken to bases that are not comparable.

3. Fixed Criterion of Learning

As noted earlier, the attainment of a fixed criterion does not ensure equality of degree of learning when there are differences in rate of acquisition. This fact militates against the use of the dropout procedure for holding the level of terminal acquisition constant (Begg & Robertson, 1973). Under this procedure, a fixed low criterion of performance, typically one correct anticipation, is adopted for eliminating items from the list. Since differences in probability of recall related to learning rate are maximal early in acquisition, the resulting biases can be quite severe.

When experimental treatments produce differences in rate of acquisition, the use of a fixed criterion is not justified even when there is no correlation between speed of learning and recall within the groups trained under a particular procedure (Nelson & Smith, 1972). The magnitude of the correlation for subjects treated alike permits no valid inferences about the covariation of the mean scores obtained under different experimental conditions. As Mandler (1959) pointed out some time ago, relationships across subjects and across situations are not functionally dependent.

4. Repeated Tests

Successive tests of retention cannot be assumed to be independent of each other for obvious reasons. Inevitably, performance on the second of two tests reflects not only the state of the trace at the end of the retention interval, but also whatever learning (of correct responses or of errors) has occurred during the first test. This state of affairs has, of course, been generally recognized for a long time, but it has been increasingly discounted in experimental practice. Thus, tests of recognition are routinely administered following tests of recall; this procedure is so common that there would be little point in citing specific instances. After a constant amount of training, recognition is typically higher than recall; hence, additional information about the state of the trace is usually obtained when the recognition test is administered second. There is no way of knowing in advance, however, whether and to what extent prior recall will distort the recognition measures under a given set of circumstances. Experiments in which the influence of recall on recognition was assessed have yielded variable results; one can find instances of both null effects (e.g., Hogan & Kintsch, 1971; Postman, Kruesi, & Regan, 1975) and of impaired recognition performance (Estes & Da Polito, 1967; Keppel, 1966). In any new experiment, the possibility that recall systematically influences recognition cannot be ruled out on a priori grounds.

The possibilities of bias are more obvious when recognition precedes recall. As expected, reexposure to the learning materials on the test of recognition normally facilitates recall (Hogan & Kintsch, 1971; Keppel, 1966; Postman et al., 1975). Nevertheless, this sequence has been consistently used to test the hypothesis that under certain special circumstances recall is higher than recognition. I am referring here to the recent experiments designed to assess the validity of the principle of encoding specificity (Reder, Anderson, & Bjork, 1974; Tulving & Thomson, 1973; Watkins & Tulving, 1975). It has since been shown that under the arrangements used in these experiments a prior test of recognition can facilitate recall (Postman, in press, b). This is not to say that the observed effects of encoding specificity are entirely attributable to artifacts entailed by the use of repeated tests. When the conditions of testing and the order of tests are confounded, an unequivocal interpretation of the results is simply not possible. From a theoretical viewpoint, it is often highly desirable to determine the relationship between recognition and recall for individual items learned by a given subject. Unfortunately, however, procedures that will serve this purpose and are also free of bias remain to be devised.

This discussion of persistent methodological problems in the measurement of retention was not intended to be polemical. A reading of the current literature sometimes leaves one with the impression of an emerging consensus that strictly methodological considerations may, if all else fails, be subordinated to the demands of theoretical analysis. This impression may, of course, be mistaken; if it is not, the long-term implications warrant serious discussion.

ACKNOWLEDGMENTS

The preparation of this chapter was facilitated by a grant from the National Institute of Mental Health.

REFERENCES

Abra, J. C. List-1 unlearning and recovery as a function of the point of interpolated learning. *Journal of Verbal Learning and Verbal Behavior*, 1969, **8**, 494–500.
Anderson, J. R., & Bower, G. H. Recognition and retrieval processes in free recall. *Psychological Review*, 1972, **79**, 97–123.

Anderson, R. C., & Watts, G. H. Response competition in the forgetting of paired associates. *Journal of Verbal Learning and Verbal Behavior,* 1971, **10,** 29–34.

Barnes, J. M., & Underwood, B. J. "Fate" of first-list associations in transfer theory. *Journal of Experimental Psychology,* 1959, **58,** 97–105.

Barrett, T. R., & Ekstrand, B. R. Second-order associations and single-list retention. *Journal of Experimental Psychology: Human Learning and Memory,* 1975, **101,** 41–49.

Begg, I., & Robertson, R. Imagery and long-term retention. *Journal of Verbal Learning and Verbal Behavior,* 1973, **12,** 689–700.

Bewley, W. L. The functional stimulus in serial learning. In R. F. Thompson & J. F. Voss (Eds.), *Topics in learning and performance.* New York: Academic Press, 1972.

Bjork, R. A., & Whitten, W. B. Recency-sensitive retrieval processes in long-term free recall. *Cognitive Psychology,* 1974, **6,** 173–189.

Bobrow, S. A., & Bower, G. H. Comprehension and recall of sentences. *Journal of Experimental Psychology,* 1969, **80,** 455–461.

Bower, G. H. Mental imagery and associative learning. In L. W. Gregg (Ed.), *Cognition in learning and memory.* New York: Wiley, 1972.   (a)

Bower, G. H. Stimulus-sampling theory of encoding variability. In A. W. Melton & E. Martin (Eds.), *Coding processes in human memory.* Washington, D.C.: Winston, 1972.   (b)

Bower, G. H., & Bostrom, A. Absence of within-list PI and RI in short-term recognition memory. *Psychonomic Science,* 1968, **10,** 211–212.

Bower, G. H., & Winzenz, D. Comparison of associative learning strategies. *Psychonomic Science,* 1970, **20,** 119–120.

Bray, N. W., & Batchelder, W. H. Effects of instructions and retention interval on memory of presentation mode. *Journal of Verbal Learning and Verbal Behavior,* 1972, **11,** 367–374.

Bruce, D., & Weaver, G. E. Retroactive facilitation in short-term retention of minimally learned paired associates. *Journal of Experimental Psychology,* 1973, **100,** 9–17.

Butter, M. J. Differential recall of paired associates as a function of arousal and concreteness-imagery levels. *Journal of Experimental Psychology,* 1970, **84,** 252–256.

Butter, M. J., & Palermo, D. S. Effects of imagery on paired-associate recall as a function of retention interval, list length, and trials. *Journal of Verbal Learning and Verbal Behavior,* 1970, **9,** 716–719.

Carey, S. T., & Lockhart, R. S. Encoding differences in recognition and recall. *Memory and Cognition,* 1973, **1,** 297–300.

Cieutat, V. J., Stockwell, F. E., & Noble, C. E. The interaction of ability and amount of practice with stimulus and response meaningfulness (*m, m'*) in paired-associate learning. *Journal of Experimental Learning,* 1958, **56,** 193–202.

Craik, F. I. M., & Lockhart, R. S. Levels of processing: A framework for memory research. *Journal of Verbal Learning and Verbal Behavior,* 1972, **11,** 671–684.

Craik, F. I. M., & Tulving, E. Depth of processing and the retention of words in episodic memory. *Journal of Experimental Psychology: General,* 1975, **104,** 268–294.

Craik, F. I. M., & Watkins, M. J. The role of rehearsal in short-term memory. *Journal of Verbal Learning and Verbal Behavior,* 1973, **12,** 599–607.

Crowder, R. G., Evidence for the chaining hypothesis of serial verbal learning. *Journal of Experimental Psychology,* 1968, **76,** 497–500.

Dallett, K. M. Implicit mediators in paired-associate learning. *Journal of Verbal Learning and Verbal Behavior,* 1964, **3,** 209–214.

Davidson, R. E., Schwenn, E. A., & Adams, J. F. Semantic effects in transfer. *Journal of Verbal Learning and Verbal Behavior,* 1970, **9,** 212–217.

Davis, J. C., Lockhart, R. S., & Thomson, D. M. Repetition and context effects in recognition memory. *Journal of Experimental Psychology,* 1972, **92,** 96–102.

Delprato, D. J. Specific-pair interference on recall and associative-matching retention tests. *American Journal of Psychology,* 1971, **84,** 185–193.

Dornbush, R. L. & Winnick, W. A. Short-term intentional and incidental learning. *Journal of Experimental Psychology,* 1967, **73,** 608–611.

Duffy, T. M. Mnemonics and intra-list interference in paired-associate learning. *Canadian Journal of Psychology,* 1971, **25,** 33–41.

Duffy, T. M., & Montague, W. E. Sentence mnemonics and noun pair learning. *Journal of Verbal Learning and Verbal Behavior,* 1971, **10,** 157–162.

Eagle, M., & Leiter, E. Recall and recognition in intentional and incidental learning. *Journal of Experimental Psychology,* 1964, **68,** 58–63.

Eagle, M. N., & Mulliken, S. The role of affective ratings in intentional and incidental learning. *American Journal of Psychology,* 1974, **87,** 409–423.

Eckert, E., & Kanak, N. J. Verbal discrimination learning. *Psychological Bulletin,* 1974, **81,** 582–607.

Ekstrand, B. R. To sleep, perchance to dream (about why we forget). In C. P. Duncan, L. Sechrest, & A. W. Melton (Eds.), *Human memory: Festschrift for Benton J. Underwood.* New York: Appleton-Century-Crofts, 1972.

Ekstrand, B. R., & Underwood, B. J. Free learning and recall as a function of unit-sequence and letter-sequence interference. *Journal of Verbal Learning and Verbal Behavior,* 1965, **4,** 390–396.

Ekstrand, B. R., Wallace, W., & Underwood, B. J. A frequency theory of verbal-discrimination learning. *Psychological Review,* 1966, **73,** 566–578.

Elmes, D. G., & Bjork, R. A. The interaction of encoding and rehearsal processes in the recall of repeated and nonrepeated items. *Journal of Verbal Learning and Verbal Behavior,* 1975, **14,** 30–42.

Epstein, W., Rock, I., & Zuckerman, C. B. Meaning and familiarity in associative learning. *Psychological Monographs,* 1960, **74,** No. 491.

Estes, W. K., & Da Polito, F. Independent variation of information storage and retrieval processes in paired-associate learning. *Journal of Experimental Psychology,* 1967, **75,** 18–26.

Forrester, W. E. Retroactive inhibition and spontaneous recovery in the A–B, D–C paradigm. *Journal of Verbal Learning and Verbal Behavior,* 1970, **9,** 525–528.

Frincke, G. Word characteristics, associative-relatedness, and the free-recall of nouns. *Journal of Verbal Learning and Verbal Behavior,* 1968, **7,** 366–372.

Galbraith, R. C., & Underwood, B. J. Perceived frequency of concrete and abstract words. *Memory & Cognition,* 1973, **1,** 56–60.

Gardiner, J. M., Craik, F. I. M., & Birtwistle, J. Retrieval cues and release from proactive inhibition. *Journal of Verbal Learning and Verbal Behavior,* 1972, **11,** 778–783.

Garskof, B. E. Unlearning as a function of degree of interpolated learning and method of testing in the A–B, A–C and A–B, C–D paradigms. *Journal of Experimental Psychology,* 1968, **76,** 579–583.

Garskof, B. E., & Sandak, J. M. Unlearning in recognition memory. *Psychonomic Science,* 1964, **1,** 197–198.

Gorfein, D. S., & Jacobson, D. E. Proactive effects in short-term recognition memory. *Journal of Experimental Psychology,* 1972, **95,** 211–214.

Greenberg, S., & Wickens, D. D. Is matching performance an adequate test of "extinction" effects on individual associations? *Psychonomic Science,* 1972, **27,** 227–229.

Greeno, J. G., James, C. T., & Da Polito, F. J. A cognitive interpretation of negative transfer and forgetting of paired associates. *Journal of Verbal Learning and Verbal Behavior,* 1971, **10,** 331–345.

Hintzman, D. L., & Block, R. A. Repetition and memory: Evidence for a multiple-trace hypothesis. *Journal of Experimental Psychology,* 1971, **88,** 297–306.

Hintzman, D. L., Block, R. A., & Inskeep, N. R. Memory for mode of input. *Journal of Verbal Learning and Verbal Behavior,* 1972, **11,** 741–749.

Hockey, G. R. J., Davies, S., & Gray, M. M. Forgetting as a function of sleep at different times of day. *Quarterly Journal of Experimental Psychology*, 1972, **24**, 386–393.

Hogan, R. M., & Kintsch, W. Differential effects of study and test trials on long-term recognition and recall. *Journal of Verbal Learning and Verbal Behavior*, 1971, **10**, 562–567.

Howe, T. S. Effects of delayed interference on List-1 recall. *Journal of Experimental Psychology*, 1969, **80**, 120–124.

Hunt, R. R., & Ellis, H. C. Recognition memory and degree of semantic contextual change. *Journal of Experimental Psychology*, 1974, **103**, 1153–1159.

Hyde, T. S. Differential effects of effort and type of orienting task on recall and organization of highly associated words. *Journal of Experimental Psychology*, 1973, **97**, 111–113.

Hyde, T. S., & Jenkins, J. J. Differential effects of incidental tasks on the organization of recall of a list of highly associated words. *Journal of Experimental Psychology*, 1969, **82**, 472–481.

Hyde, T. S., & Jenkins, J. J. Recall for words as a function of semantic, graphic, and syntactic orienting tasks. *Journal of Verbal Learning and Verbal Behavior*, 1973, **12**, 471–480.

Jacoby, L. L. The role of mental contiguity in memory: Registration and retrieval effects. *Journal of Verbal Learning and Verbal Behavior*, 1974, **13**, 483–496.

Jenkins, J. G., & Dallenbach, K. M. Oblivescence during sleep and waking. *American Journal of Psychology*, 1924, **35**, 605–612.

Johnston, C. D., & Jenkins, J. J. Two more incidental tasks that differentially affect associative clustering in recall. *Journal of Experimental Psychology*, 1971, **89**, 92–95.

Joinson, P. A., & Runquist, W. N. Effects of intralist stimulus similarity and degree of learning on forgetting. *Journal of Verbal Learning and Verbal Behavior*, 1968, **7**, 554–559.

Kammann, R., & Melton, A. W. Absolute recovery of first-list responses from unlearning during 26 minutes filled with an easy or difficult information processing task. *Proceedings of 75th Annual Convention, American Psychological Association*, 1967, **2**, 63–64.

Keppel, G. Association by contiguity: Role of response availability. *Journal of Experimental Psychology*, 1966, **71**, 624–628.

Kimble, G. A. *Hilgard and Marquis' conditioning and learning*. New York: Appleton-Century-Crofts, 1961.

Kintsch, W. Models for free recall and recognition. In D. A. Norman (Ed.), *Models of human memory*. New York: Academic Press, 1970.

Kintsch, W. Abstract nouns: Imagery versus lexical complexity. *Journal of Verbal Learning and Verbal Behavior*, 1972, **11**, 59–65.

Kolers, P. A. Remembering operations. *Memory & Cognition*, 1973, **1**, 347–355.

Kuiken, D., & Schulz, R. W. Response familiarization and the associative phase of paired-associate learning. *Journal of Verbal Learning and Verbal Behavior*, 1968, **7**, 106–109.

Kulhavy, R. W. Language mediation and paired-associate learning in college students. *Psychological Reports*, 1970, **26**, 658.

Landauer, T. K. Consolidation in human memory: Retrograde amnestic effects of confusable items in paired-associate learning. *Journal of Verbal Learning and Verbal Behavior*, 1974, **13**, 45–53.

Lesgold, A. M., & Bower, G. H. Inefficiency of serial knowledge for association responding. *Journal of Verbal Learning and Verbal Behavior*, 1970, **9**, 456–466.

Levin, J. R. Factors related to sentence facilitation of paired-associate learning. *Journal of Educational Psychology*, 1970, **61**, 431–439.

Levin, J. R., & Horvitz, J. M. The meaning of paired associates. *Journal of Educational Psychology*, 1971, **62**, 209–214.

Levin, J. R., Horvitz, J. M., & Kaplan, S. A. Verbal facilitation of paired-associate learning: A limited generalization? *Journal of Educational Psychology*, 1971, **62**, 439–444.

Light, L. L., & Berger, D. E. Memory for modality: Within-modality discrimination is not automatic. *Journal of Experimental Psychology*, 1974, **103**, 854–860.

Light, L. L., & Carter-Sobell, L. Effects of changed semantic context on recognition memory. *Journal of Verbal Learning and Verbal Behavior,* 1970, **9,** 1–11.

Light, L. L., Stansbury, C., Rubin, C., & Linde, S. Memory for modality of presentation: Within-modality discrimination. *Memory & Cognition,* 1973, **1,** 395–400.

Loftus, G. R. Comparison of recognition and recall in a continuous memory task. *Journal of Experimental Psychology,* 1971, **91,** 220–226.

Lovatt, D. J., & Warr, P. B. Recall after sleep. *American Journal of Psychology,* 1968, **81,** 253–257.

Madigan, S., & Doherty, L. Retention of item attributes in free recall. *Psychonomic Science,* 1972, **27,** 233–235.

Mandler, G. Stimulus variables and subject variables: A caution. *Psychological Review,* 1959, **66,** 145–149.

Mandler, G. Organization and recognition. In E. Tulving & W. Donaldson (Eds.), *Organization of memory.* New York: Academic Press, 1972.

Marcel, A. J., & Steel, R. G. Semantic cueing in recognition and recall. *Quarterly Journal of Experimental Psychology,* 1973, **25,** 368–377.

Martin, E. Stimulus meaningfulness and paired-associate transfer: An encoding variability hypothesis. *Psychological Review,* 1968, **75,** 421–441.

Martin, E. Verbal learning theory and independent retrieval phenomena. *Psychological Review,* 1971, **78,** 314–332. (a)

Martin, E. Stimulus component independence. *Journal of Verbal Learning and Verbal Behavior,* 1971, **10,** 715–72. (b)

Martin, E. Stimulus encoding in learning and transfer. In A. W. Melton & E. Martin (Eds.), *Coding processes in human memory.* Washington, D.C.: Winston, 1972.

Martin, E. Memory codes and negative transfer. *Memory & Cognition,* 1973, **1,** 494–498.

Martin, E., & Carey, S. T. Retroaction, recovery, and stimulus meaningfulness in the *A–B, A–Br* paradigm. *American Journal of Psychology,* 1971, **84,** 123–133.

Martin, E., & Mackay, S. A. A test of the list-differentiation hypothesis. *American Journal of Psychology,* 1970, **83,** 311–321.

Martin, E., & Noreen, D. L. Serial learning: Identification of subjective subsequences. *Cognitive Psychology,* 1974, **6,** 421–435.

McGeoch, J. A. Forgetting and the law of disuse. *Psychological Review,* 1932, **39,** 352–370.

McGeoch, J. A. *The psychology of human learning.* New York: Longmans, Green, 1942.

McGovern, J. B. Extinction of associations in four transfer paradigms. *Psychological Monographs,* 1964, **78,** No. 593.

Mechanic, A. The responses involved in the rote learning of verbal materials. *Journal of Verbal Learning and Verbal Behavior,* 1964, **3,** 30–36.

Melton, A. W. Implications of short-term memory for a general theory of memory. *Journal of Verbal Learning and Verbal Behavior,* 1963, **2,** 1–21.

Melton, A. W., & Irwin, J. M. The influence of degree of interpolated learning on retroactive inhibition and the overt transfer of specific responses. *American Journal of Psychology,* 1940, **53,** 173–203.

Modigliani, V., & Saltz, E. Evaluation of a model relating Thorndike–Lorge frequency and *m* to learning. *Journal of Experimental Psychology,* 1969, **82,** 584–586.

Montague, W. E. Elaborative strategies in verbal learning and memory. In G. H. Bower (Ed.), *The psychology of learning and motivation.* Vol. 6. New York: Academic Press, 1972.

Montague, W. E., & Kiess, H. O. The associability of CVC pairs. *Journal of Experimental Psychology,* 1968, **80**(2, Pt. 2).

Müller, G. E., & Pilzecker, A. Experimentelle Beiträge zur Lehre vom Gedächtniss. *Zeitschrift für Psychologie,* Ergänzungsband No. 1, 1900.

Murdock, B. B., Jr. *Human memory: Theory and data.* Hillsdale, New Jersey: Lawrence Erlbaum Assoc., 1974.

Murphy, M. D., & Wallace, W. P. Encoding specificity: Semantic change between storage and retrieval cues. *Journal of Experimental Psychology,* 1974, **103,** 768–774.

Nelson, D. L., Brooks, D. H., & Borden, R. C. Sequential memory for pictures and the role of the verbal system. *Journal of Experimental Psychology,* 1973, **101,** 242–245.

Nelson, T. O., & Smith, E. E. Acquisition and forgetting of hierarchically organized information in long-term memory. *Journal of Experimental Psychology,* 1972, **95,** 388–396.

Newton, J. M., & Wickens, D. D. Retroactive inhibition as a function of the temporal position of interpolated learning. *Journal of Experimental Psychology,* 1956, **51,** 149–154.

Nowaczyk, R. H., Shaughnessy, J. J., & Zimmerman, J. Proactive interference in short-term retention and the measurement of degree of learning: A new technique. *Journal of Experimental Psychology,* 1974, **103,** 45–53.

Paivio, A. Paired-associate learning and free recall of nouns as a function of concreteness, specificity, imagery, and meaningfulness. *Psychological Reports,* 1967, **20,** 239–245.

Paivio, A. A factor-analytic study of word attributes and verbal learning. *Journal of Verbal Learning and Verbal Behavior,* 1968, **7,** 41–49.

Paivio, A. *Imagery and verbal processes.* New York: Holt, 1971.

Paivio, A. Imagery in recall and recognition. In J. Brown (Ed.), *Recall and recognition.* London: Wiley, 1975.

Paivio, A. Imagery and long-term memory. In R. A. Kennedy & A. Wilkes (Eds.), *Studies in long-term memory.* New York: Wiley, in press.

Paivio, A., & Csapo, K. Concrete-image and verbal memory codes. *Journal of Experimental Psychology,* 1969, **80,** 279–285.

Paivio, A., & Csapo, K. Short-term sequential memory for pictures and words. *Psychonomic Science,* 1971, **24,** 50–51.

Paivio, A., & Foth, D. Imaginal and verbal mediators and noun concreteness in paired-associate learning: The elusive interaction. *Journal of Verbal Learning and Verbal Behavior,* 1970, **9,** 384–390.

Paivio, A., & Olver, M. Denotative-generality, imagery and meaningfulness in paired-associate learning of nouns. *Psychonomic Science,* 1964, **1,** 183–184.

Paivio, A., Smythe, P. C., & Yuille, J. C. Imagery versus meaningfulness of nouns in paired-associate learning. *Canadian Journal of Psychology,* 1968, **22,** 427–441.

Paivio, A., & Yuille, J. C. Mediation instructions and word attributes in paired-associate learning. *Psychonomic Science,* 1967, **8,** 65–77.

Paivio, A., & Yuille, J. C. Changes in associative strategies and paired-associate learning over trials as a function of word imagery and type of learning set. *Journal of Experimental Psychology,* 1969, **79,** 458–463.

Pellegrino, J. W., & Salzberg. P. M. Encoding specificity in cued recall and context recognition. *Journal of Experimental Psychology: Human Learning and Memory,* 1975, **101,** 261–270.

Pelton, L. H. Mediational construction vs. mediational perception in paired-associate learning. *Psychonomic Science,* 1969, **17,** 220–221.

Petrich, J. A. Retroactive inhibition under a multiple-choice procedure. *American Journal of Psychology,* 1974, **87,** 335–349.

Petrusic, W. M., & Dillon, R. F. Proactive interference in short-term recognition and recall memory. *Journal of Experimental Psychology,* 1972, **95,** 412–418.

Plenderleith, M., & Postman, L. Individual differences in intentional and incidental learning. *British Journal of Psychology,* 1957, **48,** 241–248.

Posnansky, C. J. Probing for the functional stimuli in serial learning. *Journal of Experimental Psychology,* 1972, **96,** 184–193.

Posner, M. I. & Konnick, A. On the role of interference in short-term retention. *Journal of Experimental Psychology,* 1966, **72,** 221–231.

Posner, M. I., & Rossman, E. Effect of size and location of informational transforms upon short-term retention. *Journal of Experimental Psychology,* 1965, **70,** 496–505.

Postman, L. Short-term memory and incidental learning. In A. W. Melton (Ed.), *Categories of human learning.* New York: Academic Press, 1964.

Postman, L. Verbal learning and memory. *Annual Review of Psychology,* 1975, **26,** 291–335.

Postman, L. Interference theory revisited. In J. Brown (Ed.), *Recall and recognition.* London: Wiley, in press.   (a)

Postman, L. Tests of the generality of the principle of encoding specificity. *Memory & Cognition,* in press.   (b)

Postman, L., & Adams, P. A. Studies in incidental learning: IV. The interaction of orienting tasks and stimulus materials. *Journal of Experimental Psychology,* 1956, **51,** 329–333.

Postman, L., Adams, P. A., & Bohm, A. M. Studies in incidental learning: V. Recall for order and associative clustering. *Journal of Experimental Psychology,* 1956, **51,** 334–342.

Postman, L., Adams, P. A., & Phillips, L. W. Studies in incidental learning: II. The effects of association value and of the method of testing. *Journal of Experimental Psychology,* 1955, **49,** 1–10.

Postman, L., & Burns, S. Experimental analysis of coding processes. *Memory & Cognition,* 1973, **1,** 503–507.

Postman, L., & Greenbloom, R. Conditions of cue selection in the acquisition of paired-associate lists. *Journal of Experimental Psychology,* 1967, **73,** 91–100.

Postman, L., & Keppel, G. Retroactive inhibition in free recall. *Journal of Experimental Psychology,* 1967, **74,** 203–211.

Postman, L., Kruesi, E., & Regan, J. Recognition and recall as measures of long-term retention. *Quarterly Journal of Experimental Psychology,* 1975, **27,** 411–418.

Postman, L., & Stark, K. Studies of learning to learn: IV. Transfer from serial to paired-associate learning. *Journal of Verbal Learning and Verbal Behavior,* 1967, **6,** 339–353.

Postman, L., & Stark, K. Role of response availability in transfer and interference. *Journal of Experimental Psychology,* 1969, **79,** 168–177.

Postman, L., & Stark, K. Encoding variability and transfer. *American Journal of Psychology,* 1971, **84,** 461–471.

Postman, L., Stark, K., & Fraser, J. Temporal changes in interference. *Journal of Verbal Learning and Verbal Behavior,* 1968, **7,** 672–694.

Postman, L., Stark, K., & Henschel, D. Conditions of recovery after unlearning. *Journal of Experimental Psychology Monographs,* 1969, **82,** 1–24.

Postman, L., & Underwood, B. J. Critical issues in interference theory. *Memory & Cognition,* 1973, **1,** 19–40.

Reder, L. M., Anderson, J. R., & Bjork, R. A. A semantic interpretation of encoding specificity. *Journal of Experimental Psychology,* 1974, **102,** 648–656.

Reitman, J. S. Mechanisms of forgetting in short-term memory. *Cognitive Psychology,* 1971, **2,** 185–195.

Reitman, J. S. Without surreptitious rehearsal, information in short-term memory decays. *Journal of Verbal Learning and Verbal Behavior,* 1974, **13,** 365–377.

Richardson, J. Cue effectiveness and abstraction in paired-associate learning. *Psychological Bulletin,* 1971, **75,** 73–91.

Richardson, J. Encoding and stimulus selection in paired-associate verbal learning. In A. W. Melton & E. Martin (Eds.), *Coding processes in human memory.* Washington, D.C.: Winston, 1972.

Roediger, H. L., III. Inhibition in recall from cueing with recall targets. *Journal of Verbal Learning and Verbal Behavior,* 1973, **12,** 644–657.

Rohwer, W. D., Jr. Constraint, syntax and meaning in paired-associate learning. *Journal of Verbal Learning and Verbal Behavior,* 1966, **5,** 541–547.

Rohwer, W. D., Jr., & Levin, J. R. Action, meaning and stimulus selection in paired-associate learning. *Journal of Verbal Learning and Verbal Behavior*, 1968, **7**, 137–141.

Rohwer, W. D., Jr., & Lynch, S. Semantic constraint in paired-associate learning. *Journal of Educational Psychology*, 1966, **57**, 271–278.

Rohwer, W. D., Jr., & Lynch, S. Form class and intralist similarity in paired-associate learning. *Journal of Verbal Learning and Verbal Behavior*, 1967, **6**, 551–554.

Rohwer, W. D., Jr., Lynch, S., Levin, J. R., & Suzuki, N. Pictorial and verbal factors in the efficient learning of paired associates. *Journal of Educational Psychology*, 1967, **58**, 278–284.

Rohwer, W. D., Jr., Shuell, T. J., & Levin, J. R. Context effects in the initial storage and retrieval of noun pairs. *Journal of Verbal Learning and Verbal Behavior*, 1967, **6**, 796–801.

Rundus, D. Negative effects of using list items as recall cues. *Journal of Verbal Learning and Verbal Behavior*, 1973, **12**, 43–50.

Runquist, W. N. Intralist interference and stimulus similarity. In C. P. Duncan, L. Sechrest, & A. W. Melton (Eds.), *Human memory: Festschrift for Benton J. Underwood*. New York: Appleton-Century-Crofts, 1973.

Runquist, W. N. Interference among memory traces. *Memory & Cognition*, 1975, **3**, 143–159.

Saltz, E. Thorndike–Lorge frequency and *m* of stimuli as separate factors in paired-associates learning. *Journal of Experimental Psychology*, 1967, **73**, 473–478.

Saltz, E., & Felton, M. Response pretraining and subsequent paired-associate learning. *Journal of Experimental Psychology*, 1968, **77**, 258–262.

Saltz, E., & Modigliani, V. Response meaningfulness in paired associates: T–L frequency, *m*, and number of meanings (*dm*). *Journal of Experimental Psychology*, 1967, **75**, 313–320.

Sandak, J. M., & Garskof, B. E. Associative unlearning as a function of degree of interpolated learning. *Psychonomic Science*, 1967, **7**, 215–216.

Sanders, A. F., Whitaker, L., & Cofer, C. N. Evidence for retroactive interference in recognition from reaction time. *Journal of Experimental Psychology*, 1974, **102**, 1126–1129.

Santa, J. L., & Lamwers, L. L. Encoding specificity: Fact or artifact. *Journal of Verbal Learning and Verbal Behavior*, 1974, **13**, 412–423.

Scarborough, D. L. Stimulus modality effects on forgetting in short-term memory. *Journal of Experimental Psychology*, 1972, **95**, 285–289.

Schulman, A. I. Recognition memory and the recall of spatial locations. *Memory & Cognition*, 1973, **1**, 256–260.

Schulman, A. I. Memory for words recently classified. *Memory & Cognition*, 1974, **2**, 47–52.

Schulz, R. W., & Martin, E. Aural paired-associate learning: Stimulus familiarization, response familiarization, and pronunciability. *Journal of Verbal Learning and Verbal Behavior*, 1964, **3**, 139–145.

Schwartz, M. Subject-generated versus experimenter-supplied mediators in paired-associate learning. *Journal of Experimental Psychology*, 1971, **87**, 389–395.

Schwartz, M., & Walsh, M. F. Identical subject-generated and experimenter-supplied mediators in paired-associate learning. *Journal of Experimental Psychology*, 1974, **103**, 878–884.

Shiffrin, R. M. Information persistence in short-term memory. *Journal of Experimental Psychology*, 1973, **100**, 39–49.

Shulman, H. G., & Martin, E. Effects of response-set similarity on unlearning and spontaneous recovery. *Journal of Experimental Psychology*, 1970, **86**, 230–235.

Silverstein, A. Long-term retention for intentionally and incidentally learned words. *Journal of Verbal Learning and Verbal Behavior*, 1964, **3**, 236–243.

Slamecka, N. J. An examination of trace storage in free recall. *Journal of Experimental Psychology*, 1968, **76**, 504–513.

Slamecka, N. J. Testing for associative storage in multitrial free recall. *Journal of Experimental Psychology*, 1969, **81**, 557–560.

Slamecka, N. J. The question of associative growth in the learning of categorized material. *Journal of Verbal Learning and Verbal Behavior,* 1972, **11,** 324–332.

Smythe, P. C., & Paivio, A. A comparison of the effectiveness of word imagery and meaningfulness in paired-associate learning of nouns. *Psychonomic Science,* 1968, **10,** 49–50.

Snodgrass, J. G., & Antone, G. Parallel versus sequential processing of pictures and words. *Journal of Experimental Psychology,* 1974, **103,** 139–144.

Suzuki, N. S., & Rohwer, W. D., Jr. Verbal facilitation of paired-associate learning: Type of grammatical unit vs. connective form class. *Journal of Verbal Learning and Verbal Behavior,* 1968, **7,** 584–588.

Till, R. E., Diehl, R. L., & Jenkins, J. J. Effects of semantic and nonsemantic cued orienting tasks on associative clustering in free recall. *Memory & Cognition,* 1975, **3,** 19–23.

Till, R. E., & Jenkins, J. J. The effects of cued orienting tasks on the free recall of words. *Journal of Verbal Learning and Verbal Behavior,* 1973, **12,** 489–498.

Treisman, A., & Tuxworth, J. Immediate and delayed recall of sentences after perceptual processing at different levels. *Journal of Verbal Learning and Verbal Behavior,* 1974, **13,** 38–44.

Tulving, E., & Bower, G. H. The logic of memory representations. In G. H. Bower (Ed.), *The psychology of learning and motivation.* Vol. 8. New York: Academic Press, 1974.

Tulving, E., & Pearlstone, Z. Availability versus accessibility of information in memory for words. *Journal of Verbal Learning and Verbal Behavior,* 1966, **5,** 381–391.

Tulving, E., & Psotka, J. Retroactive inhibition in free recall: Inaccessibility of information available in the memory store. *Journal of Experimental Psychology,* 1971, **87,** 1–8.

Tulving, E., & Thomson, D. M. Retrieval processes in recognition memory: Effects of associative context. *Journal of Experimental Psychology,* 1971, **87,** 116–124.

Tulving, E., & Thomson, D. M. Encoding specificity and retrieval processes in episodic memory. *Psychological Review,* 1973, **80,** 352–373.

Tulving, E., & Thornton, G. B. Interaction between proaction and retroaction in short-term retention. *Canadian Journal of Psychology,* 1959, **13,** 255–265.

Tulving, E., & Watkins, M. J. Structure of memory traces. *Psychological Review,* 1975, **82,** 261–275.

Tversky, B. Encoding processes in recognition and recall. *Cognitive Psychology,* 1973, **5,** 275–287.

Underwood, B. J. Speed of learning and amount retained: A consideration of methodology. *Psychological Bulletin,* 1954, **51,** 276–282.

Underwood, B. J. The representativeness of rote verbal learning. In A. W. Melton (Ed.), *Categories of human learning.* New York: Academic Press, 1964. (a)

Underwood, B. J. Degree of learning and the measurement of forgetting. *Journal of Verbal Learning and Verbal Behavior,* 1964, **3,** 112–29. (b)

Underwood, B. J. *Experimental psychology* (2nd ed.) New York: Appleton, 1966.

Underwood, B. J. Attributes of memory. *Psychological Review,* 1969, **76,** 559–573.

Underwood, B. J. Word recognition memory and frequency information. *Journal of Experimental Psychology,* 1972, **94,** 276–283. (a)

Underwood, B. J. Are we overloading memory? In A. W. Melton & E. Martin (Eds.), *Coding processes in human memory.* Washington, D.C.: Winston, 1972. (b)

Underwood, B. J. The role of the association in recognition memory. *Journal of Experimental Psychology,* 1974, **102,** 917–939.

Underwood, B. J., & Brown, A. S. Interference in recognition memory: A replication. *Bulletin of the Psychonomic Society,* 1975, **5,** 263–264.

Underwood, B. J., & Freund, J. S. Retention of a verbal discrimination. *Journal of Experimental Psychology,* 1970, **84,** 1–14.

Underwood, B. J., & Keppel, G. Retention as a function of degree of learning and letter-sequence interference. *Psychological Monographs,* 1963, **77,** No. 567.

Underwood, B. J., Runquist, W. N., & Schulz, R. W. Response learning in paired-associate lists as a function of intralist similarity. *Journal of Experimental Psychology*, 1959, **58**, 70–78.

Underwood, B. J., & Schulz, R. W. *Meaningfulness and verbal learning*. Philadelphia: Lippincott, 1960.

Underwood, B. J., Shaughnessy, J. J., & Zimmerman, J. List length and method of presentation in verbal discrimination learning with further evidence on retroaction. *Journal of Experimental Psychology*, 1972, **93**, 181–187.

Van Ormer, E. B. Retention after intervals of sleep and waking. *Archives of Psychology*, 1932, **21**, No. 137.

Wallace, W. P. Review of the historical, empirical, and theoretical status of the Von Restorff phenomenon. *Psychological Bulletin*, 1965, **63**, 410–424.

Walsh, D. A., & Jenkins, J. J. Effects of orienting tasks on free recall of incidental learning: "Difficulty," "effort," and "process" explanations. *Journal of Verbal Learning and Verbal Behavior*, 1973, **12**, 481–488.

Watkins, M. J., & Tulving, E. Episodic memory: When recognition fails. *Journal of Experimental Psychology: General*, 1975, **104**, 5–29.

Watkins, M. J., Watkins, O. C., Craik, F. I. M., & Mazuryk, G. Effect of nonverbal distraction on short-term storage. *Journal of Experimental Psychology*, 1973, **101**, 296–300.

Weaver, G. E., McCann, R. L., & Wehr, R. J. Stimulus meaningfulness, transfer, and retroactive inhibition in the A–B, A–C paradigm. *Journal of Experimental Psychology*, 1970, **85**, 225–257.

Wichawut, C., & Martin, E. Selective stimulus encoding and overlearning in paired-associate learning. *Journal of Experimental Psychology*, 1970, **85**, 383–388.

Wickelgren, W. A. Single-trace fragility theory of memory dynamics. *Memory & Cognition*, 1974, **2**, 775–780.

Wickens, D. D. Encoding categories of words: An empirical approach to meaning. *Psychological Review*, 1970, **77**, 1–15.

Wickens, D. D. Characteristics of word encoding. In A. W. Melton & E. Martin (Eds.), *Coding processes in human memory*. Washington, D.C.: Winston, 1972.

Woodward, A. E., Jr., Bjork, R. A., & Jongeward, R. H., Jr. Recall and recognition as a function of primary rehearsal. *Journal of Verbal Learning and Verbal Behavior*, 1973, **12**, 608–617.

Woodworth, R. S. *Experimental psychology*. New York: Holt, 1938.

Yaroush, R., Sullivan, M. J., & Ekstrand, B. R. The effect of sleep on memory. II: Differential effect of the first and second half of the night. *Journal of Experimental Psychology*, 1971, **88**, 361–366.

Young, R. K. Serial learning. In T. R. Dixon & D. L. Horton (Eds.), *Verbal behavior and general behavior theory*. Englewood Cliffs, New Jersey: Prentice-Hall, 1968.

Yuille, J. C. Does the concreteness effect reverse with delay? *Journal of Experimental Psychology*, 1971, **88**, 147–148.

Yuille, J. C., & Paivio, A. Latency of imaginal and verbal mediators as a function of stimulus and response concreteness imagery. *Journal of Experimental Psychology*, 1967, **75**, 540–544.

Yuille, J. C., & Paivio, A. Imagery and verbal mediation instructions in paired-associate learning. *Journal of Experimental Psychology*, 1968, **78**, 436–441.

Yuille, J. C., & Pritchard, S. Noun concreteness and verbal facilitation as factors in imaginal mediation and PA learning in children. *Journal of Experimental Child Psychology*, 1969, **7**, 459–466.

Zechmeister, E. B., & McKillip, J. Recall of place on the page. *Journal of Educational Psychology*, 1972, **63**, 446–453.

2

An Introduction to Research on Individual and Developmental Differences in Learning

William D. Rohwer, Jr.

University of California, Berkeley

In the domain of human learning and memory, the study of individual and developmental differences offers a variety of attractions. Foremost among these, if one especially values the role of explorer, is the sheer magnitude of the phenomena to be explained—the vast extent of the unknown. To be sure, what a person learns and the circumstances of his learning have substantial effects on his apparent proficiency, but the amount of variation produced by such factors typically falls far short of the amount associated with differences among learners.

For example, consider the results of an unpublished study in which a sizable sample of persons was asked to memorize a list of 50 pairs of unrelated nouns. Half of the persons were simply told to study the words during the 15 sec allotted for each pair, whereas the others were directed to use the study time by imagining a scene that related the two objects named by each pair. Performance was indexed in terms of the percentage of words correctly recalled when one word from every pair was presented as a cue for the missing word. On the average, those given study instructions recalled 21% of the missing words, whereas those who received imagery instructions produced more than 37%. As experimental effects go, this one is atypically large, but it seems less so when viewed in relation to two other aspects of the results. The average recall of some persons in the sample, first-grade children, was only 11% while that of eleventh-grade students was 51%. The performance of third- and sixth-grade students fell between these extremes. Hardly less impressive than these developmental differences were the individual differences among the eleventh graders: the most proficient third of these students recalled 66% of the missing words, far more than the 36% recalled by the least proficient third. Phenomena of this magnitude exemplify the explanatory challenge presented by the study of learner differences.

The investigation of developmental and individual differences is attractive for other reasons as well. One is the stimulation that comes from drawing on and contributing to theories of cognitive development and of human learning. The investigator can use the structures and processes posited in such theories to generate hypotheses about the sources of learner differences, design experiments to test predictions implied by the hypotheses, and construe the results as a commentary on the utility or even the validity of the guiding theoretical propositions. Inquiry into learner differences can also yield knowledge of potential use for understanding and improving the effects of educational materials and procedures. Since the effectiveness of schooling must surely depend on the compatibility of instructional provisions with the character of learning processes, and of the learners that embody them, educational assumptions can be tested against verified principles of individual and developmental differences. Thus, there are ample incentives for engaging in the study of learner differences.

The purpose of this chapter is to present one of the possible ways of converting these incentives into rewards. To delimit the discussion, the focus is initially narrowed to three restricted classes of performance, a strategy is outlined for research on learner differences in such performances, and the strategy is illustrated with reference to particular examples of research on individual and developmental differences.

I. PERFORMANCES PRODUCED BY LEARNING
FROM ITEMIZED MATERIAL

A wide variety of performance tasks can be used to evaluate explanations of individual and developmental differences in human learning and memory. These range from performances made possible by the acquisition of perceptual–motor skills to those produced by the learning of routines for problem solving. Rather than sampling exhaustively from this spectrum in an attempt to stress the potential generality of the research strategy to be presented, the discussion is anchored to a few restricted classes of performance, namely those that depend on learning from itemized material.

Since the turn of the century, tasks that require the learning of information from lists of individual items have been a mainstay of research on human learning and memory. The items on such lists are often words, although they may also be objects, pictures, syllables, letters, numbers, or abstract figures. The items may be presented singly or in groups that vary in size from two up to the simultaneous presentation of an entire list. There are also variations in what a subject is asked to learn about the items: what the items are, the order or position in which they are presented, and information about their group affiliations. (For more comprehensive treatments, see Kausler, 1974; Murdock, 1974.)

A. Information about Item Identity

Ostensibly, the most straightforward paradigm for investigating the acquisition of information about the contents of an itemized list is that of *free recall learning*. In this paradigm, the experimenter presents a list of items to the subject and afterwards asks the subject to recall the names of the objects on the list in any order he wishes. For example, the subject might hear the following sequence of words: COW, TIE, BALL, FENCE, MONKEY, BELT, TOMATO, CAGE. As in this example, typically the items are well known to the subject prior to their presentation so that the subject's main task is to learn which of the words in his vocabulary appear on the list. To assess the extent of such learning, the experimenter can test the subject by asking him to recall as many of the items as possible or by presenting the items again intermingled with other items that had not appeared on the original list and asking the subject to discriminate "old" from "new" ones.

B. Information about Order and Position

A list like that in the preceding example can also be used to study the acquisition of order information. This can be done simply by advising the subject that the task is to learn the sequence in which the items are presented and by asking the subject afterwards to recite the items in order. This paradigm, usually referred to as *serial learning,* can be varied in that the subject may be tested by being presented with one item from the sequence while being asked for the recall of the one that had succeeded it.

Another variation permits the experimenter to assess the acquisition of position information. For example, with each item printed on a separate card, the cards can be arranged in a row, and exposed to the subject's view either successively or simultaneously. Then, when the items are covered, the subject can be asked to recall the word on the card occupying position five, say, or to point to the card bearing the word "monkey." Alternatively, the cards can be shuffled and the subject asked to arrange them in replication of the original row array. Some of these variations appear to require more of the subject than others; that is, those in which the subject is given the items and asked to designate sequence or location only demand order or position information, whereas those in which the subject must produce one or more items call for the learning of item information as well.

C. Information about Group Membership

Thus far, only two of the possible ways that list items can be grouped during presentation have been discussed—individual presentation of each item and simultaneous presentation of all items. The remaining ways of subdividing a list are especially useful for studying the learning of information about group membership. In one of these, known as the method of *paired associates,* list items are presented in groups of two (for example, COW–TIE, BALL–FENCE, MONKEY–BELT, TOMATO–CAGE) and learning is assessed by giving one member of each pair as a cue for the recall of the other member.

Such versions of the task, however, demand more of the subject than information about group membership; they also require information sufficient to identify the items that have occurred on the list. To minimize this requirement, investigators have developed other means of assessing how much has been learned: the test may be conducted by presenting all of the list items simultaneously in a random arrangement and asking the subject to match them into the original pairs; or the subject can be given a test list of paired items and asked to discriminate between correct (for example, COW–TIE) and incorrect (for example, BALL–CAGE) groupings. Still another method, multiple choice, consists of presenting each cue item along with several other list items among which the subject is to identify the missing pair member.

The utility of these several test methods is not restricted to lists of paired words. Their use is equally appropriate with lists of numbers, objects, or pictures, partitioned into triads, tetrads or pentads. Whatever the content or format, a subdivided list provides an instrument for investigating the learning of information about group membership.

In the remaining discussion, performances are referred to that presumably disclose what has been learned from the presentation of itemized material. Concern is with the learning of three kinds of information—item identity, order or position, and group membership. With these performances as reference points, a strategy can be outlined for investigating the learner differences they reveal.

II. STRATEGIES FOR RESEARCH
ON LEARNER DIFFERENCES

Investigators as well as learners differ from one another. One investigator begins his inquiries because he is arrested by an empirical phenomenon, another because she seeks to verify a theoretical proposition. One intends her work as a contribution to theory construction in the domains of development, learning, or individual differences; another wants to evaluate assumptions that dictate practices of child rearing or education. Because of these and other differences among investigators and the problems they address, one cannot hope to specify a single sequence of steps that constitutes an optimal research strategy. Instead the major components of such a strategy will be described, with the knowledge that they can be assembled in a variety of combinations and orders.

A. Establishing Phenomena

At some stage of his or her work on learner differences, an investigator needs to establish firmly the existence of one or more phenomena. He or she needs evidence that performance differences are dependably associated with differences in developmental level or, within a developmental level, that some persons regularly perform differently than other persons. The establishment of such phenomena can be important for either of two purposes: for isolating an object of study or for testing predictions drawn from a theoretical hypothesis. Thus, this component may come either early or late in a program of research.

Whatever the purposes and timing of the activity of establishing a phenomenon, the investigator must be assured that the learner differences involved are (a) reliable and (b) accurately characterized. With reference to reliability, the investigator needs to ascertain that physics majors, for example, consistently learn more from itemized lists than chemistry majors, or that college students regularly learn more than sixth graders. Even if such differences are reliable, it still remains to assure that their characterization is accurate. Do the physics and chemistry majors, or the college and sixth-grade students, differ in how much they learn from itemized lists, or in how much of their learning they exhibit under a particular test condition? Although it seems rudimentary, the attainment of descriptive accuracy is essential in order to focus attention on the substance rather than the appearance of differences, and often requires an extraordinary degree of investigative endurance.

B. Formulating Hypotheses about Learner Differences

When the first step in an investigator's research strategy is the establishment of a phenomenon, the next step consists of formulating hypotheses about the sources of the learner differences that have been described. One way of generating such provisional explanations is to derive them from propositions offered by theories of individual differences, of development, or of learning and memory. Since a learning theory, for example, consists of propositions about the mental structures and processes that make learning possible in any person, differences in these structures and processes can be hypothesized as sources of performance variability across learners. For instance, if there are persuasive theoretical grounds for believing that learning the contents of a list depends on the construction of relations among the items, it can be hypothesized that performance differences among learners are due to differences in their capacity or propensity for constructing such relations.

In some cases, of course, theory construction may not be sufficiently advanced to provide the propositions needed by the student of learner differences. Even so, the investigator can make use of experimental analyses of relevant learning phenomena to establish more precisely the loci of performance differences. For example, only speculation may be available about how information previously learned from itemized lists is retrieved from memory. However, if a methodology has been developed for assessing retrieval effects independent of the amount initially learned, the investigator has an analytical tool that can be used to determine whether performance differences across persons are confined to learning proficiency or extend to retrieval proficiency as well (see Tulving & Thomson, 1973). Thus, in formulating hypotheses, the student of learner differences can exploit both the theoretical propositions and the methods of experimental analysis that come from allied research on human learning and memory.

If an investigator chooses to derive hypotheses about sources of developmental and individual differences from the results of allied research, he or she needs to be explicit about the populations to which the results pertain. Typically, propositions about human learning refer to persons in whom the postulated structures and processes are well developed and effectively engaged during work on a performance task. That is, most such propositions specify the structures and processes that produce successful performance. The assertion that persons learn group membership information by elaborating relations among items within subsets of a list, for example, refers to persons who exhibit successful test performance; it does not imply that all persons effectively elaborate relations when confronted with a request to learn group membership information. Indeed, it is this kind of boundary on such assertions that the student of learner differences uses to generate hypotheses; that is, he or she makes the provisional inference that failures to achieve successful performance result from structures or processes that are less than optimal—that a failure to learn group membership information, for example, results from ineffective elaboration of relations. By acknowledging this feature of propositions about human learning, one can adopt a relatively straightforward routine for testing hypotheses about learner differences.

C. Verifying Hypotheses about Learner Differences

The activity of verifying hypotheses about learner differences can be thought of as a three-step routine: selecting learner indices, developing compensatory conditions, and designing instructive experiments.

1. Indexing Learners

The obvious first step in this routine is to find a way of indexing populations of learners with reference to the performance levels they will exhibit on a given task. In its simplest form, this step amounts to identifying a population of persons who will perform well on a given task and one that will perform poorly. In more sophisticated forms, involving regression models of design and analysis, the step entails the use of an index that assigns values to persons on a continuous scale predictive of subsequent performance on the given task (for extended discussions, see Cronbach & Snow, 1975; Kerlinger & Pedhazur, 1974).

Investigators often settle on a learner index in the course of their efforts to establish phenomena. By the time they come to test hypotheses, they have already found, for example, that physics majors outperform chemistry majors or that college students achieve higher performance levels than sixth graders, so that the characteristic of major field or of educational level can be used to identify populations that will differ on the criterion task. Alternatively, the index may be dictated by aspects of the theory the investigator has chosen to evaluate. A developmental theory, for example, might include an implication that postadolescents will elaborate relations among list items whereas preadolescents will not, indicating that age should be used to identify populations of learners.

Learner indices have been partitioned into two classes: extrinsic and intrinsic (Jensen, 1967). The critical difference between the two classes lies in whether there are persuasive grounds for believing that the characteristic indexed is engaged during the performance of interest. With reference to the task of learning the identity of the items in a word list, for example, and depending on the guiding theory, the scores obtained by persons on the memory-span subscale of an IQ test might qualify as an intrinsic characteristic, whereas full-scale scores would probably constitute an extrinsic index. In general, for tasks that tap learning from itemized information, such characteristics as age, sex, socioeconomic status (SES), ethinicity, educational level, and intelligence test scores (IQ) may be regarded as extrinsic indices. Examples of intrinsic indices are more difficult to list since, by definition, they must be credible measures of learner differences in the specific processes believed responsible for the particular performance differences under investigation. Besides tapping learner differences in an hypothesized process or structure, to be most useful, an intrinsic index should operate in a singular way; that is, it should be sensitive to variations in the specified processes and structures, but entirely insensitive to others. Still, an index may be quite gross and still qualify as intrinsic. For example, if the criterion task were that of learning identity information from an orally presented list of randomly selected common nouns, a gross intrinsic index might be performance on an equivalent list of common nouns, whereas a purer index might be performance on a test of the tendency to process words semantically (Craik & Lockhart, 1972).

As Underwood (1975) has argued, relatively pure indices provide a bonus over and beyond their pragmatic value in identifying learner differences: they can be used early in a research program to discredit potentially untenable hypotheses. If a learner index is either patently relevant or demonstrably sensitive to hypothesized structures or processes, the differences it discloses should mirror or predict the performance differences under study. Thus, when measured learner differences fail to correlate with target performance differences, the investigator obtains an early warning that further pursuit of the hypothesis would be futile. Even in their gross forms, however, intrinsic indices are preferable to extrinsic ones precisely because they are germane to the goal of accounting for performance variation in terms of corresponding structure or process differences among learners.

To reiterate, whichever type of index an investigator decides to rely on, it is imperative for her or him to insure that it will yield samples of persons that include learners of the kind referred to in the theoretical propositions under test. If the investigator intends to test an hypothesis drawn from a theoretical model of performance in college students, for example, he or she must use a learner index that will allow for drawing at least one of the samples from a college student population. Otherwise one runs the risk that none of the learners sampled will embody the structures or processes presupposed in the relevant theoretical proposition. Thus, to warrant further inquiry, an index of learner characteristics, whether intrinsic or extrinsic, must have two properties: it must be predictive of task performance; and it must identify the populations of relevance to the hypothesis being evaluated.

2. Developing Compensatory Task Conditions

After an adequate learner index has been established, the next step in the hypothesis testing routine is to develop compensatory task conditions. The investigator's ultimate aim of verifying an hypothesis about the sources of learner differences dictates that such conditions meet three criteria: they must improve the performance of less proficient learners; they must be relevant to the guiding theoretical proposition; and they must be congruent with the hypothesis.

By itself, the first criterion is relatively easy to satisfy. The investigator simply defines a standard set of task conditions as those ordinarily imposed in previous research relevant to the theoretical proposition. He or she then modifies the conditions in ways likely to improve performance. If less proficient learners perform better under the modified than under the standard conditions, the first compensatory criterion is met.

The second criterion, however, complicates matters in that the modification must be demonstrably relevant to theoretical constructs. In an itemized information task, for example, suppose the subject is asked to listen to a list of words and then to discriminate between words that she or he had heard and similar words that had not been presented. Even though performance would surely be improved by telling the subject whether each word was "old" or "new" immediately before he or she responds, such a modification would be obviously irrelevant to the theoretical proposition guiding the investigator's research. Thus, an appropriate task modification would not only have to improve discrimination but also pertain to a process believed responsible for successful performance.

The substance of the third criterion is that compensatory conditions must be congruent with the fine grain of an investigator's hypothesis about learner differences. Such hypotheses may be divided into two classes; that is, they may relate performance differences to corresponding learner differences either in capacity or in propensity. If the investigator suspects that learners differ in capacity, she or he will develop compensatory task conditions that are *prosthetic* in character—conditions that artificially replace the structures or processes requisite for successful task performance. For example, suppose an investigator ascribes serial-order performance differences between two groups of learners to differences in the ability to retrieve previously stored item identity information. In this case, prosthetic compensation might consist of presenting all of the items so that the test would consist solely of arranging them to correspond with the original order.

In contrast, if an investigator asserts that performance differences result from corresponding differences in propensity, he or she will develop compensatory conditions that are *catalytic* in character, that is, conditions likely to trigger the processes or structures held to be responsible for successful performance. In the example, subjects might be provided with cues for retrieving item identity rather than with the items themselves.

Catalytic compensation can vary from weak to strong in terms of the degree to which it approximates prosthesis. For example, standard instructions to learn group membership information would qualify as a weak catalyst, whereas the presentation of grouped items in a relational story context would serve as a strong catalyst. Whatever the strength of the catalyst, by selecting it instead of a prosthetic condition, the investigator declares the assumption that performance differences stem from corresponding learner differences in propensity rather than in capacity.

By no means, however, are the two sources of learner differences mutually exclusive. An investigator may assume that two groups of learners differ in capacity as well as in propensity, and therefore devise a compensatory condition that provides prosthesis as well as catalysis. Alternatively, the investigator may believe that variance in performance stems from learner differences on two independent dimensions, one related to capacity, the other to propensity. For example, such a hypothesis might be that performance differences associated with age are due to developmental differences in mental capacity while those associated with social class membership arise from differences in propensity (see Case, 1975).

Finally, it is important to emphasize still another distinction among compensatory conditions. Thus far, the examples used to illustrate compensation have been uniformly positive in character, appropriate for increasing process or structural activation. Depending on the guiding theoretical proposition, however, compensation may take an alternative form. Suppose the proposition suggests that the structures and processes necessary for success are available in all persons and that performance differences stem from differences in the inhibition of dysfunctional processes. In such cases, rather than consisting of conditions that promote activation, compensation must take the form of encouraging selective inhibition.

3. Designing Instructive Experiments

Equipped with an adequate learner index and effective compensatory task conditions, an investigator can proceed to the first test of his or her hypothesis. In its simplest form, such a test requires only four groups of subjects—two samples of learners, each distributed among two experimental conditions. Using the learner index, the investigator draws a sample of proficient subjects from the reference population and another sample from one of the less proficient populations defined by the scale. Within each sample, the subjects are randomly assigned to either the standard task condition or to the compensatory condition. And, if sufficiently bold, the investigator makes the prediction that the compensatory condition will improve performance in the less proficient learners to the point that it is equivalent to that of the more proficient, both in the standard and in the compensatory conditions.

Such an experiment is instructive in the sense that its outcome can inform the investigator about the promise of an hypothesis. If the results accord with the prediction, the investigator learns that the hypothesis is at least provisionally adequate; if the results depart from the prediction in any respect, the investigator can learn that the hypothesis is inadequate.

Though instructive, this use of an experimental result is excessively coarse and the investigator can gain substantial additional profit by attending to the finer grain of the possible outcomes.

In terms of relative performance, the four-group experiment can yield only a limited number of different outcomes, provided that the investigator has effectively taken the preceding steps in the hypothesis-testing routine. These steps fix two of the relationships among the groups: in the standard condition, if the learner index is reliable, performance of the proficient subjects should exceed that of the less proficient; if the compensatory condition has been adequately developed, it should foster better performance than the standard condition among the less proficient learners. When these assumptions hold, four classes of outcome can result from the experiment.

Among the alternatives, one class, displayed in idealized form in Figure 1, consists of outcomes that accord completely with the investigator's prediction: performance of the less proficient learners in the compensatory condition is as high as that of the more proficient in the standard condition, indicating that the form of compensation provided is sufficient to produce the reference performance level, and, consistent with the presumption that the compensatory condition is isomorphic with the structures and processes normally characteristic of proficient learners, their performance in the standard and compensatory conditions should be equivalent. All three of these

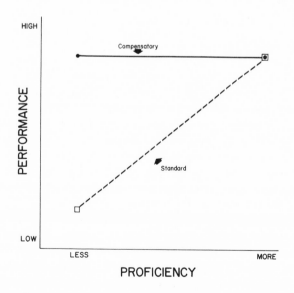

FIGURE 1.   Performance as a function of learner proficiency and conditions: a prototype of confirming outcomes.

groups, of course, exhibit performance levels superior to that achieved by the less proficient learners in the standard condition.

Even completely confirming outcomes by no means conclude the investigator's assessment of an hypothesis. The investigator should determine whether the confirming pattern can be replicated and assure that it is not due to an artifact such as a performance ceiling or a tendency of the proficient learners to ignore the compensatory provisions.

Beyond these and other necessary checks on the validity and reliability of an initial experiment, the investigator often needs to conduct additional empirical analyses in relation to an hypothesis. Suppose, for example, that a compensatory condition of the prosthetic variety has been used. The confirming experimental outcome suggests that the condition is sufficient to erase learner differences but not that it is necessary. Contrary to the investigator's hypothesis, the learner differences in question may not be in capacity but in propensity so that prosthesis should be unnecessary. To resolve this issue, the investigator can design additional experiments to assess the effects of catalytic compensatory conditions that vary in strength. Another important way of adducing support for a promising hypothesis is by demonstrating that the performance of proficient learners diminishes under conditions that block the activation of the posited structures or processes. Thus, the investigator's task is to construct and impose conditions that should interfere with a process believed responsible for high proficiency, but not with other processes relevant to performance, and show that performance decreases relative to that observed under standard conditions.

Apart from confirming outcomes, the investigator's initial experimental test can also yield a number of disconfirming ones that vary in their implications about the promise of the hypothesis. These remaining outcomes can be divided into three partially overlapping classes. One, illustrated in Figure 2, comprises cases in which the performance of the less proficient learners in the compensatory condition, although enhanced, still remains inferior to that of proficient learners in the standard condition. Such results clearly indicate that the compensatory condition is insufficient but they do not isolate the source of the problem. Among the possibilities, two prominent ones are (a) that the compensatory condition is too weak, and (b) that structures or processes in addition to those designated by the hypothesis also determine the performance differences in question. Although less likely, another possibility is that the hypothesis pertains to structures or processes that are only marginally relevant to the target performance differences. In order to choose among the possibilities, the investigator is obliged to design and conduct further experimentation.

Another class of disconfirming outcomes includes those where the compensatory condition improves performance, not only among improficient

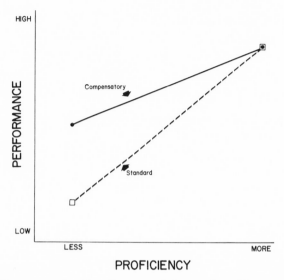

FIGURE 2.   Performance as a function of learner proficiency and conditions: prototype of one class of disconfirming outcomes.

learners, but also among proficient learners. This kind of result, displayed schematically in Figure 3, suggests two alternative interpretations. One is that the investigator's hypothesis suffers only from imprecision; that is, an overestimation of the extent or the consistency with which proficient learners activate the structures or processes responsible for performance so that the compensatory condition proves facilitating for them as well as for the improficient learners. Another interpretation is that the hypothesis is fundamentally invalid. The compensatory condition improves performance in both kinds of subjects because it activates structures or processes that are normally dormant in all learners. To choose between the two interpretations, the investigator can examine other aspects of the results. For example, weight might be added to the interpretation in terms of precision if the two groups of learners perform equivalently in the compensatory condition (Figure 3a), whereas the suspicion of a fundamental error in the hypothesis would be heightened if the performance of the proficient learners in the standard condition continued to exceed that of the less proficient, even when the latter were provided with compensation (Figure 3b).

The defining feature of the final class of outcomes, exemplified in Figure 4, is that the compensating condition diminishes the performance of proficient learners. Such results suggest that, rather than nurturing the normal operations of a skillful learner, the compensatory conditions interfere with them. A plausible inference is that the wrong structures or processes have been identified as responsible for the initial learner differences.

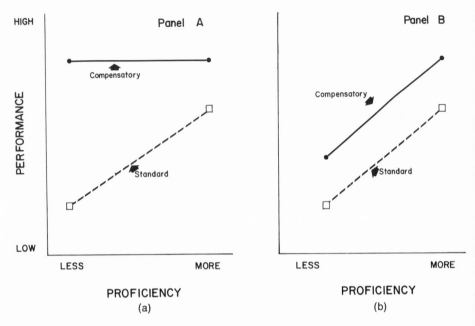

FIGURE 3.   Performance as a function of learner proficiency and conditions: prototypes of a second class of disconfirming outcomes, indicating (a) an imprecise, and (b) an invalid hypothesis.

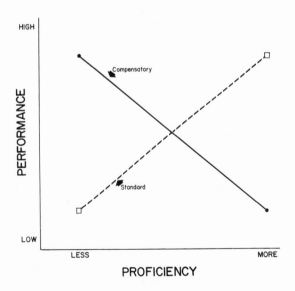

FIGURE 4.   Performance as a function of learner proficiency and conditions: prototype of a third class of disconfirming outcomes.

The extreme version of this class of outcomes occurs when the compensatory condition serves to reverse the position of the two kinds of learners such that the improficient sample achieves a higher performance level than the proficient sample. In addition to disconfirming the investigator's hypothesis, in effect, this pattern of results produces a new learner difference phenomenon that must be accommodated by a revised version of the hypothesis. Although such an outcome has certain negative implications for the effort to account for initial learner differences, it is regarded as a treasure by investigators whose goal is to identify instructional conditions that are differentially effective for various types of students (Cronbach & Snow, 1975). These investigators are intent to discover aptitude by treatment interactions (ATIs), preferably ones that are disordinal in character, in which a condition that produces a positive effect for one kind of student produces a negative effect for others. In contrast to the line I have taken here, the implicit assumption in ATI enterprises appears to be that learner discrepancies are so fundamental that performance equivalence can only be achieved through the activation of distinctly different processes and structures across individuals.

Evidently even the admittedly simple four-group design can produce results that lead in a variety of different directions. Often even more can be learned from complex designs that include several compensatory conditions and a large number of learner categories, up to the regression case where learners are identified with values on a continuous scale rather than being assigned to gross classes. However complex the design, the steps of the hypothesis testing routine remain serviceable: secure a relevant and dependable index of learner differences; develop compensatory conditions; and carry out instructive experimentation.

D. Exploiting the Results of Hypothesis Verification

Although a research strategy may be infinitely recursive in principle, at various points investigators pause to survey the implications of their efforts. As noted previously, research on learner differences can have consequences and implications for a variety of enterprises, from theory building to educational policy, and an investigator may choose to emphasize any one or all of them.

Suppose interest lies mainly in determining the merit of the theoretical propositions from which the investigator drew the hypothesis about learner differences. Then the aim would be to show how the results of his or her research bear on the propositions. If the results have confirmed the hypothesis and ruled out obvious alternative interpretations, the research provides evidence of the power and utility of the parent theory. In contrast, the results may expose the hypothesis as partially, or even totally, inadequate. Provided extrapolations from the parent theory have been made faithfully and that impeccable empirical methods have been used, research outcomes may force revisions in the propositions that guided it, and the investigator may even wish to propose other formulations. For either kind of outcome, the aim is to affect the influence of the parent theory, whether it pertains to development or to general laws of human learning and memory.

Another potential aim of research on learner differences is to increase the utility of descriptive terms and the accuracy of empirical data. At present we are far from having a productive and comprehensive taxonomy of learner difference dimensions much less the data to relate them to associated performance differences. For example, the quality of developmental investigations would be considerably enhanced by some serviceable and meaningful learner indices other than the empty variable of chronological age and the hopelessly amalgamated mental age scores derived from IQ tests (see Case, 1972, and Pascual-Leone, 1970, for a promising alternative). Similar profit would accrue from the construction of instruments for measuring varieties of learning proficiency within any given developmental level, especially if the measures were reliably related to performance differences on tasks of use in verifying theoretical propositions. As it is, investigators must either rely on omnibus tests, like the IQ batteries, that have a sorry record of utility in research on learner differences (Cronbach & Snow, 1975), or join in the proliferation of ad hoc instruments that are more specific, to be sure, but do little to foster a cumulative science. One consequence of this sad state of affairs (as is noted in Section III.C) is that learner populations can rarely be identified with enough precision to permit accurate replication, much less to provide firm evidence about developmental or individual learner differences in intellectual performance. Thus, research on learner differences might have consequences that would be salutary indeed for the achievement of descriptive and empirical objectives.

Finally, the results of learner difference research can also have implications for practical problems, such as those encountered in education. Implications of this kind may take either of two forms. One depends on choosing research paradigms directly from the pool of tasks that students perform in the public schools (for example, Estes, 1974; Hunt, Frost, & Lunneborg, 1973). Then, with some confidence, the investigator can extrapolate the results of experimental analysis and hypothesis testing to make prescriptive recommendations, that is, recommendations about administering the tasks in school in ways that defer to characteristics of the learners involved.

A second approach, although more vulnerable to criticism, is to use research results, along with confirmed or disconfirmed hypotheses, to assess the merits of implicit assumptions that underlie educational policy and practice (see Rohwer, 1973a). For example, if retention were shown to be exclusively a function of the degree, and not the method or pace of original learning, then instruction should assure high levels of initial mastery, rather than adherence to a single prescribed pattern of practice. Of course, so blunt a recommendation would hardly warrant immediate implementation without additional validation, since it would probably stem from the use of tasks different from many of those imposed in education. Nevertheless, at the time the recommendation is made, it might well be more supportable than any alternative, and its very vulnerability might provoke the investigator and others to engage in another cycle of the research strategy. Indeed, this kind of renewed need to engage in further inquiry may be the greatest benefit to be gained from pausing to exploit the implications of research results, whether the investigator's purpose is to advance theory, improve description, establish information, or to affect educational practice.

In summary, four major components of a strategy for conducting research on learner differences have been discussed: the establishment of phenomena; the formulation of hypotheses; the verification of the hypotheses; and ways of exploiting the results obtained. In the next section each of these components is illustrated by identifying their manifestations in selected research investigations.

III. SELECTED EXAMPLES OF RESEARCH ON LEARNER DIFFERENCES

Aspects of the research strategy outlined here may be discerned in a large number of studies of learner differences. However, rather than attempting a comprehensive review of all such studies, a selected few are examined here to highlight the ways that the four strategy components have been realized in practice, that is, in research on learning from itemized information. In addition to exemplifying the strategy, the studies selected meet the criteria of addressing issues of current theoretical interest, and of having a focus on individual differences, developmental differences, or a combination of both.

A. A Study of Individual Differences

Keeney, Cannizzo, and Flavell (1967) reported a study of performance differences among first-grade children in the recall of serial order information. With reference to the four components of the research strategy, the study served to: (a) establish a phenomenon; (b) verify an explanatory hypothesis; and (c) exploit the results of verification. In keeping with the principle that the strategy components can be assembled in a variety of sequences, Keeney et al. (1967) began with a preformed hypothesis that guided both the venture of establishing the phenomenon, and the construction of compensatory conditions. The hypothesis was drawn from theoretical propositions advanced to account for memory phenomena in adults (Conrad, 1964; Hintzman, 1965) and, in alternative versions, to account for developmental differences among children in performance on memory tasks (Flavell, Beach, & Chinsky, 1966; Reese, 1962). Informally phrased, the hypothesis was that differences among children in serial recall performance stem from corresponding differences in verbal rehearsal of the sequence of items to be remembered, during the interval between study and test.

Guided by the hypothesis, the investigators' first objective was to establish the implied phenomenon; that is, to ascertain whether differences in serial recall performance are associated with differences in verbal rehearsal. Each of 89 first-grade children was given 10 serial recall problems in which the task was to remember the order of designation of 2, 3, 4, or 5 of 6 pictured objects shown in a 3 × 2 array. The study trial for a problem consisted of the presentation of the array, and of the experimenter pointing to each of the given number of pictures successively at a 2-sec rate. After pointing to the last picture in the series, the experimenter screened the display from the subject's view for a delay interval of 15 sec, during which any observable lip or mouth movements were noted. At the end of the interval, the screen was removed, and the subject was asked to point to the designated pictures in the same order as that followed initially by the experimenter. When each such test trial was completed, the child was asked to state what he or she had done, if anything, to remember the pictures and their order.

Learners were classified as either Producers, Nonproducers, or mixed on the basis of observed lip movements and responses to the queries made after each test trial. The criterion for the Producer group was observable rehearsal on nine or ten of the problems while subjects regarded as Nonproducers were those who neither reported rehearsing nor were observed to rehearse on more than a single problem. Unfortunately, the remaining subjects were excluded from further analysis, so that the reported results pertain only to the extreme groups. Performance was indexed in terms of the number of test trials completed correctly and the results accorded with the prediction, disclosing that Producers achieved higher scores than Nonproducers. Furthermore, the results of a brief retest six weeks later showed that the learner index was of adequate reliability. Thus, Keeney et al. (1967) established a phenomenon: performance differences associated with differences among learners in rehearsal activity.

Since these investigators had previously formulated a hypothesis for explaining the phenomenon established, the next component in their research strategy was that of verifying the hypothesis. As they had already secured a relevant index of learner differences in rehearsal activity, their first step in the hypothesis-verification routine was to design a compensatory condition. The condition chosen was of the catalytic variety, toward the strong end of that continuum. Prior to the administration of the ten-problem serial recall task previously described, the subject was given the study and delay interval portions of two practice problems. During study, the subject was encouraged to name each of the pictured objects in the designated sequence and to whisper this sequence of names repeatedly during the delay. Additionally, at the onset of the delay interval for each of the ten test problems, the experimenter prompted the subject to engage in whispered rehearsal of the names of the pictured objects in the series.

Using this compensatory condition, Keeney et al. (1967) verified their hypothesis by conducting an experiment that may be regarded as an incomplete version of the four-group design. Six weeks after the initial administration of the ten serial-recall problems, all of the children identified as "producers" and "nonproducers" were again tested on the same set of problems. The children in the compensatory condition were prompted to engage in whispered rehearsal during each delay interval between study and test, while children in the standard condition were treated just as they had been during the first session. Half of the producers were assigned to each condition, but since the number of nonproducers was so small, the investigators decided to assign all of them to the compensatory condition, and to use their performance during the first session as an estimate of second-session performance in the standard condition. Thus, the experiment included three of the four groups appropriate for verifying the hypothesis, along with a provision for estimating the outcome for the missing group.

The results of the experiment may be seen in Figure 5, where performance is indexed in terms of the proportion of the ten problems in which recall was perfect. As the figure discloses, the outcome accorded completely with the investigators' hypothesis: the performance of the nonproducers in the compensatory condition was equivalent to that of the producers in the standard condition, and the producers performed at equivalent levels in both conditions. Thus, the experiment proved instructive in providing support for the hypothesis that differences in serial-recall performance within groups of six- and seven-year-old children stem from learner differences in rehearsal activity between study and test.

By itself, of course, this experimental outcome does not constitute a conclusive demonstration of the validity of the hypothesis—no single experiment can accomplish so much. Apart from reducing ambiguities owing to the use of an incomplete design and to the exclusion of subjects from the

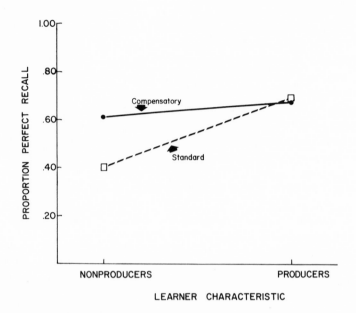

FIGURE 5.   Proportion perfect recall as a function of learner characteristic and conditions. (Adapted from Keeney *et al.*, 1967.)

middle range of the producer dimension, additional steps would be needed to bolster confidence in the hypothesis. For example, an experiment could be designed to determine the effect of a condition intended to prevent the rehearsal activity supposedly responsible for proficient performance among producers. Other experiments could be conducted to ascertain whether a catalyst as strong as the prompt used by Keeney *et al.* (1967) is necessary to effect proficiency among nonproducers. And, since the claim for the hypothesis extends beyond the performance of ordered picture recall, its utility should be examined with reference to other tasks and procedures. Finally, it would be of substantial value to construct a verifiable account of the factors responsible for differences in rehearsal activity among children in single age groups. Some of these steps have already been taken and descriptions of the results may be found in articles by Flavell (1970) and Flavell, Friedrichs, and Hoyt (1970).

These same sources may be consulted for illustrations of the ways that the results of Keeney and his associates have been exploited. In brief, the principal impact of their study has been on the construction of a developmental theory of memory; that is, the hypothesis offered to explain individual differences has also been used to account for some of the observed developmental differences in learning and memory proficiency between older and younger children. A direct attack on such developmental phenomena is illustrated in the study to be described next.

B. A Study of Developmental Differences

As has been shown, the study by Keeney *et al*. (1967) was guided by the hypothesis that individual performance differences are associated with corresponding differences in the tendency to engage in information-preserving activities between presentation and test. Similar hypotheses have been used by other investigators to account for developmental performance differences (Flavell, 1970; Hagen, 1971; Rosner, 1971). Across studies, the recurrent feature in investigators' hypotheses has been the attribution of performance differences to learner activities that presumably affect the acquisition or storage of information. Thus, developmental performance differences have been accounted for in terms of learner differences in storage processes or activities.

An alternative emphasis is evident in another set of studies. These studies were conducted to verify hypotheses that ascribe developmental performance differences to learner differences in recall or retrieval rather than storage activities (Kobasigawa, 1974; Moely, 1968; Ritter, Kaprove, Fitch, & Flavell, 1973; Scribner & Cole, 1972). Although the principal aim of these investigators has been to contribute to the construction of developmental theory, they have relied heavily on analytic conceptions and experimental methods offered by students of human learning and memory (for example, Tulving & Thomson, 1973). That is, these investigators have explicitly recognized the analytic division between storage and retrieval loci of performance effects, and, in notable cases, have sought to hold acquisition conditions constant while manipulating conditions of recall.

This approach is clearly exemplified in a study reported by Kobasigawa (1974). The target phenomenon was the relation between age and performance on a task requiring the recall of the identity of items on a previously presented list. Since other investigators had shown that the older the learner, the more proficient his recall of such information (for example, Cole, Frankel, & Sharp, 1971), thus establishing the phenomenon, Kobasigawa's research strategy began with the formulation of an hypothesis to account for developmental differences in the performance of recalling item identity information.

Evidently, the hypothesis was assembled from several sources. One is the proposition that performance depends on gaining access, at the time of a recall test, to the information previously stored in memory (see Tulving & Thomson, 1973). Another is that adult learners, provided at the time of test with retrieval cues—stimuli initially stored along with the information to be remembered—can use these cues to gain access to the target information. Evidence in support of this notion has come from experiments showing that performance is facilitated by the presentation of such cues during testing (Crouse, 1968; Tulving & Pearlstone, 1966). The very fact that the adult subjects in these studies profited from the presentation of retrieval cues also indicates that they are far from adept at producing the cues themselves. Accordingly, Kobasigawa hypothesized that developmental differences in item recall performance partly stem from learner differences in the tendency to make effective use of provided retrieval cues.

As a first step in verifying this hypothesis, Kobasigawa adopted the learner index used by previous investigators to establish the target phenomenon, chronological age, and sampled subjects from three groups: 6-, 8-, and 11-year-old children. Although the theoretical propositions used to build the hypothesis initially pertained to adult performance, the apparent risk of excluding an adult sample was minimized by other evidence showing that retrieval cues facilitated performance in children as well (Moely, 1968).

All subjects were asked to learn and recall the names of 24 pictorially represented objects under uniform conditions of storage. The 24 items to be learned were drawn from eight classes (animals, furniture, vehicles, etc.) and presented in two 4 × 3 arrays. A row of an array consisted of four item pictures, each drawn from a different class, mounted immediately below pictures representing the appropriate class (empty zoo cages, a room, a road with a sidewalk). To promote the joint storage of items and cues, the subjects were asked to name each item in response to experimenter statements such as: "In the zoo, you find ———." After naming each item in this fashion, subjects were asked to recall the entire list.

Kobasigawa took the next step in the hypothesis-testing routine by manipulating the conditions of retrieval. One condition ("cue") had the status of a standard condition in the prototypical four-group design (see Section II.C.1), and so was expected to produce substantial developmental differences. In this condition, at the time of test, subjects were given a stack of eight cards, each bearing a picture representing one of the cue classes, and told that they might look at them if they believed it would assist them in recalling the names of the list items. The second condition ("directed cue") was compensatory, of the strong catalyst variety. Here the experimenter presented each of the cue cards singly, reminded subjects of the relation between cue and items, stated the number of items related to the cue, and asked for the recall of those three items before presenting the next cue card. This directed-cue condition was predicted to attenuate the developmental differences expected in the cue condition. Finally, for purposes of reference, Kobasigawa also included an ordinary free-recall condition, although it was not germane to the test of the hypothesis.

One aspect of the hypothesis—that older children would make more use of available retrieval cues than younger children—was assessed for the cue condition by counting as "cue users" those who were observed to look at the cue cards and to recall at least one appropriate item while doing so.

From the youngest to the oldest, the proportions of the samples classified as "cue users" were .33, .67, and .83, an outcome entirely consistent with the hypothesis. Also consistent were the results obtained by computing the proportion of items correctly recalled on the test trial. As can be seen in Figure 6, where these data are plotted as a function of age and retrieval conditions, there are pronounced developmental differences in the standard (cue) condition, but not in the compensatory (directed-cue) condition. In accord with the hypothesis, when degree of initial storage is equated, developmental performance differences in item recall appear to stem from corresponding differences in making effective use of available retrieval cues.

Although the results are impressively congruent with predictions, verification of the larger claims of the hypothesis awaits further empirical analysis. For instance, it will be necessary to rule out a ceiling-effect interpretation for the results observed in the directed-cue condition. More substantively, the directed-cue condition provided multiple compensation, drawing attention to the cues, emphasizing the relation between cues and items, and designating the number of items to be recalled in connection with each cue. Accordingly, the design does not allow a decision on which of these compensatory components are necessary for the observed facilitation

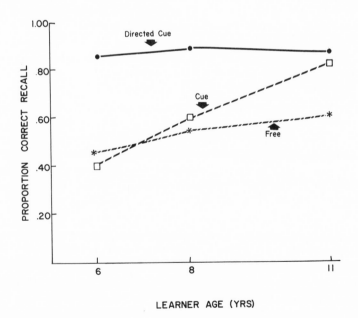

FIGURE 6.   Proportion of items correctly recalled as a function of learner age and conditions. (Adapted from Kobasigawa, 1974.)

in younger children, so that the locus of the developmental difference observed in the cue condition cannot be specified precisely. In another vein, the experiment is admittedly insufficient to explicate developmental performance differences in item recall when retrieval cues are not provided. Although such differences may be due entirely to corresponding differences in cue use, it is also plausible that they are partly due to differences in cue generation as well. To decide the issue, it would be necessary to find a means, in the form of a different kind of compensatory condition, of promoting cue generation while holding cue use constant. Finally, of course, the hypothesis would be strengthened by replication, by extension to a variety of task configurations, by assessment across a wider age range, and by the use of a more substantial index of developmental level.

C. A Study of Developmental and Individual Differences

The study to be featured here was designed and conducted in an attempt to explicate a set of apparently erratic outcomes disclosed by a series of previous investigations. The focus of the entire series was on the acquisition of group membership information from itemized lists of paired associates, and the common purpose was to verify a hypothesis about performance differences presumably associated mainly with developmental differences over the age range from preadolescence to adulthood. Thus, before the present study was even conceived, most of the components of the research strategy had already been created: a phenomenon had been established, a hypothesis had been formulated, learner indexes had been selected, compensatory conditions constructed, experiments designed and conducted, and the results had been exploited, but, as it turns out, rather prematurely (see Rohwer, 1973a).

The target phenomenon is defined principally in terms of performance on a paired-associate task. Under standard conditions, learners are instructed to study a list of pairs of unrelated nouns in such a way that when later presented with one noun from each pair, they can recall the missing pair members. The noun pairs are presented successively for study, and a cued recall test is conducted immediately afterwards. When such a task is used and performance indexed by the number of missing pair members correctly recalled, studies (for example, Jensen & Rohwer, 1965) have disclosed differences associated with learner differences in chronological age.

One attempt to account for this developmental phenomenon has been constructed from the elaboration hypothesis formulated by Rohwer (1973b), among others. This hypothesis locates the source of effective paired-associate learning mainly in processes that foster storage, rather than retrieval, of group membership information. Moreover, the hypothesis characterizes the critical storage process as one of elaborating the initially disparate nouns in each pair into an episode or situation that serves to relate the pair constituents by virtue of their joint membership in the resulting event. This characterization may be regarded as an abstraction from the substance of descriptions given by college-age subjects when asked to report on the means they use to learn group membership information from lists of paired associates (Bugelski, 1962; Martin, Boersma, & Cox, 1965; Montague & Wearing, 1967; Runquist & Farley, 1964). Extended to address the developmental phenomenon, the hypothesis contends that the propensity for engaging in elaborative activity varies directly with increasing age, a trend especially pronounced across the interval from ages 11 or 12 to 17 or 18.

Although many of the attempts to verify the elaboration hypothesis have not been developmental in character, they have established the promise of certain compensatory conditions as well as enhancing the plausibility of the developmental hypothesis itself. A frequently used compensatory condition, the construction of a sentence context for the two nouns in each pair, has appeared in two versions, one prosthetic, the other catalytic. In the prosthetic version, subjects in the compensatory condition of an experiment are presented with a sentence description of an event implicating the referents of pair members. For example, rather than simply hearing the pair, "DOG–GATE," the subject would hear, "The DOG opened the GATE." The catalytic form of this type of elaborative compensation typically consists of instructions advising the subject to form a sentence or short story that describes an event involving the referents of pair members.

The efficacy of such compensatory conditions has been established for preadolescent children for both prosthetic (Rohwer, 1966) and catalytic versions (Jensen & Rohwer, 1965). As compared with standard conditions, performance in either variety of the compensatory condition reaches substantially higher levels. Of relevance to the developmental hypothesis, college students have been shown to derive little if any profit from elaborative compensation; that is, their performance in standard conditions is virtually as high as in compensatory conditions (Bobrow & Bower, 1969; Suzuki & Rohwer, 1969). Although the results of such independent studies of learning in children and in adults were consistent with the developmental hypothesis, they were hardly conclusive in the absence of an experiment that incorporated variation in the learner characteristic along with manipulation of storage conditions. Thus, the following series of studies was conducted to provide a more convincing assessment of the hypothesis.

The first study in the series had multiple aims. One was to verify the developmental hypothesis by testing the prediction that among older subjects performance in a standard condition would approximate that in compensatory conditions, whereas among younger subjects compensation would substantially elevate performance. Another aim was to determine whether catalytic compensation is sufficient to promote adult-like performance in preadolescent children, or if prosthesis is needed as well. A final purpose of the experiment was to institute a condition intended to disrupt elaborative activity in older subjects and test the prediction that diminished performance would result. The condition was the administration of instructions to repeat each noun pair as often as possible during study. In accord with these aims, samples were drawn from populations of sixth- and eleventh-grade public school students, and each subject was asked to learn group membership information from a list of noun pairs under either standard, repetition (disruptive), catalytic, or prosthetic compensatory conditions (for a more detailed account, see Rohwer & Bean, 1973).

The results were clear and damaging to the developmental hypothesis. Performance in the compensatory conditions far exceeded performance in the standard condition not only for the younger subjects but for the older ones as well. Furthermore, for both samples, repetition instructions produced performance equivalent to that in the standard condition, offering no support for the supposition of disruption in elaborative activity. The results also indicated that catalytic compensation was sufficient to promote elaboration: presented sentences produced no more facilitation than sentence instructions.

A straightforward interpretation of the outcome is to regard it as a conclusive disconfirmation of the elaboration hypothesis in both its basic and developmental forms. However, this interpretation is difficult to reconcile with the results of previous studies showing that the performance of college students in standard conditions is as efficient as in conditions of elaborative compensation. Alternatively, it might be supposed that the learner index was defective in that it did not insure the selection of a sample from the population implicitly designated in the elaboration hypothesis, namely, persons who learn group membership information proficiently under standard conditions. Prior to the study, advocates of the hypothesis assumed that the target population could be adequately characterized simply as "adults"—persons 17 years of age or older. An examination of previous studies, however, disclosed that the adults who performed proficiently under standard conditions were uniformly drawn from populations of students enrolled in colleges having highly selective admissions policies. This disclosure prompted a replication of the study.

Whereas the public school population sampled in the first study was that of white students from lower-middle class homes, the replication was conducted with white students from a decidedly upper-middle class area, the kind of population presumed most likely to enter elite colleges. In other respects the two studies were identical.

Evidently the learner index used in the first study was indeed faulty, for the results of the replication were entirely consistent with the developmental hypothesis. In the younger sample (sixth graders) performance in the compensatory conditions was 21% higher than in the standard; in the older sample, performance in the two conditions was equivalent. Moreover, the performance of the older subjects was significantly diminished by the repetition instructions—as if elaborative activity had been disrupted—whereas for the younger learners, performance in the repetition and standard conditions was equivalent. Thus, viewed by itself, the outcome of the replication provided persuasive support for the hypothesis.

But what of the discrepancy in results between the two studies? The implication clearly runs deeper than pointing to a simple defect in the original learner index. Initially, the hypothesis pertained solely to developmental differences, but in order to obtain confirming results, it was necessary to introduce a dimension of individual differences as well. The attribute used, socioeconomic status, was gross and extrinsic, leaving much to be desired in the way of precision and relevance to the elaboration hypothesis. Nevertheless, the results were convincing enough to be exploited with reference to theory about human learning and development (Rohwer, 1973b), and in connection with issues of educational research and practice (Rohwer, 1971, 1973a). However, as subsequent studies would show, even the revised hypothesis was inadequate.

One such study, conducted by Rohwer and Eoff, was designed to examine the compensatory effects of imagery rather than sentence instructions. Performance in the compensatory condition was compared with that in a repetition and in a standard condition among sixth- and eleventh-grade students sampled from a population we regarded as comparable to that used in the Rohwer and Bean (1973, Experiment II) replication, that is, upper-middle class white. The results, however, were far from comparable: performance in the compensatory condition was much better than in the standard, not only for the younger subjects but for the older ones as well.

Unwilling to conclude that our hypothesis was essentially erroneous, we next decided to examine the merits of an alternative way of modifying the learner index used to classify subjects. Once again we retained the developmental aspect of the hypothesis, believing that children and adults differ in their propensity to engage in elaborative activity, but qualified it with reference to another extrinsic dimension of individual differences—IQ. Our prediction was that compensation would be required to provoke elaborative activity in younger students (11-year-olds) regardless of IQ level, whereas compensation would be unnecessary for high-IQ 17-year-olds. The results proved us wrong. At all three IQ levels, within both age groups, performance in the compensatory condition (sentence instructions) far exceeded performance in standard and repetition conditions. Added to the results of our preceding studies and those of others (for example, Allison, Newman, & Ford, 1973), this outcome strongly suggested that wisdom might lie in abandoning the elaboration hypothesis. Instead, however, we embarked on still another attempt to verify it.

Despite our experience to the contrary, we persisted in supposing that the hypothesis was mainly inadequate in its specification of an index of individual learner differences. We found some support for our supposition in the impressively large amount of variability that characterized the performance of older learners in the standard condition, even within IQ levels. Accordingly, in our most recent attempt to verify the hypothesis, we shifted to an intrinsic individual difference index.

The study, conducted in collaboration with James Raines and Michael Wagner, was very similar to those that had preceded it. Samples of 10- and 17-year-olds were drawn from public schools serving an upper-middle class residential community. Since previous studies had shown that prosthetic compensation was no better than catalytic at either age level, the experimental conditions consisted only of sentence, repetition and standard instructions. Prior to assignment to experimental conditions, however, all subjects were given standard instructions and asked to learn an independent list of noun pairs. Within each age level, performance on this list was used as an index of learner differences so that equal numbers of subjects from the high, middle, and low thirds of the distribution could be assigned to experimental conditions instituted in connection with the criterion list. Although plainly primitive as an index of intrinsic learner differences, this method was chosen in accord with the assumption that paired-associate performance in standard conditions varies principally as a function of elaborative propensity and therefore provides a classification scheme germane to the hypothesis.

The results, displayed in Figure 7, largely corroborated our expectations. Among subjects not predisposed toward elaborative activity—including all of the younger samples and some of the older, especially the lower third—the compensatory condition improved performance to a level approximating that attained by the proficient older subjects, whether in the standard or in the compensatory condition. Moreover, among the learners exhibiting proficiency in the standard condition, instructions intended to disrupt elaborative activity, that is, repetition, produced the predicted effect.

To be sure, the results of this latest study lend credence to the hypothesis that elaborative propensity accounts for a large share of the developmental and individual differences in performance on group membership tasks. The issue is far from resolved, however. For example, replication is imperative, especially in view of the patently discrepant outcomes observed across previous studies. If valid, the hypothesis should survive extension to tasks

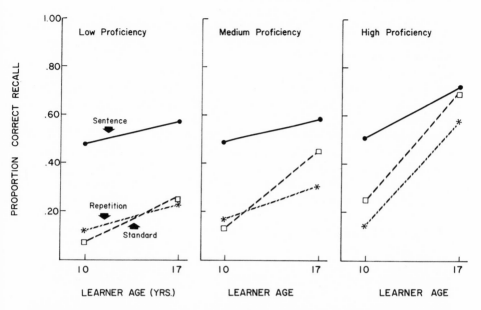

FIGURE 7.   Proportion of items correctly recalled as a function of learner proficiency, learner age, and conditions.

other than that of paired associates, and the learner indices, of both developmental and individual differences, should be replaced with alternatives that relate substantively to the elaboration hypothesis and also to more general theories of human learning and development. Thus, rather than providing an idealized illustration of the proposed research strategy, this extended example serves mainly to highlight the possibility that research on learner differences cannot be confined entirely to one or another variety; that is, the investigator may need to attend simultaneously to individual as well as developmental differences.

IV.   CONCLUSIONS

As an introduction to research on learner differences, a strategy comprised of four principal components or investigative tasks has been outlined: the establishment of phenomena, the formulation of explanatory hypotheses, verification of the hypotheses, and the exploitation of results. Certain aspects of each component have been given special emphasis. In establishing phenomena I have underlined the importance of ascertaining reliability through replication and achieving accuracy through experimental analysis. For hypothesis formulation, I have hailed the advantages that accrue when explanations of learner differences are drawn from parent theoretical propositions. It has been argued that these same propositions should be used to constrain the investigator's application of the routine for hypothesis verification: the learner index should be intrinsically related to structures and processes believed responsible for performance, and compensatory conditions should be manifestly germane to these same structures and processes. The endurance required to obtain support for a hypothesis has been high-lighted, including provisions for checking replicability, generality, and robustness. Finally, examples have been given of both the potential benefits and dangers in exploiting the results of verification.

In conclusion, it would be negligent to omit some cautionary notes. The approach described is no more than an introduction to research on learner differences, and the strategy proposed is no more than an outline. The theoretical substance and experimental skill necessary for productive investigation must be sought elsewhere. Moreover, the apparent simplicity of the approach and strategy should not be allowed to obscure the difficulties inherent in translating them into practice. Still the incentives are attractive and the attempt brings ample rewards.

REFERENCES

Allison, K. C., Newman, S. E., & Ford, W. S. Memory for noun pairs in the same or different underlying strings. *Memory & Cognition*, 1973, **1**, 205–208.

Bobrow, S. A., & Bower, G. H. Comprehension and recall of sentences. *Journal of Experimental Psychology*, 1969, **80**, 455–461.

Bugelski, B. R. Presentation time, total time, and mediation in paired-associate learning. *Journal of Experimental Psychology*, 1962, **63**, 409–412.

Case, R. Validation of a neo-Piagetian capacity construct. *Journal of Experimental Child Psychology*, 1972, **14**, 287–302.

Case, R. Social class differences in intellectual development: A neo-Piagetian investigation. *Canadian Journal of Behavioral Science*, 1975, **7**, 244–261.

Cole, M., Frankel, F., & Sharp, D. Development of free recall learning in children. *Developmental Psychology*, 1971, **4**, 109–123.

Conrad, R. Acoustic confusions in recent memory. *British Journal of Psychology*, 1964, **55**, 75–84.

Craik, F. I. M., & Lockhart, R. S. Levels of processing: A framework for memory research. *Journal of Verbal Learning and Verbal Behavior*, 1972, **11**, 671–684.

Cronbach, L. J., & Snow, R. E. *Aptitudes and instructional methods*. New York: Irvington, 1975, in press.

Crouse, J. Storage and retrieval of words in free-recall learning. *Journal of Educational Psychology*, 1968, **59**, 499–451.

Estes, W. K. Learning theory and intelligence. *American Psychologist*, 1974, **29**, 740–749.

Flavell, J. H. Developmental studies of mediated memory. In L. Lipsitt & H. Reese (Eds.), *Advances in child development and behavior*. Vol. 5. New York: Academic Press, 1970.

Flavell, J. H., Beach, D. R., & Chinsky, J. M. Spontaneous verbal rehearsal in a memory task as a function of age. *Child Development*, 1966, **37**, 283–299.

Flavell, J. H., Friedrichs, A. G., & Hoyt, J. D. Developmental changes in memorization processes. *Cognitive Psychology*, 1970, **1**, 324–340.

Hagen, J. W. The effects of attention and mediation on children's memory. *Young Children*, 1971, **26**, 290–304.

Hintzman, D. L. Classification and aural coding in short-term memory. *Psychonomic Science*, 1965, **3**, 161–162.

Hunt, E., Frost, N., & Lunneborg, C. Individual differences in cognition: A new approach to intelligence. In G. H. Bower (Ed.), *The psychology of learning and motivation*. Vol. 7. New York: Academic Press, 1973.

Jensen, A. R. Varieties of individual differences in learning. In R. Gagne (Ed), *Learning and individual differences*. Columbus, Ohio: Charles E. Merrill, 1967.

Jensen, A. R., & Rohwer, W. D., Jr. Syntactical mediation of serial and paired-associate learning as a function of age. *Child Development*, 1965, **36**, 601–608.

Kausler, D. H. *Psychology of verbal learning and memory*. New York: Academic Press, 1974.

Keeney, T. J., Cannizzo, S. R., & Flavell, J. H. Spontaneous and induced verbal rehearsal in a recall task. *Child Development*, 1967, **38**, 953–966.

Kerlinger, F. N., & Pedhazur, E. H. *Multiple regression in behavioral research*. New York: Holt, Rinehart & Winston, 1974.

Kobasigawa, A. Utilization of retrieval cues by children in recall. *Child Development*, 1974, **45**, 127–134.

Martin, C. J., Boersma, F. J., & Cox, D. L. A classification of associative strategies in the paired-associate learning. *Psychonomic Science*, 1965, **3**, 455–456.

Moely, B. E. Children's retention of conceptually related items under varying presentation and recall conditions. Unpublished doctoral dissertation, University of Minnesota. Ann Arbor, Michigan: University Microfilms, 1968. No. 68-17, 699.

Montague, W. E., & Wearing, A. J. The complexity of natural language mediators and its relation to paired-associate learning. *Psychonomic Science*, 1967, **7**, 135–136.

Murdock, B. B., Jr. *Human memory: Theory and data*. Hillsdale, New Jersey: Laurence Erlbaum Assoc., 1974.

Pascual-Leone, J. A mathematical model for the transition rule in Piaget's developmental stages. *Acta Psychologica*, 1970, **63**, 301–345.

Reese, H. W. Verbal mediation as a function of age level. *Psychological Bulletin*, 1962, **59**, 502–509.

Ritter, K., Kaprove, B. H., Fitch, J. P., & Flavell, J. H. The development of retrieval strategies in young children. *Cognitive Psychology*, 1973, **5**, 310–321.

Rohwer, W. D., Jr. Constraint, syntax and meaning in paired-associate learning. *Journal of Verbal Learning and Verbal Behavior*, 1966, **5**, 541–547.

Rohwer, W. D., Jr. Prime time for education: Early childhood or adolescence? *Harvard Educational Review*, 1971, **41**, 191–210.

Rohwer, W. D., Jr. Children and adolescents: Should we teach them or let them learn? In M. C. Wittrock (Ed.), *Changing schools: Alternatives from educational research*. Englewood Cliffs, New Jersey: Prentice-Hall, 1973. (a)

Rohwer, W. D., Jr. Elaboration and learning in childhood and adolescence. In H. W. Reese (Ed.), *Advances in child development and behavior*. Vol. 8. New York: Academic Press, 1973. (b)

Rohwer, W. D., Jr., & Bean, J. P. Sentence effects and noun-pair learning: A developmental interaction during adolescence. *Journal of Experimental Child Psychology*, 1973, **15**, 521–533.

Rosner, S. R. The effects of rehearsal and chunking instructions on children's multitrial free recall. *Journal of Experimental Child Psychology*, 1971, **11**, 93–105.

Runquist, W. N., & Farley, F. H. The use of mediators in the learning of verbal paired associates. *Journal of Verbal Learning and Verbal Behavior*, 1964, **3**, 280–285.

Scribner, S., & Cole, M. Effects of constrained recall training on children's performance in a verbal memory task. *Child Development*, 1972, **43**, 845–857.

Suzuki, N., & Rohwer, W. D., Jr. Deep structure in the noun-pair learning of children and adults. *Child Development*, 1969, **40**, 911–919.

Tulving, E., & Pearlstone, Z. Availability versus accessibility of information in memory for words. *Journal of Verbal Learning and Verbal Behavior*, 1966, **5**, 381–391.

Tulving, E., & Thomson, D. M. Encoding specificity and retrieval processes in episodic memory. *Psychological Review*, 1973, **80**, 352–373.

Underwood, B. J. Individual differences as a crucible in theory construction. *American Psychologist*, 1975, **30**, 128–134.

3

Cognitive Factors in Classical Conditioning

Leonard E. Ross

Susan M. Ross

University of Wisconsin—Madison

I. INTRODUCTION

The juxtaposition of "classical conditioning" and "cognitive processes" may appear incongruous to some since the relationship between the two has not been particularly prominent in the psychological literature. It is the thesis of this chapter, however, that a strong relationship does exist both in terms of the history of interest in the processes involved in classical conditioning and the usefulness of the conditioning paradigm in investigating many processes that fall under the rubric "cognitive."

Upon first consideration classical conditioning appears to be a very simple procedure, even when the term is used in a broad sense. Certainly many investigators over the years have characterized classical conditioning as a simple and well-controlled procedure that presumably avoids many of the complicating factors that are involved in other learning situations. Contributing to this image of classical conditioning is the history of the use of classical conditioning data in the stimulus–response learning theories of the 1940s and 1950s. The authors of these theories went to great lengths to avoid undefined constructs or processes, that is, those that were "mentalistic," or "cognitive" as the term was used at that time, and for those critical of stimulus–response theory classical conditioning was the epitome of an artificial and abstract reflexology that failed to reflect the important cognitive processes of man. Perhaps the use of the laws of classical conditioning as a model for theories of appetitive learning and the acquisition of fear and

103

frustration contributed to the idea that classical conditioning was a relatively simple but fundamental process. In this vein Lachman (1960) went so far as to suggest that it was possible the conditioning model might be destined to play the same role in psychology that the mechanical model had served in physics.

With supporters and detractors alike emphasizing the simple nature of the conditioning process it is not too surprising that the intense early interest in cognitive factors such as volition, set, and awareness was not maintained by those active in the area. The adoption of procedures that presumably minimized the effects of such factors and the ease with which classical conditioning could be conceptualized in terms of simple stimulus–response associations led investigators and theorists to ignore the possible complexities introduced by this type of cognitive subject involvement in the conditioning process.

By the late 1960s and early 1970s, when some investigators again showed an active interest in factors of awareness and set, a new and different kind of interest in cognitive processes was starting to dominate the experimental literature. This, of course, was the emergence of the information processing approach with its emphasis on the many facets of information input, transformation, storage, and retrieval. Not surprisingly in view of the identification of classical conditioning with older stimulus–response theories the usefulness of the classical conditioning paradigm as an investigatory tool in examining these processes was, and remains, relatively unexploited.

From the above, it can be seen that the relationship between cognitive processes and classical conditioning divides along two lines, depending upon the class of variables or processes that is identified as "cognitive." The history of interest in set, awareness, and other subject-involvement factors, together with the more recent recurrence of this interest, represents one tie between cognition and classical conditioning, as discussed in Section II of this chapter. Of perhaps more interest with respect to its potential for future research is the relationship between information processing and classical conditioning. This topic is considered in Section III. The final section of the chapter is concerned with the use of classical conditioning in the analysis of the processes underlying intellectual deficit.

II.   SUBJECT INVOLVEMENT IN CLASSICAL CONDITIONING: SET AND AWARENESS AS COGNITIVE FACTORS

It was Berlyne (1963) who provided a cogent reminder that the identification of Pavlov as a person who believed that all behavior consisted of isolated, automatic, reflexes is ironic indeed since he became famous in his time for the opposite viewpoint. Not only did Pavlov insist on the chronic as opposed to the acute method because of his belief in the necessity of considering the effects of other processes interacting with conditioning, but his emphasis on state as an important factor in conditioning has a very contemporary ring (for example, Sameroff, 1972).

Of even more importance for the present topic was Pavlov's recognition of the unique role of speech as stimuli in the behavior of humans. In 1932 Pavlov made the following remarks as part of his address to the fourteenth International Congress of Physiology:

> However, some particulars of this symtomatology made us guess the existence of an addition which should be taken into consideration in order to get a general idea of the human nervous activity as well. This addition relates to the speech function, which signifies a new principle in the activity of the cerebral hemispheres. If our sensations and notions caused by the surrounding world are for us the first signals of reality, concrete signals, then speech, especially and primarily the kinesthetic stimuli which proceed from the speech organs to the cortex, constitute a second set of signals, the signals of signals [Pavlov, 1955, p. 285].

Thus, in humans speech as stimuli were believed by Pavlov to play an important role in conditioning:

> Speech on account of the whole preceding life of the adult, is connected up with all the internal and external stimuli which can reach the cortex, signalling all of them and replacing all of them, and therefore it can call forth all those reactions of the organism which are normally determined by the actual stimuli themselves [Pavlov, 1927, p. 407].

Perhaps the most systematic early investigations of the role of speech in a conditioning-like paradigm was use in the Soviet Union of the Ivanov–Smolenski verbal method in which, for example, the light (conditioned stimulus, CS) would be followed by the word "press" (unconditioned stimulus, US), which was the command to squeeze a rubber bulb (unconditioned response, UR). This technique was widely used to investigate the developing role of speech in children's behavior as indexed by the control verbal commands had upon discrimination, reversal, and other conditioning phenomena. Research with the verbal method led to the conclusion that younger children, approximately 3 years old, responded in terms of the first signaling system, showing classical conditioning to CSs as a dog might respond to the beats of a metronome. Older children, 5–6 years old, were found to use speech as a mediating process, reacting to the stimuli with internal verbal responses, which in turn controlled their overt responses (see Berlyne, 1963, for a discussion of this work).

The role of verbal self-instructions also was a matter of interest to those engaged in the early classical conditioning research in this country, although the interest was more in eliminating the effects of such instructions than in studying their consequences. In fact, various methods were considered in order to eliminate voluntary influences in conditioning which interfered with the conditioning process. In this vein Hilgard and Marquis (1940) stated:

> With human subjects, the results of any conditioning experiment will tend to be complicated by the influence of voluntary factors. Since the laws of conditioning do not extend to such factors, the discovery and formulation of conditioning principles depend upon the devising of experimental situations in which voluntary influences are impossible or are eliminated [pp. 270–271].

This statement reflected the recognition that set and awareness could affect conditioning data in important ways. A number of studies carried out during the 1930s had demonstrated that instructions could increase or decrease the level of conditioning and that a conditioned discrimination was formed faster when the subject was told of the relationship between the stimuli. Further, it had been shown that the use of masking tasks, which required subjects to engage in extraneous tasks designed to hide the conditioning contingencies or to occupy the subjects' attention in order to reduce the incidence of potentially interfering activities, resulted in more systematic conditioning data. Razran (1939), for example, found that the use of masking tasks in human salivary conditioning resulted in successful conditioning that replicated Pavlov's main behavioral findings, whereas irregular and unsuccessful conditioning occurred without the masking techniques.

Among the procedures listed by Hilgard and Marquis to eliminate all variables except the "stimulus–response relationships embraced in the laws of conditioning" was the selection of naive subjects who could be instructed to maintain a passive attitude and not control their responses. This approach was widely adopted in the classical conditioning of skeletal responses in studies during the 1950s and 1960s. The fact that the eye-blink response was considered to be only semivoluntary in nature, together with the fact that some laboratories analyzed the form of conditioned responses in order to identify those subjects who presumably did not remain passive in the conditioning situation, led to the conviction that voluntary factors were under control and were not seriously confounding eyelid conditioning data, at least in the case of the simple acquisition of the conditioned response.

A somewhat different situation existed in autonomic conditioning in which such factors as expectation, relational awareness, and self-instructions were thought to have a more dominant influence upon conditioning. Freeman (1930), who found apparent conditioning of the galvanic skin response (GSR) after only one or two trials, qualified his results by pointing out that the conditioned responses he obtained might as easily have been interpreted as physiological accompaniments of the attitudes of expectation and surprise. Further, a widely cited study by Cook and Harris (1937) concluded that giving the subjects instructions such as, "the green light will now be followed by shock" resulted in as many and as large GSRs as did 30 paired presentations of light and shock. Extinction was similarly shown to be very sensitive to instructions.

Following several decades of relative inactivity in the study of such "cognitive" subject involvement factors and their effect on classical conditioning, the 1960s and 1970s showed a great increase in the number of studies dealing with this topic. With some exceptions the recent studies cluster into (a) those utilizing masking tasks in classical eyelid conditioning as a technique to manipulate subject awareness of contingencies and their changes, and (b) the use of masking tasks and questionnaires in autonomic conditioning to manipulate and/or assess the subject's relational awareness and relate such awareness to conditioning performance.

Masking tasks have a long history of use in classical conditioning dating to the late 1920s and early 1930s. Their early use was generally confined to autonomic conditioning studies, particularly those involving the salivary response and the GSR. Starting in the 1960s, however, a number of eyelid conditioning studies appeared that were specifically designed to reduce the cognitive involvement of the subject, which was found to occur when the US was omitted or delayed in extinction. The first published paper utilizing an extraneous masking task (in this case, a guessing-game masking task based on the Estes–Straughan probability-learning task) to investigate cognitive factors in extinction was, in fact, entitled "Cognitive factors in the extinction of the conditioned eyelid response" (Spence, 1963). This title was rather surprising to those who identified the theorizing of Spence with a strictly empirically based stimulus–response position, but this paper and those that followed reflected an awareness of the possible effects of such factors and led to the concept of inhibitory set, which was postulated to be a higher-order process adopted by the subject upon recognition of the change in reinforcement conditions at the onset of extinction or the introduction of partial reinforcement (see L. E. Ross, 1971, for a review of this research and the use of masking tasks in eyelid conditioning).

Later eyelid conditioning studies involving masking tasks have investigated the role of awareness in differential conditioning. The data from such a study by Nelson and Ross (1974) were interpreted as indicating that a distinction should be made between awareness defined in terms of being able to report contingencies, and functional awareness involving attentional or cognitive activities that apparently enhance differential responding.

As previously mentioned, the interest in cognitive factors and their relationship to autonomic conditioning was largely concerned with relational awareness, that is, awareness of the conditioned stimulus–unconditioned stimulus (CS–US) contingency, and the possibility that autonomic conditioning was possible only when such awareness occurred (see Grings, 1973, for a discussion of cognitive factors in electrodermal conditioning). The great majority of recent studies of this type have involved the GSR, although an experiment by Chatterjee and Ericksen (1962) studied heart rate conditioning as a function of cognitive expectancy and concluded that there was an unequivocal relationship between the two.

The elements of a typical study examining relational awareness and the GSR involves differential conditioning in which one stimulus (CS+) is paired with the US and another (CS−) is not. Subjects may or may not be given a masking task to perform during differential conditioning. Generally a questionnaire is given following conditioning (although some studies have attempted to assess awareness at various times during the conditioning session), the subjects are categorized as aware or unaware, and the conditioning performance of the two groups is compared.

The results of such studies have been somewhat contradictory, although some investigators have maintained that the evidence supports the notion that relational awareness is necessary for conditioning. The basis for this conclusion includes the finding that differential conditioning has sometimes occurred among those subjects classified as aware but not among those classified as unaware, as well as the results of masking studies in which, with awareness presumably prevented by masking tasks, conditioning was not obtained. In addition some studies in which awareness has been measured during conditioning have shown conditioning during the postaware but not the preaware periods. Contrary evidence exists in the finding that some subjects classified as unaware do show conditioning, although the adequacy of the awareness questionnaire can be questioned in such cases, and the fact that some studies in which degree of awareness on a continuously scaled measure has been correlated with degree of differential conditioning have failed to find a significant relationship.

In reviewing awareness-conditioning studies Dawson and Furedy (1973) concluded that the data could be reconciled by considering awareness as a necessary-gate variable. That is, awareness is a necessary but not sufficient condition that has an all-or-none effect with respect to differential autonomic conditioning. The necessary but not sufficient conclusion is somewhat similar to the Nelson and Ross (1974) position with respect to the role of contingency awareness in skeletal (eye-blink) conditioning previously mentioned. It thus appears possible that some type of active subject involvement or attention to the contingencies is needed for good differential conditioning of skeletal responses and is a prerequisite for differential classical conditioning in the case of autonomic responses such as the GSR.

A final point should be made that the awareness-conditioning relationship found with both skeletal and autonomic conditioning applies only to *differential* classical conditioning. There is little evidence that single-cue conditioning is similarly affected.

In view of the long history of concern with subject involvement factors it is reasonable to ask where such research may lead. Certainly there is much that remains to be determined with respect to the conditions under which subject involvement occurs and the manner in which awareness of, and attention to, stimulus contingencies interact in their effects on conditioning.

Aside from increasing knowledge about these processes, such information is necessary in interpreting conditioning differences in populations varying in age or intelligence levels.

A further fruitful area of investigation has developed in the study of multiple-response phenomena in autonomic conditioning. In GSR conditioning the identification of the independence of the individual components of multiple responses in conditioning situations (for example, Prokasy & Ebel, 1967) has opened new areas of investigation. In the long CS–US (interstimulus interval, ISI) GSR conditioning situation in which test trials are given (US omitted), three response components have generally been identified. The first of these is the response to the CS, which appears to be of an orienting response nature; the second occurs later but prior to the time a US response might occur, a pre-US response; the third occurs as a response to the omission of the US. Lockhart (1973) has pointed out the contrasting nature of the pre-US and US omission responses. Whereas, the pre-US response is not readily obtained from animals or the severely retarded, it is affected by masking tasks and seems to accompany awareness of the CS–US relationship, that is, it appears to reflect cognitive activity. In contrast the US omission response appears earlier than and even in the absence of the pre-US response. Also the omission response is evident in animals, and newborn humans (Clifton, 1974), and apparently is relatively impervious to masking and the subject's awareness of the conditioning contingencies. Further, it should be noted that the omission response cannot be interpreted solely as an orienting response to stimulus change since the omission can be responded to as an omission only if an expectancy has been established as a consequence of previous CS–US pairings. In fact, a similar paradigm in which the second stimulus is changed rather than omitted has been used to investigate preparatory set factors in autonomic classical conditioning (Grings, 1960).

Thus, analysis of the multiple-response phenomena in autonomic classical conditioning offers the rather unique opportunity to compare orienting, cognitive, and expectancy–disparity processes and their interactions.

III. COGNITIVE PROCESSES IN CLASSICAL CONDITIONING

A. Classical Conditioning in the Investigation of Learning and Memory Processes

In the previous section the cognitive aspects of conditioning under discussion were those arising from the subject's reaction to and involvement in the conditioning process, that is, awareness, attention, and set. A perhaps related, but at present quite different, interest in cognitive processes and classical conditioning is that in which the cognitive processes are derived from a view of man as an information processer. Here, concern is with the structure, functions, and interactions of the central cognitive processes by which information is received, transformed, stored, and retrieved. Whether it is believed that any particular current conception of these processes will provide the most useful conceptualization of cognitive behavior in the long run, the information processing approach has generated intense research activity directed toward a better understanding of the various input, transformation, memory, and retrieval processes that are identified as cognitive activities.

In the broad sense, any interest in these processes as they are involved in or investigated through the use of classical conditioning paradigms is germane to the topic of cognitive factors in classical conditioning. There have been several recent discussions of the relationship between classical conditioning and other learning and memory processes. Saltz (1973), for example, has proposed that, rather than attempting to use the laws of classical conditioning as a basis for explanation in other, more complex, situations, the procedure be reversed to see if other areas of human learning and memory might provide a source of basic laws applicable to conditioning. Stressing the value of the classical conditioning paradigm, Wickens (1973) has suggested that classical conditioning can serve effectively to identify the functional characteristics of basic processes, for example, stimulus selection and the nature of verbal behavior and memory. Wickens (1973) believes that classical conditioning paradigms can serve a very useful function in investigating processes which, as he states, "do not ordinarily seem to be part of the body of knowledge that we call the classical conditioning literature [p. 215]." Similarly, Estes (1973) calls for the convergence of theories of conditioning and memory and presents a model, discussed later in this section, that interprets conditioning phenomena in terms of a general theory of memory.

Clearly there is interest and concern in relating classical conditioning to more general processes, including those identified and interpreted in a cognitive, information processing, framework. The remainder of this section is focused upon three areas where classical conditioning and interest in such processes intersect. In the first, data are reviewed which deal with stimulus parameters and the distinction that emerges between stimulus detection and recognition in classical conditioning. In the second, a program of research by Grant and his co-workers dealing with the processing of information conveyed by verbal stimuli in classical conditioning is described. Finally, Estes' model of memory and conditioning is discussed.

B. Stimulus Detection and Recognition in Classical
    Conditioning

The investigation of stimulus parameters and the resulting distinction between detection and recognition processes as they are involved in single-cue and differential conditioning provides a good example of the applicability of an information processing approach to the interpretation of classical conditioning data.

An early indication that the investigation of processing demands in classical conditioning might be fruitful came from Hartman and Grant's (1962) observation that the optimal ISI for differential eyelid conditioning was longer than that found for single-cue conditioning. Hartman and Grant (1962) offered two explanations of this finding, the first suggesting that "inhibition of a response may simply require more time and be favored by longer CS—UCS intervals [p. 135]," and the second suggesting that more time was required to accommodate a "complete perceptual response to the positiveness or negativeness of the CS [p. 135]." After considering the two possibilities, they concluded that the one emphasizing inhibition seemed more plausible.

L. E. Ross and S. M. Ross (1972) discussed whether eyelid conditioning data could be more successfully integrated and explained by a conceptual framework involving inhibitory processes or one stressing information processing concepts. Consideration of research on inhibitory factors in eyelid conditioning and studies investigating the joint effects of stimulus parameters and the ISI upon differential conditioning led to the view that differential conditioning could be analyzed most fruitfully as a stimulus-processing situation. Further, Ross and Nelson (1973) concluded not only that the most useful conceptual framework for considering differential conditioning was one which treats differential conditioning as a stimulus processing situation, but that it would appear reasonable, "to consider that single cue conditioning involves a detection process, while differential conditioning involves detection plus recognition processes [p. 92]." The data that led to this position, plus additional experimental evidence which has supported it, are presented below:

1. The Hartman and Grant (1962) finding of a longer optimal ISI for differential conditioning as compared to that for single-cue conditioning suggests that a longer stimulus processing time, involving a discriminative recognition process, is required for differential but not for single-cue conditioning.

2. If an additional recognition process is required for differential conditioning any stimulus parameter which decreases the distinctiveness of the

CS+ and CS− might be expected to increase the required processing (recognition) time and thus interact with the ISI in its effect on differential conditioning performance. In classical eyelid conditioning the effects of variations of two CS parameters that would be expected to so decrease CS distinctiveness, CS complexity, and rise time have been found to interact with the ISI in the predicted manner.

With respect to CS complexity, Mayer and Ross (1969) investigated stimulus complexity by comparing the effects of two-dimensional visual stimuli (color *and* form, one dimension correlated and the other not correlated with reinforcement) with those of single dimensional (color *or* form) visual stimuli. Good differential conditioning was found at 800- and 1100-msec ISIs with the simple, one-dimensional CSs, but only at 1100 msec with the complex, two-dimensional CSs. Thus, it appears that the addition of irrelevant information to differential conditioning CSs increases the required recognition processing time so that a longer ISI is needed for good differential conditioning. An earlier study by Gynther (1957) indirectly supports this interpretation. The use of visual spatial (left versus right) CSs did not produce good differential conditioning with a 500-msec ISI, but the addition of color cues (white to right and red to left) resulted in good performance at that ISI. Presumably the redundant color information facilitated recognition and resulted in differential conditioning with a shorter ISI than would otherwise have been the case.

An interaction has also been found between ISI and the rise time of auditory CSs in differential conditioning (Wilcox & Ross, 1969). When the stimuli had a fast rise time, little differential responding was obtained with a 500-msec ISI, but good differential responding was evident with an 800-msec ISI. When the stimuli had a slow rise time, high levels of differential responding were found at both 500- and 800-msec ISI. This outcome was discussed in terms of changes in the similarity of CS+ and CS−. The sudden onset of an auditory stimulus is accompanied by onset transients, and these transients should be quite similar for CS+ and CS−, thus decreasing stimulus distinctiveness. Tones having a gradual onset do not have these large onset transients, and two tones differing in frequency thus should be less similar than the same tones presented with a fast rise time. Thus, the greater similarity in the fast rise time situation could have led to a longer processing time requirement for differential responding. The greater stimulus distinctiveness of the slow rise time tones presumably reduced the processing time requirement and led to differential responding at the shorter, as well as at the longer, ISI. Additional support for this interpretation comes from data which indicate that stimulus rise time does not affect single-cue conditioning in which only stimulus detection is required.

3. Another approach to the investigation of stimulus information processing in differential and single-cue conditioning involves the introduction
of an extraneous masking task which is intended to reduce the subject's
utilization of knowledge about stimulus contingencies during the conditioning session. Several differential conditioning studies have been conducted
(for example, Mayer & Ross, 1969; Nelson & Ross, 1974) in which the
subject was engaged in a time-estimation masking task during the eyelid
conditioning session. When differential conditioning is compared with and
without the time-estimation masking task, the masking task is found to
greatly reduce differential responding, although the same masking task has
been found to have no detrimental effects on single-cue conditioning. This
suggests that the additional task with its attentional or cognitive requirements may interfere with the recognition processes essential for differential
responding, but have little effect on the detection processes involved in
single-cue conditioning.

4. Perhaps the most direct evidence for the distinction between single-
cue and differential conditioning paradigms in terms of recognition and
detection processes comes from a study (Ross, Ferreira, & Ross, 1974)
investigating backward-masking effects in single-cue and differential conditioning.

Backward masking, the impaired identification or recognition of a brief
test stimulus when it is followed by an appropriate masking stimulus, has
been widely investigated. The reduced recognition of the test stimulus
when the interval between test stimulus onset and masking stimulus onset is
short has been interpreted as a measure of the masking stimulus' interruption of the processing of information that is retained in short term storage
following termination of the test stimulus. In the Ross, Ferreira, and Ross
(1974) study it was reasoned that if differential conditioning required an
identification or recognition process, the backward masking of the CSs
should prevent differential conditioning, but not affect single-cue conditioning where only detection is involved. Accordingly, in this study the CS+
and CS− were followed by a masking stimulus on some trials and presented alone on other trials. For some subjects the interval between the
CSs and the mask was such that CS recognition should have been un-
affected, and for these subjects differential responding on trials with the
masking stimulus was equal to that on trials without the masking stimulus. For other subjects the interval between the CS and the masking
stimulus was so short that interference in CS recognition was expected,
and for these subjects there was little evidence of differential responding on
the masked trials but good differential conditioning on trials without the
masking stimulus. Following the CS with a mask had no effect on
single-cue conditioning performance.

These data, which show the predicted effects of what is presumably the direct manipulation of the recognition process, together with the other evidence cited above, are all highly consistent with a recognition–detection process difference in differential and single-cue conditioning. Not only are the data from a number of investigations integrated by the processing analysis, but the success of this model represents the beginning of an integration of classical conditioning with some of the concepts and the theoretical framework of the information processing approach.

C. Verbal Stimuli and Their Role in Classical Eyelid Conditioning

The classical conditioning research described up to this point has generally employed relatively neutral stimuli such as lights and pure tones as CSs. However, there has been a considerable amount of research, primarily conducted by Grant and his colleagues, into the effectiveness of verbal stimuli in classical eyelid conditioning, especially the effect on conditioning of the semantic aspects of verbal stimuli. In addition, Grant (1972) has presented a preliminary version of an information processing model which accommodates the data from his research program.

Some of the initial investigations of verbal stimuli in classical eyelid conditioning (for example, Cerekwicki, Grant, & Porter, 1968) used sets of words as differential conditioned stimuli. One word was presented visually on each trial, and the members of one set were followed by the US whereas the members of the other set were not. The experimenters varied the size of the two sets of words and the relatedness among the members within the sets and found that differential responding decreased as set size increased in the case of sets of unrelated words.

The results for the sets of semantically related words were somewhat different. The effect of relatedness was found to depend upon whether the subject was classified as a conditioned form responder (C) or voluntary form responder (V), a classification based on the topography of the conditioned response. The conditioned response of the V is generally a short-latency high-amplitude eye closure that has a rapid recruitment and is sustained through the presentation of the US. The conditioned responses given by Cs generally are lower in amplitude, have a more gradual recruitment, and are less effective in avoiding the air-puff US. Cerekwicki, Grant, and Porter (1968) observed that for Cs differential responding as a function of set size was the same when the words within the sets were taxonomically related and when they were unrelated, but the differential responding of Vs was enhanced by taxonomic relatedness. Apparently, the Vs were sensitive to the relationship among the set members and were able to use this information to respond differentially.

Another of the initial investigations of verbal stimuli in conditioning (Bunde, Grant, & Frost; 1970) employed the words BLINK and DON'T BLINK, verbal commands relevant to the expected CR in the conditioning situation, as the differential conditioned stimuli. On each trial one of these stimuli was presented visually. For some of the subjects the command and the CS–US contingency were compatible (BLINK followed by the US and DON'T BLINK not followed by the US); for others the command and the contingency were incompatible (DON'T BLINK followed by the US and BLINK not followed by the US).

The results of this study also indicated that the effects of the semantic aspect of the stimuli were different for Cs and Vs. Bunde, Grant, and Frost (1970) observed that, when the command was compatible with the contingency, both Vs and Cs showed high levels of differential responding, but when the command and the contingency were incompatible, the differential responding of Vs was considerably disrupted whereas that of Cs was not affected. This finding was interpreted in terms of the Cs having a greater ability than Vs to recode the conflicting verbal information, a conclusion which even Bunde, Grant, and Frost found surprising since it was not obvious why Cs should be so able to process verbal information in this situation when they did not show such an ability in the situation presented in the Cerekwicki, Grant, and Porter (1968) study. These apparently conflicting results have proved to be replicable, and both outcomes can be derived from Grant's (1972) preliminary information-processing model of differential conditioning, which is described below.

Grant's model accounts for the effects of verbal stimuli in conditioning by providing for the processing of CS information as well as information about CS–US contingencies. The model proposes a limited-capacity central information processer that includes interaction between short- and long-term memory. The central processer receives information about the CS, the reinforcement contingency, the response given, and the consequences of the response, and it provides the internal response code that enables a response selector to output a response from the subject's response repertoire. If the immediately available response is appropriate, that is, if it has the desired consequences, the central processing capacity is available for processing CS information and analyzing the CS–US contingency. However, when an appropriate response is not immediately available, some portion of central processing capacity must be devoted to the learning of a new, more suitable response and its internal response code. Since this capacity is limited, less of the central processor is available for processing information about the CS and the CS–US contingency.

According to this model, the tradeoff between CS processing and CR learning is a factor in the performance differences between Cs and Vs. Apparently Vs have an internal code for a very effective response. Thus, they are not required to allocate central processing capacity for response learning. The Cs, on the other hand, are occupied with the refinement of an ineffective response and have relatively little capacity left for dealing with CS information and for the discovery of rules for predicting the presentation of the US. This model reconciles the BLINK–DON'T BLINK results and the taxonomic relatedness results because it suggests that the Cs in the Bunde, Grant, and Frost (1970) study were simply less sensitive to the inconsistency between command and contingency rather than better able to cope with it.

The recent research conducted in Grant's laboratory has elaborated earlier findings. For example, Zajano, Grant, and Schwartz (1974) examined differential conditioning performance of subjects shifted from original sets of reinforced and nonreinforced verbal stimuli to new sets of words from the same taxonomic categories as the original words. Under these conditions the Vs showed good transfer of differential responding while Cs did not. Neither Cs nor Vs showed transfer as a function of word length, a formal feature of verbal stimuli, and thus these results provide further support for the notion that the Vs are more sensitive than Cs to the semantic qualities of the stimuli.

The model has also led to research in two additional areas, the first of which involves the study of the topography of the conditioned response. The model provides for the feedback of information about the response given on a particular trial and the US consequences of that response, and this information should lead to the progressive refinement of the response when such a refinement increases the effectiveness of the response in reducing the noxiousness of the US. Hellige and Grant (1974) observed that response efficiency, measured in terms of the extent to which the CR occurred at the time of US presentation, increased for classically conditioned subjects but not for subjects given instrumental avoidance training. In the former case maximum eye closure precisely at the time of US presentation attenuated the effective US; in the latter case, any conditioned response given in a trial caused the US for that trial to be omitted. A surprising finding was that the response modification in classical conditioning seemed to occur to a greater extent for Vs than for Cs, and thus Hellige and Grant concluded that Vs are more actively involved than Cs in both response learning and CS information processing.

The second area of investigation involved the study of classical conditioning and reaction time as a function of the cerebral hemisphere to which the stimuli are projected (Hellige, 1974). These studies were conducted in order to investigate the parallels between C–V differences and apparent differences in information processing by the two hemispheres. The data indicate that the differences between Cs and Vs reflect general differences in the way subjects approach tasks requiring the processing of information rather than simple differences in the availability of an internal response code which apply only in the classical conditioning situation.

It is clear that Grant's "preliminary model for processing information conveyed by verbal conditioned stimuli in classical differential conditioning" has been successful in accounting for much of the data obtained in his laboratory. Although its original interpretation of C–V differences may have been inadequate, the investigations that it has precipitated seem to be providing insight into these differences. An additional point is that the model is consistent with a considerable amount of the differential classical conditioning data obtained using nonverbal stimuli including the finding that differential conditioned responding is adversely affected when stimulus complexity is increased or when the subject's processing load is increased through the imposition of a masking task. The model thus is much more general and cognitive than its name implies.

D. Estes' Model of Memory and Conditioning

Considering the central role of memory systems in information processing formulations, as well as the resurgence of interest in memory in all areas of learning, it is obvious that memory concepts will have to be integrated into any conditioning theory that possesses scope and integrative power. Happily, Estes (1973) has both elaborated this need and presented a model that is an impressive example of what may be accomplished through the coordination of learning and memory concepts.

The scope of the model can be seen from the number and variety of conditioning situations that Estes interprets in terms of his relatively simple memory model. The list includes sensitization, the establishment of an inhibitory stimulus, the interaction of the orienting reflex (OR) and UR during conditioning, experimental extinction, escape conditioning, higher-order conditioning, and sensory preconditioning. While the model is not mathematically developed, nor detailed enough at present to provide for the derivation of the effects of specific experimental variables known to affect memory or conditioning, the fact that it accounts for such a wide range of conditioning phenomena even at a very general level demonstrates its potential usefulness.

The model involves a hierarchical organization within which a control element represents an association and relates to other such elements in memory. Most important, the information stored in memory concerns attributes of behavioral events and their interrelations rather than memory of events per se. Such a representation of a stimulus is a cluster of associations of attributes with the context, that is, the background and internal stimuli, in which it occurred. This situational context is critical, as can be seen from the following details of the model.

Consider a conditioning trial during which the CS and US are presented, each with their own local context stimuli and both within common background stimulation. Control elements represent the CS and US each with their particular local context of background stimulation, in memory. The joint occurrence of the CS and US in relation to their common situational background is represented by a memory-control element superordinate to the other control elements and connected to both. The control elements for the CS and US both have output events, the OR and UR, respectively.

Any element can be activated by simultaneous input from any two connections. For example, the control element in memory representing the US has three connections, two from observables (from the US, and from its local context) and one from the control element representing common, general background stimulation. If the latter control element is itself activated by two inputs from the CS control and from background stimulation, then it and the local context stimuli of the US together will activate the US control element. Under these conditions the output response from the control element would occur without the US actually being presented.

The CR thus occurs when the control element representation of the US is activated in memory simultaneously with input from the original UR stimulus context. The form of the response that occurs depends upon the similarity of the context of the CS and that which occurred with the UR at the time of conditioning, and the degree of organization of the original stimulus–response connections. It should be noted that, if the UR is highly dependent upon context, it may be difficult to define a response, the presence of which can be used to index the presence of an association between CS and US. However, since URs evoke drive components assumed to be context free, their interfering effects on other responses can serve as a useful index of the association of the CS and US representations in memory.

Inhibitory processes are incorporated into the memory model in a manner similar to that for excitatory processes. Inhibitory associations are representations in memory of (a) reciprocal inhibition among alternative responses to a single stimulus, in which only one overt response can occur at one time, and (b) the situation in which different stimuli occur in the same context in sequence. In the former situation the interaction between responses is represented in memory by inhibitory associations running from the prepotent to the inhibited response units. In the latter situation the sequence results in both the establishment of a higher-level control element which associates the control element representations of the two stimuli, and an inhibitory association between the control elements of the stimuli such that when the higher-level element is activated both elements are, in turn, activated but with the inhibitory association of the later suppressing the earlier.

The interaction of the excitatory and inhibitory processes can be seen in the interpretation of experimental extinction. Basically the representations of the CS and US, as described above, are followed in extinction by the representation of the absence of the US in the same context as the occurrence of the US. The representations of the US and absence of the US in the same context are incompatible, leading to an interaction that inhibits the representation of the US. An inhibitory association is established so that on future trials the CS activates only the representation of the absence of the US. The reader is referred to Estes (1973), for details of the model and its extension in the interpretation of the various conditioning situations listed above.

Research involving the classical-conditioning paradigm over the last decade has not been of the simple chain-association type Estes describes in contrasting traditional conditioning theory to his memory model approach. Certainly many investigators have been concerned with the processes involved in conditioning and have theorized freely with respect to hypothetical internal stimuli, responses, drive states, and processes. Past work, however, has not utilized memory and the examination of what is learned in conditioning in the manner Estes proposes, and few in recent years have attempted to encompass such a wide range of conditioning phenomena with a single theoretical effort.

The eventual usefulness of the memory model depends upon its elaboration so that (a) the various assumptions of the model may be tested against alternative formulations of the role of memory in conditioning, and (b) testable predictions can be generated deductively and tested empirically in accordance with the increasing knowledge of memory and information analysis processes. There is no doubt that this model represents a major opportunity and challenge to those interested in cognition, memory, and conditioning.

IV. INTELLECTUAL DIFFERENCES AND CLASSICAL CONDITIONING

Research investigating developmental aspects of intellectual processes has increased tremendously in volume and scope over the last two decades. The initial growth of an experimental child psychology based largely on earlier stimulus–response learning theory has been followed by more eclectic efforts, which have, in general, tracked the methodological and theoretical changes occurring in research with adult humans and animals. Similarly, much of the research activity attempting to identify the learning and cognitive-process differences found in the comparison of normal and retarded children has drawn upon the paradigms and concepts developed in the process areas of psychology and related disciplines.

Interest in the processes underlying developmental change and intellectual difference stems from the realization that advances in understanding these phenomena can only come about through the experimental analysis of the variables affecting the underlying processes and the development of theories that integrate the process information. Without such an understanding of the changing intellectual characteristics of the child and the nature of intellectual deficit, the decisions society must face with respect to optimizing the intellectual development of children may well result in inefficient, costly, and perhaps in some cases even harmful programs. For example, intervention programs have demonstrated that intensive and comprehensive intervention procedures sometimes can produce dramatic performance changes in children. However, the particular factors that are responsible for the changes, the processes affected, and the duration of the changes have not been identified. Generally these programs have used subjective evaluation, classroom performance, intelligence tests, and other global measures to assess change. In contrast, the experimental process approach has the potential to identify the particular process changes that result from intervention and thus permit the development of an optimal intervention strategy. The long-term success of intervention programs could well depend upon the use of the process-analysis approach to refine intervention procedures so that realistic goals can be set and the chances of achieving fundamental and lasting changes in the intellectual functioning of the child be maximized.

The question considered in this section is the usefulness of the classical-conditioning paradigm in the analysis of the processes underlying intellectual growth and competence. It should be noted that there are many methodological problems in investigating such processes across age and intellectual levels. Floor and ceiling effects, motivational and reward value differences, unequal response requirements, different interpretations of instructions, and unequal transfer effects from previous learning experience can lead to instrumental task performance differences in groups differing in age or intelligence that are unrelated to the specific processes under investigation. To the extent that the classical conditioning paradigm avoids such confounding factors without introducing its own particular interpretational difficulties, valuable data can be obtained through its use.

In some cases, however, a prerequisite for the useful application of classical conditioning for this purpose is a better understanding of the conditioning process itself. When it is possible to interpret conditioning differences in terms of several processes, the simple demonstration of differences in conditioning performance may be of rather limited usefulness. Consider, for example, the finding that the severely retarded do not show the usual partial reinforcement effects in classical eyelid conditioning (Ross, Koski, & Yaeger, 1964). This normal–retardate difference could result from a lack of cognitive expectancy, an inhibition deficit, or the different sampling of contextual cues during acquisition and extinction (Estes, 1970), on the part of the retarded. Obviously identifying such conditioning differences is only a first step in analysing the underlying process differences.

Rather than working from conditioning differences to the processes underlying them, an alternative approach is to develop classical conditioning procedures to investigate the processes of interest more directly. For example, if classical conditioning can provide information concerning memory processes, it becomes an investigative tool, rather than primarily a process of interest in its own right, which then can be used to compare populations differing in age or intelligence. This would appear to be an excellent strategy that exploits the methodological advantages inherent in the use of classical conditioning with diverse populations, while investigating processes that are important for a wide range of behaviors.

Some of the issues involved in the use of classical conditioning in the comparison of normal and retarded subjects and discuss selected studies and research programs using classical conditioning procedures with such populations are considered in the remainder of this section.

A. Conditionability and Intellectual Deficit

Much of the early classical conditioning research conducted with groups of subjects varying in intellectual level was directed toward assessing "conditionability." The experimenter often selected a set of stimulus parameter values, usually those believed to be most effective for conditioning in normal adults, and compared the groups in terms of the final level of conditioned responding or resistance to extinction. Unfortunately, such comparisons are of questionable value since any differences, or lack of differences, may be due to the particular choice of parameter values, for example, ISI, CS modality, US strength, or reinforcement schedule. If the optimal parameter values differ for the groups being compared, the results could reflect this fact rather than any general conditionability difference per se. In addition, certain procedures may affect groups differently owing to other processes involved in the conditioning situation. For example, use of a visual CS may handicap those who find it more difficult to maintain attention or follow directions to maintain visual fixation. Similarly, the use of a test trial procedure introduces partial reinforcement that may differentially affect performance. If partial reinforcement effects are related to intelligence level, normal and retarded subjects could show equal performance with test trials despite the fact that a higher level of performance by normals might be found under continuous reinforcement conditions.

In view of these considerations it is doubtful that conditionability is a useful concept when used in this context. A more meaningful comparison of conditioning performance might be made by obtaining the functions for all of the relevant conditioning variables for each population and selecting the optimal values for each group. Even under such circumstances it is unclear just what use might be made of the resulting conditioning comparisons.

A more fruitful approach is the use of conditioning differences as a starting point for the investigation of the underlying processes or to vary conditioning parameters in order to determine parameter value and subject characteristic interactions. Such an emphasis on interactions rather than absolute levels of performance has long been recognized as necessary in comparative psychology (Bitterman, 1960) and has been discussed extensively with respect to developmental psychology (Gollin, 1965). Further, it may well be that the most useful data will be obtained when nonoptimal parameter values are included to determine the overload or breakdown conditions for conditioning performance. Under optimal or close to optimal conditions a lack of differences, or small differences may simply reflect ceiling effects.

While such methodological considerations as those discussed above have greatly limited the value of many conditioning studies involving the retarded, two older studies are of considerable interest despite the fact that no variation of conditioning variables was involved in either study and they involved methodological features, for example, partial reinforcement, which complicated the interpretation of their results. These studies included both "brain-damaged" and "non-brain-damaged" retardates, and although no IQ-conditioning correlation was found in either case, both studies reported a difference in conditionability as a function of central nervous system impairment. Birch and Demb (1959) compared the GSR conditioning performance of brain-damaged retarded children, young and old mongoloids, and normal children. When the performance of the older subjects (about 101–209 months) was examined, the mongoloids and normals did not differ significantly in the number of trials required to reach the conditioning criterion. Among the brain-damaged group, those classified as nonhyperactive and nondistractible performed like the normals and mongoloids; those classified as hyperactive and distractible required significantly more trials to reach the criterion. The young mongoloids in this study performed quite poorly, a finding also reported in a study comparing the eyelid conditioning performance of young and older mongoloids (Ross, Headrick, & MacKay, 1967).

While the use of a visual CS in the Birch and Demb (1959) study raises the possibility that the differences were due to visual fixation differences, similar results were reported in a study using an auditory CS. Franks and Franks (1962) conducted classical eyelid conditioning with normals, "organic" retardates and "nonorganic" retardates, in which organic retardates were those who had clearly demonstrable neurological impairment that occurred at an early age and was the probable cause of the mental deficiency. The data of this study also showed no correlation between conditionability and IQ, but those retarded subjects with central nervous system pathology conditioned to a lower level than those without such pathology. There was no difference between the normal subjects and the nonorganic retardates in the final level of acquisition. Although both studies were limited in scope, they demonstrate that there is a possible relationship between classical conditioning performance and population characteristics that are of importance, and that conditioning performance might be a function of the integrity of the central nervous system, or its developmental level, rather than of test-determined IQ.

The single-cue conditioning performance of retardates has been examined in a number of more recent studies as a function of ISI and the CS trace-delay variable. With respect to asymptotic conditioning level, the delay-CS conditioning performance of the severely retarded has been found to be considerably below that of matched chronological age normals. Despite overall level differences, the shapes of the functions relating asymptotic conditioning performance to ISIs were found to be quite similar for the two populations (S. M. Ross, 1972; S. M. Ross & L. E. Ross, 1971).

The primary interest in investigating the effects of the trace-delay and ISI variables was not one of the relative conditionability of normals and retardates but the manner in which groups differing in intellectual level retained stimulus information in the conditioning situation. Ellis (1963) proposed that retardates and young normals can be characterized as having a stimulus trace deficit. In particular, he argued that the magnitude and duration of the (hypothetical) stimulus trace was a function of central nervous system integrity and the developmental level of the organism.

The results of investigations testing this hypothesis involving delayed-reaction, reaction-time, and verbal-learning tasks were equivocal, and more recently the stimulus-trace theory has been reformulated in terms of memory processes. It appears, however, that the classical conditioning situation offers the opportunity for other perhaps more simplified tests of the basic idea that stimulus information is not retained as well by retardates, compared with normals, over short periods of time. If this is the case, trace conditioning, involving the termination of the CS some time before the occurrence of the US, should prove more difficult for retardates, and the trace-delay factor should interact with ISI. Mature normals would not be expected to show such an interaction.

The results of studies comparing the severely retarded and matched CA normals do indeed support the notion of a stimulus trace deficiency on the part of the retarded. S. M. Ross (1972) compared the trace and delay classical conditioning of severely and profoundly retarded young adults at several ISIs ranging from 350 to 1400 msec. The trace and delay CSs were found to be equally effective at the shortest ISI, but at the longer ISI values delay conditioning was found to be superior to trace conditioning. The results of this study are in clear contrast to the performance of normals of similar CA who showed no performance decrement as a function of trace conditioning across the same range of ISI values (S. M. Ross & L. E. Ross, 1971). A trace–delay difference was also found in the conditioning performance of normal preschool children (Werden & Ross, 1972). These experiments suggest that the trace–delay effect is associated with both intellectual deficit and the course of normal development as Ellis originally proposed.

These data could have been interpreted in terms of stimulus recruitment processes rather than trace-decay factors, with central nervous system integrity or developmental factors resulting in slowed recruitment processes that prevent the neural representation of the stimulus from reaching some threshold value necessary for it to become an effective stimulus. To investigate this possibility, S. M. Ross and L. E. Ross (1975) attempted to condition retarded subjects using a CS duration previously found to be sufficient for conditioning when followed immediately by the US. However, in this experiment there was an interval between CS offset and US onset equal to that found to eliminate conditioned responding when used with a short CS in the previous study. The subjects did show a trace conditioning deficit under these conditions, indicating that stimulus trace recruitment, as manipulated by varying CS duration, is less important than the length of the empty trace interval in the trace conditioning of severely retarded subjects.

It should be noted that the trace conditioning deficit effect discussed above may be specific to the particular conditioning parameters employed so that, for example, different CS or US factors could change or eliminate the trace stimulus effect. Further research is necessary to determine the conditions under which the trace deficit is obtained and how it may affect general cognitive and learning processes of the retarded.

B.   Differential Conditioning and Intellectual Deficit

While there is considerable evidence that most retardates can be classically conditioned in the single-cue delay conditioning situation, it appears that the establishment of differential conditioned responding to delay CSs is much more difficult. For example, Ohlrich and Ross (1968) examined both single-cue and differential eyelid conditioning to auditory stimuli in severely retarded subjects. Following a single-cue conditioning phase the tone CS became CS+, and a second tone of a different frequency was introduced as

CS−. The retarded subjects did show differential responding, but, since it was present from the first introduction of the CS− and did not increase with trials, Ohlrich and Ross attributed the effect to stimulus generalization processes rather than to the learning of a differential response. It was suggested that, at least under the particular conditions used, retardates lack the inhibitory or other processes necessary for differential conditioning.

A subsequent series of experiments by Ohlrich (1968) examined retardate differential conditioning as a function of ISI and intertrial interval, again employing pure tones as the differential stimuli. There was little if any differential conditioning found with 500- or 800-msec ISIs, but differential conditioning performance did appear to be a function of ISI since the largest difference, approaching 20%, was found with an 1100-msec ISI. Even this relatively small difference required 200–300 trials to develop, whereas college students tested under the same conditions showed good differential conditioning at both 800- and 1100-msec ISI values within 50 trials. Ohlrich concluded that, although these results were consistent with the idea that retardates are deficient in inhibitory processes, the data could also be interpreted as indicating that the retardate is slower than the normal in processing information about the CS. Retardates thus would be expected to show high levels of differential responding only at ISIs sufficiently long to accommodate complete processing of stimulus information.

Gendreau and Suboski (1971) differentially conditioned mildly retarded and normal subjects and also found that the retardates showed less differential responding than normals. In addition, it was found that this difference was accounted for by differences in the level of responding to the negative cue. Normals and retardates showed similar amounts of conditioned responding to the positive cue, but the retardates gave more responses to the negative cue than did the normals, a finding also consistent with an interpretation based on either a retardate deficit in inhibitory factors or the processing of stimulus information.

There is an apparent disagreement between the results of differential eyelid conditioning studies and the results of differential GSR conditioning studies carried out with retarded subjects. Grings, Lockhart, and Dameron (1962) found differential GSR responding by moderately and severely retarded subjects and concluded that differential autonomic conditioning "is not restricted by deficiencies in intellectual capacity [p. 33]." However, in this study CS+ and CS− differed to a greater extent than is the case in the differential eyelid conditioning studies. For some subjects CS+ was a visual stimulus and CS− was an auditory stimulus; for other subjects the modality of CS+ and CS− were reversed. Thus, although the study does involve differential conditioning, it might be argued that the processing required to differentially recognize CS+ and CS− in this study is considerably less than the processing necessary to differentially recognize two auditory stimuli differing in frequency. If this is the case, and if the retardate is slow or deficient in the recognition aspect of the processing of stimulus information, then the differential GSR and eyelid-conditioning data may not be at all inconsistent. Although the data are incomplete, they do suggest that retardates might be expected to show differential conditioning at relatively short ISIs only when the recognition requirements of the task are minimized by making the positive and negative stimuli quite distinct and that retardates may require a much longer ISI than normals when similarity between CS+ and CS− is increased.

The single-cue and differential conditioning performance of retardates is similar to that seen when normal subjects are conditioned using an extraneous masking task. The data from normal subjects performing a masking task during conditioning show good single-cue conditioning and relatively poor differential conditioning, and the data indicate that the optimal ISI for differential conditioning increases as the difficulty of the discrimination increases. It may be that mentally retarded subjects are performing like masked normal subjects, perhaps because retarded subjects fail to notice or fail to use their knowledge about stimulus contingencies during conditioning. Such a lack of cognitive awareness in differential conditioning on the part of retarded has been hypothesized by Grings, Lockhart, and Dameron (1962), who selected retardated subjects for study in order to minimize the effects of perception of stimulus contingencies on differential conditioning. The extent to which cognitive awareness differences might interact with slow or deficient recognition processes remains to be explored.

While there are many methodological problems that complicate the use of classical conditioning in the investigation of the processes underlying developmental and intellectual differences, they are probably fewer in number than those that arise from the use of instrumental response paradigms for the same purpose. In any case, the classical conditioning paradigm can be used from birth to old age in a manner difficult to duplicate with instrumental response situations.

As is true in other areas, there are a number of interesting and important questions regarding intellectual deficit that await examination through use of classical conditioning procedures. It is to be hoped that awareness of the flexibility of the paradigm and its potential usefulness in the investigation of various cognitive and information-processing phenomena will lead to its proper utilization in future psychological research.

ACKNOWLEDGMENTS

Preparation of this chapter was supported in part by PHS Research Grant HD 05653 from the National Institutes of Child Health and Human Development.

REFERENCES

Berlyne, D. E. Soviet research on intellectual processes in children. *Monographs of the Society for Research in Child Development,* 1963, **28**(2), 165–183.

Birch, H. G., & Demb, H. The formation and extinction of conditioned reflexes in "brain-damaged" and mongoloid children. *Journal of Nervous and Mental Disorders,* 1959, **129**, 162–170.

Bitterman, M. E. Toward a comparative psychology of learning. *American Psychologist,* 1960, **15**, 704–712.

Bunde, D. C., Grant, D. A., & Frost, M. R. Differential eyelid conditioning to stimuli that express a response-related command or convey reinforcement-related information. *Journal of Verbal Learning and Verbal Behavior,* 1970, **9**, 346–355.

Cerekwicki, L. E., Grant, D. A., & Porter, E. C. The effect of number and relatedness of verbal discriminanda upon differential eyelid conditioning. *Journal of Verbal Learning and Verbal Behavior,* 1968, **7**, 847–853.

Chatterjee, B. B., & Eriksen, C. W. Cognitive factors in heart rate conditioning. *Journal of Experimental Psychology,* 1962, **64**, 272–279.

Clifton, R. K. Heart rate conditioning in the newborn infant. *Journal of Experimental Child Psychology,* 1974, **18**, 9–21.

Cook, S. W., & Harris, R. E. The verbal conditioning of the galvanic skin reflex. *Journal of Experimental Psychology,* 1937, **21**, 202–210.

Dawson, M. E., & Furedy, J. J. The role of relational awareness in human autonomic discrimination classical conditioning. Paper presented at the thirteenth annual meeting of the Society for Psychophysiological Research, Galveston, October, 1973.

Ellis, N. R. The stimulus trace and behavioral inadequacy. In N. R. Ellis (Ed.), *Handbook of mental deficiency.* New York: McGraw-Hill, 1963.

Estes, W. K. *Learning theory and mental development.* New York: Academic Press, 1970.

Estes, W. K. Memory and conditioning. In F. J. McGuigan & D. B. Lumsden (Eds.), *Contemporary approaches to conditioning and learning.* Washington, D.C.: Winston, 1973.

Franks, V., & Franks, C. M. Conditionability in defectives and in normals as related to intelligence and organic deficit: The application of a learning theory model to a study of the learning process in the mental defective. In B. W. Richards (Ed.), *Proceedings of the London conference on the scientific study of mental deficiency, 1960.* Dagenham, England: May & Baker, 1962.

Freeman, G. L. The galvanic phenomenon and conditioned responses. *Journal of General Psychology,* 1930, **3**, 529–539.

Gendreau, P., & Suboski, M. D. Intelligence and age in discrimination conditioning of the eyelid response. *Journal of Experimental Psychology,* 1971, **89**, 379–382.

Gollin, E. S. A developmental approach to learning and cognition. In Lipsett & Spiker (Eds.), *Advances in child development and behavior.* Vol. 2. New York: Academic Press, 1965.

Grant, D. A. A preliminary model for processing information conveyed by verbal conditioned stimuli in classical conditioning. In A. H. Black & W. F. Prokasy (Eds.), *Classical conditioning II: Current theory and research.* New York: Appleton-Century-Crofts, 1972.

Grings, W. W. Preparatory set variables related to classical conditioning of autonomic responses. *Psychological Review,* 1960, **67**, 243–252.

Grings, W. W. Cognitive factors in electrodermal conditioning. *Psychological Bulletin,* 1973, **79**, 200–210.

Grings, W. W., Lockhart, R. A., & Dameron, L. E. Conditioning autonomic responses of mentally subnormal individuals. *Psychological Monographs,* 1962, **76**, Whole No. 558, 1–35.

Gynther, M. D. Differential eyelid conditioning as a function of stimulus similarity and strength of response to the CS. *Journal of Experimental Psychology*, 1957, **53**, 408–415.

Hartman, T. F., & Grant, D. A. Differential eyelid conditioning as a function of the CS–UCS interval. *Journal of Experimental Psychology*, 1962, **64**, 131–136.

Hellige, J. B. Hemispheric processing differences revealed by differential conditioning and reaction time performance. Unpublished doctoral dissertation, University of Wisconsin—Madison, 1974.

Hellige, J. B., & Grant, D. A. Response rate and development of response topography in eyelid conditioning under different conditions of reinforcement. *Journal of Experimental Psychology*, 1974, **103**, 574–582.

Hilgard, E. R., & Marquis, D. G. *Conditioning and learning.* New York: Appleton-Century, 1940.

Lachman, R. The model in theory construction. *Psychological Review*, 1960, **67**, 113–129.

Lockhart, R. A. Cognitive processes and the multiple response phenomenon. *Psychophysiology*, 1973, **10**, 112–118.

Mayer, M. J., & Ross, L. E. Effects of stimulus complexity, interstimulus interval, and masking task conditions in differential eyelid conditioning. *Journal of Experimental Psychology*, 1969, **81**, 469–474.

Nelson, M. N., & Ross, L. E. Effects of masking tasks on differential eyelid conditioning: A distinction between knowledge of stimulus contingencies and attentional or cognitive activities involving them. *Journal of Experimental Psychology*, 1974, **102**, 1–9.

Ohlrich, E. S. The effect of CS–UCS interval on the single-cue and differential eyelid conditioning of retarded children. Unpublished doctoral dissertation, University of Wisconsin, 1968.

Ohlrich, E. S., & Ross, L. E. Acquisition and differential conditioning of the eyelid response in normal and retarded children. *Journal of Experimental Child Psychology*, 1968, **6**, 181–193.

Pavlov, I. P. *Conditioned reflexes: An investigation of the physiological activity of the cerebral cortex.* London and New York: Oxford University Press, 1927.

Pavlov, I. P. Lecture two on the work of the cerebral hemispheres: Physiology of the higher nervous activity, 1932. In Gibbons, J. (Ed.), *I. P. Pavlov: Selected works.* Moscow: Foreign Languages Publishing House, 1955. Pp. 271–286.

Prokasy, W. F., & Ebel, H. C. Three components of the classically conditioned GSR in human subjects. *Journal of Experimental Psychology*, 1967, **73**, 247–256.

Razran, G. H. S. Decremental and incremental effects of distracting stimuli upon the salivary CRs of 24 adult human subjects (inhibition and disinhibition?). *Journal of Experimental Psychology*, 1939, **24**, 647–652.

Ross, L. E. Cognitive factors in conditioning: The use of masking tasks in eyelid conditioning. In H. H. Kendler & J. T. Spence (Eds.), *Essays in neobehaviorism.* New York: Appleton-Century-Crofts, 1971.

Ross, L. E., Ferreira, M. C., & Ross, S. M. Backward masking of conditioned stimuli: Effects on differential and single-cue classical conditioning performance. *Journal of Experimental Psychology*, 1974, **103**, 603–613.

Ross, L. E., Headrick, M. W., & MacKay, P. B. Classical eyelid conditioning of young mongoloid children. *American Journal of Mental Deficiency*, 1967, **72**, 21–29.

Ross, L. E., Koski, C. H., & Yaeger, J. Classical eyelid conditioning of the severely retarded: Partial reinforcement effects. *Psychonomic Science*, 1964, **1**, 253–254.

Ross, L. E., & Nelson, M. N. The role of awareness in differential conditioning. *Psychophysiology*, 1973, **10**, 91–94.

Ross, L. E., & Ross, S. M. Conditioned stimulus parameters and the interstimulus interval: The processing of CS information in differential conditioning. In A. H. Black & W. F. Prokasy (Eds.), *Classical conditioning II: Current research and theory.* New York: Appleton-Century-Crofts, 1972.

Ross, S. M. Trace and delay classical eyelid conditioning in severely and profoundly retarded subjects as a function of interstimulus interval. *American Journal of Mental Deficiency,* 1972, **77,** 39–45.

Ross, S. M., & Ross, L. E. Comparison of trace and delay classical eyelid conditioning as a function of interstimulus interval. *Journal of Experimental Psychology,* 1971, **91,** 165–167.

Ross, S. M., & Ross, L. E. Stimulus input recruitment and stimulus trace decay factors in the trace conditioning deficit of severely retarded young adults. *American Journal of Mental Deficiency,* 1975, **80,** 109–113.

Saltz, E. Higher mental processes as the basis for the laws of conditioning. In F. J. McGuigan & D. B. Lumsden (Eds.), *Contemporary approaches to conditioning and learning.* Washington, D.C.: Winston, 1973.

Sameroff, A. J. Learning and adaptation in infancy: A comparison of models. In H. W. Reese (Ed.), *Advances in child development and behavior.* New York: Academic Press, 1972.

Spence, K. W. Cognitive factors in the extinction of the conditioned eyelid response in humans. *Science,* 1963, **140,** 1224–1225.

Werden, D., & Ross, L. E. A comparison of the trace and delay classical conditioning performance of normal children. *Journal of Experimental Child Psychology,* 1972, **14,** 126–132.

Wickens, D. D. Classical conditioning, as it contributes to the analyses of some basic psychological processes. In F. J. McGuigan & D. B. Lumsden (Eds.), *Contemporary approaches to conditioning and learning.* Washington, D.C.: Winston, 1973.

Wilcox, S. M., & Ross, L. E. Differential classical eyelid conditioning as a function of CS intensity, CS rise time, and interstimulus interval. *Journal of Experimental Psychology,* 1969, **82,** 272–278.

Zajano, M. J., Grant, D. A., & Schwartz, M. Transfer of differential eyelid conditioning: Effects of semantic and formal features of verbal stimuli. *Journal of Experimental Psychology,* 1974, **103,** 1147–1152.

4

Theories of Discrimination Learning and Learning Set

Douglas L. Medin

The Rockefeller University

I. INTRODUCTION

Although historically, the study of discrimination learning has often been relegated to observations of rats in T mazes and on jumping stands, one should not thereby deduce that discrimination learning is an unimportant aspect of cognitive behavior. In its broadest sense, discrimination learning deals with how changes in behavior become associated with changes in environmental stimuli, and thus its scope certainly includes questions about the development of abstraction and generalization and the use of concepts. Even in situations as simple as a rat learning to go left in a T maze, however, a surprising number of theoretical problems have arisen, problems which have proven resistant to easy solutions.

Some of the major theories of discrimination learning advanced in the last 50 years or so are reviewed in this chapter. Since it is not feasible to cover each theory in great depth, this review focuses on key questions that have evolved around these theoretical analyses. As a by-product of this strategy, one may obtain some picture of any overall pattern of progress in this area, both with respect to understanding discrimination learning phenomena and in learning how best to use theories.

Subject populations will not receive much attention in this review. Traditionally, the area of discrimination learning has had a comparative character, and while the theories to be covered have differed in their claimed scope, evidence from a wide range of subject populations will be educed in assessing the theories.

Until around 1950 there was a clear continuity in discrimination learning theories, and the lines of opposition were neatly drawn (see the excellent review by Spence, 1950). Since then, the picture has lost most of this sharpness. Lines of development seem to have been replaced by waves of ideas, and it is most natural to characterize current theories as parallel and interactive, rather than as distinct choices. In order to muster a semblance of clarity, I shall outline the most general steps in discrimination learning from an information-processing viewpoint.

An information-processing approach will provide a global view of the main stages and processes that one may have to consider in order to understand how discrimination learning works. This sketch is essentially pretheoretical in character but may serve to clarify for the reader differences in the scope and points of emphasis in the various theories to be considered.

II. AN INFORMATION-PROCESSING VIEW
OF DISCRIMINATION LEARNING

The basic scheme is shown in Figure 1 and, to work our way through the presumed stages, it will be useful to have a concrete situation in mind. Suppose that a subject (say, a child) is presented with a choice between a red triangle on the left and a green circle on the right of the form board of a Wisconsin General Test Apparatus and that a reward is under the red triangle. On other trials the red triangle may appear on the right and the green circle on the left, but the reward (perhaps a piece of candy) is always under the red triangle (position is irrelevant).

As the first step in the process, the subject must look at the stimuli in order for the stimuli to impinge on the sensory receptors. The output or product of the orienting response is, then, stimulus reception.

The operations necessary for perceptual processing are lumped together in the second stage, which, loosely speaking, begins to tell the child what he or she sees. It is assumed that this stage produces a description of the stimuli, or in alternative phraseology, converts the nominal stimuli into functional stimuli. Theories differ widely in the assumptions as to what this stimulus description consists of, ranging from a list of stimulus components (red, green, triangle, circle, left, right), to a set of compounds (red triangle), to a single configuration (red triangle on the left and green circle on the right). Theories also differ as to whether this process is complete or selective, a distinct alternative being that only a subset of the stimulus array is processed, for example, only the color values.

The stimulus descriptions are entered into the working memory, where associated outcomes may then be activated or retrieved. In some theories this is an automatic process where the current associative strength for each

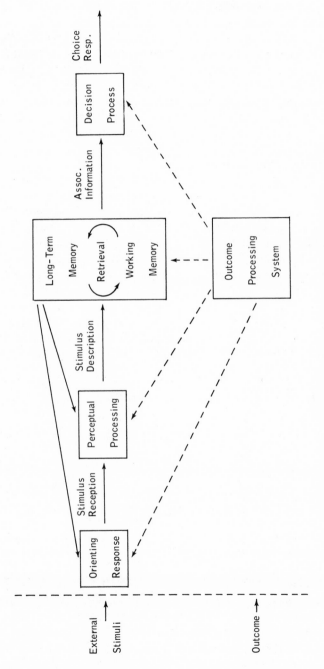

FIGURE 1. An information-processing scheme for discrimination learning.

stimulus (or stimulus component) is made available. In other theories this retrieval of information depends upon the presence of certain contextual cues and may not be automatic or inevitable.

This associative information acts as input to a decision process which generates choice responses. Again, in some theories this process is simple (for example, choose the alternative with the greatest strength), but in other theories, this process is much more elaborate and plays a major role in discriminative performance. In the latter cases it becomes more clear that the decision process might better be represented as part of working memory, since the decision process may interact closely with successive retrievals prior to a response. Such details are considered later.

Suppose now, that, however the child arrived at a decision, he or she chose the red triangle and received a reward. What does this reinforcement do? Theories differ from each other in three major ways in answering this question, corresponding to when, how, and where. Some theories imply that reinforcement operates directly and automatically, whereas others posit that reinforcement has an effect only to the extent that it was not expected. Reinforcement strengthens stimulus–response associations according to some theories, but according to other theories, reinforcement functions mainly as a source of information which does not directly influence performance. Finally, after a choice response and the subsequent outcome or reinforcement, the question arises as to where in this information-processing scheme outcomes exert their influence. Theories have assumed that different combinations of all four main stages of processing may be modified in the course of discrimination learning as the dashed lines in Figure 1 indicate.

With this general scheme and the associated alternatives for theory construction in mind, this review begins by considering the continuity–noncontinuity controversy which has dominated the area of discrimination learning.

III. EARLY DISCRIMINATION THEORIES AND ISSUES

A. Noncontinuity Theory

By the late 1920s a number of factors served to shape thinking about discrimination learning. The first was the ascendancy of J. B. Watson's brand of behaviorism, which looked askance at any appeals to unobservables in learning. In much the same vein, Thorndike's (1911) trial-and-error paradigm and Pavlov's research on classical conditioning provided two techniques that appeared promising for understanding the fundamental nature of the learning process, and, not surprisingly, the prevailing mood was that discrimination learning would be best understood by a combination of the basic processes growing out of these simple paradigms.

However, there were soon notes of discord. In Lashley's classic volume on *Brain Mechanisms and Intelligence* (1929), he reported that for rats solving brightness discriminations:

> In the discrimination box, response to position, to alternation, or to cues from the experimenter's movements usually precede the reaction to the light and represent attempted solutions. The form of the learning curve is more significant when considered in relation to such behavior. In many cases it strongly suggests that the actual association is formed very quickly and that both the practice preceding and the errors following are irrelevant to the actual formation of the association [pp. 134–135].[1]

Gestalt psychologists such as Koffka also described learning as equivalent to "perceptual reorganization," which was assumed to change abruptly rather than gradually.

Krechevsky was perhaps the most predominant spokesman for noncontinuity theory. Krechevsky (1932) began by focusing attention on the presolution period of discrimination learning, as had Lashley. Krechevsky noted that (a) the form of the learning curve was not negatively accelerated but tended to display an ogival or "S" shape, with a long period of near chance level performance followed by an abrupt rise to mastery of the discrimination and (b) during the chance period of learning, responses were not "random" but were systematic and meaningful patterns of behavior, such as consistent responses to position. From these data, he argued that learning should be viewed as systematic and intelligent attempts at problem solution involving the use of hypotheses. If the subject was not entertaining the correct hypothesis or if the relevant cues were not part of the perceptual organization or set on a trial, then that trial would be ineffective in forming the discrimination. The effects of reward, then, were not assumed to be direct and automatic but to depend upon the perceptual activity of the organism.

It is worth noting that the noncontinuity position was offered in both a weak and strong form. The weak form stressed variability in the degree to which a trial event was effective:

> Since, during this so-called presolution period, the animal does spend some time responding to "irrelevant" discriminanda, the residual neurological effect of a "rewarded" response or a "punished" response is not the same during this period as during the period when the animal is "paying attention" to the relevant discriminanda [Krechevsky, 1938, pp. 108–109].[2]

[1] From Lashley, K. S. *Brain Mechanisms and Intelligence*. Chicago: University of Chicago Press, 1929. Copyright © 1963 by Hafner Publishing Company, Inc. Reprinted by permission.

[2] Copyright 1938 by the American Psychological Association. Reprinted by permission.

The strong form of the theory argued that perceptual organization determined whether or not a trial was effective:

> The animal selects out of the welter of possible stimuli certain sets of discriminanda to which he reacts. Each time (while "paying attention to" this particular set of discriminanda) he makes what proves to be a "correct" response, he learns (wrongly perhaps) something about the significance *of this particular stimulus;* each time he makes a "wrong" response, he learns something else, *but he does not learn anything about "correctness" or "wrongness" of the to-be-finally-learned set of discriminanda.* Eventually he gives up responding to his first set of discriminanda and responds to another set, and another set, etc., until he begins to respond to the relevant set. From then on, and from then on only, is he learning anything about the discrimination involved, or, from then on only are his "bonds" being strengthened, etc. [Krechevsky, 1938, pp. 111–112].[3]

The stronger form of noncontinuity theory was the subject of almost all research relevant to the continuity–noncontinuity controversy. For example, one prediction Krechevsky and others tested was that reversing a discrimination problem while an animal was still responding at a chance level should not slow down the rate of learning. The adoption of this strong version of noncontinuity theory led to attempts to prove the null hypothesis in order to demonstrate selective learning.

Noncontinuity theory was not destined to be developed very explicitly, possibly because Lashley (1942) had suggested that quantitative models for discrimination learning would be of little use until a theory of perception became established, since what is learned depends on the organization of the perceptual field.

In capsule form, what was the viewpoint of noncontinuity theory? Its primary thrust was its emphasis on the importance of perceptual processing in discrimination learning. Reward and nonreward could modify the perceptual set or lead to the adoption of different hypotheses, according to the theory. This orientation spawned the propositions that (*a*) learning tends to be all-or-none and insightful and not rote and gradual; (*b*) presolution behavior reflects trying out hypotheses and not "chance" behavior; (*c*) hypotheses rather than excitatory and inhibitory response tendencies are modified by reward; (*d*) the comparison process involved in trying out hypotheses implies that subjects respond to relative rather than absolute cues, and finally, of course; (*e*) learning is selective rather than nonselective in character. Historically, these issues have often been treated as being so interlocking that one's position on one issue determines one's position on all other issues. More rapid progress concerning discrimination learning might have been forthcoming had these questions been treated as independent.

---

[3] See footnote 2.

B. Reply by Continuity Theorists

Noncontinuity theory represented a strong threat to the idea that discrimination learning can be conceptualized as a simple combination of basic learning processes. Two elegant and powerful theoretical analyses by Spence (1936, 1937) clearly demonstrated that continuity theory was not yet dead.

1. Basic Concepts

In Spence's theory, discrimination learning is conceived of as a cumulative process of building up the excitatory strength (associative or habit strength) of the correct stimulus compound as compared with the competing excitatory strength of the incorrect stimulus compound. When a response is not rewarded, the excitatory tendencies of the stimulus components of a compound are weakened by an active, negative process, inhibition.

Spence posited specific excitatory and inhibitory reinforcement functions in order to derive predictions concerning performance. Since the S-shaped curve typically observed in simple learning situations is similar to the integral of the normal curve, Spence assumed that the effects of reward followed this function. That is, the increment in excitatory tendency produced by a reward depends on the current strength in such a way that small increments are observed when the current strength is low, the size of the increment then rises to a maximum for middle strengths, and finally strength increments taper off again for high current strengths. The decrement in excitatory strength produced by a nonreward (inhibition) was assumed to be a linearly increasing function of the current excitatory strength. These strengths were assumed to be associated with the various stimulus components in a problem. Thus, if a subject responded to a red triangle in the left position, the excitatory strengths to red, triangle, and left would all be incremented.

In Spence's theory performance was determined by the stimulus compound of highest strength, and the strength of the compound was assumed to be just the simple sum of the strengths of the component stimuli comprising the compound. So, if red plus triangle plus left had greater total strength than green plus circle plus right, the response would be to red triangle on the left.

The role of perception in discrimination learning was minimized. Spence (1936) did maintain that the "mere presence of the cue stimulus somewhere in the experimental situation does not guarantee its impingement on the animal's sensorium at or near the critical moment of response [p. 438]," but the main appeal was to orienting or observing responses which functioned to guarantee stimulus reception (see Figure 1), and which might be learned, rather than to any modifiable perceptual processing:

> The animal learns to "look at" one aspect of the situation rather than another because of the fact that this response has always been followed within a short temporal interval by the final goal response. Responses providing other sensory receptions are not similarly reinforced in a systematic fashion and hence tend to disappear [Spence, 1937, p. 432].

In a second paper, Spence developed the idea of generalization of excitatory and inhibitory response tendencies to show how continuity theory might handle phenomena such as transposition, which others had taken as evidence that animals respond to relative rather than absolute cues (Spence, 1937).

2. Predictions from Spence's Theory

Since Spence had no recourse to today's high-speed computers, he was satisfied to provide some examples of what predictions might follow from the basic concepts and specific assumptions concerning initial strengths and strength change functions. Spence showed that, with suitable parameter values, his theory might predict that (a) position habits can develop in the course of discrimination learning; (b) when a position habit is broken, it is almost always on a trial when a correct response is made, and the problem will subsequently be solved quite quickly; (c) latencies to correct and incorrect stimuli may separate while a subject is still responding to position; (d) presolution reversals impair learning; and (e) subjects experienced with nonspatial discrimination show less position responding on a new discrimination than naive subjects. (Other predictions derived from the basic theory are considered later.) All of these predictions generally have been supported.

The analysis of generalization gradients allowed the theory to handle the phenomenon of transposition. Subjects which have been trained to choose, for example, a medium-sized stimulus over a small stimulus often prefer a large stimulus to the medium-sized stimulus on transfer or generalization tests. This pattern of results is known as *transposition* and was widely taken as evidence that animals were relying on relative rather than absolute cues. By using appropriate combinations of excitatory and inhibitory generalization gradients, Spence was able to predict that transposition might occur. The theory further predicted that transposition would break down or reverse itself when large stimulus distances were introduced, so that the medium-sized stimulus might be preferred to a very large stimulus. In a later paper Spence (1942) developed the prediction that transposition would not be observed for an intermediate-size problem where animals must choose the middle-sized of three stimuli. Transposition does seem to show a distance effect and does seem to be less obvious on intermediate-size problems (see Reese, 1968, for an extended treatment of transposition).

In short, Spence was able to derive many of the phenomena that others had thought could not be predicted by a continuity theory. Spence's theory also made several other predictions differing from those of the strong form of noncontinuity theory espoused by Krechevsky. Space does not permit a detailed review of data relevant to continuity versus noncontinuity theory (for reviews, see Spence, 1950; Sutherland & Mackintosh, 1971; Mackintosh, Chapter 5, Volume 1 of this Handbook) but for the domain staked out in these early clashes, continuity theory clearly carried the day.

Another interesting debate, considered in detail in Heinemann and Chase's Chapter 8 in Volume 2 of this Handbook, revolved around Lashley and Wade's (1946) criticism of the approach of continuity theory to stimulus generalization, in which Lashley and Wade argued that generalization was produced by failure of association or lack of discrimination rather than differential concentrations or amounts of excitation. Some of the issues raised are still unanswered, but one result of the debate was Hull's (1939, 1947, 1950) detailed analyses of stimulus generalization from a continuity orientation. This work brought out the importance of background or irrelevant cues in determining the form of generalization gradients. Hull assumed that inhibition was independent of excitation and unbounded, and so the link of this work to Spence's model is not direct.

In view of the fact that it was so simply sketched, it is surprising that Spence's theory is still being tested today. How can one account for this influence? The analysis of systematic response patterns and transposition is important perhaps less for its truth value than for the lesson that common sense is no substitute for a carefully developed and explicit theory. The consequences of a set of conceptions are never obvious until specific assumptions are stated. Many of the contributions of noncontinuity theorists were attacks on continuity theory that served to aid Spence and other continuity theorists to develop their theory further. Noncontinuity theory did not receive the attention that would have aided its own explication.

Additional aspects of Spence's theory are considered following discussion of another version of continuity theory embodying a distinctly different view of stimulus description.

C. The Gulliksen–Wolfle Theory

1. Basic Theory

Gulliksen and Wolfle (1938a, b) proposed that subjects respond to neither relative nor absolute cues but rather to the total stimulus configuration. This assumption concerning stimulus description leads to a response selection theory of learning. That is, Gulliksen and Wolfle assumed that in the standard discrimination apparatus subjects learn to respond to the left when presented with one stimulus configuration and to respond to the right when presented with the other configuration. Red triangle on the left plus green circle on the right would act as a single stimulus configuration with which directional responses could become associated. This response selection approach is in sharp contrast with Spence's stimulus selection theory, in which it was assumed that individual stimulus components acquire direct approach and avoidance tendencies.

Another salient feature of the Gulliksen–Wolfle theory was their explicit mathematical treatment of the effects of stimulus generalization both during transfer and in the course of discrimination learning. They argued that a precise treatment of stimulus similarity must involve an integration of learning theory with psychophysics. To illustrate this idea, Gulliksen and Wolfle proposed that size similarity could be represented on a log scale using distance as a measure of psychological similarity, with greater distances corresponding to less similarity. Consider a discrimination problem where a subject must choose a circle with an 8-inch area over a circle of a 2-inch area. This is shown schematically in Figure 2.

Figure 2a shows in simple summary form the two settings or stimulus configurations denoted by their setting number. During the course of learn-

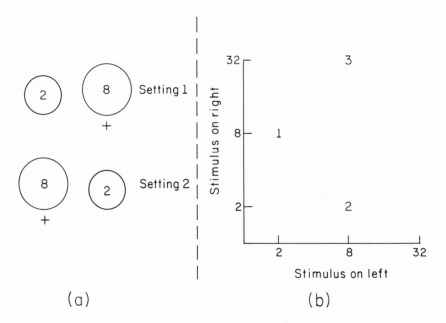

(a)   (b)

FIGURE 2.   A size discrimination problem: (a) the two types of trial settings; (b) more abstract summary of the discrimination.

ing this discrimination, the strength of the tendency to go left is influenced by the amount of reward and punishment the subject has received for making left choices. Therefore, left responses to Setting 1, which are non-rewarded, decrease the tendency to respond left to Setting 1 but also decrease the tendency to respond left to Setting 2, with the amount of this decrease for Setting 2 depending on the psychophysical similarity of the two settings. One immediate consequence of this assumption is that the difficulty of a discrimination will be a function of the similarity of the two configurations.[4]

Predictions concerning transfer can be seen in a rough way by examining Figure 2b. Configuration 3 represents the 8-inch circle on the left and a 32-inch circle on the right. Since Configuration 3 is closer to Configuration 1 than to Configuration 2, one might expect a predominance of right responses (transposition) to be observed. The theory can predict a transposition effect decreasing with distance, but it does not predict a reversal effect (or so-called absolute choices) with distance. Whether or not such a reversal effect is a reliable phenomenon is unclear (Reese, 1968).

Gulliksen and Wolfle derived a number of other predictions from the basic idea that if one knows the psychophysical function, one can predict transfer to a very broad range of stimulus configurations. Many of these predictions were more or less ignored since attention was directed toward the basic schemes of stimulus selection versus response selection, an issue to which I now turn.

2. Stimulus Selection versus Response Selection

At least for the experimental paradigms under consideration at the time, the data tended uniformly to support stimulus selection over response selection. These results have been adequately reviewed elsewhere (for example, Lovejoy, 1968; Sutherland & Mackintosh, 1971), and I mention but two main results. Nissen (1950) trained chimpanzees on a black–white simultaneous discrimination with the stimuli separated either in the usual horizontal orientation or in a vertical plane. A given animal was trained with a single orientation (for example, left, right) and then given transfer tests with the stimuli appearing in the other orientation (for example, up, down). The chimpanzees showed excellent but not perfect transfer of the discrimination across orientations. A response selection theory would have no basis for predicting above chance transfer, since during training the subject would either learn when to go left or right or when to go up or down and the new stimulus configurations were orthogonal to the old. A stimulus selection view would directly predict the transfer since, if a chimpanzee learned

---

[4] The particular form of the mathematical theory of Gulliksen and Wolfle implied that perfect discrimination learning would not be possible if the similarity of the two configurations is nontrivial.

to choose black during training, it should choose black during transfer regardless of orientation.

The theories also make different predictions for performance in simultaneous- versus successive-discrimination paradigms. In a successive paradigm the trial settings might consist of two red triangles or two green circles, with the reward being on the left for the first setting and on the right for the second setting. Response selection theories predict no special difficulty for the successive paradigm and even that successive problems would be easier than simultaneous, if the between setting similarity was less for successive than simultaneous discriminations. However, since all components are rewarded equally often in successive problems, it is difficult to see how Spence's theory could even predict that a successive discrimination would be solved.

The weight of evidence indicated that simultaneous disc¹ iminations were easier than successive problems, as stimulus selection theories predict. On the other hand, it was a somewhat awkward fact that Spence's original theory predicted that successive discriminations would be insoluable. This state of affairs can be averted by assuming (as Spence later did) that subjects may form compounds of stimuli such as "red triangle on the left" under some circumstances, namely, "when no one of the cue members is systematically reinforced more than the others" (Spence, 1952, p. 90). This really is not a very adequate solution, since the explicitness of the theory fades under such disclaimers. Later on it will be shown that a much more satisfactory modification, similar in spirit to Hull's (1943, 1952) concept of afferent neural interaction, can be made in the basic theory to increase its power and congruence with data. For the moment let us turn our attention to other developments bearing both on continuity versus noncontinuity in particular and the development of discrimination learning theories in general.

IV. RELATED DEVELOPMENTS IN DISCRIMINATION
LEARNING THEORY

A. Learning to Learn and Learning Set Theories

It is a common practice to use experimentally naive subjects in discrimination learning problems, but some interesting phenomena emerge as subjects obtain greater experience in testing situations. When monkeys are given a series of two-choice object discriminations, they show remarkable improvement in their ability to learn new problems. Initially monkeys average

50% errors on the second trial of new problems, but after a few hundred problems they average less than 10% errors on Trial 2 of new problems. This improvement in performance, or "learning how to learn," has been labeled *learning set formation* (Harlow, 1949). Learning set formation is not attributable simply to the discriminations having a common solution. For example, red may be a correct cue for one problem but, since the correct object of a pair is randomly selected, red is as likely to be an incorrect as a correct cue on a subsequent problem.

Apart from the natural interest in understanding the acquisition of learning skills, learning-set formation attracted a great deal of theoretical interest. An early hope expressed by Harlow was that learning set might bridge the gap between gradual, trial-and-error learning and all-or-none, insightful learning, thus providing a partial answer to the continuity–noncontinuity controversy.

According to this viewpoint, naive monkeys learn discriminations in an incremental (trial-and-error) fashion, whereas learning set-experienced monkeys solve discriminations in an all-or-none (insightful) manner. Learning-set data were also a means of providing consistency for those believing in a qualitative similarity between human and animal learning, since there was no longer any incompatibility between introspections and intuitions about the insightful nature of much of human learning and the trial-and-error behavior typically observed in animals. It is not surprising then, that early theories considered learning set formation to involve the development of an abstract conceptual understanding on the part of the monkey, which was often described in terms of the employment of hypotheses (for example, win–stay, lose–shift with respect to objects).

One unfortunate by-product of this great interest in describing or representing differences between initial and terminal stages of learning set formation is that very little interest has been focused on transitions between these stages. Consequently, theories of learning to learn have not been developed in very great detail, as is evidenced in the following abbreviated review of these theories.

1. Harlow's Error Factor Theory

Harlow's (1949, 1959) theory of learning set grew out of his analysis of response patterns or error factors occurring in his classic learning set experiments. His theory is a uniprocess theory since only a single process is assumed to be associated with learning to learn. This process amounts to getting rid of bad habits. Harlow proposed that the correct response strategy was immediately available, but that it had to compete with many inappropriate responses, such as a tendency to respond to positional cues, in the learning situation. Learning-set formation, according to the theory, occurred when the monkey had eliminated these error factors or inappropriate response tendencies and was left with the correct strategy (win–stay, lose–shift with respect to objects).

Harlow's theory was not developed beyond this general statement except for some work pointing out specific error factors that monkeys generally display. Levine's analysis of hypothesis behavior was a step toward greater explicitness.

2. Levine's Hypothesis Behavior Model

Levine's model (1959, 1965) refers to different classes of response patterns as hypotheses and, in this theory, learning-set formation occurs by the strengthening of the correct hypothesis by 100% reinforcement and the gradual extinction of other hypotheses because of 50% reinforcement. These hypotheses were assumed to be manifest in the response patterns on a discrimination problem. Levine gathered evidence for the theory by estimating the strength of various hypotheses (for example, stimulus preference, position alternation) at a given stage of learning set training from a subset of the observed response patterns and then using these estimates to predict the frequency of occurrence of the remaining response patterns. This enterprise was moderately successful, but the theory has not been developed to explain how reinforcement changes the status of hypotheses.

3. Restle's Mathematical Model

Restle was the first to propose an explicit theory for the acquisition of hypotheses during learning set formation. His explanation of learning set formation centers importantly on an assumption of abstract cognition: "It is assumed that monkeys use an abstract understanding of the pattern of an LS experiment, transcending the 'stimulus–response' rule familiar in most theories of learning" (Restle, 1958, p. 77). The theory assumes that three classes of cues are available during learning-set training; (1) Type a cues, which are relevant and common to all problems; (2) Type b cues, which may be relevant within any one problem but which are not valid across problems; (3) and Type c cues, which are not valid at any time (for example, position). Type a cues are abstract, and learning-set formation is assumed to involve learning to use such cues and to ignore or adapt out invalid cues (Type c) and those valid within individual problems (Type b).

Restle put this model into mathematical form and produced accurate fits to both intra- and interproblem learning curves of data from previous learning set experiments. The model predicts that, as learning set training proceeds and Type a cues become dominant, monkeys should show increasingly poorer memory for previous discriminations and less and less between problem transfer on the basis of Type b cues. Generally, the data do not support either of these predictions (for a review see Medin, 1972).

4. Modified Hull–Spence Theory

Although it is not a widely publicized fact, Spence's original discrimination learning theory is capable of predicting learning to learn effects. According to his theory, improved learning rates may result from (a) greater initial strengths associated with the two objects of a discrimination problem, (b) smaller differences in the initial strengths of relevant cues (weaker stimulus preferences), and (c) smaller differences in the initial strengths of irrelevant cues such as position that must be overcome before a problem is solved. A more extensive discussion of the application of Spence's theory to learning set is given by Reese (1964). Some of the few direct tests of this theory have failed to support it (for example, Medin, 1974).

Possibly more challenging to Spence's theory is that several experiments have demonstrated that, when an animal responds to an object and receives a reward, the probability of responding to that object does not necessarily increase. Although learning-set problems usually involve a win–stay, lose–shift solution, monkeys can solve learning set problems involving any one of four logical strategies, win–stay, win–shift, lose–stay, lose–shift (for example, McDowell & Brown, 1963, 1965; see Medin, 1972, for other studies). In addition, monkeys can solve two-trial learning-set problems when the correct solution is to choose (or avoid) a new object on Trial 2 independently of whether or not the Trial 1 response produced a reward (for example, Brown, Overall, & Gentry, 1958). The thrust of these experiments is that the effects of rewards cannot be considered to be a direct and automatic change in strength of stimulus–response associations.

5. Summary

While initially it seemed that learning set theories would provide a conceptual link between slow and fast learning, in practice this promise is still unfulfilled. The heart of the problem seems to be the lack of a conceptual link between the presumed evolution of an abstract learning strategy and performance on a single learning or generalization problem. Because hypothesis theories principally have been concerned only with representing differences in performance between initial and terminal states of learning, little attention has been directed to ways in which learning processes studied in other contexts operate in learning set formation (for an exception, see Bessemer & Stollnitz, 1971).

A greater interaction between learning-set research and the broader domain of discrimination might represent a rapprochement that could bring out relationships between research on animal discrimination learning and human discrimination learning, the latter having tended to employ concept identification paradigms and theories based on hypothesis testing (see Millward's chapter in Volume 5 of this Handbook. Further development of hypothesis theories for learning-set paradigms will determine their ultimate contribution to discrimination learning theory.

Some preliminary observations can also be made concerning how theories do and do not seem to work. One observation is that an incorrect but explicit theory proves to be more useful than a more nearly correct but less explicit theory. It has been shown how theories that are clearly stated serve to bring out more and more aspects of learning or transfer situations that normally might be ignored (for example, the breakdown of transposition for large stimulus changes). Some of these strengths are made clear in the following section on stimulus-sampling theory, which provides new standards for the evaluation of discrimination learning theories and sheds light on some aspects of the continuity–noncontinuity theory.

B. Stimulus-Sampling Theory

Stimulus sampling theory refers not to a single distinct theory of learning but rather to a general class of theories having common conceptions of how to represent a stimulus situation and the associative process. A general review of these concepts and a coverage of the history and domain of this work is available in the book by Neimark and Estes (1967).

1. Basic Concepts

A proposition set forth in W. K. Estes' seminal paper (Estes, 1950) on a statistical approach to learning is that the stimulating conditions which arise in a learning situation can be viewed as comprising a population of stimulus elements, from which only a sample is drawn (or is present) on any one experimental trial. Each element in this set is assumed to be associated with one of the members of the class of responses available, and response probabilities are determined by the proportion of stimulus elements associated with each response. The conditioning status of an element may change as a function of the outcome of a trial.

---

[5] Research on learning set formation in children has consisted mainly of applying hypothesis theories to sets of data in order to assess subject strategies rather than to evaluate the adequacy of such theories.

Stimulus-sampling models fall into two main subclasses, depending upon the presumed stimulus description. For *component* models, it is assumed that some proportion of the stimulus elements is sampled on each trial. For *pattern* models, which are similar in spirit to the Gulliksen–Wolfle configuration theory, the sample of stimulus elements is viewed as a coherent entity or pattern, rather than in terms of the individual elements that comprise it.

Generally both pattern and component models have employed a response selection rather than a stimulus selection conceptualization. This bias may have occurred primarily because a response selection approach seemed most consistent with earlier work on simple conditioning. In addition, another strong feature of these theories is that they are cast into explicit quantitative form, and response selection is easier to treat mathematically.

A final general property of stimulus sampling models is that variability is viewed as an integral part of the learning process rather than a tacked-on process (such as Hull's oscillation of inhibition). Connections between individual stimulus elements and responses are assumed to be deterministic but overt responses are not, owing to variability in the subset of the stimulus elements that are available at different times.

2. Applications of Stimulus Sampling Theory to Discrimination Learning

Initial applications of this theory were to elementary acquisition and extinction phenomena, including some especially elegant analyses of the interrelationships between trial distribution phenomena and spontaneous recovery and regression (Estes, 1955a, b). The breadth of the theory led to the hope that it might serve to integrate phenomena on simple conditioning, probability learning, stimulus generalization, and discrimination learning.

Some of the specific models initially formulated (for example, Burke & Estes, 1957) revealed some basic problems concerning the relationship between generalization and discrimination. I shall focus on one of these problems known as the "overlap problem" because it illustrates a range of stimulus sampling models and because I believe the overlap problem remains a basic issue.

Figure 3 shows a conceptual representation of the overlap problem where either the stimulus set A (S_A) or the stimulus set S_B is presented on any one trial of a discrimination problem. When S_A is presented, response R_A (for example, going left) is rewarded, and when S_B is presented, response R_B is rewarded. In the Burke and Estes model, stimulus elements may be common to both S_A and S_B, and in general, one can represent the degree of

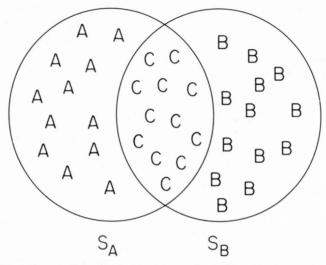

FIGURE 3.   Conceptual representation of the overlap problem. *A* refers to stimulus elements unique to stimulus setting S_A, *B* refers to stimulus elements unique to setting S_B, and *C* refers to stimulus elements common to both S_A and S_B.

similarity of S_A and S_B by the number of common stimulus elements for the two-stimulus situations.

What is the fate of these common or overlapping stimulus elements during learning? In the Burke and Estes model, common elements tend to be conditioned to R_A on S_A trials and to R_B on S_B trials, and, as long as trials on the two stimulus situations are intermixed, the common cues continue to vary in their conditioning status. Since the probability of response R_A on an S_A trial is just the proportion of stimulus elements conditioned to R_A, the probability of R_A given S_A does not approach an asymptote of unity. In other words, a perfect discrimination should not be possible, according to the Burke–Estes model, as long as common cues are present. Throughout the problem, on each trial a given common cue is either conditioned to R_A, which would tend to produce errors on S_B trials, or conditioned to R_B, which would tend to produce errors on S_A trials.

This may not seem like a very difficult problem, since one could adopt a different response rule, for example, proposing that responses are determined by the conditioning status of the majority of the stimulus elements available on a trial. However, there are two sides to the overlap problem; one needs also to represent the fact that stimulus similarity affects the rate of learning a discrimination, as well as the fact that a perfect discrimination can be obtained. This then is the problem: How can one treat stimulus similarity and stimulus generalization phenomena and still predict that a discrimination can ultimately be solved?

More than a little interest has been devoted to the overlap problem. Four general approaches have been adopted within the framework of stimulus-sampling theory, and they are considered in turn.

a. *Shrinkage or adaptation models.*   One class of models assumes that common cues become actively adapted and rendered ineffective in the course of learning. In some models this process depends on the number of transitions from one stimulus setting to the second (for example, Bush & Mosteller, 1951; Robbins, 1970, 1972); in other models (for example, Restle, 1955) common cues are adapted out because of the presence of other, more valid cues. Although the idea of shrinkage or adaptation suggests a process for overcoming the effects of overlap, the psychological rationale for these models has always been rather weak, and some direct tests of these models have been unfavorable (for example, Robbins, 1970).

b. *Observing response models.*   Another approach to the overlap problem is the idea that common cues are not actively adapted but rather that unique cues are actively selected. Atkinson (1958) assumed that if a subject makes an observing response, only nonoverlapping cues will be observed; if no observing response occurs, both common and unique cues could influence performance on a trial. For example, on a discrimination between AB and AC an observing response would make B and C the effective cues (A would not influence learning). Common cues slow learning until the subject learns to make an observing response consistently.

The basic idea in such a two-stage model is reflected in the attention theories, soon to be considered, in which selective attention allows the subject to focus exclusively on cues along the relevant dimension. Observing response models, like adaptation and shrinkage models, do not seem able to handle data showing the influence of common cues in transfer (for example, Flagg & Medin, 1973).

c. *Scanning or choice models.*   A related scheme assumes that subjects continue to learn about common cues but that the choice or decision process becomes more efficient. A prime example is LaBerge's (1962) recruitment model in which the effect of overlap is systematically reduced as the subject samples more and more information prior to an overt choice response. In this model it is assumed that subjects sample stimulus elements, accumulating associated response tendencies until the number implying some one response reaches a threshold value, k, whereupon that response is made. If $k = 1$, the model reduces to the Burke–Estes component model; if k is large, a perfect discrimination can be made, despite considerable overlap in cues (Chapter 8 by Heinemann and Chase in Volume 2 of this Handbook gives a more extensive treatment of the recruitment model).

Models based on so-called random walk processes (for example, Bower, 1959; Estes, 1960) view the choice process as a series of overt or covert steps where the information at each stage moves the subject either toward or away from a specific overt response. For example, in a simultaneous discrimination in a T maze a rat may run to the choice point, orient either to the left or the right, and thereby be exposed to stimulation associated with the corresponding arm in the maze. From this point the rat may run ahead or it may reorient, this reorientation producing new stimulation. This series of orientations proceeds until a choice response is made. In this example, taken from Bower (1959), the choice process involves two stages, first orienting and then responding when the stimulus sampled generates an overt response.

Random walk theories can take on a number of distinct forms (for example, Estes, 1962, 1966), and they have received support in a fair range of different paradigms (see Neimark & Estes, 1967, for a review). These theories have not been systematically assessed as an explanation of the overlap problem.

d. The mixed model.   The simple component model cannot handle perfect discrimination, whereas the pattern model does not predict any effects of stimulus similarity on the rate of learning. The mixed model (Atkinson & Estes, 1963; Estes & Hopkins, 1961) embodies aspects of both pattern and component models. This model assumes that responses become conditioned to stimulus patterns but that generalization will occur from the components in a conditioned pattern to components in patterns that have not yet been conditioned. For example, if a pattern AB has become associated with response i, then the subject will tend to give response i to other stimulus patterns such as AC. After the AC pattern is conditioned, there will no longer be generalization from AB to AC.

The mixed model has been applied to a number of paired-associate learning situations and seems quite promising for handling details of generalization both during learning and on transfer tests. The mixed model is not equipped to predict some discrimination transfer phenomena, which I will soon review, but it must be said that the potential of the mixed model has not been fully exploited.

In summary, the overlap problem has not been solved. The main impact of these models has been to bring out some of the alternative views concerning the relationship between discrimination and generalization. A more detailed analysis of applications of mathematical learning models to discrimination learning and the overlap problem is given by Bush (1965).

3. Contributions of Stimulus-Sampling Theory to Discrimination Learning

A new feature in the area of discrimination learning, brought about by stimulus sampling theory and still not widely used, is the idea that a model might be evaluated in terms of how well it fits the data quantitatively. The key contribution produced by this ideal is at least twofold: first, theories in quantitative form make qualitative arguments unequivocal, and, second, attention becomes focused on additional aspects of a set of data such as the learning curve, trial of last error, precriterion performance, and so on, rather than a few summary statistics such as total errors. This, in turn, greatly increases the interplay between theory and data.

A more specific contribution of stimulus-sampling theory concerns the analysis of the overlap problem discussed earlier. In particular, some of these models begin to raise the possibility that the decision or choice process may play a significant role in discrimination learning, and further that these processes may be modified in the course of learning.

Stimulus-sampling theory might have been more influential but for the revival of the issue of selective learning, to which I now turn.

V. REEMERGENCE OF ATTENTION THEORIES

A. Lawrence and Wyckoff

The groundwork for the reawakening of interest in the role of attention in discrimination learning was laid by two papers by Lawrence (1949, 1950). He demonstrated transfer effects between simultaneous and successive discriminations that continuity theories such as Spence's did not seem to predict. The first study showed that simultaneous discrimination learning with one cue facilitated subsequent learning of a successive discrimination using that same cue. The second study was more elaborate. First, Lawrence pretrained animals on a successive problem with Cue A relevant and Cue B irrelevant. Then, the subjects were trained on a simultaneous discrimination with both Cues A and B relevant and redundant. Finally, Lawrence tested to see which cue animals had used to solve the simultaneous discrimination. These tests indicated that the subjects had used Cue A much more than Cue B.

Both experiments were taken as evidence that cues do not have a fixed salience but may acquire "distinctiveness." Notice the logic of the experiments, which conforms to the weak form of noncontinuity theory. Lawrence did not attempt to demonstrate that nothing was learned about

Cue B, but simply that less was learned about Cue B and more about Cue A than would have occurred otherwise (had the initial successive discrimination not been given).

For some reason (probably best left to historians of science to dissect), Lawrence's experiments seem to have had a delayed impact. However, there was an increased immediate interest in incorporating observing responses into discrimination learning stimulated in part by Lawrence's work, but more directly by Wyckoff's (1952) formal development of the concept. An observing response is a response that results in exposure to the pair of discriminative stimuli, and one of its properties as a response is that it may be conditioned when followed by reward (as Spence had suggested).

Wyckoff demonstrated that the concept of observing responses could be used to predict ogival learning curves, improvement across repeated reversals, and an overlearning reversal effect (see Mackintosh, Chapter 5, Volume 1 of this Handbook). Wyckoff's observing response model could account for Lawrence's second experimental result only if an observing response to one cue dimension did not result in exposure to discriminable cues along the other dimension. This was not an assumption in Wyckoff's model and does not seem to be the spirit of Spence's original model. Nonetheless, it was not for another decade that theories of selective attention were to be widely reexamined.

B. Selective Attention and Analyzers

A very strong claim that perceptual processes play a vital part in learning was put forth by Sutherland (1959, 1964). In a sense, Sutherland's ideas were a natural outgrowth of his research on shape discrimination and pattern recognition (for example, Sutherland, 1959, 1968). The basic features of the theory are as follows. A stimulus input goes into a number of analyzers and the outputs from each analyzer vary with variation of the stimulus along a single dimension only. These outputs from analyzers may become associated with responses as a result of learning.

A notable property of the theory is that not all analyzers are used simultaneously, and only when an analyzer is "switched in," does its output control responses and become associated with outcomes. Discrimination learning is assumed to involve two basic processes: learning to switch in the analyzer along the relevant cue dimension and learning which responses to attach to these outputs.

In this theory, analyzers can be more or less strongly switched in, and the more strongly one analyzer is switched in, the less strongly are others switched in. That is, attending to one dimension tends to preclude attention to other dimensions.

Sutherland's ideas concerning changes in analyzer strengths represent a major departure from previous discrimination learning theories. He proposed that analyzer strength is increased only when different outputs from the analyzer are consistently followed by events of importance to the animal (Sutherland, 1964). That is, an analyzer must predict something, either of a positive or negative nature, in order for it to be used. An analyzer is not strengthened if reinforcement is given, regardless of what outputs the analyzer gives, but is strengthened if one output is usually reinforced and the other output is not. In short, analyzers were assumed to be controlled by the informational rather than the hedonic properties of outcomes.

Sutherland's analyzer theory represents a straightforward attempt to link perceptual processing with ideas concerning learning. Mackintosh (1965) in an influential review paper marshaled strong support for the general idea that the salience of stimulus dimensions can be modified by experience, as attention theories claim. Although it would be in order now to review some predictions of Sutherland's theory, let us detour for a moment to consider the related work of Zeaman, House, and Lovejoy, because their ideas concerning selective attention will yield many of the same predictions. These latter models are more formal and explicit, and it may be easier to see how various phenomena might be handled.

C. Zeaman–House and Lovejoy Attention Models

In their research on discrimination learning in normal and retarded children, Zeaman and House (1963) observed that differences between easy and hard problems and fast and slow learning were primarily in the length of the flat, chance level portion of the learning curve and not in the rate of rise to problem solution after performance departed from chance. To account for these results, they proposed a two-stage model for discrimination learning similar in spirit to Sutherland's theory.

1. Basic Theory

The main idea is that to solve a discrimination problem, subjects must learn to attend to the relevant dimension and then learn the correct response to the cues on the relevant dimension. Consider a discrimination between a red circle and a blue circle with position as the irrelevant cue and red as the rewarded color. According to the theory, the following sequence of events can happen. On each trial the animal attends to either the color or the position dimension. If color is observed, the subject responds to either red or blue, depending on the relative strengths of these approach tendencies. If the correct cue, red, is selected, both the probability of attending to color and the probability of choosing red increase. If blue is chosen, the probability of attending to color decreases, but the probability of selecting the correct cue increases, since the probability of blue being selected decreases after nonreward. If position is observed, whatever choice is made is rewarded on half the trials (in a two-choice problem) and nonrewarded on the other half. Therefore, the probability of attending increases on half and decreases on half of such trials and the probability of either positional response fluctuates around .50. No learning occurs with respect to dimensions that are not observed. The discrimination is solved when color is reliably observed and red chosen. Lovejoy (1965) has analyzed this special case of one relevant dimension and a single irrelevant dimension.

Note that as the probability of one dimension being observed increases, the probability of attending to other dimension must decrease, since only one dimension is observed on a trial. Thus, there is both direct reinforcement and extinction and indirect reinforcement and extinction, the latter resulting from changes in the status of other dimensions.

2. Comparisons with Sutherland's Model

The Zeaman–House model and Sutherland's analyzer theory represent two-stage models, and both rely on the idea that the greater the attention to one dimension, the less is the likelihood that other dimensions will be observed. There are a few differences however. Zeaman and House use "dimension" in a loose sense to refer to a broad class of cues having a common discriminative property, whereas for Sutherland, dimensions are, so to speak, "hard wired" in the form of particular analyzers and conceptually tied to pattern perception research. Second, analyzers are strengthened by their ability to abstract information which enables them to "predict outcomes of importance" according to Sutherland, but Zeaman and House assume that attentional processes are directly controlled by reward and nonreward, apart from their predictive value. In the example just considered, if the subject thought blue was less likely to be rewarded than red but nonetheless chose blue (for whatever reason), then the nonreward would strengthen rather than weaken the color analyzer in Sutherland's theory but not in the Zeaman–House–Lovejoy scheme. Whether this is a distinction of substance is unclear, since Zeaman and House may have chosen their assumption for convenience, and Sutherland's idea was not developed explicitly enough so that it would be easy to see how to test it (that is, what is the mechanism that allows an analyzer to predict outcomes, and how does it relate to choice responses?). Practically speaking, for the paradigms in which the Zeaman–House model has been applied, the two positions are indistinguishable. A third difference is that Sutherland assumed that subjects could learn about more than one dimension on a trial, whereas the original Zeaman and House model allows for learning about only a single dimension. Again, this assumption may have been made for convenience to allow the Zeaman–House model to be cast in mathematical form and to develop the predictions of the model.

3. Properties and Predictions of the Zeaman–House Model

Since explicit solutions to learning equations cannot be derived (except for some interesting special cases which Norman, 1972, has analyzed), Zeaman and House relied on computer simulations to generate predictions. These simulations suggest that four factors control the rate of learning a discrimination: (a) the number of dimensions involved, (b) the learning rate for associating responses with stimulus values, (c) the learning rate for modifying attention to dimensions, and (d) the initial probability of attending to the relevant dimension. These factors, of course, may interact, but it seems that the number of dimensions and the initial probability of observing the relevant dimensions are the two strongest factors in learning.

The model is applied to data in a manner slightly different from many other mathematical learning models. No attempt is made to fit exactly the data from any experiment, but rather Zeaman and House simply attempt to generate curves of the general observed type, a practice akin to Spence's original analyses. This may be a good strategy at the beginning stages of theory development as a device for bringing out some general properties of a model.

From their model, Zeaman and House were able to predict (a) the shape of various discrimination learning curves, (b) the effects of adding relevant and irrelevant dimensions, (c) an advantage for intradimensional shifts (in which the same dimension is correct but new stimulus values appear) over extradimensional shifts, (d) that extradimensional shifts may be either faster or slower than reversal shifts, (e) a midreversal plateau, (f) easy-to-hard transfer facilitation, and a number of other discrimination learning and transfer phenomena. Zeaman and House also suggested that a major difference between normal and retarded children might be in the initial probability of attention to relevant dimensions and not in the rate of learning appropriate attentional and choice responses, a result of considerable theoretical and applied interest.

The Zeaman–House model is not without shortcomings. It cannot handle the observation that the effects of intra- and extradimensional shifts interact strongly with dimensions. That is, an extradimensional shift to form as relevant may be learned faster than an intradimensional shift to color relevant (for a review see Medin, 1975). Nor is the model consistent with transfer tests showing that multiple cue learning may occur on a single trial (Fisher & Zeaman, 1973), and the model also fails to predict details of performance on some types of nonreversal shifts (Medin, 1973). Other difficulties are discussed by Sutherland and Mackintosh (1971) and Medin (1975), and some ways of improving the basic model are developed by Shepp, Kemler, and Anderson (1972).

However, a theory must be evaluated relative to its goals. The Zeaman–House model served to reveal many implications of attention theory that, by and large, have been supported. When the model fails, there is a good chance that one can pinpoint just why it failed; when it succeeds, one generally knows what aspect of the model predicted the observed effects. With a much more complicated model it may be difficult to pin down either success or failure and, consequently, the ability of such models to facilitate understanding of the discrimination learning process would be much curtailed. This is not to say that models should not be complicated as much as to emphasize how important it is to try to bring out and understand the implications of a theory.

I turn briefly to a more complicated attention theory, which serves to illustrate some further theoretical choice points.

4. Lovejoy's Model

Because Lovejoy's (1968) model has not received the same attention as the Zeaman–House model, we shall have to content ourselves with considering just its main ideas. Lovejoy suggested a distinction between being controlled by and learning about a dimension. In the Zeaman–House model a subject always was controlled by and learned about a single dimension. Lovejoy proposed that a subject's choice might be controlled by one dimension, but then a subject might forget which dimension controlled the response and learn about some other dimension. He also distinguished between a base-level distinctiveness or salience of a cue and directable distinctiveness, which might be modified by experience.

The choice process was assumed to be controlled by two main factors. The first was the total distinctiveness of the cue, and the second was the difference in strength or expectation concerning the two stimulus values along a dimension or what he termed the strengths of the subject's "opinions" about a dimension. On rewarded trials the directable distinctiveness along the relevant dimension increased, whereas it decreased for all other dimensions; on nonrewarded trials the directiveness of all dimensions moved toward their base level distinctiveness in Lovejoy's model.

Predictions of Lovejoy's model must be derived from computer simulations and since the model has many parameters, a very large effort would be required to analyze the model carefully. Lovejoy's model has not been very influential, at least partly because its implications may be difficult to see. A useful intermediate strategy might be to attempt to garner evidence relevant to some of the propositions Lovejoy adopted. For example, if one could arrange for, say, the color cues of red and green to be rewarded and relevant on separate preliminary discrimination problems, could one show that when these cues were the two values on a common discrimination that the probability of attending to color was lessened because of common expectations associated with the two cues? I know of no evidence relevant to this point.

To briefly summarize, the overall impact of attention models has been large, and almost all current research in discrimination learning reflects, in one form or another, an influence of these models. The next section of this chapter reviews contemporary modifications and extensions of the theories considered thus far. Two trends are evident. One is the blurring of the distinction between continuity and noncontinuity models, and the second is a broadening of the scope of various models.

VI. RECENT TRENDS IN DISCRIMINATION LEARNING THEORY

A. Modified Noncontinuity Theory

There have been several contemporary modifications in discrimination learning theory as developed by Spence and Hull, modifications that bring out new aspects of the discrimination process as outlined in Figure 1. Two of the main contributions are now reviewed briefly.[6]

1. Spiker's Stimulus-Interaction Theory

The reader may recall that a glaring problem with Spence's original theory was that it predicted that a successive discrimination (for example, black–go left, white–go right) should be impossible to learn because all of the stimulus components are associated equally often with reward. The

[6] I shall not review the Rescorla-Wagner model (Rescorla & Wagner, 1972; Wagner & Rescorla, 1972), since it is adequately described elsewhere in this series (for example, Rudy and Wagner, Chapter 7, and Rescorla, Chapter 1, Volume 2 of this Handbook). The main idea in their model is that a reinforcement is effective only to the degree that it is unexpected (see also Kamin, 1969). An interesting related line of work being explored by Wagner and his associates is that an event will interfere with rehearsal of another CS–US pairing only to the extent that that event is itself unexpected (Wagner, Rudy, & Whitlow, 1973). This procedure may prove fruitful for studying the role of memory in discrimination learning.

source of this difficulty may be the assumption that the stimulus components are treated as independent. Hull's concept of afferent neural interaction directly implied nonindependence, but Spiker (1963, 1970) was the first to systematically develop a discrimination learning theory in the Hull–Spence tradition incorporating the idea of nonindependence of stimulus components.

The key assumption in Spiker's theory is that

> . . . the strength of a habit (or inhibition) accruing to a stimulus component through direct reinforcement (or nonreinforcement) of a compound of which the component is a part will be reduced when that component appears in a different compound, the amount of reduction in the habit or inhibition strength will be an increasing function of the average dissimilarity between corresponding elements in the two compounds [Spiker, 1970, p. 500].

This means that the brightness generalization between a black triangle and a gray circle depends not only on the similarity of the black and the gray, but also on the similarity of the circle and triangle.

With the use of a few simplifying assumptions, Spiker was able to derive specific performance equations for a wide variety of situations. The theory readily predicts that successive discriminations can be solved and, in addition, predicts the relative rates of learning simultaneous and successive discriminations, including the effects of adding different kinds of relevant and irrelevant cues. These predictions and others from several other paradigms have been supported with only a few exceptions (for example, Flagg, 1974) and represent a new standard for other discrimination learning models.

To account for phenomena which appear to support attention theories, Spiker (1970; Spiker & Cantor, 1973) adds to his theory the concept of response-produced cues. The idea is this: when a subject learns to make differential responses to a set of cues on some dimension, differential response-produced cues (RPCs) become available and add to the distinctiveness of cues. In other words, RPCs act as redundant relevant cues.

As the theory has evolved, the properties attributed to RPCs have tended to be the same properties that attention theories invoke in discussing attention to dimensions. Thus, the use of RPCs is modified by reward and nonreward, RPCs are more likely to occur for salient dimensions, and when RPCs become attached to a set of cues on a dimension in one problem, they tend to be attached to cues on the same dimension during transfer. As used by Spiker, RPCs may be distinctive in two respects. First, Spiker does not assume that only some aspects (for example, those attended to) of the stimulus situation are available to be associated with reward; instead, learning is nonselective. Second, RPCs do not follow an inverse law. That is, it is not the case that the more likely RPCs are to be made to cues on one dimension, the less likely they are to be made to cues on other dimensions (although, of course he might have made this assumption).

Since RPCs can be made to mimic virtually any results growing out of an attention orientation, one wonders if there is anything at all unique about RPCs. The answer to this question is by no means obvious, but at the empirical level there is some differentiation of effort. Although RPCs need not be verbal, Spiker's work has tended to focus on paradigms requiring labeling or other forms of verbalization during learning and transfer, and perhaps this research will reveal some interesting relationships between verbalization and language habits and discrimination learning (for a general review see Cantor, 1965).

To summarize, Spiker's work represents a major advance over Spence's (1936) theory. Using the stimulus interaction principle and formulating specific prediction equations greatly expands the scope, power, and explicitness of the theory. The incorporation of RPCs in the theory blurs the distinction between continuity and attention theory, but one can hope that this represents a convergence toward better theory.

2. Kendlers' Mediation Theory

The Kendlers' work on mediation (for example, H. H. Kendler & T. S. Kendler, 1962), like Spiker's later development of RPCs, allows cue effectiveness to be modified during learning. Their original idea was that behavior may be essentially rat-like (unmediated), or human-like (mediated). In the first case, behavior is controlled in a relatively direct manner by the stimulus environment; in the latter case, however, learned behavior is assumed to depend on a symbolic representation of the relevant information in the stimulus environment.

Mediated behavior was assumed to operate as follows: The learner was assumed first to associate some mediating response (r) with the (relevant) cue (S), and then to associate the correct response (R) with the stimulus feedback from the mediating response (s). This could be represented symbolically by S–r–s–R to contrast mediated learning with unmediated (S–R) learning. Unlike Spiker's idea that RPCs simply form part of the stimulus complex, the Kendlers assumed that the cues produced by the mediating response are the effective cues.

At the time of the H. H. Kendler and T. S. Kendler (1962) paper, the general picture seemed to be that animals and young children learned nonreversal shifts faster than reversal shifts whereas the opposite was true for older children and adults. From these data it was tempting to speculate that Spence's theory was generally correct but needed to be supplemented with the concept of mediation in older children and adults. It is perhaps worth mentioning that the Kendlers did not claim that this mediation had to be verbal in character.

It is not easy to compare directly the Kendler's use of mediation with attentional constructs, since the rules for acquisition and transfer of mediating responses have not been developed to the same extent that corresponding processes have been specified in, for example, the attention model of Zeaman and House. If one sticks to the dichotomy between animals and young children on the one hand and older children and adults on the other, it is clear that mediation cannot serve as a substitute for attention constructs, since data implying selective learning and transfer are readily found in animal experiments. However, mediation may be a useful construct in discrimination learning, and the Kendlers (T. S. Kendler & H. H. Kendler, 1967; T. S. Kendler, 1972) have brought out the theoretical and practical value of distinguishing between different kinds of mediational deficiency. The analysis of such work, however, is outside the scope of this contribution.

B. Modified Attention Theories

1. Sutherland and Mackintosh (1971) Theory

As a part of an excellent review of the literature on animal discrimination learning, Sutherland and Mackintosh (1971) proposed a theory that combines some of Sutherland's earlier ideas with Lovejoy's (1968) attention model. The theory allows an animal to be controlled by and learn about more than one cue on a trial, but the more strongly one analyzer is switched in, the less strongly are others switched in. The model also provides an explicit formulation of the idea that an analyzer is strengthened only when its outputs yield correct predictions about further events of importance to an animal.

The theory accounts for a wide range of phenomena in discrimination learning, several of which have been discussed earlier. The model does not handle the effects of constant irrelevant cues (for example, Flagg & Medin, 1973), perhaps because the model contains no mechanism for stimulus generalization within a dimension. However, it is not certain that the model was meant to be tested as a formal model. The model contains 17 parameters for the simulations Sutherland and Mackintosh conducted, and it would take several years of effort just to understand how different combinations of parameter values would interact to produce a result. A different use of the model would be to try to gather direct evidence on the various subprocesses posited. One good example of this strategy is the extensive series of investigations by Thomas and his associates (for example, Thomas, 1969, 1970;

Thomas, Freeman, Svinicki, Burr, & Lyons, 1970) calling into doubt the idea that the more a subject attends to and learns about one dimension, the less it attends to and learns about other dimensions (the inverse hypothesis). This work raises the question of which data in the area of selective learning require the proposition that perceptual processing (or cue and dimension salience) can change with experience and which data seem to require an inverse principle. Such analyses should greatly sharpen the picture of discrimination learning in a way that a good fit of a 17-parameter model to data might not.

2. Attention–Retention Theory

There has been a recent trend for memory phenomena to be given greater significance in accounts of discrimination learning. One specific formalization of this evolution is a theory proposed by Fisher and Zeaman (1973) which combines the Atkinson and Shiffrin (1968) buffer model for human memory, with a multiple-look attention model.

The model has several novel features. Fisher and Zeaman's addition of a buffer system provides an explicit mechanism for rehearsal of information. The model assumes attention to dimensions but does not adopt an inverse hypothesis. The choice process is quite complicated. The dimensions observed depend on: (a) reinforcement history, (b) a stimulus similarity feedback principle according to which similar cues on a dimension are less likely to sustain attention than distinctive cues, and (c) a cue-significance feedback principle (like Lovejoy's) implying that the difference in expected outcomes associated with the values on a dimension determines whether that dimension will control performance. In addition, the expected outcomes may be generated on the basis of information in the buffer, in short-term memory, or in long-term memory.

Like Sutherland and Mackintosh, Fisher and Zeaman showed that various parameter values in the model could account for a number of discrimination learning phenomena. Also like the Sutherland and Mackintosh model, the Fisher and Zeaman model is quite complex, and it is hard (at least for me) to see why it succeeds when it succeeds and why it fails when it fails (assuming that it might fail). Again the only prescription I feel comfortable with is to try to isolate situations where one aspect of the model should be especially evident and see if the data are in accord with the imputed characteristics of that aspect.

3. A Context Model for Discrimination Learning

One concept from memory research, namely, that of retrieval, has been given prominence in a theory proposed by Medin (1975). A principal feature of the model is that, in the course of learning, information concerning both cues and the context in which they occur is stored in memory. It is further assumed that for associative information to be available (accessed), inputs from both a cue and its context must be simultaneously activated. This means that the presentation of some cue (for example, a red circle) does not produce a retrieval of the relevant associative information unless at least some of the contextual cues (for example, properties of the apparatus, the subjects physiological state) from the prior training experience are also present.

The interactive assumption takes the form of a multiplying or product rule for combining dimensional differences rather than the averaging rule used by Spiker in his theory. The difference might be represented by considering generalization from a red circle to a pink triangle along the dimension of color. In Spiker's theory the generalization from red to pink would be less the more dissimilar the circle and triangle were, but, since generalization is based on the average overall similarity, there would always be some generalization (assuming that red and pink are highly similar). In Medin's theory, if there were no similarity (or generalization) between the circle and the triangle, then there would be no generalization between the stimuli on the color dimension either, since generalization is based on a multiplicative rule.

The context model predicts the relative rates of learning in various paradigms as well as the effects of adding relevant and irrelevant cues. To account for selective attention, Medin (1975) proposed that the generalization gradient is steeper along an attended dimension than along an ignored dimension. This is a much weaker assumption than the usual hypothesis that generalization is complete along ignored dimensions and essentially absent along attended dimensions, yet this modification does give a good account of selective learning phenomena. The theory is still in its developmental stages, and the most that can be said is that the model raises the possibility that context and retrieval factors may be significant components in the discrimination learning process.

VII. SUMMARY

A. What Are the Main Questions?

I would like to return to Figure 1 to summarize some of the main questions arising from accounts of discrimination learning and try to give some indication as to the status on each issue.

1. Orienting Responses and Stimulus Reception

Aside from investigators acknowledging the importance of stimulus reception in learning and some propositions that orienting responses can be learned, discrimination learning theorists have shown little interest in orienting responses.

2. Perceptual Processing and Stimulus Description

Although Spence showed little interest in perceptual processes, there is a growing consensus today that the functional stimulus in a learning situation may not show a simple correspondence with the nominal stimulus. Here the consensus ends. Some of the major points of disagreement are (a) whether these are limitations on perceptual processing capacity; (b) whether the functional stimuli are to be viewed as the products of mediational responses, attention to dimensions (either in the loose sense or in the sense of switching in of analyzers) or as response-produced cues; (c) whether attention is preset or modified by feedback from cue similarities or anticipated outcomes; and (d) whether this stage of processing is fixed, modulated by reward and nonreward, or controlled by the ability of analyzers to predict or detect future outcomes of importance to the organism.

Component cues, configurations, and compound cues have all been offered as answers to the question of what the appropriate stimulus description should be. One new theoretical leaning is the idea that individual stimulus components may not be learned about and accessed in an independent manner. Rather, what is learned about a cue may depend heavily on what the subject knows about other cues, and the accessibility of information associated with one cue may hinge on the presence or absence of other cues.

3. Memory and Associative Information

In Spence's early theory a stimulus component automatically had access to its strength. Alternative models propose that context cues stored at the time of an earlier presentation must also be activated for a cue to access the appropriate associative information. Still other theories give the memory system a much expanded role in discrimination learning.

4. The Choice Process and Response Generation

There appears to be a consensus that stimulus selection gives a better account of performance in usual discrimination learning situations than does response selection. The choice process was not a very visible component in early discrimination learning theories, but concern with the overlap problem and mechanisms for selective learning has resulted in a growing awareness of the importance of choice behavior in discrimination learning. The more applied interest in "reflective" and "impulsive" children may serve to amplify this interest.

5. Outcome Processing

For the most part the idea that reinforcement is direct and automatic seems to have fallen by the wayside. A majority view is that reinforcement in addition or instead provides a source of information, and some have proposed that a reinforcement has an effect only to the extent that it is not anticipated. There is also an increased willingness to assume that outcomes may modify not only the strength of an association but various other stages in the discrimination learning process.

B. How Do Theories Seem to Be Working?

It seems to me that the time has come when the excitement and interest over Spence's analysis of transposition in terms of excitation and inhibition, often highlighted in reviews of discrimination learning, should be replaced by excitement and interest concerning perception, memory, and choice behavior and their modification with experience. Spence's analysis was brilliant, but it should not belie changes that the field of discrimination learning has experienced.

Aside from an accumulation of data and relevant questions, are there any lessons to be learned concerning how theories seem to have worked (or have not worked) in the past? If one is willing to tolerate blatant oversimplifications, there seem to have been three major episodes of research activity in discrimination learning.

The first episode was the continuity–noncontinuity issue which dominated the 1930s and 1940s. The center of attention was clearly Spence's theory which served to focus the efforts of both advocates and dissenters. Another concerted research effort arose with the development of statistical learning theory in the 1950s, and led to intense interest in such issues as the overlap problem. Finally, the 1960s have witnessed a shift to research on the role of attention in discrimination learning, with the Zeaman–House model acting as a major focal point.

In all three cases, the theories that dominated research activity were addressed to issues that investigators were convinced were important; the theories were fairly simple in conception and explicit in their predictions; and, perhaps most important, the theories were vulnerable to disproof.

Despite their simplicity, these theories served to call attention to details of the discrimination learning process whose significance otherwise would have continued to go unnoticed, and the theories generated predictions and implications that simply are unavailable to informal analysis. Further, because of their simplicity, when the theories could be shown to be wrong, it was possible to see where they failed, a consequence that led to further understanding and kept alive the possibility of modifying the theories so as to bring them into closer accord with the data. This seems to be a pattern worth imitating.

Today, models seem to be growing increasingly complex, and, with the advent of high speed computers and sophisticated computer simulation techniques, some of the practical constraints on complexity have been removed. There is some danger that, if the complexity of theories begins to approach the complexity of the phenomena of interest, understanding may go by the wayside. It no longer is a major accomplishment to produce a good quantitative fit to a set of data, and some theories seem to predict an impressive range of data. However, correct predictions are only one side of the coin, and the explanatory power of a theory is at least as strongly based on the set of conceivable results which it could not predict. If a theory can predict all possible results, then it explains nothing.

Partly as a precautionary measure and partly because I think it is a fruitful strategy, I would hope that more effort be devoted in the future to analysis of theories. This effort might take three basic forms. The first is simply to try to bring out the implications of a theory. In many cases a theory is formulated with a particular set of data in mind and is only assessed in light of those data. Careful analysis may reveal some new properties of the theory and suggest new applications. The second strategy is to study the effects of minor modifications of a theory in order to arrive at an idea of the range or class of models which may handle a set of data and perhaps point to aspects of a theory which are superfluous. Finally, as theories become more and more elaborate, it may be specially valuable to isolate situations in which the predictions of some one aspect of the theory can stand or fall, depending on the results, without being rescued (or obscured) by some other aspect of the theory. All of these factors might serve as a favorable influence on our attempts to understand the many intriguing questions surrounding discrimination learning.

ACKNOWLEDGMENTS

This work was supported by U.S. Public Health Service Grant MH16100 and by Grant MH23878 from the National Institute of General Medical Sciences.

REFERENCES

Atkinson, R. C. A Markov model for discrimination learning. *Psychometrika*, 1958, **23**, 309–322.

Atkinson, R. C., & Estes, W. K. Stimulus sampling theory. In R. D. Luce, R. R. Bush, & E. Galanter (Eds.), *Handbook of Mathematical Psychology*, Vol. 2. New York: Wiley, 1963. Pp. 122–268.

Atkinson, R. C., & Shiffrin, R. M. Human memory: A proposed system and its control processes. In K. W. Spence & J. T. Spence (Eds.), *The psychology of learning and motivation*. Vol. 2. New York: Academic Press, 1968. Pp. 89–195.

Bessemer, D. W., & Stollnitz, F. Retention of discriminations and an analysis of learning set. In A. M. Schrier & F. Stollnitz (Eds.), *Behavior of nonhuman primates*. Vol. 4. New York: Academic Press, 1971. Pp. 1–58.

Bower, G. H. Choice-point behavior. In R. R. Bush & W. K. Estes (Eds.), *Studies in mathematical learning theory*. Stanford, California: Stanford University Press, 1959. Pp. 109–124.

Brown, W. L., Overall, J. E., & Gentry, G. V. Conceptual discrimination in rhesus monkeys. *Journal of Comparative and Physiological Psychology*, 1958, **51**, 701–705.

Burke, C. J., & Estes, W. K. A component model for stimulus variables in discrimination learning. *Psychometrika*, 1957, **22**, 133–145.

Bush, R. R. Identification learning. In D. P. Luce, R. R. Bush, & E. Galanter (Eds.), *Handbook of mathematical psychology*. Vol. 3. New York: Wiley, 1965. Pp. 161–203.

Bush, R. R., & Mosteller, F. A model for stimulus generalization and discrimination. *Psychological Review*, 1951, **58**, 413–423.

Cantor, J. H. Transfer of stimulus pretraining in motor paired-associate and discrimination learning tasks. In L. P. Lipsitt & C. C. Spiker (Eds.), *Advances in child development and behavior*. Vol. 2. New York: Academic Press, 1965. Pp. 19–58.

Estes, W. K. Toward a statistical theory of learning. *Psychological Review*, 1950, **57**, 94–107.

Estes, W. K. Statistical theory of spontaneous recovery and regression. *Psychological Review*, 1955, **62**, 145–154.   (a)

Estes, W. K. Statistical theory of distributional phenomena in learning. *Psychological Review*, 1955, **62**, 369–377.   (b)

Estes, W. K. A random-walk model for choice behavior. In K. J. Arrow, S. Karlin, & P. Suppes (Eds.), *Mathematical methods in the social sciences*. Stanford, California: Stanford University Press, 1960. Pp. 265–276.

Estes, W. K. Theoretical treatments of differential reward in multiple-choice learning and two-person interactions. In J. Criswell, H. Solomon, & P. Suppes (Eds.), *Mathematical methods in small group processes*. Stanford, California: Stanford University Press, 1962. Pp. 133–149.

Estes, W. K. Transfer of verbal discriminations based on differential reward magnitudes. *Journal of Experimental Psychology*, 1966, **72**, 276–283.

Estes, W. K., & Hopkins, B. L. Acquisition and transfer in pattern vs. component discrimination learning. *Journal of Experimental Psychology*, 1961, **61**, 322–328.

Fisher, M. A., & Zeaman, D. An attention-retention theory of retardate discrimination learning. In N. R. Ellis (Ed.), *International review of research in mental retardation*. Vol. 6. New York: Academic Press, 1973. Pp. 169–256.

Flagg, S. F. Learning of the insoluble conditional reaction problem by rhesus monkeys. *Animal Learning and Behavior*, 1974, **2**, 181–184.

Flagg, S. F., & Medin, D. L. Constant irrelevant cues and stimulus generalization in monkeys. *Journal of Comparative & Physiological Psychology*, 1973, **85**, 339–345.

Gulliksen, H., & Wolfle, H. L. A theory of learning and transfer: I. *Psychometrika*, 1938, **3**, 127–149. (a)

Gulliksen, H., & Wolfle, H. L. A theory of learning and transfer: II. *Psychometrika*, 1938, **3**, 225–251. (b)

Harlow, H. F. The formation of learning sets. *Psychological Review*, 1949, **56**, 51–65.

Harlow, H. F. Learning set and error factor theory. In S. Koch (Eds.), *Psychology: A study of a science*. Vol. 2. New York: McGraw-Hill, 1959. Pp. 492–537.

Hull, C. L. The problem of stimulus equivalence in behavior theory. *Psychological Review*, 1939, **46**, 9–30.

Hull, C. L. *Principles of behavior*. New York: Appleton-Century-Crofts, 1943.

Hull, C. L. The problem of primary stimulus generalization. *Psychological Review*, 1947, **54**, 120–134.

Hull, C. L. Simple qualitative discrimination learning. *Psychological Review*, 1950, **57**, 303–313.

Hull, C. L. *A behavior system*. New Haven, Connecticut: Yale University Press, 1952.

Kamin, L. J. Predictability, surprise, attention and conditioning. In R. Church & B. Campbell (Eds.), *Punishment and aversive behavior*. New York: Appleton-Century-Crofts, 1969. Pp. 279–296.

Kendler, H. H., & Kendler, T. S. Vertical and horizontal processes in problem solving. *Psychological Review*, 1962, **69**, 1–16.

Kendler, T. S. An ontogeny of mediational deficiency. *Child Development*, 1972, **43**, 1–17.

Kendler, T. S., & Kendler, H. H. Experimental analysis of inferential behavior in children. In L. P. Lipsitt & C. C. Spiker (Eds.), *Advances in child development and behavior*. Vol. 3. New York: Academic Press, 1967. Pp. 157–189.

Krechevsky, I. Hypotheses in rats. *Psychological Review*, 1932, **39**, 516–532.

Krechevsky, I. A study of the continuity of the problem-solving process. *Psychological Review*, 1938, **45**, 107–133.

LaBerge, P. A recruitment theory of simple behavior. *Psychometrika*, 1962, **27**, 375–396.

Lashley, K. S. *Brain mechanisms and intelligence*. Chicago: University of Chicago Press, 1929.

Lashley, K. S. An examination of the continuity theory as applied to discriminative learning. *Journal of General Psychology*, 1942, **26**, 241–265.

Lashley, K. S., & Wade, M. The Pavlovian theory of generalization. *Psychological Review*, 1946, **53**, 72–87.

Lawrence, D. H. Acquired distinctiveness of cues: I. Transfer between discriminations on the basis of familiarity with the stimulus. *Journal of Experimental Psychology*, 1949, **39**, 770–784.

Lawrence, D. H. Acquired distinctiveness of cues: II. Selective association in a constant stimulus situation. *Journal of Experimental Psychology*, 1950, **40**, 175–188.

Levine, M. A model of hypothesis behavior in discrimination learning set. *Psychological Review*, 1959, **66**, 353–366.

Levine, M. Hypothesis behavior. In A. M. Schrier, H. F. Harlow, & F. Stollnitz (Eds.), *Behavior of nonhuman primates*. Vol. 1. New York: Academic Press, 1965. Pp. 97–127.

Lovejoy, E. An attention theory of discrimination learning. *Journal of Mathematical Psychology*, 1965, **2**, 342–362.

Lovejoy, E. *Attention in discrimination learning*. San Francisco: Holden-Day, 1968.

Mackintosh, N. J. Selective attention in animal discrimination learning. *Psychological Bulletin*, 1965, **64**, 124–150.

McDowell, A. A., & Brown, W. L. Learning mechanism in response perseveration learning sets. *Journal of Comparative & Physiological Psychology*, 1963, **56**, 1032–1034.

Mc Dowell, A. A., & Brown, W. L. Perseveration learning set formation to nonrewarded cues by normal and previously irradiated rhesus monkeys. *Journal of Genetic Psychology*, 1965, **106**, 173–176.

Medin, D. L. Role of reinforcement in discrimination learning set in monkeys. *Psychological Bulletin*, 1972, **77**, 305–318.

Medin, D. L. Subproblem analysis of discrimination shift learning. *Behavior Research Methods and Instrumentation*, 1973, **5**, 332–336.

Medin, D. L. Reward pretraining and discrimination learning set. *Animal Learning and Behavior*, 1974, **2**, 305–308.

Medin, D. L. A theory of context in discrimination learning. In G. H. Bower (Ed.), *The psychology of learning and motivation*. Vol. 9. New York: Academic Press, 1975. Pp. 263–314.

Neimark, E., & Estes, W. K. *Stimulus sampling theory*. San Francisco: Holden-Day, 1967.

Nissen, A. W. Description of the learned response in discrimination behavior. *Psychological Review*, 1950, **59**, 121–137.

Norman, M. F. *Markov processes and learning models*. New York: Academic Press, 1972.

Reese, H. W. Discrimination learning set in rhesus monkeys. *Psychological Bulletin*, 1964, **61**, 321–340.

Reese, H. W. *The perception of stimulus relations*. New York: Academic Press, 1968.

Rescorla, R. A., & Wagner, A. R. A theory of Pavlovian conditioning: Variations in the effectiveness of reinforcement and nonreinforcement. In A. H. Black & W. K. Prokasy (Eds.), *Classical conditioning II: Research and Theory*. New York: Appleton-Century-Crofts, 1972. Pp. 64–99.

Restle, F. A theory of discrimination learning. *Psychological Review*, 1955, **62**, 11–19.

Restle, F. Toward a quantitative description of learning set data. *Psychological Review*, 1958, **65**, 77–91.

Robbins, D. Stimulus selection in human discrimination learning and transfer. *Journal of Experimental Psychology*, 1970, **84**, 282–290.

Robbins, D. Some models for successive discrimination learning and transfer. *British Journal of Mathematical and Statistical Psychology*, 1972, **25**, 151–167.

Shepp, B. E., Kemler, D. G., & Anderson, D. R. Selective attention and the breadth of learning: An extension of the one-look model. *Psychological Review*, 1972, **25**, 151–167.

Spence, K. W. The nature of discrimination learning in animals. *Psychological Review*, 1936, **43**, 427–449.

Spence, K. W. The differential response in animals to stimuli varying within a single dimension. *Psychological Review*, 1937, **44**, 430–444.

Spence, K. W. The basis of solution by chimpanzees of the intermediate size problem. *Journal of Experimental Psychology*, 1942, **31**, 257–276.

Spence, K. W. Theoretical interpretations of learning. In S. S. Stevens (Ed.), *Handbook of experimental psychology*. New York: Wiley, 1950. Pp. 690–729.

Spence, K. W. The nature of the response in discrimination learning. *Psychological Review*, 1952, **59**, 89–93.

Spiker, C. C. The hypothesis of stimulus interaction and an explanation of stimulus compounding. In L. P. Lipsitt & C. C. Spiker (Eds.), *Advances in child development and behavior*. Vol. 1. New York: Academic Press, 1963. Pp. 233–264.

Spiker, C. C. An extension of Hull–Spence discrimination learning theory. *Psychological Review*, 1970, **77**, 496–515.

Spiker, C. C., & Cantor, J. H. Applications of Hull–Spence theory to the transfer of discrimination learning in children. In H. W. Reese (Ed.), *Advances in child development and behavior*. Vol. 8. New York: Academic Press, 1973. Pp. 223–288.

Sutherland, N. S. Stimulus analysing mechanisms. *Proceedings of a symposium on the mechanization of thought processes.* Vol. 2. London: Her Majesty's Stationery Office, 1959. Pp. 575–609.

Sutherland, N. S. Visual discrimination in animals. *British Medical Bulletin,* 1964, **20**, 54–59.

Sutherland, N. S. Outlines of a theory of visual pattern recognition in animals and man. *Proceedings of the Royal Society of Britain,* 1968, **71**, 297–317.

Sutherland, N. S., & Mackintosh, N. J. *Mechanisms of animal discrimination learning.* New York: Academic Press, 1971.

Thomas, D. R. The use of operant conditioning techniques to investigate perceptual processes in animals. In R. Gilbert & N. S. Sutherland (Eds.), *Animal discrimination learning.* New York: Academic Press, 1969. Pp. 1–33.

Thomas, D. R. Stimulus selection, attention, and related matters. In J. H. Reynierse (Ed.), *Current issues in animal learning.* Lincoln: University of Nebraska Press, 1970. Pp. 311–356.

Thomas, D. R., Freeman, F., Svinicki, J. G., Burr, D. E. S., & Lyons, S. Effects of extradimensional training on stimulus generalization. *Journal of Experimental Psychology Monograph,* 1970, **83**, 1–21.

Thorndike, E. L. *Animal intelligence: Experimental studies.* New York: Macmillan, 1911.

Wagner, A. R., & Rescorla, R. A. Inhibition in Pavlovian conditioning: Application of a theory. In R. A. Boakes & M. S. Halliday (Eds.), *Inhibition and learning.* New York: Academic Press, 1972. Pp. 301–336.

Wagner, A. R., Rudy, J. W., & Whitlow, J. W. Rehearsal in animal conditioning. *Journal of Experimental Psychology Monograph,* 1973, **97**, 407–426.

Wyckoff, L. B., Jr. The role of observing responses in discrimination behavior. *Psychological Review,* 1952, **59**, 431–442.

Zeaman, D., & House, B. J. The role of attention in retardate discrimination learning. In N. R. Ellis (Eds.), *Handbook of mental deficiency: Psychological theory and research.* New York: McGraw-Hill, 1963. Pp. 159–223.

5

Probability Learning and Sequence Learning

Jerome L. Myers

University of Massachusetts, Amherst

I. INTRODUCTION

In 1954, Estes and Straughan published a paper on binary prediction that proved to be the forerunner of a stream of theoretical and experimental articles dealing with such behavior. The task they employed was not new; it had been developed 15 years earlier by Humphreys (1939) as an analog to classical conditioning. However, not until publication of the Estes and Straughan (1954) paper was the binary prediction task the focus of major efforts by investigators of learning. The impact of this article undoubtedly resulted from the fact that it was one of the first published tests of Estes' statistical learning theory (SLT) which had appeared a few years earlier (Estes, 1950). "Toward a statistical theory of learning" (Estes, 1950) had held forth the promise of a learning theory capable of precise, quantitative prediction, something beyond the curve fitting which had typified previous mathematical theories. The Estes and Straughan paper began to realize that promise, not only providing support for the theory, but also presenting a simple paradigm in which it could be tested. Thus, it signaled an era in which both proponents and opponents of SLT would derive and test its consequences in a variety of prediction tasks.

In this early research on "probability learning," random event sequences were typically employed, and marginal event probability was a major independent variable. In more recent experiments, structured sequences have been employed and learning as a function of structure has been of major interest. This later work was originally motivated in large part by a desire to test alternatives to simple conditioning models of choice behavior; it has been maintained, however, by an interest in sequential information processing. In contrast to earlier research in probability learning, which was primarily concerned with the validity of a general theory of learning for which choice behavior was a convenient testing ground, current studies are focused on such issues as the acquisition and representation of sequential information in memory and the way in which such information influences choice behavior. In this chapter, these two phases of work on sequential choice behavior are reviewed. The review is not exhaustive but attempts to provide a sense of the major theoretical developments, the basic issues, and the relevant findings in probability learning and sequence learning.

II. PROBABILITY LEARNING

The basic paradigm employed in studying probability learning is quite simple. Upon presentation of the ready signal that initiates a trial, the subject is required to predict which of several events $(E_i ; i = 1, 2, . . . , r)$ will occur next; prediction of E_i is designated as A_i . The prediction is usually followed by feedback, presentation of one of the alternative events. In the simplest case, that of noncontingent events, E_i occurs with constant probability, π_i , and is independent of previous responses and events. Thus, the task is analogous to that of predicting the fall of a die or the outcome of a spin of a roulette wheel. Typically, an experimental session consists of several hundred trials, spaced at intervals of roughly 3–5 sec.

Estes and his co-workers have assumed that event prediction reflects an underlying representation of event probability which develops by means of a simple conditioning process. Several alternative models have been derived within this conditioning framework. Two of these, the linear and pattern models, have been extensively investigated. The linear model assumes that some proportion of a large population of stimulus elements is randomly sampled on each trial, that probability of response A_i on Trial n $[P(A_{i,n})]$ is equal to the proportion of the sample conditioned to that response, and that, after presentation of the reinforcing event, the entire sample becomes conditioned to the response of predicting that event. In contrast, the pattern model assumes a small set of N elements, or patterns, only one of which is sampled on each trial. The conditioning state of the sampled N pattern completely determines the response for that trial. With some probability, c, the sampled pattern becomes conditioned to the reinforced response for that trial and with probability, $1 - c$, the conditioning state is unchanged. Atkinson and Estes (1963) have provided a more formal treatment of stimulus sampling models. Despite apparent differences, the two models yield numerous predictions that are either identical or very similar. In view of the fact that much of the probability learning literature has implications for these models, it will be helpful to note certain common predictions.

A. Some Predictions from Statistical Learning Theory

One fundamental consequence of both the linear and pattern models is that $P(A_{i,n})$ should approach π_i as n increases. This prediction of asymptotic *probability matching* is of interest not only because it is a strong, parameter-free prediction, but also because it is somewhat surprising from the viewpoint of decision theory; maximization of the expected number of correct predictions requires that the subject always predict the most frequent event. A second strong prediction of both models, which follows directly from their conditioning axioms, is positive recency; if the occurrence of an event increases the probability of predicting that event, then $P(A_i)$ should monotonically approach 1.0 as the length of a run of consecutive E_i's increases.

In the following Section II.B, the status of these predictions—asymptotic probability matching and positive recency—is considered for experiments in which noncontingent event schedules have been employed. Concern here is with delineating the conditions under which these predictions are, and are not, verified, and with attempting to gain some understanding of the implications of this pattern of results for probability learning in general, and statistical learning theory (SLT) in particular.

B. Some Basic Results

1. *Asymptotic Response Probability, $P_\infty(A_i)$*

a. *Extended practice.* It is generally believed that probability matching, the asymptotic approach of $P(A_i)$ to π_i, is a robust phenomenon, readily demonstrated in probability learning studies. The facts, in contrast to the impression, are somewhat more complicated. It is true that in some studies extremely stable probability matching has been demonstrated for several terminal trial blocks; Neimark and Shuford (1959) provide an excellent example. However, it is also true that $P(A_1)$ consistently overshoots π with extended practice. An experiment by Friedman, Burke, Cole, Keller, Millward, and Estes (1964), often cited as strong evidence for probability matching, is a case in point. In each of the last 7 12-trial blocks of a series of 288 trials with $\pi = .8$, $P(A_1)$ exceeded .8; the average deviation was only .03, small but nonetheless troublesome. Similar departures from matching have been observed by other investigators, in fact, by almost anyone who has run subjects for more than 300 trials. For example, with π at .6, .7, and .8, Myers, Fort, Katz, and Suydam (1963) obtained values of $P(A_1)$ of .616, .753, and .871 for Trials 301–400.

Probability matching should hold in the noncontingent case for more than two choices. Early experiments employing three choices for 200 and 100 trials (Detambel, 1955; Neimark, 1956) did, in fact, support the probability matching theorem. However, as in binary prediction experiments, extended practice resulted in overshooting. Furthermore, experiments by Gardner (1957) and Cotton and Rechtschaffen (1958) have demonstrated that overshooting on the most frequent alternative is more pronounced in the three- than in the two-choice case. With three choices $P_\infty(A_1)$ on Trials 286–450 was about .67 and .80 for π of .6 and .7, respectively. A subsequent study by Gardner (1958), employing from 2 to 8 choices for 420 trials, reaffirmed the overshooting result and indicated that the amount of overshooting increased with number of choices. It also appears that several curves were still rising at the end of the session.

Although the basic finding that overshooting occurs with extended practice is well established, its implications for the validity of the linear and pattern models are not clear. Estes (1964, 1972), although conceding that overshooting occurs, has argued that SLT provides an essentially correct account of the course of probability learning. He ascribes the apparent failure of the probability-matching theorem under extended practice to extraneous factors that influence predictive behavior so that it is no longer an adequate reflection of the underlying state of learning. One possibility is that the theory describes predictive behavior quite accurately as long as the probability of a correct response continues to increase. When the basic learning process asymptotes at π and, consequently, there is no further increase in probability of a correct response, the subject may test various strategies designed to further improve his performance. According to this analysis, overshooting should be more likely to occur and should be of greater magnitude in conditions under which it represents a large improvement in probability correct, relative to probability matching. This seems to be the case. The difference in probability correct between matching and optimization (100% prediction of the most frequent event) is a quadratic function of π, and also increases with number of choices when there is a uniform distribution over the less frequent events; the degree of overshooting follows the same pattern.

Measures other than prediction probabilities may be helpful in assessing Estes' interpretation of overshooting. In particular, reasons advanced for overshooting—boredom, fatigue, experiments in which subjects make attempts to increase the percentage correct—do not obviously apply to direct estimates of π. If SLT provides a valid account of probability learning, as opposed to predictive behavior, such estimates of π might well prove more stable over prolonged series of trials than choice proportions. Whether this will, in fact, occur remains to be seen. Neimark and Shuford (1959) and Beach, Rose, Sayeki, Wise, and Carter (1970) have found that estimates of π match π in the last few blocks of a 300-trial sequence. Unfortunately, more trials are required to resolve the issue of asymptotic stability.

As one might expect, degree of practice is not the only variable that constrains the applicability of the probability matching theorem. Investigators who are determined to do so can produce overshooting in a variety of ways; undershooting is somewhat more difficult to achieve, but possible. Most of these departures from probability matching have been obtained under experimental conditions outside of the intended scope of SLT and are thus not relevant to evaluating the validity of the theory. Nevertheless, there are implications for alternative models, for an understanding of decision making capabilities, and for methodology in probability learning experiments. Therefore, two other factors are now considered that produce departures from matching.

b. *Instructions.* The premise underlying this research appears to be that subjects are capable of more intelligent decisions than SLT, and early findings of probability matching, imply. In particular, probability matching has been assumed to be a result of the subject's failure to detect the randomness inherent in the event sequence and his consequent attempts to find a perfectly predictable pattern (Flood, 1954). This assumption gains support from the finding of 5–10% overshooting when events are displayed in such a way as to appear randomly sequenced (Nies, 1962; Peterson & Ulehla, 1965). Under these conditions of apparent randomness, explanations which emphasize that the odds are constant over trials and that event runs are irrelevant cues have no additional effect. Nies found no difference between two groups differing only with respect to the presentation of such an explanation, and Beach and Swensson (1967), who employed such an explanation in addition to random shuffling of an event deck, obtained the same 8% overshooting observed by Peterson and Ulehla (1965) without such instructions. In the absence of a clear appearance of randomness, explanations must be very strongly worded to have an effect. Studies by McCracken, Osterhout, and Voss (1962), and Braveman and Fischer (1968) have demonstrated that merely telling subjects that the sequence is random or that there is no fixed pattern has little effect, nor are subjects unduly influenced by being instructed to avoid a trial-by-trial approach or by being told that it is impossible to be correct on every trial. Subjects appear to understand what is expected of them only when both knowledge of randomness and the desirability of maximizing correct responses over blocks of trials is communicated; then, terminal values of $P(A_1)$ are obtained that exceed, by 10–20%, those for subjects merely instructed to attempt to predict correctly on each trial.

Although carefully worded instructions, or displays of randomness, can elicit overshooting, the results cited above hardly stand as a testimonial to man's decision making capabilities. Under conditions in which the subject is all but instructed to predict the more frequent event, overshooting by only 10% is obtained. Individual subject protocols are not more impressive. For example, only 29 and 27% optimalize (always predict the more frequent event) in the last trial block of the Peterson and Ulehla (1965) and Beach and Swensson (1967) studies, respectively; this result occurs despite the fact that the former experiment involved monetary incentives, which by them-selves elicit overshooting, and in the latter study, subjects were reminded throughout the session "to ignore the runs and to avoid the gambler's fallacy." To be fair, subjects are not quite as dense as these data would suggest. Nies (1962) reported that, although only 3% of his subjects op-timized, 60% were able to verbalize the optimal strategy in a post session interview.

There are several reasons why many subjects fail to learn the optimal strategy and why most of those who do learn it fail to use it. First, as Siegel (1959) has suggested, there may be a certain utility in varying one's re-sponse, in attempting to outguess the experimenter. Second, subjects be-lieve that patterns are present in the event sequence (for example, Nies, 1962) and exaggerate the likelihood of short runs (Tune, 1964). Third, these beliefs are essentially correct in many of the experiments in which instruc-tions have been manipulated. Nies, who randomized in 50-trial blocks, reported that more short runs were present in his event sequence than would be expected for unconstrained random event sequences. This is undoubt-edly even truer in studies by Goodnow (1955), McCracken et al. (1962) and Braveman and Fischer (1968), in which event proportions were fixed for blocks of 10, 20, and 30 trials, respectively. As Jones and Myers (1966) have demonstrated, when the sequence is randomized in such short blocks, subjects can outguess the experimenter, achieving considerably more cor-rect responses than would be expected on a chance basis. With such constrained sequences, the "gambler's fallacy" (the other event is due) is not a fallacy, and the strategy of uniformly predicting the higher probability event is not necessarily optimal. Jones (1971) has pointed out that sequence structure is a form of instruction; if so, subjects in experiments such as those just cited receive conflicting messages.

c. *Monetary payoffs.*   In the studies just considered there was no tangi-ble incentive for subjects to optimize. Those who still have faith in the decision-making capabilities of human subjects might expect the introduc-tion of monetary gains and costs to markedly increase probability of pre-dicting the more frequent event. This expectation is confirmed. Comparing subjects who won one cent for correct predictions and lost one cent for incorrect predictions with subjects who had no monetary incentive, Myers et al. (1963) found $P(A_1)$ to be significantly higher for the one-cent group. The differences in terminal (Trials 301–400) response probabilities were .03, .12, and .06 at π values of .6, .7, and .8, respectively.

An additional expectation—that $P(A_1)$ would be a monotonic increasing function of incentive magnitude—at best receives weak confirmation. In the Myers et al. (1963) experiment cited above, the average value of $P(A_1)$ was .03 higher in ten-cent than in one-cent groups. More generally, a review of eight experiments in which two nonzero payoff levels were compared reveals differences in terminal values of $P(A_1)$ ranging from essentially zero (Jones & Myers, 1966) to about .05 (Suppes & Atkinson, 1960; Castellan, 1960). One point is evident: while instructional and motivational manipulations can yield increased probability of predicting the more frequent event, subjects consistently fall short of the optimal strategy of always predicting that event. What is less clear is the extent to which this reflects a failure to learn the optimal strategy as opposed to a failure to use that strategy.

Rather substantial effects of payoff magnitude can be produced by employing a within-subject paradigm in which each subject makes predictions under two payoff levels. This has been done by randomly sequencing equal number of trials at each payoff level (Schnorr, Lipkin, & Myers, 1966; Schnorr & Myers, 1967) or by changing the payoff level partway through the sequence of trials (Castellan, 1969; Halpern, Schwartz, & Chapman, 1968; Swensson, 1965). Under either approach, choice data reflect a "negative contrast" effect. On high-payoff trials, $P(A_1)$ is at about the same level as in payoff groups in the studies cited above; however, on low-payoff trials, $P(A_1)$ is considerably depressed, typically below the probability matching level. Schnorr and Myers (1967) demonstrated that, on high-payoff trials $P_\infty(A_1)$ is independent of payoff magnitude whereas, on low-payoff trials, $P_\infty(A_1)$ decreases as the difference between high and low payoff decreases. Schnorr et al. (1966) and Swensson (1965) have also found that estimates of event probability, obtained at the end of the experimental session, are considerably under the true value of π for low-payoff trials. This may indicate that subjects based their estimates on their response sequences. Alternatively, incentive may influence the underlying probability learning process and negative contrast may reflect basic differences in learning, rather than in strategies, on high- and low-payoff trials.

Whatever the explanation, the negative contrast effect is a phenomenon of some generality, not a peculiar consequence of the probability learning task or the subject population used. The effects observed in experiments with humans rather neatly parallel those obtained with rats in runways and T mazes (Black, 1968), both response times and choice proportions being depressed on low-incentive trials as a function of the difference in magnitude of the two amounts of reward.

Several models have been proposed to account for the effects of payoffs upon human probability learning (Luce & Suppes, 1965). Three of these will be considered, chosen for discussion because they are capable of generating predictions for both the learning curve and the sequence of responses, have provided good fits to several data sets, and represent somewhat different assumptions about the choice process.

Both Siegel (1959, 1961) and Estes (1962) have proposed models which incorporate two independent processes, probability learning and decision. Both assume that the underlying learning process asymptotes at π and is described by some variant of SLT. With respect to the decision process, Siegel has assumed that subjects choose a strategy that maximizes the sum of the expected utility of payoffs and the expected utility of varying one's response. This quantity is maximized when

$$P_\infty(A_1) = (k_1 + k_2)\pi + (.5 - k_2),\tag{1}$$

where the k_i are functions of utilities of payoffs and response variation. Siegel's key contribution, the notion that response variation has value for a subject, is consistent with both intuition and the finding that subjects who have not optimized have frequently indicated knowledge of the optimal strategy. Nevertheless, the results of direct attempts to test the validity of the concept of utility of response variation have been mixed (Messick, 1965; Halpern & Dengler, 1969; Halpern, Dengler, & Ulehla, 1968). Fits to asymptotic choice proportions support the model; for example, setting k_1 equal to k_2 in Equation (1), the Myers et al. (1963) data have been fit and an average absolute deviation of observed from predicted values of .022 obtained. Further direct tests of the basic assumptions would be useful, as would fits to choice proportions obtained with nonsymmetric payoff matrices. Of particular interest would be a test of a stochastic version; if SLT describes the learning of subjective probability (Siegel, 1961), sequential statistics and learning curves can, and should, be fit.

Random walk models (Bower, 1959; Estes, 1960, 1962) provide a more molecular analysis of choice behavior. In one such model, it is assumed that on any trial, n, the subject has probability $\phi_{i,n}$ of orienting toward A_i ; once the subject is oriented toward a response, the probability of making it is $p_{i,n}$.

Consideration of the following diagram may make the model clearer. Let S denote the starting position on a trial, O_i indicate orienting toward response i, and A_i represents execution of response i. Then the process on a single trial may be represented by

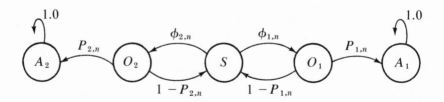

If $\phi_{i,n}$ and $p_{i,n}$ are independent functions of n described by SLT, then both have asymptotes at π_i and $P_\infty(A_1) = \pi^2/(1 - 2\pi(1 -))$. For π of .6, .7, and .8, predicted $P_\infty(A_1)$ are .692, .845, and .941, respectively; these values closely approximate those obtained by several investigators who used monetary payoffs. In the case in which no payoffs are at stake, $p_1 = p_2 = 1$ will yield $P_\infty(A_1) = \pi$.

The model has a certain appeal; it is conceptually simple and permits derivations of learning curves and sequential statistics (Cole, 1965, has fit such statistics), as well as response times (the expected number of orienting responses prior to reaching an A_i state is easily derived), and is thus subject to test in a variety of ways. However, the predicted lack of influence of payoff magnitude upon $P_\infty(A_i)$ is too strong a result; choice proportions are known to be a function of payoff magnitudes (markedly so when gains, or losses, depend upon the particular response), and the model should be modified to be responsive to this fact.

In contrast to the two models just considered, both of which postulate independent probability learning and decision processes, Myers and Atkinson's (1964) weak–strong model assumes that the response depends directly on the conditioning state of a sampled stimulus element; the element is either strongly or weakly conditioned to some A_1. Following an incorrect response, the sampled element changes conditioning state with probability δ; following a correct response, the transition to a new state occurs with probability μ. The model has yielded good fits to asymptotic choice proportions and sequential statistics in experiments employing a wide range of payoff matrices (Myers & Atkinson, 1964; Myers, Suydam, & Heuckeroth, 1966). Like the models considered previously, it is applicable to more than two-choices and, like the random walk models, it is also capable of describing choice latencies (Myers, Gambino, & Jones, 1967).

d. Discussion.   Our review of asymptotic choice proportions raises two questions. First, is there a fundamental probability learning process that develops with practice, asymptotes at π, and is directly manifested in prediction behavior in early trials, given proper instructions and no tangible payoffs? If so, overshooting is merely the result of conditions in which the subject is led to incorporate such probabilities into complex response strategies and decision rules. The Estes and Siegel models for choice under payoff are two representations of this view. On the other hand, the Myers–Atkinson model assumes a single learning process the rate and asymptote of which is determined by payoff parameters. The duoprocess position would be enhanced if estimates of event probability were demonstrated to develop in accord with SLT under conditions in which asymptotic choice proportions deviated from π; for example, under extended practice, instructions to optimize, or monetary payoffs.

A second unresolved issue is the extent of the decision making capabilities of subjects. Is the optimal strategy as difficult to learn as the widespread failure to optimize would suggest? Or is it that subjects perform more intelligently than it appears, maximizing an expected utility based on something more than monetary payoffs, and responding to reliable sequential cues that we have unthinkingly built into our sequences? With respect to this last point, a clearer picture of decision making capabilities should evolve with the use of unconstrained random sequences rather than sequences randomized in very small blocks.

One final point is in order. Evaluation of models of choice has too often rested solely, or at least primarily, on fits to marginal response probabilities from terminal trial blocks. It was noted earlier that this approach has a problem; the predicted asymptote may be exceeded not because the model is wrong, but because extended practice represents some second phase of performance not reflected in the model. On the other hand, good fits to such terminal choice proportions are hardly grounds for euphoria. The true learning process may not yet have asymptoted, and the fits may be fortuitous. The same model that fits ''asymptotic'' probabilities at 300–400 trials may also fit, with a change in parameter values, a higher ''asymptote'' obtained with still more practice. There is no clear way to define the true asymptote; consequently, good fits to terminal trial block proportions are by themselves, at best, weak support for a model. Sequential statistics would appear to provide more information about the status of stochastic models. Such data are considered next.

2. Sequential Dependencies

Fine-grain analyses of the data that focus on the dependency of responses upon preceding patterns of responses and events are considerably more informative than marginal probabilities. Such sequential dependencies provide a measure of trial-to-trial changes in performance and are, therefore, more direct tests of basic assumptions about reinforcing effects of trial outcomes. Furthermore, where earlier there was one marginal probability to predict for a single trial block, there now is a large array of probabilities conditional on the preceding pattern of responses, or events, or both.[1]

a. Runs of events. The run curve, response probability conditional upon the length of the preceding run of events, most directly reflects the

---

[1] Not all of these quantities will be independently distributed, and we will often require more parameters to fit them than to fit marginal statistics. Nevertheless, the main point is important; the use of conditional statistics typically increases the number of free predictions.

validity of the assumption that event occurrence is the effective reinforcement. According to SLT, with each successive repetition of the preceding event, probability of predicting that event should increase by some fraction of the distance to the upper bound of unity. Thus, the run curve should be a monotonically increasing, negatively accelerated, function of run length with asymptote of 1.0. It has long been apparent that this prediction of positive recency is not usually supported by data; negative recency, descent of the run curve after several event repetitions, has been observed in numerous studies (for example, Anderson & Whalen, 1960; Jarvik, 1951). Indeed, positive recency is ordinarily obtained only when the average run length is long—a condition met by intentionally constructing sequences with this property (Derks, 1963; Jones & Myers, 1966), or by using π of .7 or higher—and subjects have had at least 100 trials in the task (Derks, 1962; Edwards, 1961) or have had several hundred trials of event observation prior to prediction trials (Reber & Millward, 1968). Even in these cases, the asymptote of the run curve is consistently 10–15% below unity.

Findings of negative recency are not quite as disastrous for SLT as they might at first appear. Recognizing that the "gambler's fallacy" is strongly entrenched in the belief systems of most college students, one might argue that it plays a role in the probability learning task; subjects enter the experiment with a firm conviction that events come in short runs, a conviction that is largely reinforced at low π levels and generally takes several hundred trials to negate. This line of reasoning led Friedman and five coinvestigators (1964) to run subjects for three sessions of 384 trials each. The first two sessions presumably provided an opportunity to wash out the gambler's fallacy; 48-trial blocks with π of .5 were alternated with randomly sequenced blocks with π values ranging from .1 to .9 in increments of .1. In the critical third session, subjects experienced 288 trials with π of .8, preceded and followed by a single block with π of .5. Fits to a wide array of statistics were generally good and, most importantly, positive recency was obtained for both the .8 and terminal .5 series in the third session.

These results, together with other data in which negative recency is replaced by positive recency during the course of the session (Derks, 1963; Edwards, 1961), are consistent with the proposition that extended practice eliminates preexperimental biases, permitting the basic conditioning process envisaged within SLT to be revealed. Anderson (1964) has put forth an alternative interpretation of the results of Friedman and his co-workers. He noted that the probability of an event repetition was greater than .5 over the first two sessions. The schedule, rather than extinguishing preexperimental biases, may have built in a bias to expect runs to continue. According to this interpretation, the good fits of the third session are not the product of an ongoing conditioning process, but rather reflect the subject's memory of the event sequence of previous days. That subjects can learn event repetition probabilities, and that such learning is readily transferred in the presence of new schedules, has been amply demonstrated in several experiments (Anderson, 1960; Witte, 1964).

This argument led Friedman, Carterette, and Anderson (1968) to run subjects for 25 350-trial sessions under a 50 : 50 schedule. Analyses carried out for individual subjects, week by week, revealed a high degree of variability among subjects and over time, as well as a tendency to alternate responses that was at odds with the limited-memory assumption of the linear and pattern models presented earlier. Few subjects exhibited consistent positive recency and run curves typically asymptoted below the predicted value of unity. These failures of SLT were evident within the first week of the experiment.

It is not clear that these data provide broad grounds for rejecting SLT. Rather, they might be viewed as further restricting its range of application. Both the experimenters and Estes (1972) have noted that the use of 50 : 50 schedule may yield unrepresentative results. Prolonged practice with a low degree of success may motivate the subject to seek alternative strategies that will be more productive; this would account for the marked variability in the Friedman *et al.* (1968) study. Furthermore, long runs are infrequent with such a schedule, and thus, the event sequence may have reinforced those biases with which subjects entered the experiment.

b. Runs of successes. In the studies reviewed thus far noncontingent event schedules have been employed. In such schedules, the event, E_1 or E_2, is independent of trial number or of any aspect of the preceding sequence of responses or events. In contrast, Yellott (1969) employed a noncontingent success schedule in which the trial outcome, success or failure of the prediction, was independent of previous outcomes. The probability of a successful outcome—that is, that the event on a trial matched the response—was referred to as δ and was constant over responses. The advantage of such a "noncontingent success" schedule is that it provides a unique opportunity to differentiate the pattern and linear models. In the pattern model, learning occurs only following errors; following a correct response, the sampled element cannot change state and so the proportion of elements conditioned to each response (and, accordingly, response probability) does not change. As a consequence, the pattern model predicts that alternation responses in the noncontingent success task will be independent of the length of the preceding run of successes. On the other hand, in the linear model, only the event and not the outcome, dictates changes in response probability. The linear model predicts that the probability of alternation responses in the noncontingent success task will decrease as the run of preceding successes increases. Using δ of .8 and 1,

Yellott clearly demonstrated the correctness of the pattern model prediction. Furthermore, both variances and a variety of sequential statistics were well fit by the pattern model for the .8 block, and the estimate of the learning rate was .173, a value very close to that obtained in experiments using noncontingent event sequences.

These results clearly differentiate between alternative models and also provide strong support for the general proposition that a simple conditioning process underlies probability learning. There is, however, one departure from this pattern of support for SLT. Under the $\delta = 1$ schedule, some subjects exhibited very structured patterns of responding, consistent with the view that they had actively processed the event sequence, encoded it into structured chunks, and then had engaged in hypothesis testing. That sequential information is generally encoded in memory is also suggested by results of the few studies in which direct probes of memory have been employed (Millward & Reber, 1968; Vitz & Hazan, 1969). Perhaps one can best reconcile such evidence of memory processes with the generally excellent account of Yellott's data provided by the pattern model by concluding that his subjects utilized the information stored about the sequence only under the rather artificial $\delta = 1$ condition.

The overall implications of sequential dependency data for SLT are mixed. The form of event–run curves in the Friedman et al. (1964) study and of success-run curves in Yellott's study, and quantitative fits to these statistics support SLT. On the other hand, repeated findings of negative recency, the influence of event alternations in the Friedman et al. (1968) study, results of memory probes, and Yellott's $\delta = 1$ data also make it clear that information about the pattern of prior events is stored in memory and, except under carefully restricted conditions, influences predictive behavior.

C. Discussion

The broad impact of two decades of theoretical work on predictive behavior is evident. The conceptual and mathematical apparatus developed during the course of this work comprises a major general contribution to psychological theorizing. Regardless of evaluation of the success of SLT in explaining probability learning, the theoretical enterprise demonstrated the viability of an approach in which predictions of the fine details of the course of learning can be derived from a relatively small and basic set of assumptions.

It is more difficult to assess the outcome of the specific issue that generated the bulk of the prediction research. Is binary prediction the result of "the pervasive operation of a rather simple form of conditioning" (Estes, 1964, p. 121)? Certainly, the conditioning framework accounts for much of the data under a wide range of reinforcement schedules, and in several extensions of the simple noncontingent-event task. Nevertheless, fundamental predictions do frequently fail. Most critical for a simple stimulus–response theory is evidence that subjects remember (Millward & Reber, 1968) and respond to (Friedman *et al.* 1968) local event patterns, learn something about the probabilities of such patterns and transfer this knowledge to new sequences (Anderson, 1960; Witte, 1964), and formulate and test hypotheses based on event patterns (Yellott, 1969). In view of the successes of the theory, particularly in its application to the Friedman *et al.* (1964) data and to the early phases of the Yellott (1969) study, it may be that the failures cited serve not to invalidate the theory, but rather to circumscribe its range of application. In short, there is evidence of an underlying probability learning process which may best be characterized as associative learning, but whose operation is easily obscured by the propensity of subjects to seek sequential cues and to incorporate such information into their decision making process.

In retrospect, the need to distangle processing of event probabilities and sequential information is evident. Probability learning may be more directly investigated by collecting subject's estimates of event probabilities. There is already some evidence (Shanteau, 1970) that such estimates are described by Anderson's (1968) linear integration model, which simply assumes that the response is a weighted average of the preceding set of events. Since both Estes' linear model and a Bayesian revision model (Beach *et al.*, 1970) are special cases of the linear integration model (Anderson, 1968; Messick, 1970), they are also tenable. Further investigation of probability estimates may provide a better understanding of the process by which we develop subjective probabilities. Furthermore, such research may well converge with recent work in verbal learning addressed to the general issue of how information about stimulus frequency and recency are represented in memory (for example, Hintzman, 1969; Howell, 1973).

Sequential information processing may be studied profitably in the binary prediction situation with the use of considerably more constrained sequences than have been employed in the research described thus far. By systematically manipulating salient characteristics of the event sequence, such as length of runs or alternations, one is more likely to discover how subjects learn to respond to such sequential stimuli than if one employs random sequences and post hoc analyses of responses to patterns which chanced to occur. Such experimentation has been carried out concurrently with the development of models in which constructs such as encoding, memory, and hypothesis testing play a central role. The remainder of this chapter will deal with such developments.

III. SEQUENCE LEARNING: CONDITIONAL
EVENT SCHEDULES

In contrast to earlier research with noncontingent event schedules, no single theoretical position has dominated the research considered next. Consequently, several alternative models of prediction will be described first. These differ in orientation and detail but have the common goal of accounting for such sequential effects as negative recency and the common view that subjects remember event patterns and base their predictions upon that memory. The account of these models will be followed by a summary of relevant experimental findings. Then, armed with the facts, or some approximation thereof, I will attempt to evaluate the models under consideration.

A. Models

1. Fixed Memory-Span Models

In the simplest such model (Burke & Estes, 1957), the trace of the immediately preceding event is represented as a unique set of stimulus elements. Thus, on each trial, the subject samples from one of two distinct sets of elements. Application of the conditioning axioms of SLT reveals that the asymptotic probability of a repetition response, $P(A_{i,n}|E_{i,n-1})$, should slightly exceed the true probability that an event will be repeated on the next trial.

Restle (1961, pp. 109–111) has suggested an extension of the event-trace model capable of accounting for the ability of subjects to learn to respond to patterns spanning several trials. He assumes that the last k events are in memory; the response is based on a sample of elements drawn from a set corresponding to that pattern of k events. One strong prediction of the model is that subjects learn to respond without error to any pattern of length k or less that perfectly forecasts the next event. For example, if runs longer than length three never occur, the subject should learn not to make a repetition response following three events of the same type.

2. Determining the Structure of Sequences

Feldman and Hanna (1966) have assumed that subjects keep track of the changing conditional probabilities of E_1 following all possible event patterns of length k (five in their paper) or less. The subject first learns to discriminate the longest pair of subsequences S and S' such that the two differ only in the first, or earliest, position (for example, $E_1E_2E_1E_1E_2$ and $E_2E_2E_1E_1E_2$) and $P(E_1|S)$ differs significantly from $P(E_1|S')$. Discrimination is equivalent to probability matching at the level of subsequences; thus, $P(A_1|S)$ and $P(A_1|S')$ would match $P(E_1|S)$ and $P(E_1|S')$, respectively. Shorter subsequences would be discriminated later in learning. This structural-analysis model appears to credit subjects with more memory and computational power than they possess, but it may prove a useful baseline against which to evaluate performance.

3. Encoding Event Runs

The models just described place a considerable strain on subject's memories and one's credulity. The strain on memory at least is reduced if one takes a very different tack and assumes that subjects encode only certain types of patterns. In view of the considerable evidence attesting to the salience of event runs (Myers, 1970), a reasonable assumption is that the subject remembers only the type of event he has just seen and the number of times in a row that it has just been presented. The two models presented next assume just such a short-term memory as well as some long-term information about the distribution of run lengths.

a. Restle's (1961) schema model.   Restle assumed that the subject attempts to match the run in progress against some schema stored in memory. For example, if the events for the last four trials were $E_2E_1E_1E_1$, the probability of an A_1 response is the probability that the schema $E_2E_1E_1E_1E_1$, rather than $E_2E_1E_1E_1E_2$, is found in long-term memory. The probability of finding a particular schema was assumed to be a function of both its relative frequency of occurrence in the past and its length; Restle assumed that long runs are more salient than short runs in memory. Depending upon the distribution of runs in the event sequence, the schema model can predict either positive or negative recency. The overshooting observed in noncontingent event experiments is also predicted, particularly the pronounced overshooting observed with more than two choices. The schema model makes two qualitative predictions that were also noted for the k-span model; first, the probability of a repetition response will exceed the actual probability of an event repetition because of the weight given long runs, and second, subjects will learn always to predict the continuation of a run that has always continued, and the breaking off of a run that has always broken off in the past.

b. Gambino and Myers' (1967) generalization model.   These investigators assumed that the subject has a set of expectancies, one for each possible run length that he might encounter in the experiment. If the subject has just seen m consecutive events of a particular type, his expectancy that runs of length m will continue is increased or decreased by a fraction, depending upon whether the current run does continue. Furthermore, the continuation (breaking off) of a run of length m results in a generalized increase (decrease) in expectancies that runs of other lengths will continue; as one might expect, generalization is assumed to be greatest for run lengths close to m in value. The generalization assumption is the critical difference between this and other models capable of predicting negative recency. It provides a mechanism for generating errors at points in the sequence at which the next event is perfectly predictable. For example, suppose the event sequence contains no runs longer than five; the generalization model, in contrast to the models previously described, predicts a greater-than-zero error probability because of generalized expectancies resulting from the continuation of runs of lengths one through four.

B. Results

1. Responding to Event Contingencies

A direct test of the Burke–Estes trace model is provided by manipulating π_{11} , the probability that an event occurrence is repeated on the next trial. As the model predicts, the asymptotic probability of a repetition response is close to, but slightly above π_{11} for values of .3 and greater (Anderson, 1960; Engler, 1958; Witte, 1964); this result can also be predicted by the Restle and Gambino–Myers models. A result contrary to the prediction of over-shooting was obtained by Anderson who found that the probability of predicting an event repetition was below the event repetition probability for π_{11} of .1 and .2. Further evidence against the Burke–Estes and Restle models is provided by the run curves in Witte's experiments; the Burke-Estes model generally predicted too much positive recency, and the Restle model predicted too much negative recency. These data also are inconsistent with the Feldman–Hanna model; since the occurrence of an event depends only upon the preceding event, the structural analysis model would incorrectly predict flat run curves.

The runs model stimulated several studies in which the event sequences were constructed of a limited number of run lengths. In a typical sequence, equal numbers of runs of lengths 2 and 5 might be randomly ordered; following any run length except two, the next event is perfectly predictable. At the uncertainty point, that is, after a run of length 2 in the example, the probability of a repetition response exceeds the probability of an event repetition (Gambino & Myers, 1966; Restle, 1966), a result predicted by both run models. In addition, the probability of a repetition response increases with the number of long runs (for example, length 5) and decreases with the number of short runs (for example, length 2) immediately preceding the run in progress (Butler, Myers, & Myers, 1969), a result demanded by the reinforcement axioms of the Gambino–Myers model.

However, when contingencies among run lengths are not random, the results are more difficult for any runs model. For example, if the probability is high that long and short runs will alternate, repetition response probability will be higher when the run preceding the current run was short than when it was long (Butler *et al.*, 1969).

The event contingencies considered thus far only scratch the surface of the sequential processing capacity of human subjects. In an attempt to evaluate their structural analysis model, Feldman and Hanna generated a sequence with some contingencies complex enough to defy brief description here. The subjects learned to respond differentially to different patterns; in fact, the probability of predicting an event following each of 62 different patterns of length 5 or less is related to the true probability of the event following that pattern by a linear regression line having slope of .998 and intercept of .013. While Feldman and Hanna have taken this result as evidence of contingency matching, a prediction of their model, it should be noted that there is considerable scatter about this best-fitting function. Nevertheless, the main point is well taken; while runs are extremely salient sequential cues, other patterns can also serve as a basis for prediction.

2. Errors of Prediction

All of the models described in the preceding section, except the Gambino–Myers generalization model, predict that the subject will learn to eliminate errors at those points at which the sequence is perfectly predictable. Thus, in a sequence resulting from the random ordering of runs of lengths 2 and 5, subjects should learn to always predict the preceding event if the ongoing run is of length 1, 3, or 4, and to predict the alternate event if the current run is of length 5. Inappropriate failures to make a repetition response will be referred to as anticipatory errors while inappropriate repetition responses will be referred to as perseverative errors. While such errors are clearly less frequent than would be expected if subjects were guessing or merely matching the overall probability of an event repetition, they continue to occur after as many as 700 trials with no indication that further practice would result in improvement; indeed, error rates appear to asymptote within the first 100 trials (Gambino & Myers, 1966; Restle, 1966; Rose & Vitz, 1966). Typically, anticipatory errors increase as mean run length decreases and perseverative errors are an increasing function of the number of run lengths present and of the difference in lengths when only two are present. These error data, as well as repetition responses at the uncertainty point, are well fit by the generalization model (Gambino & Myers, 1967).

Contrary to the predictions of the generalization model, or of any run model, rules about patterns other than runs can also be learned although, again, not to an errorless criterion. Rose and Vitz (1966) found better than chance acquisition of such rules as "if the current pattern is 1121, predict a 2." Wolin, Weichel, Terebinski, and Hansford (1965) have also reported some learning of responses to patterns other than runs.

3. The Acquisition of Sequential Information

Of the models considered, only the Feldman–Hanna structural analysis model predicts differential rates of learning different contingencies; the schema and generalization models envisage the encoding only of runs and no one has hypothesized any relationship between learning rates and event patterns for the k-span model. Hanna and Feldman's assumption that long subsequences are discriminated first appears to be incorrect; their own data analyses revealed that subjects first responded differentially to patterns which span fewer events. For patterns of the same length, the order in which subjects learned to respond with different probabilities appeared to depend upon how much the patterns differed with respect to probability of the next event.

In contrast to the precise pattern analysis assumed by Feldman and Hanna, Wolin et al. (1965) characterize their subjects as first learning general, inexact, aspects of the sequence and later more specific rules. For example, a subject might learn first that the sequence was composed of runs and single alternations and later learn that runs of E_1's had to be an odd-numbered length or even some specific length. Still another view of the learning process is provided by Butler et al. (1969). In their data, it appeared that learning of recurrent sequential units (runs of different lengths) and learning of contingencies between such units proceeded concurrently; however, learning the units, as indicated by anticipatory and perseverative errors, appeared to stabilize well before contingency learning was complete.

4. Transfer

Once probabilistic contingencies are learned, their effects persist for many trials after the sequence has been changed. At the end of 200 trials of π_{11} of .5, Anderson (1960) observed that the probability of a repetition response was approximately .7 for subjects originally trained with π_{11}'s ranging from .6 to .9 and approximately .5 for subjects originally trained with π_{11}'s of from .1 to .4; there was no indication that the two groups of curves were converging. Still more impressive evidence of transfer was obtained by Witte (1964), who found that run curves still differed as a function of original training after four once-a-week sessions at π_{11} of .5. Such persistent effects of original training are difficult for any of the models under consideration.

Using a four-choice prediction task, Jones and Erickson (1972) have demonstrated transfer of still other types of contingencies. Groups trained to attend to the length and event class of two preceding runs performed better in a transfer task incorporating multirun contingencies than did groups trained only to attend to current run length or given no training. None of the four models presented thus far can account for these results because what was transferred was not knowledge of the consequences of specific patterns—be they runs or various other configurations over several event positions—but rather an abstract rule, perhaps "pay attention to the last two run lengths and the positions in which they appeared."

Following Yellott's (1969) lead, Colker and Myers (1971) employed a transfer phase in which all predictions were correct. Prior to this all-correct phase, subjects experienced one of four types of sequences composed of two run lengths; these varied with respect to length of the two event runs and probability that a run of a particular length would be followed by a run of the same length. Protocols for the all-correct phase were divided into two categories—simple periodic solutions which required that the subject remember only the run in progress and the length of the immediately preceding run (for example, 2/5/2/5/2 . . . , the digits represent run lengths) and complex solutions which encompassed all response patterns that required the subject to remember more than the immediately preceding run length (for example, 2/2/5/5/2//5/5/2/2/5//2/2/ . . .). Within each experimental group, there were significantly more errors in the training phase for subjects who subsequently exhibited complex solutions. Furthermore, those groups with higher mean error rates in training had more complex solutions in the transfer phase. None of the models we have considered encompass such results. They seem to require us to conceptualize a limited-capacity information processing organism; when, either because of preexperimental biases or experimental influences, strategies are pursued which place a heavy load on short-term memory, more predictive errors are made. Butler's (1969) finding that a display of prior events beyond the current run results in more errors than a display of only the current run is also consistent with the limited capacity hypothesis; give a subject information and he will try to use it and, if the information is irrelevant, as prior runs were in Butler's study, the subject's processing will be impaired.

5. Memory for Binary Patterns

It is clear that subjects do not learn perfectly in the face of patterns that are perfect predictors of the next event, at least in the sequences under consideration, all of which contain some points at which there is stimulus uncertainty. The Gambino–Myers model provides one mechanism for errors; an alternative explanation is simply that short-term memory is not perfect under the processing load placed upon the subject with such sequences. This possibility suggests that one look at memory for event patterns.

Glanzer and Clark (1963) provided subjects with brief exposures to sets of eight binary figures. Accuracy of subsequent reproduction was best for runs of eight like figures, deteriorated as the number of runs increased, but was considerably improved again for single alternations. Millward and Reber (1968) obtained similar results in the context of a binary prediction task, probing on each trial for a specific event k trials back. As would be expected, recall accuracy decreased as a function of depth of probe. Of somewhat greater interest is the finding that, with depth held constant, recall accuracy decreased as a function of the number of runs intervening between the target item and the probe, with one exception: when a single alternation intervened, there was a decided upturn in the recall function. The results of these two experiments suggest that the amount remembered depended upon the patterning of events, a result at odds with both the fixed-span and Feldman–Hanna models. Furthermore, as Restle and Gambino and Myers have assumed, runs were basic units of information storage. On the other hand, other patterns were recalled above a chance level.

Vitz and Hazan (1969) also probed memory in the context of the typical binary prediction task. They, however, probed only three times during the session, asking subjects to recall as much as they could of the preceding event series. Consistent with the implications of several transfer studies cited earlier (Anderson, 1960; Witte, 1964), rather accurate long-term memory was exhibited.

The relationship between prediction and memory is clearer in another study (Myers, 1970). Probes of memory for recent events yielded more errors for those experimental conditions in which errors of prediction were greatest. Thus, contrary to all of the models considered, short-term memory is fallible and, in fact, correlated with predictive errors. Of additional interest is the distribution of remembered run lengths. In more than 97% of 1,440 probes of memory, the preceding run length was either remembered correctly or was remembered as shorter than it actually was. As might be expected, the distribution function was monotonic; the correct run was reported most often and the probability of a particular run length being reported decreased as a function of distance from the correct value.

C. Discussion

It is clear that, as Restle, and Gambino and Myers, have hypothesized, event runs are units of encoding and information about the events following each run length is available in long-term memory. It is equally clear that, contrary to the runs models, other patterns of events are encoded. It appears that an appropriate model will incorporate the assumption that what is remembered and responded to is not a fixed-span of events but rather a variable event span whose length depends upon the particular pattern of events. Furthermore, such a model will be all too human; unlike the current model, it will have a fallible short-term memory.

Two possible mechanisms for memory failure are suggested by the Myers (1970) data, in particular, by the finding that run lengths were almost always remembered as shorter than they actually were if they were remembered incorrectly. First, errors may occur at event input; with some probability, a counter may fail to register the incoming event. Second, errors may occur at retrieval. For example, suppose the subject has correctly registered a run of length five. Then, he has recently registered a run of length four, before that, a run of length three, and so on. Assuming that traces of inputs vary in strength as a function of proximity to the probe, and that the probability of retrieving a trace when probed is proportional to strength, something very much like the observed distribution of reported run lengths would be obtained. Distinguishing between these two positions will be of interest. In addition, memory probe experiments employing other sequential constraints are required to determine whether the apparent information loss is a general phenomenon, or is peculiar to the run-structured sequences employed in the experiment described.

Transfer studies demonstrate long-term perseverative effects of training with event contingencies, effects that seem to be beyond the scope of the models considered. It appears that, having once formed hypotheses about the sequences, subjects give greater weight to those event patterns that support their hypotheses, only slowly changing their response pattern as evidence accumulates that the sequential structure has changed. In line with this view, probes of memory during transfer might reveal that subjects trained differently would differ in what they recall of the common transfer sequence; subjects trained with high event repetition probabilities might be more accurate in recalling prior run lengths, whereas subjects trained with low event repetition probabilities might be more accurate in recalling event alternations.

The Colker and Myers (1971) results suggest a limited-capacity information processing system. If this is so, failures in short-term memory, and perhaps the amount of experience required for appropriate revision of hypotheses during transfer, will be a function of the amount of material stored in short-term memory and the complexity of rules for response selection. This suggests that part of the subject's problem in eliminating anticipatory and perseverative errors may lie in striving for perfection. As numerous investigators have noted, even in the face of more clearly random sequences subjects believe that there is a solution, a strategy that will completely eliminate errors. Presumably, the subject develops and tests progressively more complex hypotheses, and, therefore, stores more information, in an attempt to find the solution. The result is a loss of information from an overburdened processing system with the consequence that errors which could be eliminated are not. One further implication of this view of the subject as a limited-capacity information processing system is that a sufficient model cannot merely incorporate a mechanism for memory failures (whether at input or retrieval) but must also specify how such failures depend upon the information processing load. This implies, in turn, a need for a more precise definition of such terms as "processing load" and "sequence complexity."

A clearer picture of sequential processing has emerged from studies in which the number and complexity of hypotheses has been reduced through the use of repeated event patterns. In particular, such studies have provided further data relevant to two related questions: What determines the subject's response at any position within the pattern? What determines the relative level of difficulty of responses at different positions within a pattern? The next section provides a discussion of models and data within the context of such deterministic sequences.

IV. SEQUENCE LEARNING: DETERMINISTIC SCHEDULES

In this section, how subjects learn to predict sequences that consist of repetitions of a single pattern is considered. The pattern could be a simple binary one, for example, *aaabb*. At the other extreme, it may involve more than two events and be generated by a relatively complex set of rules. Regardless of the complexity of the sequence, interest here will focus on the serial position function. Of primary concern will be the ability of different models to predict variation in error rate over positions in the pattern as a function of pattern structure.

A. Models

1. An Association Model

Vitz and Todd (1967) have proposed a model to account for prediction of repeated simple binary patterns of the form *m a*'s followed by *n b*'s, for example, *aaabb*. They assume that the pattern can be viewed as a set of stimuli where each stimulus is the run preceding a position. Thus, if the pattern *aaabb* is repeatedly presented, the stimuli and responses are: $a \rightarrow a, aa \rightarrow a, aaa \rightarrow b, b \rightarrow b, bb \rightarrow a$. The stimulus–response connections are assumed to be learned all-or-none with probability c, as in Bower's (1961) one-element model of paired-associate learning. If the association is not learned, the subject guesses the correct response with probability g. Such a model predicts stationarity, constant probability of a correct response over trial blocks prior to the last error to a stimulus, as well as independence of responses. Furthermore, assuming that c is constant over positions, error rates should not vary significantly with position in the sequence or with length of runs of a's and b's.

The scope of the model is quite limited; for example, it fails to account for patterns such as $aabab$ because the stimulus a is followed by an a at Position 2, and by a b at Position 5. Thus, the preceding run does not contain sufficient information to allow the subject to learn the entire pattern. Nevertheless, if the model successfully accounts for learning of the simple patterns for which it was designed, it might be elaborated to deal with the more complex patterns much in the way that Bower's one-element model for paired-associate learning was extended to account for additional stages such as stimulus differentiation and response integration.

2. A Two-Stage Model

Restle (1967) has provided one possible elaboration of the model sketched above. He distinguishes between "mandatory" and "optional" positions; in the pattern $aabab$, Positions 2 and 5 are optional in the sense that the subject's response is not completely determined by the preceding run length. Restle's account of the learning of mandatory positions is essentially the same as Vitz and Todd's although he prefers to speak of learning mandatory rules rather than forming associations. Responses at optional positions are assumed to require a second all-or-none stage to be learned; thus, error rates should be higher at optional than at mandatory positions.

3. Hierarchical Rule Learning Model

The two models described above deal with prediction of binary sequences. A richer conceptualization incorporating more, and more complex, hypotheses, becomes possible when one considers multichoice tasks. Restle (1970), and Restle and Brown (1970), have analyzed the learning of such tasks. They have assumed that subunits are learned first and then higher-order rules, which integrate such subunits. The model has great scope, predicting the relative difficulty of sequences, the relative difficulty of positions within sequences, the effects of manipulations within a few positions in sequences, and transfer effects. Three operators are defined (others are possible); $T(X)$ is a transposition operator and implies incrementing each element in X by one; if X is the single element 4, $T(X)$ implies 45, and if X is the subunit 123, $T(X)$ is 123234. The second operator, $R(X)$ is a repetition operator; thus $R(5)$ implies 55 and $R(23)$ implies 2323. The third operator is a mirror-image operator which implies subtracting each element in X from 7 (or in general, from one more than the total number of events); thus, $M(2)$ implies 25 and $M(14)$ implies 1463. Now consider the sequence 12126565. This may be generated by letting $X = 1$, applying T, then R, then M; one may represent this sequence of operations as $M(R(T(1)))$. Restle and Brown assume that error rates will be a function of the level of the rule applied to generate a response for a position in the sequence; level corresponds to distance to the left of X in this notation. Thus, Position 5, which is generated by the leftmost, or M, operation, should prove most difficult. Positions 3 and 7, which require the R operation to generate a correct response, should be next in error rate. Events at Positions 2, 4, 6, and 8 are generated by the transposition operation which is the lowest level (rightmost) operation, and should, therefore, be easiest to learn. Two additional predictions are immediately evident. First, if one divides the pattern into subunits and rearranges these so that the new sequence is no longer generated by a single rule hierarchy, the sequence should be considerably more difficult to learn. Second, transfer to a new sequence employing the same rule hierarchy but a different element X should be positive.

B. Results

1. Binary Event Sequences

a. Mandatory positions.   Both Vitz and Todd (1967) using patterns with only mandatory positions, and Restle (1967) using more complex patterns, have found that an all-or-none learning model provides a reasonable fit to data at such positions. Furthermore, Vitz and Todd tested two critical predictions of the all-or-none model, stationarity of error probabilities and independence of responses, and obtained no significant difference. Nevertheless, there is at least one problem with the model. Both Vitz and Todd, and Derks and House (1965), have noted higher error rates at the first and last positions in a run than at other positions. One not very plausible interpretation of such a result is that c, the conditioning probability, varies as a function of position in the run. It is more likely that subjects lose track of the preceding run length; several of Vitz and Todd's subjects reported miscounting, and data considered in Section III clearly demonstrate that this happens in nondeterministic sequences.

Another possible source of difficulty, even in simple patterns, is suggested by a result obtained by Garner and Gottwald (1967). Using a simple *aaabb* pattern, they found that prediction errors were most frequent following a run of two *a*'s. The pattern provided greater difficulty when the second *a* was presented on trial 1, that is, *aabbaaa* . . . On the other hand, *aaabbaaa* . . . was relatively easy for subjects. Apparently, subjects develop expectancies which conform to some simple hypothesis about the structure of the pattern; in this case, subjects appear to expect a double alternation. Errors pile up at positions that deviate from the expected structure. Furthermore, the extent to which early trials confirm the subject's expectancy influences difficulty of learning the pattern.

  b. Optional positions. As Restle (1967) hypothesized, optional positions, those at which the response is not completely determined by the immediately preceding run length, do have higher error rates than mandatory positions. This is evident in both his own data and those obtained by Derks and House (1965). Furthermore, the frequency distribution for errors is well fit by Restle's two-stage model. However, in both studies there is variation in error rates among optional positions and, in some of the Derks and House sequences, some mandatory positions have high error rates. These are generally at the end of runs longer than length three, suggesting miscounting. In short, there is support for the hypothesis of all-or-none learning of stages but Restle's model, like Vitz and Todd's, fails to provide a complete account of variations in error rate over positions in the pattern.

  A closer look at how the second, optional position, stage is learned is instructive. Consider one sequence employed by Restle:

Event: *a*   *a*   b   *b*   a   *b*   b   a   *b*
Position: 1   2   3   4   5   6   7   8   9

Italicized letters denote optional positions. Note that Positions 1 and 7 demand different responses, but the preceding five events, or three runs, are identical. No other pairs of positions require this much information in order to be discriminated. Nevertheless, only Position 1 was clearly more difficult than other optional points; there were actually slightly more errors at Positions 2 and 9 than at 7. These results argue against an associative theory in which combinations of preceding events or runs are a discriminative cue for prediction. If such a theory were correct, one would expect both Positions 1 and 7 to be considerably more difficult than other positions on two grounds. First, it is reasonable to assume that it takes more trials to integrate a longer discriminative cue; if this were not true, there is no reason for the consistent differences in error rate between mandatory and optional positions. Second, longer discriminative cues place a greater burden on memory and should result in more miscounting and thus more errors. That this relationship between memory load and processing exists was amply documented in Section III. Restle has proposed an alternative account of Stage 2 learning. He assumes that following the learning of mandatory positions the subject develops some general rule that integrates the individual runs. Errors should develop at positions which depart from the general rule since such positions have to be learned as exceptions. In the example under consideration, the sequence can be described as a repetition of the simple pattern *bba* except for Position 1, which has a notably higher error rate than other positions. This analysis is consistent with Garner and Gottwald's account of simple pattern learning and confirms their emphasis on the role of expectancies.

2. N-ary Sequences (N > 2)

Restle and Brown (1970) have reported a series of ten experiments in which a six-choice task was employed. Such experiments are an advance over binary choice experiments because they permit greater variation in the rules used to construct sequences and because errors are more informative; one notes not only where errors occur, but also which erroneous response occurred.

Learning of such sequences is dictated by abstract properties of the sequence, such as scales (for example, 2345) and trills (for example, 2323), rather than by specific events or numerical intervals between events. Restle and Brown first demonstrated this by comparing learning of an initial sequence with learning of three other sequences derived from it by either transposing the initial sequence by one event (for example, 123 becomes 234), inverting it (123 becomes 654, or by transposing and inverting it (123 becomes 543). Sequence had little effect on error rates. More important to the point at issue, sequences did not differ with respect to the profiles of error rates over positions.

Errors in this study were typically most frequent at the beginning of the scale and trill subunits and were the result of overextension of the previous subunit. Thus, in a sequence beginning 234654, the fourth position would have a high error rate and the error would frequently be the prediction of a 5 instead of 6. Fritzen and Johnson (1969) have shown that at least one cause of such errors is the subject's failure to recognize the end of the subunit; error rates were lower when all subunits in a sequence were of the same length or when subunits could not physically be continued (for example, 321).

Additional evidence for the importance of subunits such as runs and trills was obtained by using an ambiguous sequence. For example, 6543432345 may be chunked either as 6543/432/345 (scales) or as 65/434/323/45 (trills). Different error profiles can be produced by pretraining on sequences clearly composed of scales or of trills, or by pretraining on an ambiguous sequence with pauses introduced which chunk the sequence into scales or into trills. It is quite evident that the errors produced in transfer are a result of the induced expectancy. For example, in the ambiguous sequence presented above, subjects trained to expect scales should make more errors at Position 5 than subjects trained to expect trills, and the error for the scales group should usually be a 2; this is what was observed.

Given that subjects learn rules which guide them through subunits of the overall pattern, how are the subunits integrated? Restle's (1970) hierarchical rule learning model provides an answer which receives considerable support from the data of the last five Restle and Brown experiments. Several results are of particular relevance. First, the error rate at a position in a sequence appears to depend not upon the particular rule required to generate the response at that position, but rather upon where that rule lies in the rule hierarchy. For example, given the sequence 12122323121223236565545465655454, which is so much more elegantly represented by $M(R(T(R(T(1)))))$, we find most difficulty at the seventeenth position, where the M operation must be applied, somewhat less at Positions 9 and 25, where the higher-order (leftmost) R operation must be applied, and so on. The sequence generated by $T(M(R(T(R(1)))))$ has much the same error profile indicating that position in the rule hierarchy, rather than the specific rule applied, is critical.

Second, there is some evidence that when a sequence can not be described by a hierarchy of rules, performance at transition points between subunits is poor. Restle and Brown found that a sequence obtained by randomly ordering subunits of a sequence generated by a rule hierarchy had more errors at the first position within subunits; typically, these were due to overextension of the previous subunit. This result not only confirms the importance of the rule hierarchy in integrating subunit learning but also indicates that lower-order regularities can be learned in the absence of higher-order rules.

Third, there is evidence that rule hierarchies are learned from the bottom up, or from right to left in terms of the operator notation we have used. In essence, subjects appear to first determine the lowest element X, then to learn the operation on it, for example $T(X)$, gradually building up the hierarchy. At each level, the repetition operator R is tried out first, resulting in errors. This is natural since the subject knows that the whole pattern is repeated and does not know the pattern length. This interpretation suggests that subjects should learn a complex pattern most readily if small subunits are first learned and then the pattern is extended by introducing rules gradually in a lower- to higher-order direction. The conjecture was borne out; subjects had less difficulty in learning the sequence $T(M(T(R(T(1)))))$ when preceded by a series of training blocks in the order $T(1)$, $R(T(1))$, $T(R(T(1)))$, $M(T(R(T(1))))$ than when preceded by training blocks in the order $T(1)$, $T(M(1))$, $T(M(T(1)))$, $T(M(T(R(1))))$.

It is possible that the results considered are specific to the prediction task, that they depend upon verbal rehearsal and a conscious and deliberate encoding and storing of information. Two experiments, employing rather different methodologies, have addressed this issue. Garner and Gottwald (1968) required subjects to observe repeating patterns of eight binary events, presented either visually or auditorily, and at one of five rates of presentation. Subjects stopped the presentation when they felt able to provide a description of the pattern. Stopping point and accuracy of description were differently affected by the independent variables at high and low speeds, a result which led the authors to conclude that processing at low speeds ("learning") is an active intellectualized process, while at high speeds ("perception") it is a passive experience of an integrated sequence. Restle and Burnside (1972), who required subjects to track six-event sequences by pushing the appropriate button when a light came on, reached a very different conclusion. Redoing several of the Restle and Brown prediction experiments with the tracking task, they found similar effects on error profiles. In contrast to Garner and Gottwald, they concluded that learning and perception of serial patterns are closely related, that both involve a rather rapid organization of serial information, an organization controlled by rule hierarchies.

C. Discussion

The data present difficulties for associative models. The generally intricate profiles of errors argue against simple conditioning of responses to serial positions. Simple conditioning on the basis of last event, the models with which we began this chapter, also clearly does not stand up to the results. Conditioning of responses to the immediately preceding run, essentially the Vitz–Todd model, does not completely describe even data from simple binary patterns, although the addition of some forgetting mechanism might suffice to resolve the problem. Nevertheless, it is evident that a complex conditioned stimulus must be assumed if one is to cope with optional positions in binary sequences, or with the results obtained in multichoice prediction tasks.

Conceivably, the conditioned stimulus may be some preceding set of events or runs. However, as was noted in considering the Restle (1967) data, and as Restle and Brown (1970) have also found in their six-choice experiments, there is no clear relationship between errors at a position and the memory load required for accurate response discrimination. Furthermore, Restle and Brown have also noted that changes in the sequence may have effects at some position quite distant from the locus of change. Developing an adequate account of the data from an associative framework may prove quite challenging.

Restle and Brown's (1970) rule hierarchy model provides an alternative frame of reference. It is assumed that subjects discriminate some basic element, learn to operate on this, and proceed to concatenate operators until the sequence is learned. Operators that are applied to larger subsequences are learned later. Errors occur at the beginning of subunits and these are erroneous extensions of the currently applied operator. Errors also apply at points where there is ambiguity about the nature of the subunit and the subject makes the wrong decision on the basis of prior expectations. Finally, errors occur because of premature attempts to apply the repetition operator, presumably owing to a lack of definition of the pattern length.

Several issues merit consideration. First, why do errors accumulate at initial positions in subunits? Fritzen and Johnson (1969) have noted several possible sources of such errors. The subject may not know when to terminate the preceding subunit. Their data indicate that this is a problem for the subject. It is not clear whether this is because the subject has miscounted the length of the preceding subunit or has not learned what its length should be. Furthermore, some errors may occur when subjects know that a new operator is to be applied but are not sure which operator or know which operator but are not sure of which number to begin with. The relative contributions of these factors should be assessed.

Second, what is the nature of the learning process? How is each new rule acquired? Is the process all-or-none, as Restle (1967) at one time hypothesized? Are all rules equally easy to learn? Or does the ease of acquiring a rule depend upon the rule and perhaps upon the nature of the rules that have already been learned? There is little information on this, but it would be surprising if all rules were really equivalent in difficulty and if difficulty of a particular rule did not depend upon the overall configuration of rules.

Third, the Garner and Gottwald (1968) and Restle and Burnside (1972) results on perception versus learning of patterned information lead to discrepant conclusions. These studies differ in many ways—in the sequences, independent variables, and dependent variables. Determining the conditions under which the same sequences yield equivalent results with fast and slow event input rates seems fundamental to delineating the generality of any theory of sequential information processing and to defining the boundary conditions for its application. With respect to generality of such theories, Jones' (1974) discussion of serial patterns provides a useful consideration of a wide range of theories and their validity for tasks ranging from prediction to perception to recall of sequences.

Finally, given some representation of rules, how does the subject generate his response? Greeno and Simon (1974) have noted that the same pattern description can be a base for very different procedures for deriving the appropriate response. These procedures differ in short-term memory requirements—how many and which elements must be immediately available—and in the number of operations which must be applied in order to arrive at the appropriate response. Experimental investigation of the process of response generation appears to be a logical next step for investigators in this field.

V. CONCLUSIONS

The course of prediction research and theorizing has been a steady progression through three overlapping stages. The first was marked by the use of random sequences in experimentation and very simple associative models in theorizing. It served to set boundary conditions on the applicability of the models under consideration. That early work has generated two paths— more direct studies of how event probabilities are represented and of how patterns of events are processed.

The second stage was marked by the introduction of constrained sequences in which stimulus uncertainty was reduced but not eliminated. Associative models became more complex than previously, with the run, rather than the event, being a candidate for the discriminative stimulus. In addition, models were introduced that were more oriented toward the information processing approach developing in other fields of learning and in perception. The importance of a run of events as a salient stimulus became clear but at the same time it was also evident that subjects could encode, remember, and respond to considerably more complex patterns. In addition, the need to consider the capacity of the information processing system became apparent.

In the current, third, stage of investigation, subjects have been faced with recurrent patterns of events. The resulting data place the difficulties encountered by an associative theory in full perspective. Progress toward an information-processing model has been made. Prediction of future stages of theoretical development is a risky affair, but it would seem that such work will center about delineation of rules not yet considered, the relative difficulty of learning different rules, the nature of the rule-learning process, the generality across paradigms of various models, and a clearer definition of the information processing stages, with particular emphasis on the relationship between pattern representation and response generation.

REFERENCES

Anderson, N. H. Effect of first-order conditional probability in a two-choice learning situation. *Journal of Experimental Psychology,* 1960, **59,** 73–93.

Anderson, N. H. An evaluation of stimulus sampling theory. In A. W. Melton (Ed.), *Categories of human learning*. New York: Academic Press, 1964.

Anderson, N. H. A simple model for information integration. In R. P. Abelson *et al.* (Eds.), *Theories of cognitive consistency: A source book*. Chicago: Rand-McNally, 1968.

Anderson, N. H., & Whalen, R. E. Likelihood judgments and sequential effects in a two-choice probability learning situation. *Journal of Experimental Psychology*, 1960, **60**, 111–120.

Atkinson, R. C., & Estes, W. K. Stimulus sampling theory. In R. D. Luce, R. R. Bush, & E. Galanter (Eds.), *Handbook of mathematical psychology*. Vol. II. New York: Wiley, 1963.

Beach, L. R., Rose, R. M., Sayeki, Y., Wise, J. A., & Carter, W. B. Probability learning: Response proportions and verbal estimates. *Journal of Experimental Psychology*, 1970, **86**, 165–170.

Beach, L. R., & Swensson, R. G. Instructions about randomness and run dependency in two-choice learning. *Journal of Experimental Psychology*, 1967, **75**, 279–282.

Black, R. W. Shifts in magnitude of reward and contrast effects in instrumental and selective learning. *Psychological Review*, 1968, **75**, 114–126.

Bower, G. H. Choice-point behavior. In R. R. Bush & W. K. Estes (Eds.), *Studies in mathematical learning theory*. Stanford, California: Stanford University Press, 1959.

Bower, G. H. Application of a model to paired-associate learning. *Psychometrika*, 1961, **26**, 255–280.

Braveman, N. S., & Fischer, G. J. Instructionally induced strategy and sequential information in probability learning. *Journal of Experimental Psychology*, 1968, **76**, 674–676.

Burke, C. J., & Estes, W. K. A component model for stimulus variables in discrimination learning. *Psychometrika*, 1957, **22**, 133–146.

Butler, P. A. The role of information in choice behavior. Unpublished doctoral dissertation, University of Massachusetts, Amherst, 1969.

Butler, P. A., Myers, N. A., & Myers, J. L. Contingencies among event runs in binary prediction. *Journal of Experimental Psychology*, 1969, **79**, 424–429.

Castellan, N. J., Jr. Effect of change of payoff in probability learning. *Journal of Experimental Psychology*, 1969, **79**, 178–182.

Cole, M. Search behavior: A correlation procedure for three-choice probability learning. *Journal of Mathematical Psychology*, 1965, **2**, 145–170.

Colker, R., & Myers, J. L. Effects of sequential structure upon binary prediction under an all-correct procedure. *Journal of Experimental Psychology*, 1971, **89**, 416–418.

Cotton, J. W., & Rechtschaffen, A. Replication report: Two- and three-choice verbal conditioning phenomena. *Journal of Experimental Psychology*, 1958, **56**, 96–97.

Derks, P. L. The generality of the "conditioning axiom" in human binary prediction. *Journal of Experimental Psychology*, 1962, **63**, 538–545.

Derks, P. L. Effect of run length on the "gambler's fallacy." *Journal of Experimental Psychology*, 1963, **65**, 213–214.

Derks, P. L., & House, J. I. Effect of event run structure on prediction of recursive binary sequences. *Psychological Reports*, 1965, **17**, 447–456.

Detambel, M. H. A test of a model for a multiple-choice behavior. *Journal of Experimental Psychology*, 1955, **49**, 97–104.

Edwards, W. Probability learning in 1000 trials. *Journal of Experimental Psychology*, 1961, **62**, 385–394.

Engler, J. Marginal and conditional stimulus and response probabilities in verbal conditioning. *Journal of Experimental Psychology*, 1958, **55**, 303–317.

Estes, W. K. Toward a statistical theory of learning. *Psychological Review*, 1950, **57**, 94–107.

Estes, W. K. A random walk model for choice behavior. In K. J. Arrow, S. Karlin, & P. Suppes (Eds.), *Mathematical methods in the social sciences*. Stanford, California: Stanford University Press, 1960.

Estes, W. K. Theoretical treatments of differential reward in multiple-choice learning and two-person interactions. In J. H. Criswell, H. Solomon, & Suppes (Eds.), *Mathematical models in small group processes.* Stanford, California: Stanford University Press, 1962.

Estes, W. K. Probability learning. In A. W. Melton (Ed.), *Categories of human learning.* New York: Academic Press, 1964.

Estes, W. K. Research and theory on the learning of probabilities. *Journal of the American Statistical Association,* 1972, **67,** 81–102.

Estes, W. K., & Straughan, J. H. Analysis of a verbal conditioning situation in terms of statistical learning theory. *Journal of Experimental Psychology,* 1954, **47,** 225–234.

Feldman, J., & Hanna, J. F. The structure of responses to a sequence of binary events. *Journal of Mathematical Psychology,* 1966, **3,** 371–387.

Flood, M. M. Environmental non-stationarity in a sequential decision-making experiment. In R. M. Thrall, C. H. Coombs, & R. L. Davis (Eds.), *Decision processes.* New York: Wiley, 1954.

Friedman, M. P., Burke, C. J., Cole, M., Keller, L., Millward, R. B., & Estes, W. K. Two choice behavior under extended training with shifting probabilities of reinforcement. In R. C. Atkinson (Ed.), *Studies in mathematical psychology.* Stanford, California: Stanford University Press, 1964.

Friedman, M. P., Carterette, E. C., & Anderson, N. H. Long-term probability learning with a random schedule of reinforcement. *Journal of Experimental Psychology,* 1968, **78,** 442–455.

Fritzen, J., & Johnson, N. F. Definiteness of pattern ending and uniformity of pattern size: Their effects upon learning number sequences. *Journal of Verbal Learning and Verbal Behavior,* 1969, **8,** 575–580.

Gambino, B., & Myers, J. L. Effect of mean and variability of event run length on two-choice learning. *Journal of Experimental Psychology,* 1966, **72,** 904–908.

Gambino, B., & Myers, J. L. Role of event runs in probability learning. *Psychological Review,* 1967, **74,** 410–419.

Gardner, R. A. Probability-learning with two and three choices. *American Journal of Psychology,* 1957, **70,** 714–185.

Gardner, R. A. Multiple-choice decision behavior. *American Journal of Psychology,* 1958, **71,** 710–717.

Garner, W. R., & Gottwald, R. L. Some perceptual factors in the learning of sequential patterns of binary events. *Journal of Verbal Learning and Verbal Behavior,* 1967, **6,** 582–589.

Garner, W. R., & Gottwald, R. L. The perception and learning of temporal patterns. *Quarterly Journal of Experimental Psychology,* 1968, **20,** 97–109.

Glanzer, M., & Clark, W. H. The verbal loop hypothesis: Binary numbers. *Journal of Verbal Learning and Verbal Behavior,* 1963, **2,** 301–309.

Goodnow, J. J. Determinants of choice distribution in two-choice situations. *American Journal of Psychology,* 1955, **68,** 106–116.

Greeno, J. G., & Simon, H. A. Processes for sequence production. *Psychological Review,* 1974, **81,** 187–198.

Halpern, J., & Dengler, M. Utility and variability: A description of preferences in the uncertain outcome situation. *Journal of Experimental Psychology,* 1969, **79,** 249–253.

Halpern, J., Dengler, M., & Ulehla, Z. J. The utility of event variability in two choice probability learning. *Psychonomic Science,* 1968, **10,** 143–144.

Halpern, J., Schwartz, J. A., & Chapman, R. Simultaneous and successive contrast effects in human-probability learning. *Journal of Experimental Psychology,* 1968, **77,** 581–586.

Hintzman, D. L. Apparent frequency as a function of frequency and the spacing of repetitions. *Journal of Experimental Psychology,* 1969, **80,** 139–145.

Howell, W. C. Representations of frequency in memory. *Psychological Bulletin,* 1973, **80,** 44–53.

Humphreys, L. G. Acquisition and extinction of verbal expectations in a situation analogous to conditioning. *Journal of Experimental Psychology,* 1939, **25,** 294–301.

Jarvik, M. E. Probability learning and a negative recency effect in the serial anticipation of alternative symbols. *Journal of Experimental Psychology,* 1951, **41,** 291–297.

Jones, M. R. From probability learning to sequential processing: A critical review. *Psychological Bulletin,* 1971, **76,** 153–185.

Jones, M. R. Cognitive representations of serial patterns. In B. R. Kantowitz (Ed.), *Human information processing: Tutorials in performance and cognition.* Hillsdale, New Jersey: Lawrence Erlbaum Assoc., 1974.

Jones, M. R., & Erickson, J. L. A demonstration of complex rule learning in choice prediction. *American Journal of Psychology,* 1972, **85,** 249–259.

Jones, M. R., & Myers, J. L. A comparison of two methods of event randomization in probability learning. *Journal of Experimental Psychology,* 1966, **72,** 909–911.

Luce, R. D., & Suppes, P. Preference, utility, and subjective probability. In R. D. Luce, R. R. Bush, & E. Galanter (Eds.), *Handbook of mathematical psychology.* Vol. III. New York: Wiley, 1965.

McCracken, J., Osterhout, C., & Voss, J. F. Effects of instructions in probability learning. *Journal of Experimental Psychology,* 1962, **64,** 267–271.

Messick, D. M. The utility of variability in probability learning. *Psychonomic Science,* 1965, **3,** 355–356.

Messick, D. M. Learning probabilities of events: A discussion. *Acta Psychologica,* 1970, **34,** 172–183.

Millward, R. B., & Reber, A. S. Event-recall in probability learning. *Journal of Verbal Learning and Verbal Behavior,* 1968, **7,** 980–989.

Myers, J. L. Sequential choice behavior. In G. H. Bower & J. T. Spence (Eds.), *The psychology of learning and motivation: Advances in research and theory.* Vol. 4. New York: Academic Press, 1970.

Myers, J. L., & Atkinson, R. C. Choice behavior and reward structure. *Journal of Mathematical Psychology,* 1964, **1,** 170–203.

Myers, J. L., Fort, J. G., Katz, L., & Suydam, M. M. Differential monetary gains and losses and event probability in a two-choice situation. *Journal of Experimental Psychology,* 1963, **66,** 521–522.

Myers, J. L., Gambino, B., & Jones, M. R. Response speeds in probability learning. *Journal of Mathematical Psychology,* 1967, **4,** 473–488.

Myers, J. L., Suydam, M. M., & Heuckeroth, O. Choice behavior and reward structure: Differential payoff. *Journal of Mathematical Psychology,* 1966, **3,** 458–469.

Neimark, E. D. Effects of type of nonreinforcement and number of alternative responses in two verbal conditioning situations. *Journal of Experimental Psychology,* 1956, **52,** 209–220.

Neimark, E. C., & Shuford, E. H. Comparison of predictions and estimates in a probability learning situation. *Journal of Experimental Psychology,* 1959, **57,** 294–298.

Nies, R. C. Effects of probable outcome information on two-choice learning. *Journal of Experimental Psychology,* 1962, **64,** 430–433.

Peterson, C. R., & Ulehla, Z. J. Sequential patterns and maximizing. *Journal of Experimental Psychology,* 1965, **69,** 1–4.

Reber, A. S., & Millward, R. B. Event observation in probability learning. *Journal of Experimental Psychology,* 1968, **77,** 317–327.

Restle, F. *Psychology of judgment and choice.* New York: Wiley, 1961.

Restle, F. Run structure and probability learning: Disproof of Restle's model. *Journal of Experimental Psychology,* 1966, **72,** 382–389.

Restle, F. Grammatical analysis of the prediction of binary events. *Journal of Verbal Learning and Verbal Behavior,* 1967, **6,** 17–25.

Restle, F. Theory of serial pattern learning: Structural trees. *Psychological Review*, 1970, **77**, 481–495.

Restle, F., & Brown, E. R. Organization of serial pattern learning. In G. H. Bower & J. T. Spence (Eds.), *The psychology of learning and motivation: Advances in research and theory*. Vol. 4. New York: Academic Press, 1970.

Restle, F., & Burnside, B. L. Tracking of serial patterns. *Journal of Experimental Psychology*, 1972, **95**, 299–307.

Rose, R. M., & Vitz, P. C. The role of runs in probability learning. *Journal of Experimental Psychology*, 1966, **72**, 751–760.

Schnorr, J. A., Lipkin, S. G., & Myers, J. L. Level of risk in probability learning: Within- and between-subjects designs. *Journal of Experimental Psychology*, 1966, **72**, 497–500.

Schnorr, J. A., & Myers, J. L. Negative contrast in human probability learning as a function of incentive magnitudes. *Journal of Experimental Psychology*, 1967, **75**, 492–499.

Shanteau, J. C. An additive model for sequential decision making. *Journal of Experimental Psychology*, 1970, **85**, 181–191.

Siegel, S. Theoretical models of choice and strategy behavior: Stable state behavior in the two-choice uncertain outcome situation. *Psychometrika*, 1959, **24**, 203–216.

Siegel, S. Decision making and learning under varying conditions of reinforcement. *Annals of the New York Academy of Science*, 1961, **89**, 766–782.

Suppes, P., & Atkinson, R. C. *Markov learning models for multiperson interaction*. Stanford, California: Stanford University Press, 1960.

Swensson, R. G. Incentive shifts in a three-choice situation. *Psychonomic Science*, 1965, **2**, 101–102.

Tune, G. S. Response preferences: A review of some relevant literature. *Psychological Bulletin*, 1964, **61**, 286–302.

Vitz, P. C., & Hazan, D. N. Memory during probability learning. *Journal of Experimental Psychology*, 1969, **80**, 52–58.

Vitz, P. C., & Todd, T. C. A model for simple repeating binary patterns. *Journal of Experimental Psychology*, 1967, **75**, 108–117.

Witte, R. S. Long-term effects of patterned reward schedules. *Journal of Experimental Psychology*, 1964, **68**, 588–594.

Wolin, B. R., Weichel, R., Terebinski, S. J., & Hansford, E. A. Performance on complexity patterned binary event sequences. *Psychological Monographs*, 1965, **79**, 1–18.

Yellott, J. I., Jr. Probability learning with noncontingent success. *Journal of Mathematical Psychology*, 1969, **6**, 541–575.

6

Reinforcement and Human Memory

Thomas O. Nelson

University of Washington

I. INTRODUCTION

This chapter begins with the assumption that the behavior of humans and the behavior of (nonhuman) animals abide by a common set of reinforcement principles. To the degree that this assumption is valid, the reinforcement phenomena observed in the animal domain should also be evident in the human domain. More specifically, reinforcement is known to play a major role in animal learning, but what is its corresponding role in human learning and memory? In this chapter, a review is presented of efforts to generalize the reinforcement principles derived from animal learning situations to human learning situations, especially human verbal learning. An examination of the successes and failures at generalization not only should help to delimit the domain of reinforcement principles common to animal learning and human learning, but also should allow for a more precise specification of the theoretical mechanisms underlying reinforcement. In particular, memory must be one of these mechanisms because, without memory, there would be no reinforcement phenomena in either humans or animals (that is, without memory, the organism would respond to each recurrence of a stimulus situation as if nothing like it had ever occurred in the past). What specific roles does memory play in the various phenomena of reinforcement? The human learning situation is especially well suited for investigating this question because memory factors are generally easier to observe and manipulate in humans than in animals (for example, via instructions to the subject). Thus, this chapter examines the bidirectional interplay between reinforcement and memory. Although intermingled

207

throughout the chapter, the role of memory in various reinforcement phenomena is emphasized in Sections III and IV, and the influence of reinforcement on verbal learning and memory is predominant in Sections II and V.

The language used here to discuss reinforcement and to integrate various findings comes from the theoretical framework proposed by Tolman (1932). The highlights of this account of reinforcement are as follows. The organism stores in memory an *expectancy* that arises from an environmental contingency between the stimulus situation (S), the response (R), and the outcome (O). This expectancy takes the form "In situation S, response R will be followed by outcome O." For example, suppose an organism attends to the environmental contingency that bar pressing (response R) in an operant chamber where there is a bar (stimulus situation S) is followed by the occurrence of food (outcome O). Then the organism might store in memory the $S–R–O$ expectancy, "When in an operant chamber where there is a bar, bar pressing will be followed by food." Subsequently, the organism utilizes his stored $S–R–O$ expectancy to behave purposefully in a goal-directed fashion so as to produce a particular outcome (for example, given the previously stored $S–R–O$ expectancy, the goal of obtaining food would induce the organism to bar press when he is in an operant chamber where there is a bar). Thus, the function of outcome O during learning is to *emphasize* some particular $S–R–O$ contingency in the environment, giving rise to the storage of an $S–R–O$ expectancy in memory; subsequently, the function of outcome O is to *induce performance* (via the $S–R–O$ expectancy stored in memory) of response R in situation S when the organism's goal is to obtain outcome O.

II. LEARNING VERSUS PERFORMANCE

A. Necessity of Reinforcement for Learning

As indicated above, reinforcement can emphasize particular $S–R–O$ contingencies and thereby increase the likelihood that expectancies about them will be stored in memory (that is, learned). However, just because reinforcement can facilitate learning, it does not follow that reinforcement is necessary for learning. (Analogously, just because italicizing one word in a series of to-be-learned words may facilitate the learning of that particular word, it does not follow that italicizing was necessary for the learning of that particular word—other words, which are not italicized, will also be learned.) There are a number of situations in which learning and/or behavioral changes seem to occur in the absence of external reinforcement. A classic example is the "latent learning" experiment by Tolman and Honzik

(1930). Three groups of rats were used, and each rat was individually placed in a maze once daily for 17 days. The maze consisted of a series of choice points where the rat had to turn either left or right, with incorrect turns leading to blind alleys and correct turns eventually leading to the goal box at the end of the maze (one-way doors prevented backtracking after correct turns). The three groups, partially deprived of food so that they would be hungry, differed in terms of the outcome received when they finally entered the goal box. One group always received food reinforcement upon reaching the goal box; another group never received food in the goal box (they were simply removed to their home cage); the final group did not receive food in the goal box for the first 10 days but did receive food there beginning with the 11th day. Performance, in terms of the number of wrong turns (errors) made before the rat reached the goal box, is shown in Figure 1. The always-rewarded group reduced their errors dramatically during the course of the experiment, whereas the never-rewarded group showed only a small decrease in errors. However, and most important, the group that did not receive reward until the eleventh day suddenly performed like the always-rewarded group from the twelfth day on. Thus, the eleventh-day group apparently learned as much during the first 11 days as the

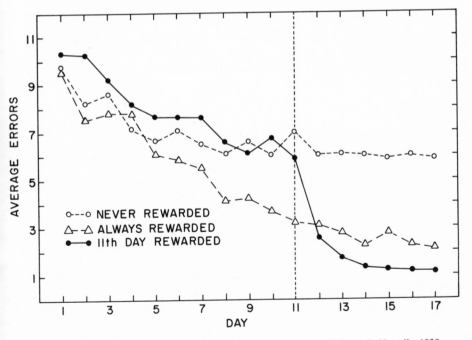

FIGURE 1.   Average errors for each group on each day. (From Tolman & Honzik, 1930. Originally published by the University of California Press; reprinted by permission of the Regents of the University of California.)

always-rewarded group, even though the eleventh-day group's performance on the early trials did not show evidence of their learning (hence the term "latent learning"). There are two important conclusions to be drawn from this experiment. First, external reinforcement is not necessary for learning but, instead, may exert its primary effect on performance (for other examples, see Bolles, 1972). That is, even without external reinforcement during early trials, the eleventh-day group apparently learned how to traverse the maze as well as the always-rewarded group. After a food reward appeared in the goal box on the eleventh day, the now-rewarded rats began to utilize their previously learned knowledge about the maze—they began going directly to the goal box instead of taking a roundabout route. This leads to the second conclusion, viz., the level of performance does not always show what has been learned. Although the reliable occurrence of correct performance implies that learning has occurred, poor performance does not necessarily imply poor learning (that is, correct performance implies learning, but not vice versa). Poor performance will result either (a) if learning has not occurred or (b) if learning has occurred but the learned knowledge simply is not being utilized.

B. Sufficiency of Reinforcement for Learning

It was shown in the previous section, that reinforcement is not *necessary* for learning, that is, learning can occur in the absence of external reinforcement. Now consider whether or not reinforcement is *sufficient* for learning, that is, whether reinforcement by itself will produce learning. Historically, the view that reinforcement is sufficient for learning was embodied in Thorndike's Law of Effect, which stated that the outcome "wrong" automatically weakens the prior stimulus–response connection, whereas the outcome "right" automatically strengthens it, acting ". . . unconsciously and directly, much as the sunlight acts upon plants, or an electric current upon a neighboring current, or the earth upon the moon . . . a satisfying after-effect can strengthen its connection with no paraphernalia to help it" (Thorndike, 1933, p. 48).

To test his Law of Effect in the human domain, Thorndike developed a paradigm that is now known as Thorndikian paired-associate learning. The primary difference between Thorndikian paired-associate learning and standard paired-associate learning is the kind of outcome: In standard paired-associate learning, a stimulus occurs, followed by the subject's response, followed by the outcome of the correct stimulus–response pair (regardless of the correctness of the subject's response); in Thorndikian paired-associate learning, the stimulus occurs, followed by the subject's response, followed by the outcome of "right" or "wrong" (depending upon the correctness of the subject's response).

The results of Thorndikian paired-associate learning experiments led to disconfirmations of various versions of the Law of Effect. For example, consider the findings of a well-known study by Wallach and Henle (1942, Experiment 1), who used a modified form of Thorndikian paired-associate learning. The subject's task was to state the correct digit response when presented with each of 20 stimulus words. Following every response, the experimenter said either "right" or "wrong" according to a predetermined sequence. The sequence was arranged so that, on each of the four trials through the list, exactly four of the subject's 20 responses would be called "right" regardless of the subject's actual response. After the fourth trial, the stimuli were presented again, and the subject was asked to recall the response he[1] had just given to each stimulus word. To maintain the subject's motivation, he was paid a half-cent for every correctly remembered response. The critical variable in this study was the kind of instructions that had been given to the subject at the beginning of the experiment. Half of the time, the subjects had been told that they were participating in an experiment on EXTRASENSORY PERCEPTION (ESP) and that, consequently, there were no correct responses for them to learn (that is, the outcome of "right" versus "wrong" purportedly had no future utility for subjects in the ESP condition). The remaining half of the time, the subjects had been told to LEARN the correct response to each stimulus word (that is, the outcome of "right" versus "wrong" purportedly did have future significance for subjects in the LEARN condition). How should the two conditions compare on the recall of "right" versus "wrong" responses after the fourth learning trial? If reinforcement is sufficient for learning (that is, the reward "right" automatically produces learning via the Law of Effect), then more "right" than "wrong" responses should be recalled, regardless of the instructions about ESP versus LEARN. If future utility is critical (that is, reinforcement alone is not sufficient for learning), then the recall advantage for "right" over "wrong" responses should be prominent in the LEARN condition but should decrease, and in the limit be absent, in the ESP condition.

The results, shown in Table 1, are quite straightforward. Although there was noticeable incidental recall (chance = 10%), the effect of the reinforcement of "right" versus "wrong" was significant only in the LEARN condition. In the ESP condition, there was no recall advantage whatsoever of "right" over "wrong"—the two percentages are nearly identical.[2] These

[1] For brevity, "he" refers throughout to both male and female subjects.

[2] The lack of effect of reinforcement in the ESP condition does not seem to occur when the subject is given only one trial (for a review, see Postman, 1962), perhaps because some interference from prior trials is necessary or perhaps because more than one trial is needed to convince the subject that he is not actually in a learning experiment. However, the finding about reinforcement having a negligible effect in the absence of future utility is otherwise robust and occurs in many different situations (for example, the number-estimation experiments in Nuttin & Greenwald, 1968, Chapter 5; the random-assignment condition in Wallach & Henle, 1942, Experiment 2).

TABLE 1
Percentage of "Right" and "Wrong" Responses
Recalled in Each Condition in Wallach
and Henle's (1942) Experiment 1

| | Outcome | |
Condition	"Right"	"Wrong"
ESP	21	22
LEARN	67	23

results support two conclusions. First, future utility plays an important role in the effect of reinforcement on learning, perhaps via the mechanism of differential rehearsal, that is, perhaps the learner devotes extra rehearsal to "right" responses only when he believes they will have some kind of future utility (for more discussion of differential rehearsal, see Section III.B.1.c). Second, reinforcement alone is not sufficient for learning, that is, learning does not occur automatically whenever a response is reinforced by "right." Other examples of the insufficiency of reinforcement are given in Levine (1971) and in the next section, in which the critical conditions for the effectiveness of reinforcement are described.

C. Awareness and Intention

1. Verbal Operant Conditioning

In 1955, Greenspoon conducted a pioneer experiment on verbal operant conditioning. A human subject was told to say anything he wanted, and the experimenter reinforced the subject by casually saying "mmm-hmm" whenever the subject said a plural noun. During the course of the session, the frequency of plural nouns increased substantially (relative to an unreinforced control group whose performance provided a baseline). At the end of the session, when asked the purpose of the experiment, most subjects did not verbalize the contingency between saying plural nouns and being reinforced with "mmm-hmm." This suggests that they might have learned to say the correct response without awareness of the $S-R-O$ contingency. However, subsequent studies have shown that the assessment of awareness was insufficient in Greenspoon's study (for a review of the role of awareness in conditioning, see Brewer, 1974). Evidently, the impression of learning without awareness is dispelled when the subject's awareness is assessed by a questionnaire which, in essence, asks (a) whether the subject noticed any contingency between his response in this situation and the outcome of "mmm-hmm" (that is, awareness of the S–R–O contingency) and (b) whether the subject wanted the outcome of "mmm-hmm" to occur.[3] Using this kind of questionnaire, Dulany (1962) was able to predict the subject's verbal operant conditioning performance very accurately. If the subject was both aware of the S–R–O contingency and wanted the "mmm-hmm" outcome, then his frequency of plural-noun responses increased; however, if the subject was aware of the S–R–O contingency but did not want the "mmm-hmm" outcome, his frequency decreased; finally, if the subject was unaware of the S–R–O contingency, then, regardless of his desire for the "mmm-hmm" outcome, his frequency of plural nouns remained approximately constant at the baseline level. The conclusion to draw from these results (assuming, of course, that the subject remains capable of performing the reinforced response) is that the combined conditions of awareness and intention are typically both necessary and sufficient for reliable performance of the reinforced response.

2. Correlated S–R–O Expectancy and Contingency

Seemingly contrary to the above, the subject's performance sometimes increases steadily even though he has not learned the "correct" S–R–O expectancy. This situation is demonstrated in an experiment by Philbrick and Postman (1955). The subject heard a sequence of 216 different words, each being presented only once. After every word, the subject responded with a digit from 1 to 9 and the experimenter said "right" or "wrong," depending upon whether or not the response was in accord with a contingency undisclosed to the subject ("number of letters in the word minus one," for example, FROG-3). Whenever the subject had four or more correct responses in a block of nine words, he was asked to state the S–R–O expectancy on which his responses were based. The finding of interest was that, throughout the sequence, the subject's responses systematically improved long before his S–R–O expectancy coincided with the actual S–R–O contingency. What was the reason for this? The subject's S–R–O expectancy was correlated with the actual S–R–O contingency (for example, "the digit 2 goes with short words"). Performance improves progressively as the subject's S–R–O expectancies become progressively more correlated with the actual S–R–O contingency, even though the subject is not yet aware of the actual S–R–O contingency.

---

[3] Asking the subject about his intentions does not require the assumption that he has free will. Such asking can be thought of as a request for him to tell what is deterministically occurring within him, that is, he may be monitoring rather than making a free choice.

In one of the verbal operant conditioning studies alluded to in the previous section, Dulany (1961) noticed extraordinary performance in some subjects who were not aware of the actual $S-R-O$ contingency. The subjects had correlated $S-R-O$ expectancies consisting of response classes that were subordinates of the actual reinforced response classes. For example, the reinforced response class "plural nouns" might be misconstrued as "gems" (DIAMONDS, PEARLS, etc., each of which is also a plural noun), or the reinforced response class "animals" might be misconstrued as "mammals." Such a correlated subordinate $S-R-O$ expectancy, together with a desire for the outcome of the $S-R-O$ expectancy, is sufficient for correct performance.

III.   INFORMATION VERSUS AFFECT

A.   Direct versus Vicarious Reinforcement

Reinforcement can provide information leading to a correct $S-R-O$ expectancy. Then, via this $S-R-O$ expectancy, reinforcement can induce the organism to perform the response R if the organism desires the affective consequences (outcome O) of the $S-R-O$ expectancy. However, to maximize acquisition of the $S-R-O$ expectancy, is it necessary for the organism to actually experience, during learning, the affective consequences of outcome O? In one investigation of this question, Hillix and Marx (1960) compared the influence of vicarious versus direct reinforcement. The subject's task was to learn five complex patterns of lights. On the study trial for the first light pattern, the subject continued to guess various numbered lights until the reinforcement occurred, indicating that he had guessed the correct lights (the reinforcement consisted of the correct lights becoming illuminated as the subject guessed them). Next, the study trial for the second pattern occurred, and so on, until there had been a study trial on all five light patterns. During study, half of the subjects were directly reinforced (that is, they were the subjects described above who did the guessing and were reinforced whenever they guessed correctly). The other half of the subjects were vicariously reinforced (that is, they observed the directly reinforced subject's guesses and reinforcement, saying aloud all of the directly reinforced subject's guesses to ensure complete perception). Following study, a test trial occurred in which the directly and vicariously reinforced subjects attempted to correctly recall the five light patterns. The results showed better recall for the vicariously reinforced subjects! These subjects had been exposed to the informational aspects of the reinforcement but had never themselves been reinforced for guessing correctly during the study trial.

This counterintuitive advantage of vicarious reinforcement over direct reinforcement has also occurred in a clinical setting (Marlatt, 1970). Vicariously reinforced subjects heard a tape recording of other subjects being directly reinforced by "mmm-hmm" for describing personal problems. Subsequently, these vicariously reinforced subjects were more likely to describe their own personal problems than were the directly reinforced subjects, and this effect was still present one week later in a follow-up interview. It is not clear why vicariously reinforced subjects actually perform better than (rather than just as well as) directly reinforced subjects. At the very least, these results from two quite different situations do show that the subject does not have to experience directly the affective pleasure of reinforcement to maximize subsequent performance; information about the $S-R-O$ expectancy seems more critical. It should be pointed out, however, that subsequent performance does seem better when the subject induces the $S-R-O$ expectancy than when he is simply told the $S-R-O$ expectancy—the so-called "I'd rather do it myself" phenomenon (for a literature review, see Marlatt, 1972).

B. Magnitude of Reward

One of the classic variables influencing animal behavior is magnitude of reward. The general finding (for a review, see Bolles, 1967) is that reward magnitude exerts its effect on performance rather than on learning (see the discussion of latent learning in Section II.A). Similarly, the effect of reward magnitude on human memory seems indirect and on performance rather than directly on learning. Furthermore, the mechanisms underlying the influence of reward magnitude seem different for storage and retrieval. Therefore, storage and retrieval will be considered separately.

1. Storage of Expectancies

a. Determinant of expectancy.   Typically, an $S-R-O$ expectancy is stored in memory when the subject experiences (either directly or vicariously) the affect of outcome O and incorporates information about the occurrence of outcome O into his $S-R-O$ expectancy. However, which of these—affect or information—determines the actual $S-R-O$ expectancy that the subject acquires? The relative contributions of affect and information were separated experimentally in a study reported by Estes (1969). The subject, whose goal was to accumulate as many points as possible during the experiment, had repeated cycles through eight pairs of stimulus cards (each card displayed a different nonsense syllable). For each pair of cards, the subject attempted to choose the "correct" card and predict its reward value (0–4 possible points), after which the experimenter told the subject how many points the chosen card was actually worth. Every pair contained one incorrect card that was always worth 0 points. However, the subject received points only if he had both chosen the correct card *and* accurately predicted its point value. Unknown to the subject, the correct cards were divided into three different conditions, as shown in Table 2. The Uniform cards had a constant reward value throughout the experiment (for example, as Table 2 indicates, correct card *b* was always worth 2 points); consequently, through learning, the subject could receive 100% reinforcement on these cards. The Random cards had one reward value on some trials and another reward value on the remaining trials, with each reward value occurring randomly and approximately equally often (for example, correct card *e* was worth 1 point on some trials and 2 points on other trials); consequently, the subject could receive 50% reinforcement on these cards. The Never-Right cards, as the name suggests, had one reward value on some trials and another reward value on other trials, but the designated value was never the one that the subject predicted (for example, if the subject chose card *h* and predicted 3 points, the experimenter said its point value was 4 points; if the subject had predicted 4 points, the experimenter would have said 3 points); consequently, the subject could never receive any reward on these cards. Thus, in this experiment, one not only examines the influence of reward magnitude on learning; one also compares a situa-

TABLE 2
Design and Results of Estes' (1969) Experiment

Design				Results	
Correct stimulus	Value assigned	Condition	Reward if correct	Acquisition errors	Chosen (%)
a	1	Uniform	1	9.45	7
b	2	Uniform	2	7.40	41
c	3	Uniform	3	9.05	64
d	4	Uniform	4	5.35	98
e	1, 2	Random	1, 2	5.62	25
f	3, 4	Random	3, 4	6.70	74
g	1, 2	Never Right	0	6.92	17
h	3, 4	Never Right	0	5.88	73

tion in which the subject receives information only (in the Never-Right condition, the subject never experienced the affect of being rewarded) with a situation in which the subject receives both information and affect (for example, in the Random condition, approximately half of the subject's correct responses were rewarded). The acquisition phase of this experiment continued until the subject went through an eight-pair cycle without making any errors, that is, the subject chose the correct card and predicted its point value for Uniform cards, and chose the correct card and predicted either of its two possible point values for Random and Never-Right cards (this differential criterion disallows a direct comparison of the acquisition performance for Uniform versus either Random or Never-Right). The average number of acquisition errors is shown in Table 2. Notice that acquisition errors did not systematically decrease as reward magnitude increased, either for the Uniform condition or for the Random and Never-Right conditions. Thus, there is no evidence that learning is differentially influenced by the affect of receiving large, small, or even no rewards. In fact, acquisition in the Never-Right condition (no rewards) was nearly identical to that in the Random condition (50% rewards). Evidently, the subject used the (sometimes misleading) information stated in the experimenter's feedback, rather than the affect of being reinforced, to construct $S–R–O$ expectancies about the various cards.

These $S–R–O$ expectancies, determined by information rather than affect, influenced not only acquisition but also subsequent choice behavior as well. Following the acquisition phase, choice tests were given on only the eight "correct" cards (the eight "incorrect" cards were discarded). All possible pairs were constructed from these eight cards, and the subject chose one member of each pair and predicted its reward value. As before, the subject would receive the point value associated with the chosen card whenever that point value was correctly predicted (however, the experimenter's feedback was withheld during these choice tests). The percentage of times that each card was chosen over its pair mate, collapsed over all possible pair mates, is shown in the last column of Table 2. Choice performance was completely in accord with the expectancies based on information (as opposed to affect) from the acquisition phase. The choice percentage increases with reward magnitude for all three conditions (Uniform, Random, and Never-Right). Furthermore, all of the values for the latter two conditions fall roughly midway between the corresponding Uniform conditions, for example, the Random 1, 2 value of 25% is midway between the Uniform 1 value of 7% and the Uniform 2 value of 41%. Specifically, notice that the values for the Never-Right condition, in which no affect from reinforcement had ever occurred previously, are both greater than zero and in accord with expectancies determined solely by information.

Thus, although acquisition was not influenced by reward magnitude (see the next two sections, however), subsequent performance was, and the influence seems to result from expectancies based on information rather than affect. Of course, the latter result is almost certainly of limited generality because once the subject realizes that he can never be right on Never-Right cards, he can incorporate this information into his expectancy. That is, the subject was "hustled" by the inaccurate information stated in the experimenter's feedback about the outcomes for Never-Right cards; the correct information is that Never-Right cards actually have an outcome of 0 points. If the subject should acquire this correct information (for example, via instructions or extended training), then his performance in the Never-Right condition would undoubtedly change. Nevertheless, the results of Estes' "hustler" experiment clearly demonstrate that expectancies are based not on the actual affect of reinforcement but instead on (sometimes misleading) information. The implication of this finding for typical learning situations, which confound information and affect, is that affect determines the subject's expectancies only indirectly (via information about possible subsequent affect). Thus, the critical determinant of $S-R-O$ expectancies seems to be information rather than affect itself.

b. Completeness of expectancy.   Depending on certain factors, reward magnitude may or may not influence acquisition. One of these factors is the completeness of the subject's expectancies. In an experiment by Keller, Cole, Burke, and Estes (1965), undergraduate subjects earned points by learning a list of 25 paired associates in which the stimuli were single letters of the alphabet and the two possible response alternatives were "left" and "right." For each stimulus, one response alternative always had one reward value, whereas the remaining response alternative always had another reward value (for example, G–left was worth 4 points, whereas G–right was worth 6 points; T–left was worth 2 points, whereas T–right was worth 1 point). The range of possible points, over all stimulus–response combinations, was from 1 to 8 points. As each stimulus was presented, the subject indicated either "left" or "right" and then was informed of the number of points for his choice (that is, the subject always received points, the number depending upon which of the two responses he had chosen). Two groups of subjects differed in the information they received about the *nonchosen* response. The Correction subjects were informed of the points not only for the chosen response, but also for the nonchosen response; the Noncorrection subjects were informed only of the points for the chosen response, and were not informed of how many points the nonchosen response was worth. Thus, during any given learning trial, the Correction subjects could establish complete $S-R-O$ expectancies for each stimulus, whereas the Noncorrection subjects could establish only partial $S-R-O$ expectancies. To illustrate this, let a given stimulus be designated S_i, a response of "left" or "right" be designated by R_L or R_R, and an outcome following R_L or R_R to S_i be designated by O_{iL} or O_{iR}. Then the information received by a Correction subject when he responds "left" during any given trial is complete and can be represented as follows: S_i–R_L–O_{iL} and S_i–R_R–O_{iR}. A Noncorrection subject who responds "left" would receive only incomplete information: S_i–R_L–O_{iL} and S_i–R_R–?. Therefore, the Correction subject has received enough information to respond correctly the next time this stimulus appears (where "correct" is defined as choosing the higher-valued response to the particular stimulus). Because the Correction subject has complete expectancies, reward magnitude might have no effect (that is, regardless of the reward magnitude, the Correction subject has enough information to know whether he should respond "left" or "right" next time). In contrast, the Noncorrection subject has only partial information and is not guaranteed to be correct the next time the same stimulus appears. The Noncorrection subject should make the same response if the previous outcome was high but change if the previous outcome was low because the average gain from changing his response increases as the reward magnitude of his previous outcome decreases (for example, changing his response is generally more beneficial when the previous outcome was 2 points rather than 6 points). Naturally, this "low, shift–high, stay" strategy sometimes produces errors (for example, changing a previous 2-point response is not beneficial when the remaining response for the item is worth only 1 point). These errors should cause the Noncorrection subject to have worse performance overall than the Correction subject. Furthermore, the "low, shift–high, stay" strategy should produce marked effects of reward magnitude on the Noncorrection subject's acquisition performance (for example, acquisition of the correct response should be more rapid when the two response alternatives for an item are worth 1 versus 8 points than when they are worth 4 versus 6 points).

The results were quite straightforward. First, acquisition performance was better for the Correction subjects, who had complete S–R–O expectancies, than for the Noncorrection subjects, who had incomplete S–R–O expectancies. Second, reward magnitude had no systematic influence on acquisition in the Correction condition; for example, the items acquired fastest had responses worth 4 versus 8 points, the slowest had responses worth 1 versus 4 points, and items acquired intermediately included responses worth 1 versus 8 points and 1 versus 2 points. This result confirms the notion that the affect from receiving large versus small rewards is less important than the information about S–R–O expectancies. Third, reward magnitude did systematically influence acquisition performance in the Noncorrection condition: Acquisition performance increased (a) as reward magnitude decreased for the lower-valued response and (b) as reward magnitude increased for the higher-valued response; for example, Noncorrection subjects displayed better acquisition performance on those items with responses worth 2 and 8 points than on those worth 4 and 6 points. This finding demonstrates how reward magnitude, coupled with incomplete S–R–O expectancies, influences acquisition performance. This influence does not seem to result from differential learning (otherwise the Correction condition also would have been influenced), but rather results from gambling via the "low, shift–high, stay" strategy when the subject's expectancies are not complete enough to dictate how he should perform. Thus, reward magnitude influenced performance rather than learning.

c. Giving priority to items for differential rehearsal. If information rather than affect determines the influence of reward magnitude on acquisition, then reward magnitude should exert its greatest influence in situations in which the subject can utilize the information about reward magnitude in some way. For instance, when the subject believes that some particular items are worth more than others (that is, during acquisition, the subject expects that subsequently remembering certain items will be rewarded more highly than subsequently remembering other items), then he can devote extra processing to the high-reward items. The extra processing does not consist simply of "trying harder," but instead seems to be a learner-controlled process of differential rehearsal. For example, more rehearsal can be given to certain items than to others, which will tend to improve subsequent recall of the items receiving extra rehearsal (Rundus, 1971). However, differential rehearsal is of major use only when the subject can devote extra rehearsal to certain items at the expense of others. Unless the information about reward magnitude specifies which particular items are to be given priority for differential rehearsal, it will be of little use. Evidence that giving priority to particular items underlies the influence of reward magnitude comes from a free-recall experiment conducted in my laboratory at the University of Washington. Reward, magnitude was manipulated in two different experimental designs: between subjects (in which all items have equal priority) and mixed list (in which different items have different priorities).[4]

In the between-subjects design, one group of 20 undergraduate subjects was told in advance that they would receive one cent for every correctly

[4] The choice of the term "mixed list" (as opposed to "within subjects") is intentional. In a mixed-list design, items in the various conditions are intermingled in the same list. This allows for prioritizing (stealing processing from some items and giving extra processing to other items). The more general term "within-subjects design" can refer either to a mixed-list design or to a blocked design, in which the subject goes through first one condition and then another condition (hence, the items from various conditions are not intermingled, and the results would probably be more like those from a between-subjects design—see Weiner, 1966, Experiments 6–8).

recalled item; another group of 20 undergraduate subjects was told in advance that they would receive ten cents for every correctly recalled item. The items were 40 common words, 20 from each of two taxonomic categories (OCCUPATIONS and ANIMALS). These items were alternately ordered (for example, LAWYER, TIGER, PHYSICIST, BUFFALO) and visually presented at a rate of 8 sec per item. Then, 5 min were allowed for written recall of the items in any order that the subject remembered them. The percentage of items correctly recalled is shown in Table 3. In the between-subjects situation, where reward magnitude gave the same priority to all items, a t test for independent scores showed that reward magnitude did not reliably influence recall ($t < 1$). This result (like all others I know of from between-subjects designs, for example, Harley, 1965a) suggests that the *direct* influence of reward magnitude on verbal learning is negligible.

Although reward magnitude does not seem to influence acquisition directly, it can have an indirect effect by giving priority to particular items so that they can be differentially rehearsed (see Rundus, 1971). This is evident in the mixed-list situation, in which the same general procedure and the same reward values of one cent and ten cents were employed. Ten undergraduate subjects were told in advance that they would receive one cent for every correctly recalled OCCUPATION item and ten cents for every correctly recalled ANIMAL item; for counterbalancing purposes, ten other undergraduate subjects were told in advance that they would receive ten cents for every correctly recalled OCCUPATION item and one cent for every correctly recalled ANIMAL item. Here the influence of reward magnitude was so pronounced that not one of the 20 mixed-list subjects recalled more one-cent items than ten-cent items. For comparability with the between-subjects situation and in the interest of conservativism, the same t test for independent scores (with the same degrees of freedom) was used to analyze the mixed-list data, summarized in the bottom row of Table 3. Reward

TABLE 3
Percentage of Items Recalled as a
Function of Reward Magnitude in
Two Experimental Designs

Experimental design	Reward magnitude		Difference (10¢ − 1¢)
	10¢	1¢	
Between subjects	55	51	4
Mixed list	66	49	17

magnitude reliably influenced recall ($t = 4.06$, $p < .001$) and is estimated (ω^2) to account for a remarkable 84% of the total variance.

These results support the notion that giving priority to particular items underlies the influence of reward magnitude on acquisition. Although the total rehearsal for a given acquisition period may be limited, the subject can spread that rehearsal over the to-be-remembered items in any way he chooses. When the S–R–O expectancy is the same for every item (as in the between-subjects situation), the subject has no basis for differential rehearsal. However, when the S–R–O expectancy differs from item to item (as in the mixed-list situation), thereby giving priority to particular items, the subject can differentially rehearse the high-reward items.

This influence of reward magnitude occurs in paradigms other than free recall, as long as a mixed-list design is used so that the subject can give priority to particular items (for example, for reward-magnitude effects in paired-associate learning with between-subjects versus mixed-list designs, see Harley, 1965a, b). A general model of memory that emphasizes the role of differential verbal rehearsal has been applied by Atkinson and Wickens (1971) to reinforcement effects in various verbal-learning paradigms.

The differential processing that underlies the effect of reward magnitude can also be nonverbal, as shown in a mixed-list study by Loftus (1972). Pairs of scenic pictures were presented for study, and the subject was told the point value of each member of the pair (for example, the left picture might be worth 9 points, whereas the right picture might be worth 1 point). Loftus recorded the number of eye fixations on each picture and found that reward magnitude influenced the number of eye fixations, which, in turn, influenced subsequent recognition memory for the pictures. When the number of eye fixations was held constant, reward magnitude had no residual effect. Thus, analogous to the verbal situation, the influence of reward magnitude on the acquisition of pictures seems indirect, with the underlying direct influence being the number of eye fixations (a visual analog of verbal rehearsal).

2. Retrieval of Expectancies

a. Typical results.   Suppose that storage has already occurred and retrieval is about to begin. What will be the effect of introducing different reward values now? The typical result is that reward magnitude does not reliably influence retrieval. For example, at the beginning of a free-recall experiment, Weiner (1966, Experiment 9) gave the subject either intentional-learning instructions (telling him to learn the 36 words about to be presented) or incidental-learning instructions (telling him that 36 words would be presented to illustrate the procedure to be used in a later phase of the experiment). Immediately following presentation of the words, the subject was offered either nothing or five cents for every word that he could recall during the next five minutes. Although the intentional-learning instructions yielded better recall than the incidental-learning instructions, there was no significant influence of reward magnitude.

Essentially the same result occurs when the retention test is delayed. Birnbaum (personal communication) gave subjects a mixture of ten study and test trials on a 75-word list in a categorized free-recall experiment. One week later, the subjects returned and recalled as many words as possible for approximately 2.5 min. Then, half of the subjects were told simply to continue recalling additional items during the next 3 min, and the remaining subjects were offered the substantial inducement of one dollar for each additional item that they recalled during the next three minutes. The average number of additional words recalled was 5.2 for each group!

b. The exception.   Loftus and Wickens (1970) did find an effect of reward magnitude on retrieval and also seem to have isolated the locus of the effect. In a mixed-list situation, continuous paired-associate learning occurred on pairs of nonsense syllables and letters of the alphabet (e.g., DAX–P). Each pair was assigned either a high or low reward value (in terms of points that would eventually determine the amount of the subject's payment for participation). This point value either was or was not disclosed to the subject as he studied each pair, and either was or was not disclosed to the subject as he attempted retrieval during the test of each pair.

The results are shown in Table 4 (two conditions, high–low and low–high, could not logically occur in this experiment and consequently have no cell

TABLE 4
Percentage of Correct Responses and Latency
of Errors for Each Condition in Loftus and
Wickens' (1970) Experiment

Reward value disclosed during acquisition	Reward value disclosed during retrieval		
	High	Not disclosed	Low
High	68 (7.6)	62 (6.0)	—
Not disclosed	52 (8.2)	49 (6.0)	48 (5.8)
Low	—	47 (5.9)	47 (6.0)

Note: Main entry is average percentage correct and entry in parentheses is average error latency (in seconds).

entries). An important dependent variable is the error latency, which may be taken to represent the maximum amount of time that the subject searches his memory before he terminates retrieval. Consider both the error latency and the percentage correct as conclusions are drawn from this experiment. First, nowhere was there a reliable difference in performance between the not-disclosed condition and the corresponding low-reward condition, suggesting that the subject functionally treated no information as representing low reward. Second, a high reward disclosed during acquisition had the facilitory effect typical of mixed-list designs: The percentage-correct entries in the first row (high reward disclosed during acquisition) are much higher than the corresponding percentage-correct entries in the rows below them (low reward or reward not disclosed). However, there is no parallel effect on error latency. This pattern of results can be explained simply by assuming that the high-reward items were differentially rehearsed during acquisition (Section III.B.1.c). Now consider the very different situation in which a high reward was disclosed during retrieval (compare the entries in the first column with the corresponding entries in the columns to the right). Again, there is a facilitory effect on percentage correct for high reward, but this effect is much smaller during retrieval than during acquisition. Furthermore, during retrieval, the facilitory effect on percentage correct is accompanied by a parallel effect on error latency: The error latency is longer when the reward value disclosed during retrieval was high. This suggests that high reward exerts its influence not by making retrieval more efficient but, rather, by encouraging extra searching before retrieval is terminated (that is, the subject does not give up as quickly during retrieval if the item has a high reward value). In studies where reward magnitude has no effect on retrieval (see the previous section, III.B.2.a), the subject probably searches for the same amount of time, regardless of the item's reward magnitude, thereby eliminating the effect of reward magnitude on retrieval. Thus, while indirectly facilitating storage via mechanisms such as giving priority to particular items, reward magnitude typically does not facilitate retrieval; in those rare cases where there is some facilitation of retrieval, the effect is small and seems due to extra searching before retrieval is terminated.

IV. DELAY OF REINFORCEMENT

One of the classic findings in the animal literature is that delay of reinforcement retards learning (for a review, see Renner, 1964). Attempts at generalizing this finding to the human domain sometimes have succeeded and at other times have failed. Perhaps, although a common set of principles underlies the delay effect in both domains, procedural differences between the two domains have obscured the basic principles and produced artifactually different results. The attempt here is to isolate these procedural differences and describe a set of basic principles underlying the effect of delay of reinforcement.

A. Inference Factors

1. Response Inference

To form an $S–R–O$ expectancy, the organism must infer the response to which the reinforcing outcome pertains. For example, consider a rat that receives a food pellet after pressing the bar in a discrete-trials bar-pressing situation. As the rat constructs the $S–R–O$ expectancy, it must infer the response to which the reinforcement pertains. The difficulty of this inference task increases proportionally with the delay between the pertinent response and the reinforcement. In part, this difficulty occurs because the delay interval is filled with other responses that the rat is continually making, for example, grooming, scratching, sniffing, or even doing nothing (which sometimes is defined by the experimenter as the correct response!). How does the rat determine which of these many responses the reinforcing outcome pertains to? One possibility is that it retrieves one of its responses from memory, forms an $S–R–O$ expectancy, and tests the $S–R–O$ expectancy at its next opportunity (see Levine, 1971). The longer the delay of reinforcement, the less likely the pertinent response is to be the one included in the $S–R–O$ expectancy. Sometimes, however, the outcome itself restricts the set of possible responses which the rat must consider (for example, only ingestion responses when the outcome is illness—see Garcia & Koelling, 1966); then, lengthening the delay interval does not have as much of a negative effect. An extreme case can occur in the human situation if the reinforcing outcome is so restrictive (of the previous responses to which it can apply) that there is absolutely no inference problem. The importance of this inference factor has been demonstrated in an experiment by Nelson (1971). Four groups of undergraduate subjects had the task of learning a six-item list of consonant–digit pairs (e.g., H–5). The subject was told in advance that the correct response would always be a digit from 3 to 9, and he was to learn which digit was paired with each consonant stimulus. For two groups, the reinforcing outcome following the correct response was the appearance of a red light; for the remaining two groups, the reinforcing outcome was the appearance of the correct consonant–digit pair. Within each pair of groups, one group received the outcome immediately after the correct response; the other group received the outcome 2 sec after the correct response. All groups were told that the appearance of the reinforcing outcome indicated that the correct response had occurred, but no groups were informed of the delay. The unusual feature of the experiment was the procedure for responding. When the consonant stimulus appeared, the subject *continuously responded* in time to a metronome, saying a digit every 2 sec until the reinforcing outcome appeared. Thus, on every trial the subject would eventually make the correct response; his task was to make it as early as possible in the response sequence (that is, give it first). For instance, if 5 were the correct response for the stimulus H, then the following might occur in each group when H was presented: (*a*) for the group with the immediate consonant–digit outcome: H, "6, 2, 5," H5; (*b*) for the group with the immediate LIGHT outcome: H, "6, 2, 5," LIGHT; (*c*) for the group with the 2-sec delayed consonant–digit outcome: H, "6, 2, 5, 8," H5; (*d*) for the group with the 2-sec delayed LIGHT outcome: H, "6, 2, 5, 8," LIGHT. Thus, in both delay groups, the reinforcing outcome always occurred after the digit *following* the correct digit. The results, in terms of the percentage of first responses that were correct across trials, are shown in Figure 2. The 2-sec delay had no effect whatsoever when the consonant–digit outcome specified the correct response. In contrast, the 2-sec delay had a debilitating effect for the LIGHT

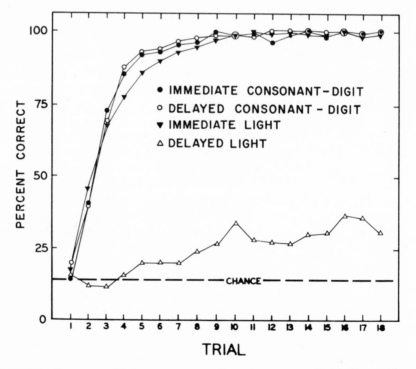

FIGURE 2.   Percentage of first responses correct for each group on each trial. (From Nelson, 1971.)

outcome, which did not itself specify the correct response—13 of the 20 subjects in this group were still performing at a chance level after eighteen reinforced trials on a six-item list! These results support four conclusions. First, reinforcement alone is not sufficient for learning (Section II.B). Second, to form the correct $S-R-O$ expectancy, the subject must infer the particular response to which the outcome pertains. Third, such inference is facilitated when the information contained in the reinforcement emphasizes the correct $S-R-O$ expectancy.[5] Fourth, the effect of delay of reinforcement depends not so much on the type of organism (human versus animal) but, rather, on how completely the reinforcing outcome specifies the correct response.

2. Stimulus Inference

To form an $S-R-O$ expectancy, the organism must not only infer the correct response; he must also infer the stimulus serving as a cue for the response-reinforcement contingency. The reasoning about stimulus inference is the same as the reasoning about response inference in the previous section.

B. Memory Factors

The importance of inference factors was highlighted in Section IV.A. In addition to being inferred, each of the three components (S, R, and O) must also be remembered throughout the formation of the $S-R-O$ expectancy. Then, once formed, the $S-R-O$ expectancy must be retained so that the organism can retrieve and utilize it subsequently. This notion is illustrated schematically in Figure 3.

1. Formation of Expectancy

To infer the stimulus and response that the reinforcing outcome pertains to, the organism must remember those components as he is forming his $S-R-O$ expectancy. First, consider memory of the response. Suppose, for

[5] This may help to explain why the anticipation method of paired-associate learning does not promote faster acquisition than the study–test method. In the former, the test and study phases are integrated, that is, the first stimulus occurs, followed by the subject's response, immediately followed by the correct stimulus–response pair, then the next stimulus occurs, and so on. In the latter, the test and study phases are segregated, that is, the first stimulus occurs, followed by the subject's response, the next stimulus occurs, and so on, then the first stimulus-response pair occurs—hence, there is a filled delay between the response and the stimulus–response pair. However, because the stimulus–response pair completely specifies the correct response to the stimulus, there should be no disadvantage for the study–test method. Such is the case empirically, and often there is actually an advantage for the study–test method, perhaps due to memory factors (Izawa, 1974).

FORMATION   RETENTION

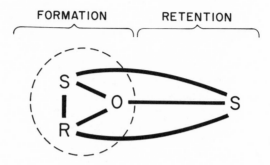

FIGURE 3. Three components must be remembered during formation of the *S–R–O* expectancy (dashed circle) and retained for utilization during the subsequent occurrence of the same stimulus situation.

instance, that in Nelson's delay experiment (Section IV. A) the 2-sec LIGHT group had been told in advance that the reinforcing LIGHT outcome pertained to the next-to-last response. This information would have eliminated the inference problem, but the subject would still have had to remember which response was next to last. Remembering back through only two responses might not be too difficult, but the difficulty would quickly become overwhelming if the subject had to remember back through more than about three or four responses (see Pollack, Johnson, & Knaff, 1959); this is probably a standard problem for animals when reinforcement is delayed. Of course, the difficulty of remembering the correct response—and, hence, the delay effect—can be short-circuited if the reinforcing outcome contains information specifying the identity of the correct response.

Not only must the response be remembered while the organism is forming the *S–R–O* expectancy; the stimulus, too, must be remembered unless information about its identity is contained in the reinforcing outcome. When the reinforcing outcome is delayed, remembering the stimulus can be a problem, particularly if the delay interval is filled with intervening activity (as is nearly always the case for the animal). This problem is demonstrated in the human domain by a continuous paired-associate learning experiment reported by Atkinson (1969). The subject saw a nonsense-syllable stimulus and guessed a response from the digits 2 to 9. Then a delay interval occurred (ranging from 0 to 12 sec), which either was or was not filled with the intervening activity of number counting. Following the delay interval, one of two possible outcomes occurred: (*a*) the correct response only or (*b*) the correct response paired with the nonsense-syllable stimulus. Subsequently (after at least ten other items), the stimulus reappeared and the subject tried to recall the response that had been specified by the outcome. Memory performance, in terms of the percentage of correct responses on this sub-

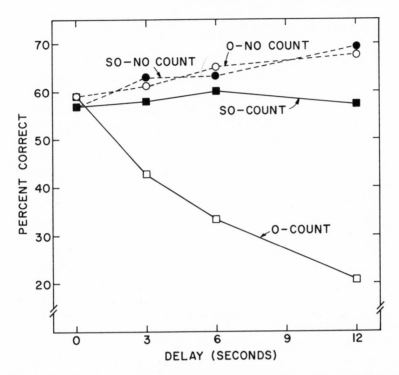

FIGURE 4.   Percentage of correct responses on the subsequent trial for each condition as a function of delay interval. (From Atkinson, 1969.)

sequent trial, is shown in Figure 4. Notice that the effect of delay of reinforcement depends upon the particular experimental situation. Delay has a detrimental effect only when the identity of the stimulus is not specified by the outcome *and* when the delay interval is filled with intervening activity (which increases the likelihood that the stimulus will be forgotten from memory). Delay does not have a detrimental effect if the outcome contains information specifying the identity of the stimulus, even though the subject himself may have forgotten the stimulus while he was number counting. Surprisingly, delay can actually improve performance when the delay interval is not filled with intervening activity; perhaps this improvement occurs because extra rehearsal of the stimulus makes it more resistant to forgetting during the subsequent retention of the *S–R–O* expectancy (see Section IV.B.2) or perhaps it is due to other retention factors (see Section IV.B.3). In any case, once again it is clear that delay of reinforcement does not automatically hinder memory performance. The effect of delay is partially determined by the accessibility of the stimulus and response components while the *S–R–O* expectancy is being formed.

2. Retention of Expectancy

Once formed, the $S-R-O$ expectancy must be remembered until the same stimulus situation recurs. At that time, the subject must recognize the stimulus situation as having occurred previously; this will happen only if he has remembered the stimulus component of the $S-R-O$ expectancy. Also, he must remember the response and its associated outcome so that he can decide how to respond. If any of the three components of the $S-R-O$ expectancy is forgotten, an error is likely to result.

There is one situation in which it is not necessary to remember the $S-R-O$ expectancy until the stimulus recurs, and this situation actually arises *because* the reinforcing outcome is delayed! Notice that there is a time continuum from the initial stimulus–response occurrence to the recurrence of that stimulus. The reinforcing outcome can occur at any time during that time interval. The farther it is from the initial stimulus–response occurrence, the greater is the delay of reinforcement. However, if the delay is great enough, the reinforcing outcome will occur at the time when the stimulus is about to recur! Buchwald (1969) investigated this situation by using Thorndikian paired-associate learning. A stimulus word was presented, and the subject guessed one of two response alternatives (the digit 3 or 5). The reinforcing outcome of "right" or "wrong" was either given immediately or delayed until the stimulus word recurred. For example, in the former condition, the sequence of events might be: The experimenter presents FROG, the subject says "3," the experimenter says "wrong," . . . other items . . . , the experimenter re-presents FROG, and the subject must decide whether to say 3 or 5. In the latter condition, the sequence of events might be: The experimenter presents FROG, the subject says "3," . . . other items . . . , the experimenter re-presents FROG and tells the subject, "You made the wrong response to this stimulus last time," and the subject must decide whether to say 3 or 5. The results were that the delayed-outcome subjects, who had to remember only two previous components (the stimulus and response), performed better than the immediate-outcome subjects, who had to remember three previous components (the stimulus, response, and outcome). In another experiment, Buchwald (1969) showed that reminding the subject of his old response when the stimulus recurs also tends to improve performance (that is, the subject has to remember the old stimulus and the old outcome but not his old response). Thus, short-circuiting the requirement of remembering all of the components in the $S-R-O$ expectancy improves retention of the $S-R-O$ expectancy, just as it improves formation of the $S-R-O$ expectancy (Section IV.B.1). In general, whenever a particular situation eliminates the need for a critical memory (shown by the solid lines in Figure 3), performance increases; whenever a strain is placed on a critical memory, performance decreases.

The factors of inference and memory (during both formation and reten-tion of the *S–R–O* expectancy) seem to be important determinants of the delay-of-reinforcement effect. When the human subject has to overcome problems of inference and/or memory, delay hinders his performance just as it hinders animal performance. In those situations in which delay does not hinder performance, a careful analysis will generally reveal that an infer-ence problem or a memory problem has been short-circuited—such short-circuiting seldom occurs in animal studies (but see Garcia & Koelling, 1966), so the usual finding is a strong delay effect.

3. The Delay–Retention Effect

There is a delay situation, perhaps the most important of all for applica-tions to education, where delay of the reinforcing outcome facilitates sub-sequent retention because of memory factors. However, the facilitation results from neither rehearsal during the delay interval (Section IV.B.1) nor the old outcome's being coincident with the subsequent test of the item (Section IV.B.2). Rather, the facilitation seems to occur because delaying the outcome helps the subject isolate the correct response (as specified by the reinforcing outcome) from his previous incorrect response. This effect is most pronounced when there is a fairly lengthy retention interval between the outcome-specified correct response and the occurrence of the sub-sequent test—hence the name "delay-retention effect." Consider the time intervals shown in Figure 5. When the outcome-specified correct response occurs immediately after the subject's response (that is, a near-zero delay interval), the subject may subsequently have difficulty remembering which of the two responses was his and which was the one specified as correct by the reinforcing outcome. Such discrimination is easier when there is a temporal separation between the subject's response and the outcome-

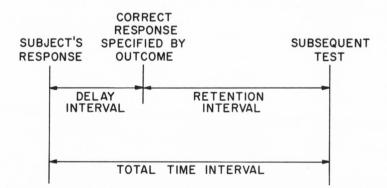

FIGURE 5.   Time intervals between the subject's response, the correct response as specified by the reinforcing outcome, and the subsequent test of the correct response.

specified response (that is, when the delay interval is substantially greater than zero). However, to insure that the delay-retention effect is not simply a result of a shorter retention interval for the outcome-specified response, the confounding of delay interval with retention interval must be eliminated by keeping the length of the retention interval constant while the delay interval increases. This occurred in an experiment by Sturges (1969). Undergraduate subjects made guesses on 38 four-alternative multiple-choice items. Then one group immediately saw the 38 multiple-choice items with the correct response underlined for each item; another group did not see them until 24 hr later. One week after seeing the correctly underlined items, each group was again tested on the 38 multiple-choice items. The percentage of correct responses on the retention test was 92% for the 24-hr delay group and 79% for the immediate group—delaying the outcome obviously facilitated subsequent retention.

Notice, however, that when the length of the retention interval is held constant and the delay interval is increased, a new confounding occurs: As the delay interval increases, so does the total time between the subject's incorrect response and the retention test. Rather than resulting from delay of the outcome, the delay-retention effect may occur simply because, as the total time interval increases, the subject is more likely to forget his previous (potentially interfering) incorrect response. Therefore, the delay-retention effect must be demonstrated in a situation where the total time interval is held constant as the delay interval increases. This occurred in an experiment by Kulhavy and Anderson (1972). The subjects made guesses on 35 four-alternative multiple-choice items. Then, one group immediately saw the 35 items with the correct response underlined for each item; another group did not see the underlined items until the next day. One week after the initial guessing session (as opposed to the correctly-underlined-item session), each group was again tested on the 35 multiple-choice items. The percentage of correct responses on the retention test was 66% for the one-day delay group and 50% for the immediate group, again showing the delay-retention effect.[6] To determine the locus of the delay-retention effect, retention performance was conditionalized on the correctness of the subject's initial guess. The results are shown in Table 5. The effect of delay

[6] To ensure that the delay-retention effect did not simply result from better memory for the outcome-specified correct response (the retention interval was shorter in the delay group than in the immediate group), two control groups were included. These control groups did not have an initial test and, hence, did not make initial responses. Instead, they received only the outcome-specified correct responses given to the experimental groups. For one control group, this occurred at the same time as for the one-day-delay experimental group; for the other control group, this occurred at the same time as for the no-delay experimental group; the retention test occurred the same day for both control groups (viz., 7 days later for the no-delay control group and 6 days later for the one-day-delay control group). The difference between the percentages correct on the retention test was small and not statistically significant (62% for the no-delay control group versus 57% for the one-day-delay control group). Thus, these control groups show that the delay-retention effect occurring in the experimental groups cannot be attributed simply to differential retention due to retention intervals of slightly different lengths.

TABLE 5

Percent Correct Retention Conditionalized on
Delay Interval and on Correctness
of Initial Response in Kulhavy and
Anderson's (1972) Experiment

Initial response	Delay interval (days)	
	Zero	One
Correct	70	78
Incorrect	31	61

interval was fairly small and not statistically reliable when the initial response was correct, but was massive and highly reliable when the initial response was incorrect. These findings support the notion that the delay-retention effect results from isolation of the outcome-specified correct response from the subject's initial incorrect response. (Put differently, there is less proactive interference when the amount of time increases between the occurrence of a potentially interfering response and the subsequent acquisition of the target response—see Underwood & Freund, 1968.)

It should be mentioned that, to optimize retention, there may be limits on how long the delay interval should be between the initial incorrect response and the outcome-specified correct response (More, 1969). The exact length of the optimal delay interval depends on boundary conditions such as length of the retention interval, type of outcome, and nature of the information to be remembered. Because of some of these boundary conditions, the delay-retention effect is more likely to occur in the human domain than in the animal domain (for example, the outcome of the $S–R–O$ expectancy may have to completely specify both the stimulus and the correct response—it is difficult to provide such specific information to an animal). However, this certainly does not mean that the basic processes underlying delay of reinforcement differ from humans to animals. The processes may be the same, but the boundary conditions for particular delay-of-reinforcement phenomena such as the delay-retention effect may be more difficult to maintain in the animal domain.

V. CHANGING CONTINGENCIES OF REINFORCEMENT

Thus far, the focus has been on the formation and retention of individual $S–R–O$ expectancies. Furthermore, in the previous situations, the organism behaved in accord with the assumption that the environmental reinforcement contingency would continue to remain in effect (that is, would not change). But what happens when the reinforcement contingency does change? Do humans and animals respond in the same basic way to changed reinforcement contingencies?

Before examining answers to these questions, it is important to realize that in every response-contingent reinforcement situation, there seems to be not just one $S-R-O$ expectancy but, rather, two (the second expectancy pertains to the outcome following the *nonoccurrence* of the critical response—see Section III.B.1.b). For example, during the acquisition of a lever-press response in a Skinner box, the rat is assumed to acquire the following two $S-R-O$ expectancies. First, the response of lever pressing (when the rat has access to the lever) is followed by food, yielding an $S-R-O$ expectancy of "lever, press, food." Second, any response other than lever pressing (when the rat has access to the lever) is followed by the outcome of nothing, yielding an $S-R-O$ expectancy of "lever, no press, nothing." Thus, the two assumed expectancies are "lever, press, food" and "lever, no press, nothing."

What is the theoretical utility of assuming multiple $S-R-O$ expectancies? These multiple expectancies aid in explaining and integrating three changing-reinforcement phenomena: extinction, the partial-reinforcement effect, and learned helplessness. Let us consider the common mechanisms underlying these phenomena in the animal domain and the human verbal domain, beginning with the phenomenon of extinction.

A. Extinction

Extinction is defined as a decrement in the performance of an acquired response. During extinction trials in the animal domain, the previously correct response is no longer followed by the reinforcing outcome; instead, the outcome of nothing occurs (for example, the lever-press response is followed by nothing instead of by food). Extinction also occurs in the domain of human verbal learning, but only when the situation is comparable to that in the animal domain. Analogous to the animal lever-pressing situation, a critical prerequisite for the extinction of a human verbal response is the establishment of a response-outcome contingency during acquisition.

1. Contingent versus Noncontingent Reinforcement

During the acquisition phase of the animal-extinction situation described above, the animal had received food when it pressed the lever but received nothing when it made any other response (that is, the outcome was contingent upon the response). The importance of an analogous response-outcome contingency for the subsequent extinction of a human verbal response has been demonstrated by Nelson (1971). Undergraduate subjects learned a list of consonant–digit paired associates and then went through a series of extinction trials. There were three groups, differing only in terms of the procedure during acquisition. For the first group (Noncontingent Consonant–Digit), as each consonant appeared during acquisition, the subject guessed a digit from the pool of digits from 3 to 9; then, regardless of the correctness of the subject's response, the correct digit paired with the consonant appeared. The procedure was identical for the second group (Contingent Consonant–Digit) except that the correct digit paired with the consonant appeared only if the subject's response was correct; if the subject's response was incorrect, then nothing appeared. For the third group (Contingent Light), the procedure was the same as that for the Contingent Consonant–Digit group except that the outcome following a correct response was the illumination of a light signifying "Right"; following an incorrect response, nothing occurred. For all three groups, acquisition continued until the correct response was made on three consecutive trials. Then, without any warning to the subjects, eight extinction trials occurred where the outcome of nothing followed correct responses, that is, the acquisition outcome that previously followed correct responses was withdrawn. The results of interest, shown in Figure 6, concern the performance of each group during the eight extinction trials.[7] Extinction is defined as a decrease in the percentage of correct responses across extinction trials. Notice that the noncontingent group did not extinguish at all, whereas there was marked extinction in the two contingent groups, who extinguished at approximately the same rate.

These results support two conclusions about the extinction of a human verbal response. First, the amount of extinction is not determined by the specificity of the reinforcing outcome that follows correct responses. The Contingent Consonant–Digit outcome completely specified the correct response whereas the Contingent Light outcome simply indicated that the correct response had occurred (see Section IV.A.1), yet the rates of extinction were not significantly different for these two groups. Second, to obtain subsequent extinction of a verbal response, a response–outcome contingency has to be established during acquisition.[8] The withdrawal of a

---

[7] In terms of acquisition performance, the Noncontingent Consonant–Digit group was fastest (15.3 trials to criterion) because information specifying the correct response occurred even if the subject's response had been incorrect. The remaining two groups required more acquisition trials (23.6 for the Contingent Consonant–Digit group and 24.9 for the Contingent Light group) because, after an incorrect response, they knew only what response *not* to make—their outcome of nothing following an incorrect response did not specify what response they should make (see Section III.B.1.b). After a correct response, however, the specificity of the outcome is irrelevant; the subject needs only to know that he is correct (see Section IV.A.1). Consequently, the Contingent Consonant–Digit group and the Contingent Light group did not differ during acquisition.

[8] This implies that paired-associate learning in particular, and verbal learning in general, should be conceptualized as instances of instrumental conditioning rather than classical conditioning (for more discussion of this point, see Nelson, 1971).

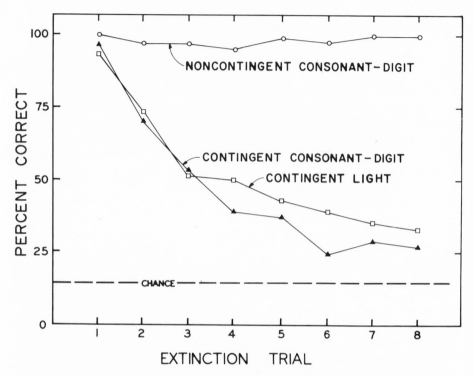

FIGURE 6.   Percentage of correct responses for each group on each extinction trial as a function of the reinforcement during prior learning. (From Nelson, 1971.)

noncontingent reinforcing outcome does not extinguish a verbal response; this result is very robust (for example, Goss, 1965, demonstrated that verbal responses acquired by noncontingent reinforcement do not extinguish during even as many as 56 extinction trials).

2. Kind of Response-Outcome Contingency

The previous section demonstrated the importance of a response-outcome acquisition contingency (that is, contingent reinforcement) for producing subsequent extinction of a verbal response. But is any kind of response-outcome contingency sufficient? Evidently not. To obtain extinction of a verbal response, the outcome following correct responses during extinction trials—typically the outcome of nothing—must also have followed wrong responses during acquisition. It is not sufficient simply to make the reinforcing outcome contingent upon correct responses during acquisition without considering the outcome that follows wrong responses. Put differently, the outcome of nothing that is usually employed during extinction trials does not extinguish a verbal response unless it has followed wrong responses during acquisition.

This principle is made clear in an experiment by Buchwald (1959). The subject's task was to choose the correct nonsense syllable in each of 18 pairs of nonsense syllables. During acquisition, three groups had different kinds of response-outcome contingencies. The Right–Wrong group was told "right" after correct responses and "wrong" after wrong responses. The Right–Nothing group was told "right" after correct responses and nothing was said after wrong responses. The Nothing–Wrong group was told nothing after correct responses but was told "wrong" after wrong responses. Thus, a response–outcome contingency of one kind or another was established for all three groups during acquisition. After acquisition, all three groups went through a series of extinction trials where the outcome of nothing occurred regardless of the correctness of the response. The results were straightforward. Of the subjects who attained the acquisition criterion (correct responding on 36 consecutive trials), the percentages who subsequently displayed extinction were: 3% of the Nothing–Wrong subjects, 6% of the Right–Wrong subjects, and 71% of the Right–Nothing subjects. Obviously, a substantial percentage of subjects displayed extinction only in the Right–Nothing group. These results support three conclusions about the extinction of a verbal response. First, the outcome of nothing during extinction trials does not necessarily produce extinction; the occurrence of extinction depends upon the events that took place during acquisition. Second, not any kind of response-outcome contingency during acquisition is sufficient for subsequent extinction. Third, and perhaps most critical, substantial extinction occurs only when the outcome that previously followed wrong responses during acquisition subsequently follows correct responses during extinction.

Now consider the following theoretical analysis of extinction in terms of the multiple $S–R–O$ expectancies that arise and change during changing contingencies of reinforcement (see Figure 7). Essentially, extinction entails changing the multiple $S–R–O$ expectancies from (a) the contingent-reinforcement situation to (b) the noncontingent-reinforcement situation where the extinction outcome which follows both wrong *and* correct responses is the same as that which followed only wrong responses during acquisition. In terms of Figure 7, O_w (which might represent the outcome of nothing) followed only wrong responses during acquisition but subsequently follows both wrong and correct responses during extinction. Therefore, during extinction, the organism stores in memory a new correct-response expectancy (that is, $S–R_c–O_w$) which, in essence, induces it to stop making the previously correct response (that is, it stops performing R_c). Instead, perhaps in an attempt to find some new correct response that actually will be followed by O_c, the organism tries other

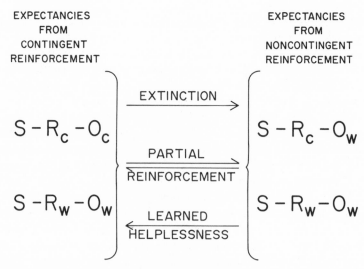

FIGURE 7. Multiple S–R–O expectancies arising and changing during extinction, partial reinforcement, and learned helplessness. (The subscript "c" pertains to "correct" and the subscript "w" pertains to "wrong.") For the animal domain, O_w might refer to nothing and O_c to food in an appetitive situation, whereas O_w might refer to shock and O_c to avoidance of shock in an aversive situation.

responses and, thus, the previously correct response becomes extinguished. Eventually, after many extinction trials, the organism stores in memory the multiple S–R–O expectancies of S–R_c–O_w and S–R_w–O_w; these expectancies can induce an animal to stop responding entirely (for their effect on a human subject, see the final paragraph of the next section, V.B).

B. Partial-Reinforcement Effect

The prior section highlighted the importance of a response-outcome contingency during acquisition. The contingency was described as if correct responses are always followed by the reinforcing outcome throughout acquisition (wrong responses being followed by another outcome, usually the outcome of nothing)—this situation is known as continuous reinforcement. In contrast, sometimes the response-outcome contingency is not completely consistent throughout acquisition. In the situation known as partial reinforcement, the reinforcing outcome occurs after only some percentage of the correct responses during acquisition. This situation, initially examined by Humphreys (1939) in human probability learning, has been studied extensively in the animal domain (for a review, see Lewis,

1960). In a typical animal experiment, during acquisition of a lever-pressing response, some percentage of a rat's lever presses are reinforced by food, whereas the remainder of its lever presses are followed by the outcome of nothing (which also follows wrong responses). What influence does this partial reinforcement have on acquisition and subsequent extinction? The typical findings from the animal domain are that (a) partial reinforcement retards acquisition of the correct response and (b) extinction occurs more slowly after partial reinforcement than after continuous reinforcement. How do these findings about partial reinforcement in the animal domain arise from the $S–R–O$ expectancies stored in memory?

First, consider the finding that partial reinforcement retards acquisition. Essentially, the response-outcome contingency operates only sporadically throughout acquisition (see Figure 7). During the remaining time, the correct response is not followed by the reinforcing outcome; instead, the correct response is followed by the same outcome that follows wrong responses (that is, O_w). Thus, the response-outcome contingency is established, then broken, then reestablished, and so on. Consequently, as Figure 7 indicates, the organism stores in memory a series of multiple $S–R–O$ expectancies, some containing $S–R_c–O_c$ and others containing $S–R_c–O_w$. This could retard acquisition performance for at least two reasons. First, initial occurrences of the correct response may not be reinforced (if the response-outcome contingency happens not to be operative) so that, initially, the only expectancies stored in memory about the correct response are $S–R_c–O_w$ expectancies; these expectancies would induce the organism not to repeat the correct response. Second, even when some occurrences of the correct response are reinforced, the organism may try other responses in an attempt to discover a response that is always reinforced.

Next, consider the finding that extinction is slower following partial reinforcement than following continuous reinforcement. Unlike the continuously reinforced subject, the partially reinforced subject previously stored in memory a series of different correct-response expectancies ($S–R_c–O_w$ and $S–R_c–O_c$) implying that the nonoccurrence of the reinforcing outcome is only short-lived (that is, nonreinforced correct responses eventually were followed by reinforced correct responses). Therefore, during extinction, the partially reinforced subject requires many nonreinforcements (and, hence, many extinction trials) to disconfirm the implication of the series of correct-response expectancies stored in memory. After disconfirmation occurs, the previously acquired expectancies no longer induce the organism to perform the correct response (Section V.A). In contrast, the continuously reinforced subject's series of correct-response expectancies consist only of reinforced correct responses. Therefore, during extinction, even a single nonreinforced correct response can be sufficient for disconfirmation.

If the above analysis applies to humans as well as to animals, then both acquisition and extinction in human learning should be slower under partial reinforcement than under continuous reinforcement. Such is the case empirically, as illustrated in an experiment by Nelson (1971). Two groups of undergraduate subjects, a continuously reinforced group and a partially reinforced group, acquired a list of consonant–digit paired associates. On every trial, the subject had to guess a digit response from the digits 3 to 8. For the continuously reinforced group, the occurrence of the correct response was always followed by the reinforcing outcome of the correct consonant–digit pair (incorrect responses were followed by the outcome of nothing). For the partially reinforced group, only two-thirds of the correct responses were reinforced (the remaining responses were followed by the outcome of nothing). Both groups had 18 acquisition trials and, without forewarning, 18 extinction trials, in which all responses were followed by the outcome of nothing. The results are shown in Figure 8. These data demonstrate clearly the effects of partial reinforcement. The responses of the partially reinforced group were learned more slowly and were extinguished more slowly than those of the continuously reinforced group.

Notice one particularly interesting feature of the results shown in Figure 8. The performance of the continuously reinforced group first decreased over extinction trials and then increased (that is, nonmonotonic extinction). This increase remained above chance after Trial 25, which happens to be

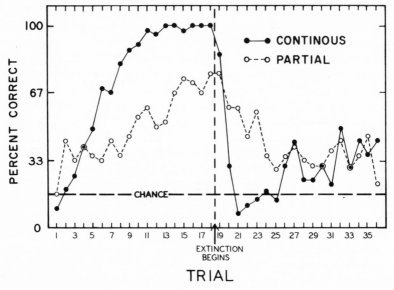

FIGURE 8.   Percentage of correct responses for each group on each acquisition trial and extinction trial. (From Nelson, 1971.)

the sixth trial after the first extinction trial (and there were only six possible responses in the response pool). Evidently, after exhausting the response pool without ever being reinforced, the subjects began a return to their well-learned acquisition responses. Postexperimental interviews of the subjects confirmed this strategy. This result highlights an important point: Extinction should be construed as a decrement in performance rather than as a decrement in memory. That is, the occurrence of extinction does not necessarily imply that the organism has forgotten the $S-R_c-O_c$ expectancies; instead, the $S-R_c-O_c$ expectancies may remain stored in memory but not induce performance (perhaps because new $S-R_c-O_w$ expectancies become predominant). The occurrence of nonmonotonic extinction demonstrates that at least some of the $S-R_c-O_c$ expectancies remain stored in memory during extinction.

C. Learned Helplessness

The final animal-learning phenomenon to be considered in terms of changing contingencies of reinforcement is learned helplessness (for a review, see Maier, Seligman, & Solomon, 1969). An animal, typically a dog, goes through a series of trials in which it receives painful electric shocks that it can neither avoid nor escape. After an initial series of frantic responses, the animal eventually stops responding. Subsequently, when placed in a standard shuttle box where it can avoid shock, the animal displays impaired avoidance learning, sometimes to such a degree that it never does learn the avoidance response. Thus, as indicated in Figure 7, the prior experience of noncontingent reinforcement (electric shock, regardless of the response) impairs subsequent learning when reinforcement is contingent upon a particular response (avoidance of shock contingent upon a shuttling response). In essence, the noncontingent-reinforcement expectancies seem to induce a mental set for nonlearning (see lack of future utility in Section II.B; also Levine, 1971).

Does learned helplessness occur in human verbal learning when the situation is analogous to that in the animal domain? A rough analogy is provided by an unpublished verbal learning experiment conducted in my laboratory at the University of Washington. The subject's task was to guess the digit (from the pool of digits 1–5) that was paired with each of five letters. First, a letter appeared and the subject guessed a digit. A "correct" guess was reinforced (a buzzer sounded and a visible counting device incremented one step, indicating to the subject that he had just earned one cent); nothing happened after an "incorrect" guess. Next, another letter appeared, and so on, until the subject had gone through all five letters, which ended the first trial. Then a second trial occurred on the same five letters, and so on, until five complete trials had occurred on the same set of letters, which ended the first block of trials. Following the first five-trial block, there was a second five-trial block with an entirely new set of letters. Finally, there was a third five-trial block with a third set of letters.

There were three groups of undergraduate subjects, one "Helpless" experimental group and two control groups. In the Helpless group, there was no correct response for the subject to learn during the first two blocks, but he could learn during the third block. That is, during the first two blocks, the digit response to be reinforced was randomly determined anew on every trial. Consequently, from the Helpless subject's perspective, the occurrence of the reinforcing outcome was not contingent upon any particular digit response (in terms of the noncontingent-reinforcement expectancies in Figure 7, the outcome—the chance probability of reinforcement—was identical for all possible response alternatives). After the first and second blocks had been completed, the third block began. Across the five trials of the third block, the correct digit response to a given letter stimulus was *unchanging*. Would the Helpless subject's noncontingent-reinforcement expectancies from the first two blocks impair his performance during the third block, in which he could learn contingent-reinforcement expectancies? To answer this question, baseline learning data were obtained from two control groups. One control group (C1) went through all three blocks, with the correct digit response unchanging across the trials of each block (that is, contingent-reinforcement expectancies were established); the third block consisted of the same letter–digit pairings as the Helpless group's third block. The second control group (C2) worked on arithmetic problems instead of going through the first two blocks; their only block was identical to the Helpless group's third block. To maintain correspondence with the animal situation, none of the groups was informed in advance about changing/unchanging correct responses—they formed their own expectancies as the experiment progressed.

The crucial results, shown in Figure 9, concern performance across the five trials of the third block, in which learning could occur for all three groups. The influence of prior experience on subsequent learning is obvious. In particular, whereas both control groups showed substantial learning across all five trials, the Helpless group's first evidence of learning occurred on the fifth trial—the Helpless subjects showed no learning whatsoever across the first four trials! Apparently, the Helpless group's noncontingent-reinforcement expectancies from the first two blocks interfered with the establishment of contingent-reinforcement expectancies during the third block. These findings in human verbal learning are analogous to those from learned helplessness in animals,[9] in which prior noncontingent reinforce-

---

[9] Recently, learned helplessness has also been demonstrated for human nonverbal responses in an escape-avoidance aversive situation (Hiroto, 1974).

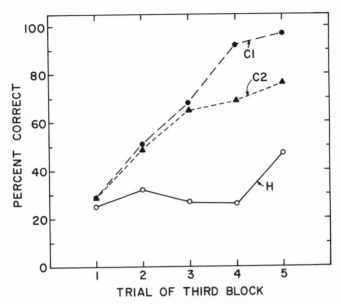

FIGURE 9.   Percentage of correct responses on each trial of the third block for each group (C1 = control with unchanging correct response on all three blocks; C2 = control with arithmetric on first two blocks and unchanging correct response on third block; H = "Helpless" group with changing correct response on first two blocks and unchanging correct response on third block.)

ment interferes with the subsequent learning of a contingently reinforced avoidance response. Thus, in the human domain as well as in the animal domain, changing the contingencies of reinforcement (as in Figure 7) profoundly influences behavior, and humans and animals exhibit comparable responses to changed contingencies of reinforcement.

VI. SUMMARY

The research reviewed in this chapter supports the following propositions relating reinforcement and human verbal memory:

1. The same basic reinforcement principles apply in both the animal domain and the human verbal domain; however, these principles may be obscured if critical boundary conditions are violated.

2. External reinforcement is neither necessary nor sufficient for memory or memory performance; hence, reinforcement does not automatically strengthen a particular memory.

3. Reinforcement has two primary functions (one informative and the second motivational): (a) to emphasize particular environmental reinforcement contingencies, thereby providing information that can be used (directly or vicariously) to establish S–R–O expectancies in memory; (b) to induce subsequent performance based on remembered S–R–O expectancies.

4. For reinforcement to induce "correct" performance, the organism must remember an S–R–O expectancy that is identical to (or correlated with) the environmental reinforcement contingency.

5. When performance is goal directed, reinforcement induces "correct" performance only if the organism wants the outcome of a remembered S–R–O expectancy. If the organism wants the opposite outcome, it will purposefully make an "incorrect" response. Therefore, a lack of "correct" performance does not necessarily imply a lack of memory for the S–R–O expectancy.

6. Magnitude of reward has an indirect effect on acquisition by prioritizing particular items for differential rehearsal, which, in turn, has a direct effect on information storage.

7. Magnitude of reward usually does not influence the retrieval of information from memory. In those rare instances when it does, the influence is small and results from more extended searching rather than from more efficient searching.

8. Delay of reinforcement can either retard, facilitate, or have no effect on performance. Two critical determinants of the delay effect are inference (of the S and R to which the O pertains) and memory (during both formation and retention of the S–R–O expectancy).

9. Extinction, partial-reinforcement effects, and learned helplessness are due to changing contingencies of reinforcement:

a. Extinction (a decrement in performance rather than memory) occurs when contingent reinforcement ceases and the outcome that previously followed wrong responses subsequently follows correct responses.

b. Partial reinforcement, a vacillation between the presence and absence of contingent reinforcement, retards both acquisition and subsequent extinction.

c. Learned helplessness is an impairment in acquisition (during contingent reinforcement) due to prior noncontingent reinforcement.

ACKNOWLEDGMENTS

Preparation of this chapter was supported by grant MH-21037 from the National Institute of Mental Health. The chapter was written in part at the University of Washington and in part during a visiting appointment at the University of California, Irvine. I thank R. C. Bolles,

W. K. Estes, and G. R. Loftus for providing valuable comments, and A. P. Fries and C. E. Larson for collecting data for the two new experiments.

REFERENCES

Atkinson, R. C. Information delay in human learning. *Journal of Verbal Learning and Verbal Behavior,* 1969, **8,** 507–511.

Atkinson, R. C., & Wickens, T. D. Human memory and the concept of reinforcement. In R. Glaser (Ed.), *The nature of reinforcement.* New York: Academic Press, 1971. Pp. 66–120.

Bolles, R. C. *Theory of motivation.* New York: Harper & Row, 1967.

Bolles, R. C. Reinforcement, expectancy, and learning. *Psychological Review,* 1972, **79,** 394–409.

Brewer, W. F. There is no convincing evidence for operant or classical conditioning in adult humans. In W. B. Weimer & D. S. Palermo (Eds.), *Cognition and symbolic processes.* Hillsdale, New Jersey: Lawrence Erlbaum Assoc., 1974. Pp. 1–42.

Buchwald, A. M. Effects of "right" and "wrong" on subsequent behavior: A new interpretation. *Psychological Review,* 1969, **76,** 132–143.

Dulany, D. E., Jr. Hypotheses and habits in verbal "operant conditioning." *Journal of Abnormal and Social Psychology,* 1961, **63,** 251–263.

Dulany, D. E., Jr. The place of hypotheses and intentions: An analysis of verbal control in verbal conditioning. In C. W. Eriksen (Ed.), *Behavior and awareness.* Durham, North Carolina: Duke University Press, 1962. Pp. 102–129.

Estes, W. K. Reinforcement in human learning. In J. Tapp (Ed.), *Reinforcement.* New York: Academic Press, 1969. Pp. 63–94.

Garcia, J., & Koelling, R. A. Relation of cue to consequence in avoidance learning. *Psychonomic Science,* 1966, **4,** 123–124.

Goss, A. E. Manifest strengthening of correct responses of paired-associates under postcriterion zero percent occurrence of response members. *Journal of General Psychology,* 1965, **72,** 135–144.

Greenspoon, J. The reinforcing effect of two spoken sounds on the frequency of two responses. *American Journal of Psychology,* 1955, **68,** 409–416.

Harley, W. F. The effect of monetary incentive in paired associate learning using an absolute method. *Psychonomic Science,* 1965, **3,** 141–142.   (a)

Harley, W. F. The effect of monetary incentive in paired associate learning using a differential method. *Psychonomic Science,* 1965, **2,** 377–378.   (b)

Hillix, W. A., & Marx, M. H. Response strengthening by information and effect in human learning. *Journal of Experimental Psychology,* 1960, **60,** 97–102.

Hiroto, D. S. Locus of control and learned helplessness. *Journal of Experimental Psychology,* 1974, **102,** 187–193.

Humphreys, L. G. Acquisition and extinction of verbal expectation in a situation analogous to conditioning. *Journal of Experimental Psychology,* 1939, **25,** 294–301.

Izawa, C. Retention interval hypotheses and list lengths: Comparison of anticipation and study-test procedures. *Canadian Journal of Psychology,* 1974, **28,** 214–224.

Keller, L., Cole, M., Burke, C. J., & Estes, W. K. Reward and information values of trial outcomes in paired-associate learning. *Psychological Monographs,* 1965, **79**(Whole No. 605).

Kulhavy, R. W., & Anderson, R. C. The delay-retention effect with multiple-choice tests. *Journal of Educational Psychology,* 1972, **63,** 505–512.

Levine, M. Hypothesis theory and nonlearning despite ideal S–R reinforcement contingencies. *Psychological Review,* 1971, **78,** 130–140.

Lewis, D. J. Partial reinforcement: A selective review of the literature since 1950. *Psychological Bulletin*, 1960, **57**, 1–28.

Loftus, G. R. Eye fixations and recognition memory for pictures. *Cognitive Psychology*, 1972, **3**, 525–551.

Loftus, G. R., & Wickens, T. D. Effect of incentive on storage and retrieval processes. *Journal of Experimental Psychology*, 1970, **85**, 141–147.

Maier, S. F., Seligman, M. E. P., & Solomon, R. L. Pavlovian fear conditioning and learned helplessness: Effects on escape and avoidance behavior of (a) the CS–US contingency and (b) the independence of the US and voluntary responding. In B. A. Campbell & R. M. Church (Eds.), *Punishment and aversive behavior*. New York: Appleton-Century-Crofts, 1969. Pp. 299–342.

Marlatt, G. A. Comparison of vicarious and direct reinforcement control of verbal behavior in an interview setting. *Journal of Personality and Social Psychology*, 1970, **16**, 695–703.

Marlatt, G. A. Task structure and the experimental modification of verbal behavior. *Psychological Bulletin*, 1972, **78**, 335–350.

More, A. J. Delay of feedback and the acquisition and retention of verbal materials in the classroom. *Journal of Educational Psychology*, 1969, **60**, 339–342.

Nelson, T. O. Extinction, delay, and partial-reinforcement effects in paired-associate learning. *Cognitive Psychology*, 1971, **2**, 212–228.

Nuttin, J., & Greenwald, A. G. *Reward and punishment in human learning*. New York: Academic Press, 1968.

Philbrick, E. B., & Postman, L. A further analysis of 'learning without awareness.' *American Journal of Psychology*, 1955, **68**, 417–424.

Pollack, I., Johnson, L. B., & Knaff, P. R. Running memory span. *Journal of Experimental Psychology*, 1959, **57**, 137–146.

Postman, L. Rewards and punishments in human learning. In L. Postman (Ed.), *Psychology in the making*. New York: Knopf, 1962. Pp. 331–401.

Renner, K. E. Delay of reinforcement: A historical review. *Psychological Bulletin*, 1964, **61**, 341–361.

Rundus, D. Analysis of rehearsal processes in free recall. *Journal of Experimental Psychology*, 1971, **89**, 63–77.

Sturges, P. T. Verbal retention as a function of the informativeness and delay of informative feedback. *Journal of Educational Psychology*, 1969, **60**, 11–14.

Thorndike, E. L. An experimental study of rewards. *Teacher's College Contributions to Education* (No. 580). New York: Teacher's College Bureau of Publications, 1933.

Tolman, E. C. *Purposive behavior in animals and men*. New York: Appleton-Century-Crofts, 1932.

Tolman, E. C., & Honzik, C. H. Introduction and removal of reward, and maze performance in rats. *University of California Publications in Psychology*, 1930, **4**, 257–275.

Underwood, B. J., & Freund, J. S. Effect of temporal separation of two tasks on proactive inhibition. *Journal of Experimental Psychology*, 1968, **78**, 50–54.

Wallach, H., & Henle, M. A further study of the function of reward. *Journal of Experimental Psychology*, 1942, **30**, 147–160.

Weiner, B. Motivation and memory. *Psychological Monographs*, 1966, **80**(Whole No. 626).

7

Motivation and Reward in Human Learning: A Cognitive Approach

Joseph R. Nuttin

University of Louvain, Belgium

I. INTRODUCTION

Three decades ago it was rather revolutionary and shocking to emphasize the cognitive or informative aspect of reward in human learning. On the contrary, in current psychological research cognitive interpretations have become fashionable, with the result that Right and Wrong are often presented to the subjects as mere cues signaling which responses are to be learned and which are not; the reward aspect of the successful outcome for all practical purposes is neglected. Therefore, in this chapter I propose to link the motivational and informational aspects of outcomes in learning tasks because I am convinced that, in the context of current cognitive psychology, these aspects of behavior are too often disassociated from one another. In fact, I assume that humans are at the same time cognizing their world and in search of objects satisfying their cognitively elaborated needs. The conceptualization of human behavior in terms of *open-task systems* may be useful in interpreting cognition and motivation, processes that pervade every behavioral act, including those of learning.

The assumed complexity of human behavior bears a direct relation to the astonishing flexibility and versatility of the human's higher cognitive functioning (information processing) and motivation. Whereas there is little difficulty in defining the few rewards used by animal psychologists (see

Miller, 1963, p. 97), almost anything can be either a reward or a punishment to human subjects, according to its motivational and cognitive context. The *interruption* of a task can mean failure as well as success, according to instructions and interpretations. One person may conceive of an event as self-enhancing, whereas another may perceive it to be deprecating, and so on. Whatever the conditions, variables, and instructions with which one is working, their behavioral context and interpretation can be structured in several different ways (Spence, Armstrong, & Conrad, 1969). This cognitive elaboration has its behavioral impact: it is found that task interruptions signifying failure to a subject influence behavior in a different way from interruptions signifying success (see, among others, Atkinson, 1953; Marrow, 1938).

In psychophysical and psychophysiological experiments, researchers are extremely careful and precise when defining the physical stimulus impinging on the subject's sense organs. As much care and precision should be used when defining the meaningful situations, motivational conditions, and instructions in behavioral investigations. Contradictory results in behavioral experiments may often originate from factors of this kind, as is shown in Section VII.

One aspect of human cognitive flexibility is the diversity of relationships continuously constructed between objects and events. Context and informational meaning are related to the active relational network that is assumed to codetermine behavior. Until recently, behavioral scientists were very reluctant to consider any parameters other than physical (that is, temporal and spatial) in learning (see Section V.A.2). It is not clear now what will ultimately prove to be the best way for them to deal with the more complex relations characteristic of the behavioral and cognitive realm. On the basis of results obtained up to now, it should not be assumed that subjective differences in terms of context, meaning, and cognitive processing have no impact (see, among others, Bandura's recent presidential address, 1974; cf. also Jenkins, 1974). At this stage, however, there may be some advantages in presenting subjects with instructions and tasks that do not allow for an uncontrolled variety of information-processing and response strategies as situations and variables based in, or suggested by, the nature of the task itself are preferable to conditions artificially, or at least superficially, induced by complex instructions.

II. BASIC CONCEPTS

Let us state what is meant by the terms *motivation* and *reward* in *learning,* when discussing their role in the context of this chapter.

A. Motivation as a Cognitive–Dynamic Structure

In many learning experiments, motivation has been manipulated in such terms as deprivation time with regard to physiological needs, amount of reward, less or more severe electric shocks, and so on. With human subjects, threat of failure and other situations inducing stress and anxiety have been studied as motivational factors in learning. I refer to a rather different concept of motivation in the title of this chapter. It is assumed that in human beings motivational and cognitive functions collaborate in building up object-directed means–end structures, such as tasks, projects, plans, intentions, and interests. Cognitive–dynamic structures of this kind seem to have special relevance in human behavior, since most of human activity is made up of super- and coordinated plans or interests. Later in this chapter (Section IV), I will go into more detail with regard to motivational concepts, but it should be made clear from the beginning that, as long as motivation refers undifferentially to hours of food deprivation, weight of food pellets, anxiety, task instructions, intentions, and the like, and as long as learning is measured in terms of running speed, response rate, frequency of repetition, as well as acquisition of information, one cannot expect agreement in the results and interpretations as concerns learning–motivation interaction.

B. Cognitive Learning in Its Behavioral Context

In this chapter, *learning* is conceived of as the acquisition process by which new behavioral information and response abilities are made available to the behaving subject. In this sense, learning is an intervening variable. Operationally, it must be defined in terms of actual responses or performances made in specific informational and motivational conditions. The problem is which performance the subject is motivated to make. Human subjects can be instructed (motivated) to perform the whole range of responses available in their behavioral and cognitive repertory; thus, a discussion of *recall performance* (Section VIII) is necessary. In contrast, nonhuman subjects have a more limited range of motivation. In humans, the relative frequency of repetition of rewarded (Right) and punished (Wrong) responses is not the direct result of learning per se; performances are codetermined by cognitive–dynamic processes interacting with the behavioral repertory of a given subject in a given situation.

A few remarks concerning the broader behavioral context in which learning and its different forms are to be situated are necessary at this point.

Learning is a function that accompanies every behavioral process. After doing, perceiving, thinking, or fearing something, humans are usually able to communicate what they have done and how they did it. In many cases, long intervals of time do not destroy the "traces" left in memory. Experiences and acts ending in failure are remembered as well as successes (Turner & Barlow, 1951). Moreover, earlier experiences remain available to be used as components of present behavior. Some more or less laborious retrieval and reconstruction processes (Bartlett, 1950) may be required to that end, but it also happens that earlier events and thoughts come up again and again without any special motivation for such recurrence.

On the basis of information gained by experience or received from others, and with the help of new skills mastered—either occasionally or intentionally—human behavior is modified in the direction of relationships required or wanted for optimal functioning (needs). Besides learning about their own responses and their outcomes, individuals gain information about the sequences of events occurring in the physical or social world. In this context, humans learn to prepare for unrewarding as well as rewarding events. The farmer learns to protect his harvest at the first signs of storm; the child is conditioned to "take" a box on the ears. In a more creative mood, individuals learn to react to their environment by changing either the natural or social sequences of events rather than merely preparing to accept them. Thus, they modify not only their behavior but also their world in the direction of the "needed" relationships. Outcomes that are rewarded or punished, as well as information gained by experience and by communication from others, are found to play a role in the various ways of learning and behaving. The mechanisms involved are the main topic of this chapter, but let us keep in mind the context in which they are assumed to operate.

C. Reward, Its Complexity and Double Function

Coming to the concept of *reward*, it appears from what has been said previously that the complexity of reward in humans makes it impossible to confine reward to a fixed category of objects and events (cf. Meehl, 1950). Stated in a positive way this conclusion means that, generally speaking, the variety of available rewards depends on the complexities of the motivational system in a specific category of living beings. In the context of the human cognitive-dynamic system, every object can become a *means* to something else. In particular, the same outcome can be rewarding and punishing at the same time in the context of conflicting tendencies, as I have stated elsewhere (Nuttin, 1973, pp. 243–257). The rewarding means object is not to be thought of as a secondary reward since, in many cases, it has never before been associated with an experienced primary reward (Longstreth, 1971). The link between means and goal objects is constructed cognitively, or known by information received from other people. It is assumed, for instance, that a student is actually motivated to, and rewarded by, passing exams successfully as a means to get a degree; the degree itself may be a means to practice a profession, to play a role in social life, and so on. Besides its reward value as a means, passing (succeeding in) the exam may be a "primary" reward for the student's achievement need.

One of the main points with regard to reward in human learning is its double function—emotional or motivational and informative. Reward and punishment elicit an emotional or affective response insofar as they satisfy the motivation the subject has invested in the act; as such, they refer to the response the subject has made. Their informative function refers to responses still *to be made* in the frame of a broader behavioral unit. The informative function is specific to what I call an *open* task (Section III). The emotional aspect is common to *open* and *closed* tasks, but may be expected to predominate in closed tasks, in which failure and success are final, in contrast to their tentative and provisional character in the first steps of an open task. My first experimental investigation of the double aspect of reward and its relation to learning was carried out in my doctoral thesis (Nuttin, 1941), in which reward was placed in the framework of the open-task concept. My present position on that issue is discussed in Section V below. Another important point—the distinction between extrinsic and intrinsic reward, or between reward and the successful outcome of an act—is only mentioned briefly here with respect to the differential impact of each on learning (see Nuttin & Greenwald, 1968, pp. 2–8, about the distinction itself). It has been found that extrinsic reward shifts the subject's interest from the task to the reward itself (usually some sensory pleasure). Thus, the subject's enjoyment and gradually his efficiency in performing the task tends to disappear (Lepper, Greene, & Nisbett, 1973). It was shown in Harlow's laboratory that monkeys working at the well-known hasp and latch puzzle performed better when rewarded with food, but the group receiving no extrinsic reward (manipulation pleasure being the intrinsic reward) continued to display interest in the puzzles, whereas the extrinsically rewarded subjects discontinued their problem-solving activity as soon as the food reward was removed (see Gately's unpublished thesis as reported in Levine & Fasnacht, 1974).

D. Response Repetition, Behavioral "Techniques," and Changing Rewards

One preliminary remark should be made concerning the impact of reward in general. The repetition of previously rewarded responses is a less predominant feature in human behavior than that of animals. The explanation is not that humans are not affected by reward contingencies, but that the expected reward itself changes in terms of ever-changing human goals and means. The psychological needs of an animal are rather stable in terms of its search for need-satisfying objects, and the ways in which these needs are satisfied are kept unchanged, whereas human striving for achievement, consideration, power, affection, and knowledge follows ever-changing routes to ever-receding concrete goals.

Researchers in learning have been more efficient in examining the use of techniques of goal attainment, that is, the *how* of human behavior, than explaining *what* humans really do. The latter is determined to greater extent by the development of cognitive–dynamic structures in which learning is only one of the components. Therefore, the distinction between the two aspects of behavior, how versus what, should be kept in mind when studying the role of learning and reinforcement in human conduct. (See, also, Bindra, 1974.)

It is now becoming clear that for several decades learning theorists have been obsessed by the reward factor. The etiology of this "rewarditis" is not difficult to discover; it is connected with the types of organisms and the limited range of responses originally studied, the particular motivational variables manipulated, and the theoretical concept of learning itself. It is not certain that the best remedy to this situation is simply to change the definition of reward (reinforcement), defining it as everything that is shown to produce learning in its traditional senses of behavior modification. Reward, of course, can be correlated with motivation, and its role in learning and behavior should be placed in the context of the human complex motivational system. If it is necessary to maintain the classical terminology, *reward* and *reinforcement* will have to be understood in very heterogeneous contexts. This is already the case in social psychology with such concepts as self-reinforcement (see Bandura, 1971; Mischel, 1973; Kanfer, 1971).

III. OPEN TASKS AND THE INFORMATIVE FUNCTION OF OUTCOMES AND EVENTS

Terms such as *intentional* and *incidental* learning, *open* and *closed* tasks, and *instructions* and *intent* to learn all refer to the role of motivation in learning. Two issues are at stake in this context: (1) the motivation to learn, and (2) the impact of motivation on learning. In fact, humans usually learn while doing something else, that is, they learn from what they do, or from what they perceive others to be doing, most often without any explicit instruction or intention to learn. When learning something is what the individual is primarily doing (learning behavior), he or she is considered to be explicitly motivated to learn. This motivation may or may not have been induced by instructions. In any case, it is a type of motivation and be-havior assumed to exist only in humans.

In experimental settings it seems easy to separate the two extreme conditions. The presence or absence of motivation to learn (intentional versus incidental learning) is generally assumed, not always rightly, to correspond to the presence or absence of learning instructions. The motivation-learning problem is narrowed down still further when the differential influence of reward and punishment in incidental and intentional learning alone is under investigation. Therefore, it is preferable to formulate the motivation-learning problem in terms of the motivational nature of the task in its behavioral context. This is what the concepts of *open* and *closed* tasks relate to. The term *task* is used to refer to any small or large behavioral unit that an individual intends (Section IV) to perform. A task may be either self-assigned or accepted through instructions received from others (auto-or heteromotivated). As a preliminary definition, a task is *closed* when its end result is reached by giving a single response to the stimulus, which is expected not to be presented again; a task is *open* when giving a response is perceived by the subject as a substructure of a broader behavioral system. In the latter context, similar situations may recur, and each individual response given or event perceived may have a role to play in further steps in the task to be fulfilled. A classical learning task with successive presentations of the same series of stimuli is a good illustration of this, but is not the only type of open task (see Section IV.D).

A. The Underlying Concept of Behavior

Formulating the motivation-learning problem in terms of task openness implies a special approach to human behavior itself. Instead of confining behavior within the stimulus–response structure and insisting on the subject's intention (or lack thereof) to learn the association between these two elements, the open-task concept implies that the stimulus–response unit is integrated into a broader cognitive–dynamic structure (a behavioral project or plan). Such motivational structures are future oriented; they are conceived as the normal motivational orientation of humans in the sense that most human activities and responses appear to be means to reach further end results (that is, substructures in the framework of larger behavioral units, interest systems, or tasks). This behavior orientation, insofar as it is found actually to exist, endows reward with an additional function, as stated above. Besides its reference to the response given (to the past), it also refers to the utility or instrumental value of the same response in the framework of the future task (Nuttin, 1964, p. 74). Although the first function is predominantly motivational or affective and the latter informative, it cannot be denied that receiving information for future task fulfillment is rewarding to a certain extent, whereas being rewarded for a specific response has obvious informative value, and this is precisely the informational aspect, or second function, of reward. (See also Nelson's remarks, 1971, p. 213.)

B.   A Continuum of Open-Task Conditions

The important point, then, is to find out to what extent a specific act is part of a broader behavioral structure or, on the contrary, constitutes an independent unit in itself. Artificial tasks without relation to the subject's everyday life—as is the case with many experimental tasks—are likely to remain disconnected units without a perceived relation to further work, save possibly within the experimental task itself. In the latter case, the task is *open* within the narrow limits of the experimental task (for example, a learning task).

In my opinion, the concepts of *open* and *closed* tasks are to be conceived of as a dimension allowing variation along a continuum. This dimension is defined in terms of a cognitive–dynamic orientation going beyond the present act itself. At both ends, the condition is clear: the present experience or response is perceived as having, or not having, potential utility (interest) in a further context. These clear-cut conditions are labeled "open" and "closed" tasks in the strict sense. It is assumed that behavioral elements perceived as steps to further end results are participants in the dynamics of the broader structure. The degree of this dynamic investment depends on the probability and closeness of the relationship being perceived. Not only the rewarded outcome, but every event happening in the context of an open task, may be perceived as potentially of further interest or use. In this context, some responses and events are capable of alerting the subjects, that is, arousing their attention and interest, as is shown below (Section V.A). Between the ends of the continuum, a large variety of more or less latent orientations and interests, and more or less perceived relationships, endow present behavior with a certain degree of "openness" toward the future. In experimental situations, as opposed to real-life behavior, instructions will, of course, play a major role in determining the relationship between present responses and further tasks; the nature of the task and its "real-life" context, however, should be taken into account, as will be evidenced from illustrations given below (Section IV.D). It should be noted, for instance, that some laboratory tasks, by the arbitrary quality of the instructions given, are perceived by the subjects as being meaningless in themselves. It is not clear what events are to follow; hence, a nonfocused open-task condition is created.

IV. THE ORIGIN OF COGNITIVE–DYNAMIC STRUCTURES: TASKS, INTENTIONS, AND TASK TENSION

The cognitive approach to behavior that is the basis of this chapter assumes a few general tenets that will not be discussed here (see Nuttin, 1974). A few words should be said, however, in order to provide the cognitive–dynamic structures mentioned—*tasks, task tension, projects, plans,* and *intentions*—with a proper theoretical status (see also Heider, 1960; Lewin, 1926, 1938; Ryan, 1970 about the problem of intentions and tasks).

The massive injection of ideational processes into human behavior affects an individual dealing with the world in various ways. Imagined and expected reinforcers or noxious stimuli influence behavior in the same manner as those perceptually present (Cautela, 1971). Behavioral acts proceed by manipulation of the perceived physical objects as well as by thinking about them. Developmental psychologists have shown how images, generalized schemes, and ideas about events develop. Children gradually become able not only to physically put together two or more perceived objects, but to combine them cognitively in such a way that new structures emerge, and operations are performed on the "combined" objects (Bruner, 1964, 1974; Chomsky, 1957; Luria, 1961; Piaget, 1937; Vygotsky, 1962). At that stage of development, behavior has become a complex performance in which both its cognitive and its motor components codetermine human performance as a whole. Moreover, thought processes seem to have some functional properties capable of affecting the course of ideational behavior in specific ways. One of them is mentioned here.

A. Task Tension: A Dynamic Gap

It is a common-sense fact that goals are easier to conceive and set than to work out at the level of reality. Dealing with objects[1] on the representational level of behavior seems easier to do than actually changing the situations in the real world. Some of the objects and skills needed for real performance are difficult to acquire and to master, whereas their ideational

---

[1] Throughout this chapter the term *object* is taken in its broadest sense, including not only physical objects and people, but also all kinds of meaningful situations, patterns of relationships, activities and, generally speaking, whatever one is perceiving, thinking about, feeling, and doing.

substitutes are easily at our disposal. As concerns the dynamic side, motivational states are assumed to elicit behavior on both the ideational and motor level. On the basis of what has been said, however, ideational processes are expected to proceed faster in reaching their end result. Even when difficult planning and problem solving are implied, ideation is only one part of the behavioral act as a whole. Thus, a lag is created between the ideational and "executive" phases of performing an act. The motivational state, however, is assumed to continue to act on the behavioral process as long as the real change is not achieved. Thought processes, therefore, are usually preparatory stages to action. The discrepancy (or distance) between the end result as conceived and the actual situation as perceived is assumed to produce a state of dynamic tension (the so-called *task tension*), which activates and directs behavior toward the intended change.

B.   The Dynamic Roots of Task Tension

The dynamics of task tension ultimately reside in the need that originated the thought process itself. Additional sources, however, may increase its dynamic power. On the one hand, a subject who succeeds in elaborating his need in a cognitive task or plan has come closer to the behavioral realization of the object needed. Several experiments have shown that behavior dynamics increase as a function of the subject coming closer to the end result in view (see, among others, Miller, 1944). On the other hand, by setting a personal goal or accepting a task, the subject is assumed to become ego involved in the behavioral process itself, and, as a result, deeper layers of ego-motivation are contacted. Further, it is assumed that the motivational tension originating in the mismatch between the perceived and the conceived situation will continue to elicit and direct behavior as long as a dynamic balance is not achieved. Research hypotheses in this area could be tested, for instance, in relation to a dynamically optimal distance between a perceived and conceived state of affairs; in fact, it is probable that too great a distance between them must have a paralyzing effect on behavioral activity.

It follows from what has been said that tasks, intentions, and plans have their ultimate dynamic origin in the basic needs from which they spring via information processing and learning in general. They are conceived as cognitive-*dynamic* structures through which these needs find a personal outlet. Tasks, intentions, and plans can be distinguished from purely "cognitive maps" conceived of in terms of computer programs (Miller, Galanter, & Pribram, 1960, p. 61); for instance, the latter are found in plans given by experts to consultants, but are not to be identified with intentions and projects in which subjects try to concretize their own goals (Nuttin, 1964, pp. 66–67).

C. Task Tension in Open and Closed Tasks

In opposition to Lewin (1938), task tension (that is, the dynamic element of a cognitive-dynamic structure) is conceived as being intrinsically object directed, its end result being the object of the task itself. A *closed task* is a cognitive-dynamic structure with a task tension having its end result in the first (and unique) response to be made in a given situation. The end result of an *open task*, on the contrary, goes beyond the behavioral or perceptual response under consideration. In situations in which the relationship between a response given and any further end result of the open task remains uncertain (for example, when the subject, suspects, or is told, that a previously right response may or may not be right in any further presentations of the same stimulus, as is the case in ESP experiments), the open or closed nature of the task itself becomes uncertain, and various strategies may be used according to the subject's interpretations, abilities, and expectations. When the previously right response is certain not to be correct on the following trial, the task with regard to this response is not closed insofar as it contains useful information about the response not to be given later on.

It appears from these few examples that the concept of open and closed tasks accounts for complexities that cannot be formulated in terms of intentional and incidental learning instructions alone. Motivational, informational, and situational factors work together in creating a specific kind of task (see Section V.B.2). In other cases, tasks have been shown to be subjectively open without learning instructions.

The major importance of the cognitive and motivational "openness" of behavioral units (tasks) in the framework of this theoretical outline consists of the focused attention and state of alertness it is assumed to create in the behaving subject. It is shown in the next section how reward and other informative cues affect cognitive learning by alerting the subject and focusing his activity on specific responses and events. Another characteristic of an open task resides in its greater independence from stimulus conditions and time limits as compared with physiological needs. These tasks are to be conceived of as more or less continuously active dynamic systems. Therefore, their impact on behavior and learning is not restricted to periods of actual need. An open task or interest system, even when in a latent state, is always ready to be activated by relevant incentives and cues. For example, even when hunger is satiated, the self-assigned task to earn a living may still be active. The same holds, a fortiori, for psychological needs—the end result is never completely achieved (Section II. D). Thus, human readiness to get activated in a specific direction and, hence, their increased ability to learn, depends to a large extent on the direction taken by the cognitive elaboration of their needs. This is the process that gives rise to *intrinsic* motivation and reward in learning; extrinsic rewards, built up on the basis of a small range of "lower" needs, do not function as adequate substitutes in learning (Section II.C).

V. THE ROLE OF MOTIVATION IN ATTENTIONAL LEARNING

The role of motivation in human learning is not limited to the question whether rewarded responses are learned better than punished ones in either open or closed tasks, or in intentional versus incidental learning.

In the Hullian and Thorndikian traditions, motivation was recognized as an essential condition of learning insofar as need reduction or reward was its main factor. It is interesting to see that another aspect of the motivational state was mentioned as an essential condition from the very beginning in Pavlov's (1927) work on conditioning. An animal has to be *alert* and *attentive* to certain stimuli and cues. Alertness (referred to, of course, as an alert state of the nervous system) was considered to be an essential condition for making new associations, that is, learning a new conditioned reflex. As a result of more recent research on the orienting reaction interest in arousal and attentional factors in these areas has been broadened considerably. At the other extreme of the learning field, educationalists have always known that lack of attention and interest results in bad learners. In their opinion, extrinsic reward has to be added to stimulate motivation if intrinsic interest fails. At the same time, it has been shown that motivation is a variable to be manipulated with care. High degrees of motivation may be more helpful in performance than in learning per se. The Yerkes–Dodson law, originally established on the basis of animal studies with electric shock (Yerkes & Dodson, 1908) and later hunger (Dodson, 1917) as motivational variables, has been applied largely to humans; it is generally accepted that intermediate degrees of motivation create optimal conditions for learning and that this optimal motivation itself varies as a function of such variables as the difficulty of the task and personality factors (anxiety proneness, etc.).

Before outlining my theoretical hypothesis, I should mention that the effect of motivation of major importance in this scheme is the "orienting" or attentional effect, as suggested by Pavlov, whereas the function of need *reduction* and reward will be treated in a different context. Let it also be made clear that the learning and motivation processes discussed here are those defined in Section II. It is not my purpose to introduce this theoretical outline by showing once more that a large amount of experimental evidence supports the thesis that a rewarding aftereffect does not produce learning per se, as defined in this chapter. This has been done in many studies. The contiguity factor, however, will be considered briefly. My main goal, is to investigate a mechanism of learning in which motivational and cognitive processes are supposed to play a role via selective attention and informative cues (including reward). This hypothesis about attention learning in open-task conditions is delineated in three steps. A more direct impact of the affective aspect of reward (success and failure) will be considered in the section on affective learning (Section VI).

It should be said from the beginning that motivation to learn, or to do anything else, is not assumed to have any direct impact on retention, but it is hypothesized that motivation plays an important role in retaining information by creating selective attention in the context of an individual's limited capacities to register, process, and store all the information presented to him. These limited capacities of processing and retention are well established; I propose to consider this fact as the starting point for my study of the factors and mechanisms in selective attention learning.

A. The Need for Selectivity and Strategies

1. Coping with Information Complexity: Selective Attention

Humans behave in a world in which the number and complexity of events occurring at a given moment are overwhelming—most of these events are not even actually perceived; they are not brought to the individual's attention. In any case, the limited channels at their disposal and the inhibitory and gating mechanisms at work prevent humans from registering and processing the bulk of informational data available. At the same time, humans are confronted with a number of things to do, needs to satisfy, tasks to fulfill, and interests to pursue. Thus, the concrete learning problem in this behavioral context is to know *how*, that is, via what processes, humans gather, process, and retain the information needed for efficient behavior in their complex environment; how will they deal with this situational and behavioral complexity? The human's motivational state requires that he be selective, that is, preferentially oriented toward certain types of data and use strategies in making choices, as is actually the case in many experiments (Section V.A.4.b) on perceptual selectivity (see Ryan, 1970, pp. 249–276). Moreover, in this complex situation humans often find themselves in a state of *uncertainty* about the relevance and utility of many of the events that are happening, especially with regard to their own responses as long as the outcome is not known. All this applies to subjects in experimental learning conditions as well as real-life situations. (See, also, Broadbent, 1970.)

2. Contiguity and Uncertainty

If *contiguity* is considered to be a sufficient condition of learning (see, among others, Estes, 1969), it is in the context of subject's oriented motivation and attention as just described that it should be situated. In that context, contiguity is an active process, that is, *perceived* contiguity, and not just a physical fact of temporal or spatial "togetherness" of events. Active or latent motivational interest in, or directedness toward, some categories of events is implied. Moreover, some cognitive relationships between perceived contiguous events are established. For instance, human response and its outcome often are contiguous events actively related (or *belonging*) to each other. Things are even clearer when active *uncertainty* is involved. Berlyne and Normore's (1972) experiment using blurred pictures is interesting in that respect. When uncertainty is actually provoked in a subject by showing him blurred pictures, a guessing activity is initiated to solve the task of finding the object represented in the picture. The right answer is given by showing the clear picture. This situation is similar to a subject looking forward to be informed about the outcome of his uncertain response. Uncertainty creates searching and directed attention. To use Woodworth's (1958, p. 240) suggestive terminology in this respect: the first element perceived evokes, as it were, an implicit question and directs the subject's attention to some concurring or following events. These events are related to each other as an answer is related to a question.

Behavioral scientists tend to consider only the temporal aspects of relations between behavioral elements following each other; the cognitive relationships actively established between such elements are overlooked. However, the latter play an important role, not only in contiguity perception as stated here, but in encoding and retrieving as well. Actively establishing relationships between elements to be learned is of special importance when the unit to be encoded is in itself a larger whole, such as a poem or a speech. The element selected for attention is the unit as a whole; networks of relationships have to be established within the unit in order to master it. The network of relations can be of either a purely associative or a more cognitive nature. The importance of establishing cognitive relations for encoding and learning in general has been emphasized by Ehrlich (1968) and several Russian authors such as Smirnov (1966, p. 351) and Zinchenko (1962). This viewpoint is in agreement with Pavlov's more general thesis that, besides analysis, synthesis is necessary for associative learning.

3. The "That's It" Reaction

Coming back, now, to the main point: on the basis of what has been said, it is assumed that the learner's motivational state in open-task conditions elicits a directed and selective activity, called *selective attention*. The kind of stimuli chosen as signals or cues for events to be selected depends on the strategy adopted by the subject. In many learning conditions *reward* is assumed to function as a signal pointing to the most relevant response. Other signals and cues, even punishments, are able to play the same role (cf. Nuttin & Greenwald, 1968, pp. 98–102). As a result of the attentive activity, thresholds for perceiving signals referring to relevant objects and events are lowered. The level on which this discriminative or selective perception takes place is not a sensory but a more central one. Events thus signaled and perceived are at the same time actively contiguous. It is in this context that the first step of our theoretical outline is to be understood: Any perceived signal or cue referring to the relevant event will alert the subject, arouse his object-directed activity, and, with regard to that event, elicit a response that can be called a *"that's it reaction."* The event signaled is recognized as the event of interest at the moment. Among the numerous events occurring, this one will be picked up as having special relevance or utility value in the framework of the open-task system.

Before passing on to the second step of our theoretical construct, I will briefly touch upon some recent data on strategies concerning the informative versus affective function of reward.

4. Strategies in Information Processing and the Emotional Value of Reward

a. *Private versus public communication of outcomes.*   For a long time one of my main concerns has been to distinguish between the emotional and informational aspects of reward and to investigate their mutual interaction in different behavioral conditions. At Louvain, in this context, we are now conducting a series of experiments in which public communication of successful and unsuccessful outcomes is being compared with privately giving reward and punishment to a subject. An additional variable, the relative frequency of personal successes as compared to those of fellow subjects is also introduced. We hypothesize that conditions in which subjects receive public communication of, say, relatively higher numbers of failures (social isolation), produce more emotionally loaded outcomes. This increased emotional aspect will lower the informative function of outcomes and, hence, reduce cognitive learning. On the other hand, it is well known that emotional involvement favors retention (Section VI). To date, results obtained using closed-task conditions, which were investigated first, have not yielded clear-cut results.

b. *Performer's versus observer's strategy.*   Meanwhile, another experiment has been conducted in the same laboratory by Eelen (1974) showing the differential effect of reward on subjects according to their participation either as performers or as observers in the learning experiment. The idea is that performers (receiving rewards and punishments for personally made responses) are more emotionally involved in the outcomes received than observers, who merely perceive another performer's outcomes. The experiment runs as follows. Subjects (performers and observers) are presented with 20 cards on which the following type of letter constellation is printed:

$$ GO \; \frac{N}{P}. $$

The task for both, performers and observers, is to learn the correct nonsense syllable to be formed by adding either N or P to the two initial letters. Each response is followed by Right or Wrong (in three different proportions, 25%, 50%, and 75% for different groups of subjects). Immediately following the learning trial, a recognition test trial is applied as follows. Observers and performers are presented with cards on which the two initial letters are printed together with *four* other consonants, including the two from which the choice has been made during the learning trial. The task now is to recognize among the four consonants the two originally presented. Thus, for each card the subjects are asked to communicate the letter chosen (by the performer) independent of the fact that it was rewarded or punished, and the second letter originally presented but not chosen. The usual precautions (inversion of punished and rewarded letters, buffer items, etc.) have been taken. Among the results obtained those of interest for this problem are given in Table 1 and they can be summarized as follows.

In all conditions, the letter chosen by the performer and followed by either Right or Wrong is recognized more often than the letter not chosen. This holds for the observer as well as for the performer, with one striking exception: when the letter chosen during the first trial has been followed by

TABLE 1

Mean Proportions of Performer's and Observer's
Recognition of Letters Chosen Versus Letters Nonchosen
and Followed by Either *Right* or *Wrong* [a, b]

	Response followed by Right		Response followed by Wrong	
	Chosen	Nonchosen	Chosen	Nonchosen
Performers	.72	.48	.78	.50
Observers	.80	.48	.56	.77

[a] Adapted from Eelen (1974)
[b] Proportions shown are obtained in the 50% Right condition.

Wrong, it is the nonchosen (and, hence, Right) alternative that is significantly recognized more often by the observer. The performer, on the contrary, continues to recognize the wrong letter chosen, more often than the nonchosen (Right) alternative. The proportions shown in Table 1 are taken from the 50% Right condition; they are practically the same for the two other conditions (that is, 25 and 75% Right choices).

These results very strongly suggest that observers apply a special strategy when perceiving a fellow performer choosing a response that appears to be Wrong. Instead of learning the letter chosen and its wrong outcome, they immediately shift attention to the other (Right) alternative. Thus, the observers' strategy consists in learning the Right responses only, whereas the performers continue to recognize the responses personally given more often. One can assume that their personal involvement in the response given prevents the performer from shifting attention with as much ease as the less involved observer. What is learned is affected by the cognitive processes during the first trial (that is, by the subject's performance; see also Postman, 1968) and by the strategy used in processing the information given. The latter is more "rational" in the observer. Some authors (among others, Shiffrin & Atkinson, 1969) assume that in similar learning conditions *performers* tend to follow that same strategy, a hypothesis, however, that is not confirmed in this experiment.

B. The Learning Effect of Activity and Attention

The second step of our theoretical outline is the assumption that a behavioral unit which is the object of active focusing by the alerted subject (active attention) is learned better. Some experimental evidence supporting this thesis will be referred to briefly. The older literature will not be mentioned, but it is well known that James (see Trabasso & Bower, 1968, pp. 2–3) as well as Wundt (compare his concept of apperception), attached a major importance to focalization, concentration, or attention in registering events. In recent years, data coming from the psychoneurological as well as the behavioral fields have pointed not only to the differential effect of selective attention and aroused activity on neurological and sensorial processes (see among others Spong, Haider, & Lindsley, 1965; and reviews by Moray, 1970), but also to their impact on learning. It should be made clear that the activity meant in this context does not refer to subjects having many things to do and many decisions to make. In fact, that kind of increased activity may interfere with learning, as has been suggested by some experimental results (Hillix & Marx, 1960). The increased activity meant here primarily refers to intensified, focused attention and originates in object-directed motivation. (See Le Ny, 1967, on activity in learning.)

1. The Psychophysiological Approach

The facilitative effect of selective attention on learning is generally admitted. Psychoneurologists currently refer to it. Olds (1973, pp. 56–57) speaks of "higher" attention learning as opposed to "lower" learning of skills and reinforcement learning. In the former case, Olds imagines that "engrams are induced," not by application of reward, but instead by prior attention. Berlyne (1967, p. 50), reviewing the literature on arousal in its relation to reinforcement, concludes that arousal immediately following the response to be learned is responsible for facilitating learning. In experiments on discrimination in rats, the French psychoneurologist Bloch and his collaborators found that stimulation of the reticular system, immediately following the only learning trial, significantly increases learning of the response (cf. Bloch, Denti, & Schmaltz, 1966; Deweer, Hennevin, & Bloch, 1968; Lecomte, Deweer, & Bloch, 1969). Russian authors (among others, Anokhin, 1958) have shown how activation and attention in terms of orienting reactions contribute to the formation of new connections.

2. Behavioral Research

On the level of psychological research with verbal learning tasks, several experiments suggest that motivation (meaning also increased activity) affects the capacity to retain material in storage (see, among others, Weiner & Walker, 1966), whereas Trabasso and Bower (1968) report several studies in which attentional processes are shown to affect classifying, encoding, and learning. Results obtained by Schönpflug (1966) and by Schönpflug and Beike (1964) support the thesis that what they call "organismic activation" (in casu emotional activation as measured by electrodermal skin resistance) produces better retention and recall of the material learned. Similar results were obtained by Kleinsmith and Kaplan (1964) with high as compared to low arousal stimuli. Here, however, some contradiction between findings of different authors still exists with regard to the impact of immediate versus delayed recall testing (see also Florès, 1975, pp. 280–299, on motivational activity in learning). Studies related to the positive learning effect of non-oriented arousal states (as produced for instance by white noise in experiments by Berlyne, Borsa, Hamacher, & Koenig, 1966) are probably less to the point in our present context, but it could be hypothesized that subjects have to raise their level of focused activity and effort in order to encode the items presented to them under conditions of disturbing noise.

As to the influence of activity-inducing and arousal-producing instructions, I refer only to one older study by Alper (1948). Subjects working at a paired-associate learning task under neutral instructions showed more forgetting and less reminiscence than the more aroused group (with intelligence test instructions) when results of an immediate test trial were compared with those of a one-day delayed trial. Moreover, I am inclined to admit that the Lewinian factor of persisting task tension (as manipulated, for instance, by the ambiguous "interruption" condition) is very close to the activity variable discussed here. In fact, task tension is nothing else than object-oriented motivation by which the subject is activated until subjective task completion. The main difficulty, however, with this issue is that the interruption procedure—which is nothing other than a technique, and, I repeat, a very ambiguous one—has been considered to be the variable itself. It has been shown that task interruption and completion have many meanings according to the context and the subject's expectations. In an interesting experimental study by Ferdinand (1959) it was found that the perception of experience of completedness or uncompletedness of a task tends to be independent of the material fact of task interruption and completion. In an ego-involved test situation, for instance, the task was not perceived as completed when the test items were solved, but only after the results or marks had been communicated. Unimportant tasks, on the contrary, were perceived as being completed even when interrupted, save when the subjects were instructed that they had to be resumed later.

In any case, the major factor involved in a persisting task tension and in task interruption is the subject's oriented motivation insofar as it is stimulated and persists at a certain level of arousal. Thus, the concept of an uncompleted task has to be integrated into the broader notion of what I have called an *open* task. A task remains open to the extent that its components are of persisting interest to the subject. Many of the conflicting results in this area (see, among others, Ryan, 1970; Van Bergen, 1968) probably could be partially explained in terms of the ambiguities mentioned.

3. The Impact of Activity and Attention on Fixation and Retrieval Processes

As concerns the more specific processes by which intensified activity exerts its influence on learning, it is hypothesized that encoding processes (including categorizing and establishing relationships) as well as retrieval processes can be affected. Only a few data from my own laboratory will be mentioned here.

At the level of retrieval processes, it is found, for instance that after identical learning trials, outcomes are recalled more often by subjects who have to use this recall for the accomplishment of a further important task (the repetition of correct responses only). It is assumed that these subjects were more motivated and spent more effort in retrieving the outcome than those who had no further need of it (d'Ydewalle & Eelen, 1975).

The different degrees of attention paid to the presentation of data have an impact on recall via better registration or encoding of the data presented. In one experiment, the subject was presented with a series of 144 pairs of block letters printed on cards; his task was to compare the relative size of the black surface of the two letters. He had to respond ''R larger (or smaller) than H,'' etc. The response proper was in the evaluations of ''larger'' or ''smaller.'' Each pair of letters appeared 12 times in 12 different shapes in the series as a whole. The association (R always followed by H) was followed 12 times either by reward or by punishment in a closed-task condition. In a parallel series of experiments, subjects had to compare pairs of irregular geometrical forms as to their relative size. Each form was labeled after a letter printed on the top of the form. The same pairs of letters (e.g. R smaller, or larger, than H) were repeated 12 times and followed 12 times by either reward or punishment. After evaluating the relative sizes, the subjects were asked to respond to the first letter of each pair, presented again, with the second letter of that pair.

The main result with regard to the problem discussed here is that a significantly higher percentage of correct repetition of the second letter was given in the first condition (letters) compared than in the second (forms). The average percentages for several groups in each condition were 41.0 and 15.6%, respectively (Nuttin, 1953, pp. 334–335; Nuttin & Greenwald, 1968, pp. 77–78). Our hypothetical explanation is that much more attention and activity is invested in the pairs of block letters to be compared than in the labels surmounting the geometrical forms. In the latter case, attention was focused on the geometrical forms and not on the letters themselves; they are less actively related to each other. As to other aspects of the results obtained, it should be mentioned that, in both conditions, the pairs of letters followed 12 times by reward were not connected more often with each other than those followed 12 times by punishment. The percentages for the block letters were 40.4% after reward and 42.0% after punishment; for the geometrical forms, they were 16.0% and 15.2%, respectively. Thus, even in conditions of active contiguity, the addition of reward following the occurrence of two elements does not add anything to the likelihood that an association will be found.

Summarizing, psychoneurological and behavioral research supports the thesis that intensified and object-oriented activity affects learning in general as well as its constituent processes (encoding and retrieval). Reward is one of the possible alerting signals that increases cognitive activity with relation to the rewarded responses (that's it reaction). This accounts for the fact that, in some open-task conditions, rewarded responses are learned better although reward per se does not directly affect cognitive learning.

C. Retention as a Function of Motivational Investment

Our main problem, however, is the general mechanism by which selective attention learning can be conceptualized. How can one explain the experimental observation that increased cognitive–dynamic activity or attention tends to affect the retention of materials on which it has been focused? The learning situation examined here is the open-task condition in its broad behavioral context (Section III), as well as the classical learning experiment. In Section VI, the same basic hypothesis will be applied to affective learning.

The *"that's it"* reaction, mentioned above, as its essential function, directs the subject's active or latent motivational system toward a specific, identifiable response or event (see Section V.A.3). Thus, the intended event becomes an object of the actor's interest and his motivation is invested in it. Therefore, the motivational system (interest) and its object (response or event) are conceptualized as an integrated dynamic unit. The lower thresholds of excitability and readiness for reactivation characterizing any active or latent motivational system are conveyed to the intended object as part of the dynamic structure. As a consequence, the interesting response or event will easily tend to come up into the subject's actual awareness and behavior. Each time an occasionally met object or a more central event and a task to be performed orient the subject's attention and searching activity in the direction of that system, the entire structure (including the invested object) will tend to be reactivated insofar as neurological and behavioral conditions allow. This is often observed when subjects "search their memory" in order to reevoke and retrieve "traces."

In this context, the spontaneous as well as provoked reappearances of objects in the subject's awareness are explained. They constitute the minimal form of what has been labeled *rehearsal* and is considered to be responsible for the acquisition process (Postman, 1964). However, as Estes (1971) remarks, the problem is why some elements tend to be more rehearsed than others. In our hypothesis, the same dynamic process underlying spontaneous and semispontaneous rehearsal has to be considered the basis of better retention as well. It is assumed that the more a dynamic system maintains a higher activation level, the more likely it is to survive the many other dynamic structures and substructures continuously overflowing the human behavioral and neurological system. The objects integrated in a dynamic structure will share in the activity of the system itself. It is admitted that repeated reactivation (in particular, by rehearsal) of verbal or behavioral units is an additional condition for retention and active reintegration. (For some experimental support, compare Nuttin & Greenwald, 1968, pp. 82–87.)

VI.   RETENTION OF SIGNIFICANT EVENTS AND
AFFECTIVE LEARNING

The mechanisms described up to now apply to cognitive learning in the whole field of open-task situations. This field has been shown to be much broader than the intentional learning area proper, that is, explicit learning behavior (Section III). In fact, whatever task an individual is actively engaged in, many other dynamic orientations are present in a *latent* state. The casually met event can arouse this latent interest and create a temporarily active open task in the alerted direction. In such cases, the mechanisms at work are assimilated to the ones described above. The only difference is that before being alerted, the subject's attention and motivation in that direction were in a latent state. It is well known that all motivational states can be present in an actively searching, as well as in a latent, form. In the latter case, it is the occasionally encountered event instead of the actively searched signal that alerts the subject and evokes his latent interest. This implies that a certain readiness to perceive potentially relevant objects is preserved in a latent motivational state.

Besides the many specific interests existing in a given individual, one more general motivational system seems to be continuously maintained in a state of latent vigilance and readiness; it is related to the so-called central areas of personality. Every event concerning an individual in his biological or social identity elicits affective and emotional responses that are found to have an impact on their retention. This constitutes a new category of *significant* or *important* objects, the impact of which on learning appears to be related to the motivation-learning problem. The difference with the relevant and, hence, also significant events mentioned up to now (in active and passive attention learning), resides in the fact that their importance is not connected with their utility value in the framework of any future-oriented means–end structure, project, or open task. It is assumed that the significance of these events originates in a system of interest and motivation, the object of which is the individual himself. These types of significant and ego-involved events may occur in any situation—in the framework of closed as well as open tasks. Once more, the learning and retention of these events cannot be accounted for in terms of reward.

An important aspect of these affectively significant events deserves special attention in the context of this chapter. A cognitive-dynamic structure in the form of a project or task is always more ego involved than an impersonal need. Therefore, the accepted or self-assigned task results in an ego-involved *failure* or *success,* and not merely in a punishment or reward. Failure may be ego threatening, whereas turning away from failure and clinging to success may be a reaction of self-defence. Such an affective response has been observed even in experimental learning studies with children (cf., among others, Nuttin, 1953, p. 337). In this context, success and failure may become affectively significant events, differentially related to learning and to personality factors (see Rosenzweig, 1933), and extensive research has been done on fear of failure and hope of success in the need for achievement area (see, among others, Atkinson & Raynor, 1974; Heckhausen, 1970; Weiner, 1972).

There is an impressive amount of observational and experimental data pointing to the impact of significant events on retention. Only a few are mentioned here, as they round off our thesis on the role of motivation in learning. They point, among others, to the possible impact of reward and punishment (success and failure) on affective learning insofar as ego involvement is implied.

The ego-involved character of a task and the reward value of its outcome depends, of course, on the importance given to the task. In an older Lewinian study, carried out by Brown (1933), the retention of unimportant stopgaps (in-between tasks that Brown considered to be more "unreal") was compared with the recall scores of important tasks. The ego-involved importance variable was manipulated by instructions in terms of significance for the subjects. The important tasks yielded significantly better results after 30 min, 36 hr, and 1-week intervals, respectively. This was still the case, although the differences were smaller, in groups in which former in-between tasks were presented as the important ones, and vice versa. Ferdinand (1959) repeated Brown's experiments in a new theoretical context, with several new conditions. As concerns to the significance of the task, it is interesting to note that the unimportant in-between tasks are nevertheless recalled better when subjects are informed that they are to be resumed later. This points to a more objective and instrumental form of significance in terms of our open-task factor, as opposed to affective importance and ego involvement in both open and closed tasks.

Several experimenters in Eastern European countries also stress the factor of personal significance in learning. Mittag (1955), studying young workers in the context of some of Gottschaldt's theories, showed that in ego-involved conditions (tests of general knowledge), personally important tasks, although completed, were recalled better than unimportant ones (even when uncompleted). Significant differences in results were obtained in recall tests immediately afterward, as well as 24 hr, 1 week, and 1 month later. In neutral conditions, on the contrary, uncompleted tasks were recalled better than completed ones. A correlation of .68 was obtained between interest in the task and recall. Therefore, tasks strongly tied to real-life interests produce better learning than tasks with no importance beyond the experimental situation (compare our concept of closed tasks, Section III). As to the difficulty of the task, a medium degree of difficulty (within the range of subjects' abilities) tends to activate the subjects most and favors recall.

The affective importance of success as independent of open-task situations is shown in a Japanese study by Ito (1957; summarized by Van Bergen, 1968). In an experiment with school children, in relaxed and cooperative working conditions, failed tasks were recalled better than successful ones. This was the case with uncompleted as well as completed tasks. On the contrary, in ego-threatening and competitive conditions, successful items seemed to have a special significance for these children: They were recalled better than the punished ones in completed and uncompleted task conditions. Thus, the impact of ego-involved success (and failure) on what is termed *affective learning* seems to depend on the stressful and ego-threatening nature of the task and personality traits. It may be one of the factors intervening in the better recall of successful responses in closed tasks. In fact, reward and success are adhered to more spontaneously and affectively in many conditions by many people. Moreover, by the very fact that an important task implies a certain degree of ego involvement, anything with utility value for accomplishing that task will have some affective and ego-involved value connected with its utility or means–end character in open tasks.[2]

VII. CONTRADICTORY RESULTS

Several experiments on the learning effect of focused motivational activity and intent to learn have yielded contradictory results. Therefore, it may be helpful to point to a few limitations, additional conditions, and sources of error in this respect. First, some general conditions affecting the possible impact of other factors will be mentioned.

A. Identifiability and Structure

The *identifiability* of responses and situations to be learned is considered to be an important condition for attention, motivational activity, and intention to have an impact on retention. Imagine the kind of experiment in which a response to a series of, say, 24 letters has to be chosen from among two digits. The two digits presented 24 times together with the various letters are the same for each item of the series. One does not see how concentrated activity, attention, or intent to learn will bear upon each stimulus–response unit individually, in the absence of special strategies that may require time to develop. To have any impact, intending and attending activities should have something identifiable to relate to. Conditions such as those in the example given are often used for well-defined methodological purposes. The import, however, of the results obtained may be limited to the conditions used. Even in much more identifiable conditions with two *different*

---

[2] Thus, the general idea implied in our hypothesis is not that reward has an influence on learning in open-task conditions and not in closed tasks, but that subjects tend to be less alerted by reward in closed tasks, except when success is emotionally important to the subject, for example, in ego-threatening and self-defensive conditions.

alternatives presented for each stimulus, it is found that the subjects use various strategies (Section V.A.4; see also research done on stimulus variables and reviewed among others by McLaughlin, 1965, p. 368).

From recent research (Anderson & Bower, 1973) it seems plausible to infer that information gained in a list context is stored in different ways than materials presented in a story context. Further, the serial nature of the behavioral units to be learned may seriously limit the applicability and impact of factors playing a major role in the selective learning of the daily life. For instance, among the many behavioral units performed in a day, a person may retain for years his visit to the laboratory to learn lists of digits and words. Although his intent to learn was directed toward the stimulus–response units and not to the visit as such, only the latter was retained.

A condition closely related to the identifiability factor discussed here is isolation and structure in general. Many contradictory results have been obtained in this area (see d'Ydewalle, 1974; Köhler, 1958; Nuttin, 1953; Oléron, 1968; Park, 1966; Postman & Adams, 1955; von Restorff, 1933; cf. also reviews by McLaughlin, 1965, p. 369; Wallace, 1965). It appears from the conflicting results that isolation is not effective in all conditions. One exceptional failure in an important task of eight items may have a strong affective impact and, therefore, more of an isolating effect than eight Wrongs in merely guessing the matches for, say, 24 stimulus words. On the other hand, a strongly isolated item in space and time is bound to concentrate upon itself all the subject's activity and attention since nothing else is presented. I therefore am inclined not to isolate completely the effect of structural and affective or dynamic factors when isolation of outcome is at stake (see earlier experiments in that area, Nuttin & Greenwald, 1968, pp. 103–122).

B. Incomparability of Experiments and Results

In interpreting conflicting results, attention should be paid to many other conditions. It seems easy to admit, for instance, that randomly guessing and matching letters and numbers in an extrasensory perception experiment, and being "rewarded" and "punished" for each guess, may have small behavioral effects when compared with failure and success in important ego-involved tasks (affective value of success versus reward). The nature and complexity of the task has been shown to affect learning in different ways. Having to perform a meaningful task (a so-called *orienting task,* for instance) and, additionally, to learn (intentionally) the responses given in solving that task, a subject may be affected by the relative importance given to both tasks. The so-called orienting task may be considered to be the primary objective, whereas learning some attributes (Underwood, 1969) of the materials presented and the responses given may be considered secondary. The opposite may be true when the orienting task is rather meaningless.

In some research it was hypothesized that both tasks may interfere with each other. In fact, Gleitman and Gillet (1957) found a decrease in learning, which they attributed to a conflict between the orienting and the learning tasks. A similar interference effect, obtained in a different context by Wallace (1968), is interpreted by the author in terms of subjective response tendencies toward different kinds of material (words versus nonsense material). Contradictory results in that same area were obtained in recent experiments by d'Ydewalle and Eelen (1975). An increase in retention was found and interpreted as confirming the hypothesis that the subject's degree of activity involved in the orienting task tends to increase learning.

As to the many contradictory results concerning the influence of the intent-to-learn factor, a good illustration is given by two series of experiments carried out in the Louvain laboratories. De Montpellier (1972) obtained the clear-cut superiority of intentional learning, whereas in the experiments just mentioned d'Ydewalle and Eelen (1975) did not find that the intent factor had any learning effect per se.

An important source of contradictory results is found in the nature of the dependent measures taken. Testing the recognition of stimulus material used in the training trial, as in some of de Montpellier's experiments, just mentioned, and also in Wallace (1968), yielded different results than recalling the responses given. Nevertheless, both kinds of results are often lumped together under the heading of "recall tests." In other experiments, the recall activity itself is mixed with other processes. When in an evaluation task, for instance, the stimulus material is presented again during the recall trial, the subject may tend to evaluate once more the same stimulus instead of merely recalling the response previously given. Contradictory results in such cases obviously result from the different processes underlying the recall performance. The various information-processing strategies shown at work as a function of partially uncontrolled variables are also an important source of contradictory results. The noncomparability of experiments and results may result from many factors, indeed.

VIII. PERFORMANCE AND RECALL: THE LAW OF INSTRUMENTALITY

A. Recall Performance

One does not see how to motivate an animal to repeat its previously punished responses, whereas a human subject, owing to his more flexible cognitive-dynamic structures, can easily be instructed to do so in a test of retention. The high degree of autonomy of human cognitive behavior makes the distinction between cognitive learning and performance very important. Showing what one is able to do can readily be distinguished from doing what normally one would want to do in a given situation. One can ask a person to describe, successively, all of the routes that, in a given city, as far as he knows (has learned), allow him to drive from *A* to *B*, even though he may not currently wish to follow any of the routes. Therefore, the classical distinction between measuring man's *learning* versus measuring his *performance* should be revised to a certain extent in the human context. In any case, overtly tested recall (in cognitive learning) is performance and as overt as the repetition of a "learned" (that is, reinforced) response. In humans, the distinction between testing cognitive learning and measuring performance amounts to providing them with different motivations. A recall performance is a performance in which one is motivated (instructed) to do or say (repeat) all one is able to repeat relating to previous responses or events; a performance in the classical sense (usually called *learning performance*) is what a subject actually does when he is motivated to repeat previously rewarded responses only, that is, the only kind of responses an animal is naturally motivated to perform.

B.   The Law of Instrumentality

The main law governing human performance in general is assumed to be the *law of instrumentality*. Its formulation is as follows: To the extent that conditions for cognitive functioning are fulfilled, an individual performs the act which is expected to be most probably instrumental in obtaining the motivational end result predominating at a given moment. The difference from the law of reinforcement in instrumental conditioning is obvious. When a person is motivated or instructed to show retention of previous failures, the instrumental act is to reproduce (repeat) them. When a person is motivated to satisfy hunger, it will be safest and most instrumental simply to repeat previously rewarded responses (that is, responses that already have proved to be instrumental to that end), save when other motives, such as exploration, are strong enough to risk a certain delay without too high a probability of having hunger frustrated too long.

The fact that the same reward is effective or ineffective in strengthening the same response depending on the subject's information, as shown by Estes (1972), can be interpreted, I think, in terms of instrumentality. The information given to the subject in an ineffective reward condition is such that the previously rewarded response is perceived as no longer, or less probably, instrumental in pursuing the effect to be obtained. In other words, rewarded responses tend to be repeated as a function of their perceived instrumentality. The same can be said of such cognitive learning models as those developed by Buchwald (1969) and confirmed among others by d'Ydewalle and Eelen (1975). Repetition of verbal responses can be predicted in terms of recall of the response itself and the outcome received (Right or Wrong). It should be emphasized, however, that this cognitive model implies an additional cognitive element—the (at least) implicitly given information that correct responses remain the same in different trials.

Experimental evidence supporting a cognitive explanation of learning performance and behavior in general (not excluding, of course, many other determinants) is accumulating very rapidly in recent research. This applies to Western and Eastern European countries (where the cognitive view never vanished completely) as well as to the American scene, where its development is more explosive. An important aspect of the trend is found in the fact that psychoneurological investigators are no longer reluctant to investigate such cognitive processes as symbols, thought, planning, and programming behavior (see, among others, Luria, 1966; Pribram, 1971). The tendency to talk about the neurological correlates of cognitive and psychological processes, rather than "epiphenomenalizing" the latter, was characteristic of many of the psychoneurological sections of the Moscow International Congress of Psychology in 1966. The peaceful coexistence of Vygotsky and Pavlov is an eloquent symptom of this trend.

C.   Instrumental versus Reinforced Responses:
     The Use of Repetition

Coming back to our specific learning problem, one of the most striking facts in favor of a strict reinforcement theory of behavioral performance has been that animal reinforcement procedures (rather than theories) have proved to be fruitful in the human psychotherapeutic and educational context. The fact, however, that human behavior can be modified by reward contingencies in much the same ways as animal behavior does not astonish a cognitive psychologist. One cannot see why an intelligent person, using the best of his intelligence, should not repeat responses that have proved to be instrumental to obtain objects wanted, and why he should not stop to avoid or to fear objects perceived as no longer noxious. It is not implied that the same behavioral changes cannot be obtained by other, and usually more slowly working, mechanisms in less cognitively developed organisms. The point is as follows. First, rewarded responses tend to be quickly abandoned in men when they are merely perceived as no longer instrumental. This perception is based on information given, and not necessarily on an experience of failure of reward (that is, an extinction procedure; see Estes', 1972, experiment). This functional substitution of various forms of cognitive information for overt behavioral reward in different circumstances, is what is meant among others by *cognitive functioning*. Second, and most important, humans themselves often change the instrumental character of previous responses by changing the concrete objects (rewards) wanted and the cognitive means–end structures relating specific responses (means) to specific rewards. Repetition of responses is less functional and instrumental in living beings continuously changing the objects (rewards) to be obtained in order to satisfy their growing needs for achievement, affection, knowledge, power, and the like, then is the case in hungry animals looking only for food and a few other things (cf. Section II. D).

In a word, the effect of reward and absence of reward, as well as repetition behavior, are not fully accounted for by reinforcement processes in terms of automatic strengthening and inhibition. More flexible cognitive functions in terms of instrumental means–end relations appear to play a major role in human performance, not excluding, I repeat, the more automatic influence of other factors, especially those in cognitively unfavorable conditions.

D.   Cognitive Processes in Recall and Repetition Performances

Two of our associates at the Louvain Laboratory, d'Ydewalle and Eelen (1975), recently investigated, in relation to Buchwald's (1969) model, the extent to which cognitive recall of a response and its outcome actually influences the repetition of that response in a classical learning experiment (performance learning). After a first learning trial, subjects went through a test trial in which some of them were instructed (Recall-plus-Repeat condition), first, to recall the previously given response and its outcome for each stimulus presented again, and, second, to perform according to the original learning instructions, viz. repeating as many correct responses as possible. Among the many interesting results obtained in several experimental conditions (for example, changing the proportion of Right outcomes: .25, .50, and .75), the following data are instructive in this context:

1.   When recall of the outcome (Right or Wrong) fails, subjects guess the outcome "Right" as a function of the proportion of right responses obtained in Trial 1. The hypothetical explanation is that they keep in mind a general cognitive image (a pattern of relative frequencies) of the proportion of right outcomes received in Trial 1. Similar conclusions were reached in research on the "spread of effect" by Nuttin (1949; cf. also Eelen, 1974).

2. The proportion of right responses in Trial 1 positively affects the repetition of previously given responses (Right and Wrong ones). The hypothesis is that, when recalling the response given and not recalling the outcome received, the subjects repeat responses previously given on the basis of their guesses about the outcome. Since guessing *Right* occurs more frequently in the 75% than the 25% Right condition (according to Point 1), the proportion of repetition of responses is actually found to be higher in that condition. No effect of the intent to learn was found (see, however, Section VII.A). It can be added that subjects tend to guess the outcome Right for correctly recalled responses. A similar tendency was found in earlier experiments for relatively higher degrees of clear recognition of stimulus situations (Nuttin & Greenwald, 1968, pp. 38–43).

From these and other results obtained, it was concluded that the effects of Right and Wrong on subsequent performance or responding can be explained in cognitive terms, that is, in terms of what subjects retain (recall) from previous experiences or guess on the basis of these experiences. In fact, when cognition fails, a cognitive substitute, for example, guessing, enters the scene and is called upon to regulate performance. A short note on this interesting cognitive process and its role in behavioral performance may be to the point.

E. The Use of Guessing

In many experiments and real life situations, subjects are presented with such an abundance of informational data and a complexity of situations and tasks that guessing activities play an important role in responding. Guessing is an alternative way of dealing cognitively with informational complexity. Selective attention and strategies operate at the level of information registration and processing (as shown above), whereas guessing is a codeterminant in decision making and performance. Its role in behavior points to the importance of cognitive activity. When actual knowledge is not available, subjects cannot help using cognitive substitutes! Experimenter's instructions may even encourage or urge them to do so. Both "automatic" response tendencies and cognitive guessing activities cooperate and interact in the same way as motor and cognitive components in behavior usually do. In any case, the relationship found between the frequency of guessing Right and the proportion of Right's actually received (including their approximate localization; cf. Nuttin, 1949), compels one to accept the impact of some cognitive (perceptual and representational) patterns in performance and recall. (See, also, Gladstone, 1974; Gladstone & Miller, 1968.)

IX. CONCLUSION: DIVERSITY AND CONTINUITY IN THE LEARNING PROCESS

The cognitive learning process and the role of reward as described in this chapter are not considered to be the only form of learning. The cognitive development of organisms varies along a continuum; the role of that flexible and expeditious way of dealing with objects that constitutes cognitive functioning varies together with it. Affective learning (cf. Section VI), learning of skills, and canalization of needs in behavioral habits (Nuttin & Greenwald, 1968, pp. 129–132) are forms of learning in which the automatic influence of reinforcing factors is supposed to play a more important, although not exclusive, role. It is assumed that dynamic activation and the relatedness of a behavioral unit to that dynamic system are the basic processes involved in cognitive and noncognitive learning. While focused (object-directed) activation is assumed to be instigated by the that's-it reaction in cognitive-attention learning, reinforcement itself is believed to elicit automatic activation of the rewarded behavioral unit. Miller's (1963, p. 94) behavioral observation is interesting in that respect: a naive animal that happens to rotate a wheel which turns off an electric shock is found to intensify that rewarded response. Miller assumes that the sudden reinforcement produces an automatic increase in the organism's activity and favors learning. Dynamic activation in terms of facilitating and "amplifying" elements coming from "drive sources" is also introduced in Estes' (1969) hypothesis; these amplifying elements, however, are conceived as more directly related to the stimulus side of the behavioral unit. In any case, activation rooted in "drive sources" and related in one or other way to a behavioral unit, is assumed to be at the basis of better retention and reproduction readiness of that unit. Thus, the learning process is conceived of as having some fundamental unity and continuity throughout the phylogenetic and ontogenetic sequences of more or less cognitively functioning organisms, together with a large diversity of concrete mechanisms involved in the various phases of the process as a whole.

REFERENCES

Alper, T. G. Task-orientation and ego-orientation as factors in reminiscence. *Journal of Experimental Psychology,* 1948, **38**, 244–238.

Anderson, J. R., & Bower, G. H. *Human associative memory.* Washington, D.C.: Winston, 1973.

Anokhin, P. K. *Internal inhibition as a physiological problem* (in Russian). Moscow: 1958 (quoted after Berlyne, 1967).

Atkinson, J. W. The achievement motive and recall of interrupted and completed tasks. *Journal of Experimental Psychology,* 1953, **46**, 381–390.

Atkinson, J. W., & Raynor, J. O. *Motivation and achievement.* Washington, D.C.: Winston, 1974.

Bandura, A. Vicarious and self-reinforcement process. In R. Glaser (Ed.), *The nature of reinforcement.* New York: Academic Press, 1971.

Bandura, A. Behavior theory and the models of man. *American Psychologist,* 1974, **29,** 859–869.

Bartlett, F. C. *Remembering. A study in experimental and social psychology.* Cambridge, England: Cambridge University Press, 1950.

Berlyne, D. E. Arousal and reinforcement. In D. Levine (Ed.), *Nebraska symposium on motivation,* 1967, Lincoln, Nebraska: University of Nebraska Press, 1967.

Berlyne, D. E., Borsa, D. M., Hamacher, J. H., & Koenig, I. D. V. Paired-associate learning and the timing of arousal. *Journal of Experimental Psychology,* 1966, **72,** 1–6.

Berlyne, D. E., & Normore, L. F. Effects of prior uncertainty on incidental free recall. *Journal of Experimental Psychology,* 1972, **96,** 43–48.

Bindra, D. A motivational view of learning, performance, and behavior modification. *Psychological Review,* 1974, **81,** 199–213.

Bloch, V., Denti, A., & Schmaltz, G. Effets de la stimulation réticulaire sur la phase de consolidation de la trace mnésique. *Journal de Physiologie,* 1966, **58,** 469–470.

Broadbent, D. E. Stimulus set and response set: Two kinds of selective attention. In D. I. Mostofsky (Ed.), *Attention: Contemporary theory and analysis.* New York: Appleton-Century-Crofts, 1970. Pp. 51–60.

Brown, J. F. Über die dynamischen Eigenschaften der Realitäts- und Irrealitätsschichten. *Psychologische Forschung,* 1933, **18,** 2–26.

Bruner, J. S. The course of cognitive growth. *American Psychologist,* 1964, **19,** 1–15.

Bruner, J. S. The growth of representational processes in childhood. In J. S. Bruner, *Beyond the information given.* London: Allen & Unwin, 1974. Pp. 311–324.

Buchwald, A. M. Effects of "right" and "wrong" on subsequent behavior: A new interpretation. *Psychological Review,* 1969, **76,** 132–143.

Cautela, J. R. Covert conditioning. In A. Jacobs & L. B. Sachs (Eds.), *The psychology of private events.* New York: Academic Press, 1971.

Chomsky, N. *Syntactic structure.* The Hague: Mouton, 1957.

de Montpellier, G. Nature et méchanisme de l'apprentissage intentionnel. *Psychologica Belgica,* 1972, **12,** 33–44.

Deweer, B., Hennevin, E., & Bloch, V. Nouvelles données sur la facilitation réticulaire de la consolidation mnésique. *Journal de Physiologie,* 1968, **60**(Supplement 1-2), 430.

Dodson, J. D. Relative values of reward and punishment in habit formation. *Psychobiology,* 1917, **1,** 231–276.

d'Ydewalle, G. Een experimentele studie van de herhaling van juiste en verkeerde antwoorden. Unpublished doctoral dissertation, University of Louvain, 1974.

d'Ydewalle, G., & Eelen, P. Repetition and recall of "right" and "wrong" responses in incidental and intentional learning. *Journal of Experimental Psychology, Learning and Memory,* 1975, **1,** 429–441.

Eelen, P. Een experimentele studie van de invloed van "juist" en "verkeerd" op het verwerken van de informatie in twee leerparadigma's: Performantie-leren versus observatie-leren. Unpublished doctoral dissertation, University of Louvain, 1974.

Ehrlich, S. *Les mécanismes du comportement verbal.* Paris: J. Vrin, 1968.

Estes, W. K. Reinforcement in human learning. In J. T. Tapp (Ed.), *Reinforcement and behavior.* New York: Academic Press, 1969. Pp. 63–94.

Estes, W. K. Reward in human learning: theoretical issues and strategic choice points. In R. Glaser (Ed.), *The nature of reinforcement.* New York: Academic Press, 1971. Pp. 16–44.

Estes, W. K. Reinforcement in human behavior. Reward and punishment influence human actions via informational and cybernetic processes. *American Scientist,* 1972, **60,** 723–729.

Ferdinand, W. Experimentelle Untersuchungen über den Einfluss der persönlichen Wichtigkeit des Materials auf das Behalten. *Psychologische Forschung*, 1959, **25**, 455–517.

Florès, C. La mémoire. In P. Fraisse & J. Piaget (Eds.), *Traité de psychologie expérimentale*, Vol. IV. Paris: Presses Universitaires de France, 1975.

Gladstone, R. On "Learning Theory." *American Psychologist*, 1974, **29**, 847.

Gladstone, R., & Miller, M. Rationality, motivation, and extinction. *Journal of Psychology*, 1968, **68**, 33–38.

Gleitman, H., & Gillet, E. The effect of intention upon learning. *Journal of General Psychology*, 1957, **57**, 137–142.

Heckhausen, H. Change in attractiveness of task after failure: Cognitive dissonance theory vs. achievement motivation theory. *Proceedings of the international conference on psychology of human learning*. Vol. 1. Prague: Institute of Psychology, 1970. Pp. 195–203.

Heider, F. The Gestalt theory of motivation. In M. R. Jones (Ed.), *Nebraska symposium on motivation*, 1960. Lincoln, Nebraska: University of Nebraska Press, 1960. Pp. 145–172.

Hillix, W. A., & Marx, M. H. Response strengthening by information and effect in human learning. *Journal of Experimental Psychology*, 1960, **60**, 97–102.

Jenkins, J. J. Remember that old theory of memory? *American Psychologist*, 1974, **29**, 785–795.

Kanfer, F. H. The maintenance of behavior by self-generated stimuli and reinforcement. In A. Jacobs & L. B. Sachs (Eds.), *The psychology of private events*. New York: Academic Press, 1971.

Kleinsmith, L. J., & Kaplan, S. Interaction of arousal and recall interval in nonsense syllable paired-associate learning. *Journal of Experimental Psychology*, 1964, **67**, 124–126.

Köhler, W. Perceptual organization and learning. *American Journal of Psychology*, 1958, **71**, 311–315.

Lecomte, P., Deweer, B., & Bloch, V. Consolidation et conservation de la trace mnésique: Effets respectifs de la stimulation réticulaire. *Journal de Physiologie*, 1969, **61**(Supplement 1-2), 334–335.

Le Ny, J.-F. *Apprentissage et activités psychologiques*. Paris: Presses Universitaire de France, 1967.

Lepper, M. R., Greene, D., & Nisbett, R. E. Undermining children's intrinsic interest with extrinsic rewards: A test of the "overjustification" hypothesis. *Journal of Personal and Social Psychology*, 1973, **28**, 129–137.

Levine, F. M., & Fasnacht, G. Token rewards may lead to token learning. *American Psychologist*, 1974, **29**, 816–820.

Lewin, K. *Vorsatz, Wille und Bedürfnis. Mit Vorbemerkungen über die psychischen Kräfte und Energien und die Struktur der Seele*. Berlin: Springer-Verlag, 1926.

Lewin, K. The conceptual representation and measurement of psychological forces. *Contributions to Psychological Theory*, 1938, **1**, No. 4.

Longstreth, L. E. A cognitive interpretation of secondary reinforcement. In J. K. Cole (Ed.), *Nebraska symposium on motivation, 1971*. Lincoln, Nebraska: University of Nebraska Press, 1971. Pp. 33–80.

Luria, A. R. *The role of speech in the regulation of normal and abnormal behavior*. New York: Liveright, 1961.

Luria, A. R. *Human brain and psychological processes*. New York: Harper & Row, 1966.

Marrow, A. J. Goal tensions and recall. *Journal of General Psychology*, 1938, **19**, 3–64.

McLaughlin, B. "Intentional" and "Incidental" learning in human subjects: The role of instructions to learn and motivation. *Psychological Bulletin*, 1965, **63**, 359–376.

Meehl, P. E. On the circularity of the law of effect. *Psychological Bulletin*, 1950, **47**, 52–75.

Miller, G. A., Galanter, E., & Pribram, K. H. *Plans and the structure of behavior*. New York: Holt, 1960.

Miller, N. E. Experimental studies of conflict. In J. Mc. V. Hunt (Ed.), *Personality and the behavior disorders*. New York: Ronald Press, 1944. Pp. 431–466.

Miller, N. E. Some reflections on the law of effect produce a new alternative to drive reduction. In M. R. Jones (Ed.), *Nebraska symposium on motivation, 1963*. Lincoln, Nebraska: University of Nebraska Press, 1963. Pp. 65–112.

Mischel, W. Toward a cognitive social learning: Reconceptualization of personality. *Psychological Review*, 1973, **80**, 252–283.

Mittag, H. D. Ueber personale Bedingungen des Gedächtnisses für Handlungen. *Zeitschrift für Psychologie*, 1955, **158**, 40–120.

Montgomery, K. C. The relation between exploratory behavior and spontaneous alternation in the white rat. *Journal of Comparative and Physiological Psychology*, 1951, **44**, 582–589.

Moray, N. *Attention: Selective processes in vision and hearing*. New York: Academic Press, 1970.

Nelson, T. O. Extinction, delay, and partial-reinforcement effects in paired-associate learning. *Cognitive Psychology*, 1971, **2**, 212–228.

Nuttin, J. De wet van het effekt en de rol van de taak in het leerproces. Unpublished doctoral dissertation, University of Louvain, 1941. 189 pp.

Nuttin, J. Spread in recalling failure and success. *Journal of Experimental Psychology*, 1949, **39**, 690–700.

Nuttin, J. *Tâche, réussite et échec. Théorie de la conduite humaine*. Louvain: Publications Universitaires, 1953.

Nuttin, J. The future time perspective in human motivation and learning. In *Proceedings of the XXIInd International Congress of Psychology, Washington, 1963*. Amsterdam: North-Holland Publ., 1964. Pp. 60–82. Also published in: *Acta Psychologica*, 1964, **23**, 60–82.

Nuttin, J. Pleasure and reward in human motivation and learning. In D. E. Berlyne & K. B. Madsen (Eds.), *Pleasure, reward, and preference*. New York: Academic Press, 1973.

Nuttin, J. A relational theory of motivation and the dynamic function of cognitive contents. Paper presented at the Montreal Congress of Applied Psychology, 1974. (Louvain, Report No 4.)

Nuttin, J., in collaboration with Greenwald, A. *Reward and punishment in human learning. Elements of a behavior theory*. New York: Academic Press, 1968.

Olds, J. Brain mechanisms of reinforcement learning. In D. E. Berlyne & K. B. Madsen (Eds.), *Pleasure, reward, and preference*. New York: Academic Press, 1973. Pp. 35–63.

Oléron, G. Influence de la structuration des données sur la mémoire à court et à moyen terme. *Année Psychologique*, 1968, **68**, 83–95.

Park, T.-Z. Zur Frage der psychologischen Grundlagen der Wort-Wort-Verbindung. *Psychologische Forschung*, 1966, **29**, 89–111.

Pavlov, I. P. *Conditioned reflexes*. London: Clarendon Press, 1927.

Piaget, J. *La construction du réel chez l'enfant*. Neuchâtel-Paris: Ed. Delachaux & Niestlé, 1937.

Postman, L. Short-term memory and incidental learning. In A. W. Melton (Ed.), *Categories of human learning*. New York: Academic Press, 1964. Pp. 145–201.

Postman, L. Association and performance in the analysis of verbal learning. In T. R. Dixon & D. L. Horton (Eds.), *Verbal behavior and general behavior theory*. Englewood Cliffs, New Jersey: Prentice-Hall, 1968.

Postman, L. Experimental studies of long-term retention. Unpublished paper presented at the Frascati Symposium on Recent advances in learning psychology, 1972.

Postman, L., & Adams, P. A. Performance variables in the experimental analysis of the law of effect. *American Journal of Psychology*, 1954, **67**, 612–631.

Postman, L., & Adams, P. A. "Isolation" and the law of effect. *American Journal of Psychology*, 1955, **68**, 96–105.

Pribram, K. H. *Languages of the brain. Experimental paradoxes and principles in neuropsychology.* Englewood Cliffs, New Jersey: Prentice-Hall, 1971.

Rosenzweig, S. Preferences in repetition of successful and unsuccessful activities as a function of age and personality. *Journal of Genetic Psychology* 1933, **42**, 423–441.

Ryan, T. A. *Intentional behavior. An approach to human motivation.* New York: Ronald Press, 1970.

Schönpflug, W. Paarlernen, Behaltensdauer und Aktivierung. *Psychologische Forschung,* 1966, **29**, 132–148.

Schönpflug, W., & Beike, P. Einprägen und Aktivierung bei gleichzeitiger Variation der Absichtlichkeit des Lernens und der Ich-Bezogenheit des Lernstoffs. *Psychologische Forschung,* 1964, **27**, 366–376.

Shiffrin, R. M., & Atkinson, R. C. Storage and retrieval processes in long-term memory. *Psychological Review,* 1969, **76**, 179–193.

Smirnov, A. A. *Psychological problems of memory* (in Russian, with title and summaries in English). Moscow: Prosveshcheniye, 1966.

Spence, J. T., Armstrong, J., & Conrad, R. Contribution of instructions to the effects of two types of symbolic reinforcers on the discrimination learning of children. *Psychonomic Science,* 1969, **17**, 107–108.

Spong, P., Haider, M., & Lindsley, D. B. Selective attentiveness and cortical evoked responses to visual and auditory stimuli. *Science,* 1965, **148**, 395–397.

Trabasso, T., & Bower, G. H. *Attention in learning.* New York: Wiley, 1968.

Turner, N. H., & Barlow, J. A. A memory for pleasant and unpleasant experiences: Some methodological considerations. *Journal of Experimental Psychology,* 1951, **42**, 189–196.

Underwood, B. J. Attributes of memory. *Psychological Review,* 1969, **76**, 559–573.

Van Bergen, A. *Task interruption.* Amsterdam: North-Holland Publ., 1968.

von Restorff, H. Über die Wirkung von Bereichsbildungen im Spurenfeld. *Psychologische Forschung,* 1933, **18**, 299–342.

Vygotsky, L. S. *Thought and language.* (Edited and translated by E. Hanfmann & G. Vakar.) New York: Wiley, 1962.

Wallace, W. P. Review of the historical, empirical, and theoretical status of the von Restorff phenomenon. *Psychological Bulletin,* 1965, **63**, 410–424.

Wallace, W. P. Incidental learning: The influence of associative similarity and formal similarity in producing false recognition. *Journal of Verbal Learning and Verbal Behavior,* 1968, **7**, 50–54.

Weiner, B. *Theories of motivation. From mechanism to cognition.* Chicago: Markham Publ., 1972.

Weiner, B., & Walker, E. L. Motivational factors in short-term retention. *Journal of Experimental Psychology,* 1966, **71**, 190–193.

Woodworth, R. S. *Dynamics of behavior.* New York: Henry Holt & Comp., 1958.

Yerkes, R. M., & Dodson, J. D. The relation of strength of stimulus to rapidity of habit-formation. *Journal of Comparative Neurology and Psychology,* 1908, **18**, 459–482.

Zinchenko, P. I. *Involuntary remembering* (in Russian). Moscow, 1962. (Quoted after Berlyne, in *Contemporary Psychology,* 1964, **9**, 323.)

8

Motivation from the Cognitive Perspective

Bernard Weiner

University of California, Los Angeles

There are two broad interrelationships between motivation and cognition: (*a*) the influence of motivation upon cognitive processes, and (*b*) the influence of cognitive processes upon motivation. The questions raised when considering the motivation → cognition linkage include, for example, whether the range of information that is registered, processed, and used is augmented or restricted when individuals are highly motivated; whether we are able to learn more when the to-be-learned material is "interesting" or of personal value; and whether we are better able to retrieve information when there is something at stake, such as the potential reward desired by a quiz show contestant. That is, are information search, storage, and retrieval, perception, judgment, and decision making, and the remaining wide array of cognitive processes affected by motivational states? Of course, psychologists would like to do more than merely demonstrate that such as influence exists. The goal is to develop general laws that relate motivation to cognition and to understand the mechanisms responsible for this association.

It might surprise the reader to learn that extremely little is known about the influence of motivation upon cognition. The data are sparse and often unreliable; the methodologies frequently are subject to criticism; and there is a paucity of theoretical networks to account for the few observed relationships. Indeed, even the demonstration stage has not been reached in this difficult and complex area. I therefore have decided not to review and analyze this psychological literature here, although the reader should be less fearful than me of these murky, important, and almost virginal waters.

We then turn to the second of the proposed general interrelationships between motivation and cognition: the influence of cognitive processes upon motivation. The kinds of questions raised under this rubric include, for example, whether cognitions can arouse motivation, what roles are played by cognitive processes in the maintenance of goal-directed activity and the attainment of the goal, and whether cognitions can function as goal satisfiers and lead to a cessation of behavior.

I. THE MIND–BODY PROBLEM

The questions listed above thrust us directly into the middle of what is known as the mind–body problem, for the influence of thought (the mind) on action (the body) is under consideration. A number of hypotheses or presumptions relating central and peripheral processes have been entertained. One dualistic supposition is that the mind and the body are completely independent, with distinct functions that do not interact:

$$\text{Thought:} \quad A \; \cdots \; B \; \cdots \; C$$
$$\text{Action:} \quad A' \cdots B' \cdots C' \tag{1}$$

The processes of the mind and the body may be correlated, however. For example, deprivation may lead one to think about food, to experience an "intention" to obtain food, and produce approach behavior toward food. But the thoughts and the intention do not *affect* the action; the central representations are *epiphenomena (epi = upon)*.

In contrast to the independence depicted above, it has been proposed that the mind and the body interact. There are various interactionist positions. One group of interactionists contends that thoughts are the product of action:

$$\text{Thought:} \quad A \cdots \; B \cdots \; C$$
$$\text{Action:} \quad A' \cdots \; B' \cdots \; C' \tag{2}$$

Sequences of events illustrating this position are: "I am eating a great deal; I must be hungry"; or "I just argued for the passage of this controversial bill; I must be in favor of it"; or "I am running; I must be afraid." In these examples thoughts are not causes; they are behavioral by-products and once more might be considered epiphenomena, for they do not influence action.

The following schema depicts a contrasting interactionist position:

$$\text{Thought:} \quad A \; \cdots \; B \; \cdots \; C$$
$$\text{Action:} \quad A' \; \cdots \; B' \; \cdots \; C' \tag{3}$$

Thoughts are causes that in part determine action (for example, ''I am in favor of this bill; I will argue for it''). This is the belief espoused by cognitive motivational theorists (see Weiner, 1972, 1975). Although thoughts are presumed to influence action, it is generally accepted that not all behaviors must be mediated by thoughts (for example, reflex actions), that not all of the determinants of behavior need to have a conscious or a cognitive representation (for example, hormonal influences), and that behaviors may also have informational value and influence thought processes (see Eqs. 2 and 3).

The belief that behavior is mediated or influenced by thoughts certainly is in accord with common sense; one may wonder how it could be otherwise argued. Yet in the crucial formative years of the experimental study of motivation between, say, 1930 and 1955, most motivational psychologists did not accept the cognitive viewpoint. Rather, it was contended that behavior could be explained with a simple language system that primarily included the terms ''stimulus'' and ''response.'' Humans were conceptualized as machines; the task of the psychologist was to understand the structure and the function of the machine, using objective language and anchoring input–output relationships to observables. Machines do not think (or at least they did not before the advent of computers!), and there was no need or place for cognitive constructs.

Since the late 1950s the limitations of the mechanistic conception of motivation have become increasingly evident, and the efficacy of the cognitive viewpoint has been repeatedly demonstrated. The interactionist position (Eq. 3) therefore has gained ascendency in the field of motivation. But the reader should realize that cognitive approaches to the experimental study of motivation are relatively new; the scientific progress of the field must be considered with this fact in mind.

II. A GUIDING FRAMEWORK

A convenient unit of behavior includes the initiation of goal-directed activity, maintenance or persistence of behavior in service of the desired goal, attainment or abandonment of the goal, and the consequences of goal attainment or nonattainment. For example, assume that one is home studying when the telephone rings, bringing an invitation to join some friends at a party. This request arouses a desire to affiliate, and initiates a change of activity. Behaviors are now undertaken that are instrumental to the satisfaction of the aroused affiliative concerns. For example, the books are put away, clothes are changed, the car is taken from the garage and driven to the party, and conversation is exchanged with friends at the party. After a certain period of time these affiliative desires are partially or wholly satisfied, and the person leaves for home (although, of course, there are many possible causes of the cessation of the affiliative-related activity; see Atkinson & Birch, 1970). During the return trip there may be feelings of satisfaction that produce an increment in the likelihood of attending the next party. This action sequence, or "behavioral episode," is illustrated in general form in the left hand column of Table 1.

During this behavioral sequence cognitions play essential motivational roles. For example, the voice heard over the phone initiates an *intention* to go to the party; while dressing, *social comparison processes* dictate our choice of clothes; when driving to the party, it is *decided* what road to follow, *utilizing information* about road conditions and *knowledge* of the shortest path; during a conversation at the party, *cues are detected* that someone does or does not like us; a *strategy is selected* to win friends; when driving home, the conversation is *recollected;* and so on. The sequence of thought processes that occurs during a behavioral episode is depicted in general form in the right hand column of Table 1.

Table 1 outlines parallel thought and action sequences. If the interactionist position (see Eq. 3) is accepted, that is, if it is presumed that thought may influence action, then it is evident from Table 1 and the previous paragraph that cognitive activity can affect motivated behavior during various phases of a behavioral episode.

In this chapter some of the functions of cognitive processes in relation to an action sequence are examined. Of necessity, only a brief introduction to interesting empirical data and promising conceptual frameworks are presented. In a major portion of the chapter I examine the effects of thoughts on

TABLE 1

The Sequence of Action and Thought
during a Behavioral Episode

Behavioral activity		Cognitive activity	
A.	Motivational arousal	A'.	Registration of new information and/or the onset of a new intent
B.	Instrumental activity and persistence of goal-directed behavior.	B'.	Cognitive activities related to the attainment of the goal.
C.	Goal attainment or nonattainment.	C'.	Cognitive activities during goal expression.
D.	Behavioral consequences of goal activity.	D'.	Postgoal thoughts.

action following motivational arousal but prior to goal attainment (B' and B in Table 1). This linkage has been of particular concern to investigators in the field. The chapter concludes with a detailed examination of one currently popular cognitive approach to motivation, labeled attribution theory.

III.   COGNITIONS AND THE INITIATION OF BEHAVIOR

A.   The Need for Cognitive Activity

As already intimated in Section I, the mechanists conceptualized humans as passive organisms, at rest until "goaded" by an external stimulus, such as a hot stove, or by an internal stimulus, such as the pangs produced by food deprivation. Behavior then persists until the stimulus is "turned off," thus returning the organism to the prior level of equilibrium. At the point of equilibrium the level of stimulation is zero. Both Sigmund Freud (1915) and Clark Hull (1943) advocated such a homeostatic conception of behavior, with stimulus reduction having hedonic consequences.

The cognitivists, on the other hand, conceive of humans as active, information processing organisms, seeking stimulation and knowledge, acting to master the environment and to fulfill their potential. Zero-level stimulation is an aversive state to be avoided.

The necessity of varied stimulation was dramatically illustrated by Donald Hebb and his colleagues in what is known as the study of "sensory deprivation" (see Schultz, 1965). In one type of deprivation procedure, the subject lies alone in a white room with goggles over his or her eyes that permit only homogeneous light. In addition, padding is put on both arms and legs, thus decreasing tactile stimulation. College student subjects in an experiment using this procedure reported an inability to think when external input was so severely limited. Some also told of hallucinations. Few of the subjects remained in the experiment for more than 8 hr, although they were highly paid.

B.   Cognitive Consistency

The processing of information, as well as many other cognitive activities, has affective significance. For example, assume that a student finds that he or she has failed an exam. This information naturally is aversive. Further information then is sought, and the score is compared with the scores of other students. The comparison may reveal that the score is the lowest in the class. When introspecting about the test performance the student concludes that the grade was due to low ability, thus decreasing his or her self-concept. It is evident that in this cognitive–behavioral sequence a variety of cognitive activities have emotional significance.

The affective significance of cognitions at times is determined not only by the particular content of a cognition, but also by the relationship or the "fit" between new information and the prior cognitive structures. Cognitions inconsistent with current beliefs may create an "imbalance" that has motivational consequences (see Zajonc, 1968).

The most widely known and investigated theory of cognitive consistency or cognitive balance was formulated by Leon Festinger (1957). According to Festinger, if the implications of two or more cognitions are mutually exclusive, then cognitive dissonance is created. For example, if an individual smokes and then reads that smoking causes cancer, dissonance is aroused. These elements of knowledge are incongruent and mutually incompatible; if smoking causes cancer, then one should not smoke. Dissonance, according to Festinger, is unpleasant; the individual therefore is motivated to resolve or to reduce the dissonance.

Dissonance may be reduced in a number of ways. Using the smoking example, the best way to reduce dissonance would be to stop smoking. But many people find this behavioral change quite difficult. Another way to reduce dissonance is to alter cognitions. For example, it might be contended that the evidence associating cancer with smoking is inconclusive. If one perceives that cancer is not caused by smoking, then it is not dissonant to smoke. A survey asking respondents if they thought the linkage between smoking and cancer had been sufficiently proven revealed that the greater the smoking habit, the greater the percentage of individuals who do not believe that smoking causes cancer. Apparently, when cognitions are not in harmony, processes are instigated to help bring these cognitions into balance or consonance. To bolster one's consonant beliefs, one can seek data indicating that smoking does not cause cancer, one can affiliate with others who smoke, one can ignore articles that discuss the smoking–cancer linkage, or one can remember the 100-year-old who smokes a cigar a day.

Experimental Studies

A few experimental methodologies have been used extensively to demonstrate the motivating effects of cognitive dissonance. In one well-known procedure (Festinger & Carlsmith, 1959), subjects in a dissonance-arousing experimental condition were given a small reward to perform a task that was inconsistent with their beliefs; subjects in a second experimental condition were given a large reward for their performance. In this particular investigation the subjects were either paid $1.00 or $20.00 to recruit other subjects for a boring experiment. It was reasoned by the experimenters that lying for only a small reward is dissonance producing. On the other hand, little dissonance is aroused for lying if one is given a large reward. Thus, only the subjects in the $1.00 reward condition would be motivated to alter their belief systems and bring their cognitions into balance.

One way to reduce the dissonance between the cognitions is to perceive the experiment for which the new subjects are being recruited as more interesting that it really is. If the experiment is perceived as interesting, then the recruiters are not lying, and their behavior is consistent with the small reward. The data in this study indeed revealed that subjects in the $1.00 condition rated the experiment as more interesting than subjects in the $20.00 condition.

In a similar series of experiments that are more closely related to traditional motivational phenomena, subjects were asked to refrain from eating or drinking for a period of time (Brehm, 1962). When the subjects reported back to the experimenter, they were requested to undergo further deprivation. Some subjects were given reasonable pay for their discomfort, whereas others were asked to comply without reward. Receiving no reward, coupled with the cognition of continued hunger or thirst, theoretically creates a state of cognitive dissonance. One way to reduce the dissonance is to perceive the deprivation as not being particularly aversive. To test this notion, the subjects were given an opportunity to eat or drink prior to leaving the experimental room. It was found that the subjects in the dissonance-producing or no-compensation condition ate and drank less than subjects in the no-dissonance or reward condition. That is, the dissonance-aroused subjects evidently believed that they were not very hungry or thirsty.

One final experiment is reported here to indicate further the type of data gathered by dissonance theorists. The experiments are often intriguing as well as novel. In this experiment (Aronson & Mills, 1959) female subjects volunteered to participate in a supposedly frank discussion of sex. Before the discussion they were required to undergo an interview. In one condition the interview was embarrassing, with the subjects required to repeat "dirty" words. In the second experimental condition a routine interview was conducted. All the subjects then heard a boring and intellectualized sexual discussion. It was reasoned that it is dissonant to undergo a difficult "initiation" and then receive a small reward. Thus, the subjects given the embarrassing interview would be in a state of dissonance. One way to reduce this dissonance is to perceive the boring discussion as worthwhile and interesting. If that were the case, then the initial interview would have been "worth it." The data supported this hypothesis; the women given the embarrassing interview liked the discussion more than women given the routine interview.

In sum, the dissonance research demonstrated that the relationships between cognitions have motivational implications. In addition, some of the data (e.g., Brehm, 1962) suggest that a motivational state, such as that produced by food deprivation, must be cognized to affect behavior. That is, *perceptions* of internal states, whether accurate or not, control behavior. Furthermore, if the cues of the viscera are contradicted by other information emanating from "higher" centers, then the latter information is more heavily weighted in judging one's state of motivation. Note that this conception, and the data springing from it, are far removed from the typical infrahuman studies of motivation in which experimenters manipulate hours of deprivation and examine the effects of tissue deficits on performance. Furthermore, the basic assumptions about motivation accepted by most animal psychologists are called into question.

C. Intentions

The cognitions most influencing action according to "naive" inner experience are "intentions." For example, one suddenly intends to go to a movie, to buy clothes, and so on, and then one acts upon those intentions. That is, one's actions are regulated by conscious plans. Intentions were the main object of psychological consideration early in the history of psychology, but they vanished from study with the rise of mechanism and behaviorism. Intentions are now making a slow comeback into psychological research and are increasingly becoming the subject of investigation. They have even heavily influenced educational practices since the advent of "performance contracts" made between the teacher and his or her pupils. In these agreements the student pledges to reach a certain goal or performance standard within a specified period of time.

Data have revealed that conscious goals do regulate action (see Locke, 1968). For example, accepting hard goals produces a higher level of output than accepting easy goals. In a field research experiment illustrating this point, it was found that the higher the goals set in a fund-raising drive, the more money was collected, relative to the amount collected the prior year. Perhaps, then, incentives exert their influence on performance through the manipulation of conscious intentions or performance plans. All this may smack of "common sense"; however, such an allegation does not disavow the effect of conscious plans on behavior. Research in this area is minimal, and basic empirical data, as well as conceptual advances, remain to be introduced.

D. Summary

In sum, cognitions play important roles as motivators of behavior. There is a "need" for cognitive activity, for individuals seek out stimulation and boredom is an aversive state. The relationships between new cognitions and prior cognitive structures can produce motivational states, and intentions, or conscious goals, in part regulate action. These are, of course, just a few selected examples of the capacity of cognitive activity (or inactivity) to influence the initial phase of a behavioral episode.

IV. COGNITIONS AND GOAL ATTAINMENT

A change in motivational dominance generally is followed by an alteration in the direction of behavior. Activities are typically undertaken that are instrumental to the satisfaction of the newly activated motivational system.

The most evident function of cognitive processes during the instrumental phase of a behavioral episode is to guide the individual toward the goal. For example, to attain an affiliative-related goal the person may perceive it necessary to dress properly, to arrive at the party on time, or to interact in a friendly manner. The cognition or the belief that "A leads to B" has been labeled an "expectancy." An expectancy has an "if–then" logic, for example, "If I turn left at the corner, then I will arrive at the party" or "If I dress well, then I will attract new friends." Thus, an expectancy can be considered a subjective probability regarding the efficacy of certain behaviors, or a perceived contingency between a behavior and goal attainment. It is intuitively evident that subjective expectancy is a significant determinant of action, for behaviors that are perceived as instrumental to the attainment of a desired goal usually are exhibited in action.

In addition to expectancy, a second determinant of performance is the incentive value or the perceived attractiveness of a goal. Cognitive theorists generally postulate that motivated behavior is determined jointly by the subjective expectancy of goal attainment and by the anticipated value of the goal. This is in accord with our common sense, which dictates that what we do depends on the likelihood of getting something and just how good that something is. Decision theorists use the same fundamental rule to predict choice in gambling situations: the bet selected depends upon the odds given and the amount of the payoff. Of course, the expectancy of success and the value of the goal must be defined operationally and specified prior to the behavior being predicted, or else merely a tautological system has been constructed. These are difficult problems that remain to be solved. Lewin (1938), Tolman (1952), Rotter (1966), and Atkinson (1964) are among the prominent motivational psychologists who have formulated Expectancy × Value theories of behavior.

The Expectancy of Success

A great deal of research has been conducted demonstrating that the expectancy of success in an achievement-related context influences choice (the direction of behavior), how hard one will work (the intensity or magnitude of behavior), and how long one will perform the task (the persistence of behavior). Choice, intensity, and persistence generally are considered to be the main indicators of motivation. To understand this body of research, Atkinson's theory of achievement motivation must first be examined (see Atkinson, 1964; Weiner, 1972). A small portion of that theory is presented in detail here so that the reader will gain some familiarity with one relatively formal cognitive theory of motivation.

According to Atkinson, the motivation to approach an achievement-related goal is determined by three interacting factors: the motive or the desire for success, the expectancy of successful performance at that activity, and the incentive value of the success. The motive for success (M_s) is considered to be a relatively stable individual difference, often labeled the need for achievement. The expectancy of success refers to the subjective probability (P_s) of reaching the goal. As any probability figure, P_s can vary in magnitude from zero to one. Finally, the incentive value of success (I_s) is conceptualized as the amount of pride that one anticipates given a successful accomplishment. In achievement-related contexts, incentive value has a special relationship with subjective probability: $I_s = 1 - P_s$. That is, the easier the task, the less is the pride that is experienced for success, and the more difficult the task, the greater the feeling of accomplishment given a success.

It is assumed by Atkinson that these three motivational determinants relate to one another multiplicatively, that is, motivation is a product of the motive for success × the probability of success × the incentive value of success ($M_s \times P_s \times I_s$). In Table 2 values are assigned to these three concepts to examine the effects of M_s and P_s on strength of motivation and, therefore, choice, intensity, and persistence of behavior. Table 2 reveals that there is a bell-shaped relationship between P_s and the strength of motivation, with motivation maximal at the level of intermediate difficulty ($P_s = .50$). Furthermore, when the need for achievement increases, as in the right half of Table 2, the relative motivation to undertake tasks of intermediate difficulty grows in strength.

The derivations made on the basis of Atkinson's model that are revealed in Table 2 have been tested and confirmed in many investigations. In a

TABLE 2

The Strength of Approach Motivation (M) in
Achievement-Related Contexts as a Function of the Need for
Achievement (M_s), the Probability of Success (P_s),
and the Incentive Value of Success (I_s)

	M_s P_s I_s M	M_s P_s I_s M
Easy task (P_s = .90)	1 x .90 x .10 = .09	2 x .90 x .10 = .18[a]
Intermediate task (P_s = .50)	1 x .50 x .50 = .25	2 x .50 x .50 = .50
Difficult task (P_s = .10)	1 x .10 x .90 = .09	2 x .10 x .90 = .19

[a]Note that the difference between .18 and .50, which is .32, is twice the difference of .09 and .25, which is .16. Thus, the preference for intermediate risk increases as Ms increases.

typical study, subjects are asked to choose to perform one among a number of tasks that differ in perceived difficulty. The findings in these studies reveal an overall tendency for individuals to undertake tasks intermediate in difficulty. For example, they stand at a middle distance from the peg in a ring-toss game; they prefer participating in (and watching) an athletic event in which the opposing teams or contestants are about equal in ability; and so forth. In addition, the preference for tasks of intermediate difficulty is most pronounced among subjects labeled as high in achievement needs (see Atkinson, 1964; Weiner, 1972). Thus, derivations from an abstract motivational model are supported by empirical evidence, hence lending validity to the proposed model.

1. Intermediate Difficulty

Intermediate difficulty tasks have unique motivational significance. As already indicated, they arouse the greatest amount of achievement-related motivation. In addition, commerce with such tasks provides the most information about an individual's ability and/or effort expenditure. This follows because most individuals succeed at easy tasks and fail at difficult tasks. Hence, outcomes at these extreme tasks generally confirm one's beliefs about the nature of the environment, that is, the ease or difficulty of the tasks. No information is then gained by the actor about himself. On the other hand, outcomes at tasks of intermediate difficulty, in which about one-half the individuals undertaking the task succeed and the other one-half fail, yield information about personal competence. To illustrate this point somewhat differently, generally little is learned about the "quietness" of a person if observations are made at the library, where everyone is quiet, or at a football game, where everyone is noisy. The behaviors in these situations are attributable to the "demands" or the "press" of the environment. To learn about particular individuals, the behaviors exhibited in a given environment have to vary among people.

There is accumulating evidence to support the view that tasks of intermediate difficulty are chosen because of their informational value. Of course, such a position is quite consistent with the basic assumptions about humans espoused by cognitivists (see Sections I and III.A). In one representative experiment demonstrating the informational value of performance at intermediate difficulty tasks, policemen first rated their overall shooting ability. The policemen also rated their subjective probability of hitting targets that varied in their level of difficulty. The policemen then were offered one opportunity for target feedback. The clear choice was for performance feedback at a target that was perceived as intermediate in difficulty, relative to one's perceived ability. Thus, the high ability shooters wanted feedback at the most difficult target, the intermediate ability shooters wanted performance feedback at the intermediate-difficulty target, and the poor shooters desired knowledge of results at the objectively easier targets (Meyer, Folkes, & Weiner, in press).

It is apparent, then, that there are competing interpretations of the empirical observation that individuals prefer to undertake tasks of intermediate difficulty. On the one hand, according to Atkinson's theory, performance of these tasks theoretically produces the greatest amount of positive affect. Yet tasks of intermediate difficulty also generate maximum information and self-evaluative feedback. One is then challenged to discover if either of these interpretations is more "correct" or "better" than the other.

In an ingenious experiment, Trope and Brickman (1975) pitted "hedonic" versus "informational" explanations of task choice. In their investigation, Trope and Brickman (1975) simultaneously varied the difficulty of tasks as well as their "diagnosticity." Here diagnosticity referred to the difference between the proportion of individuals high versus low in ability who succeed at the task. Thus, for example, a task at which 90% of individuals high in ability succeed, whereas 60% of the persons low in ability succeed has greater diagnostic value than a task accomplished by 52% versus 48% of the individuals respectively high or low in ability. However, the 52%–48% task is more intermediate in difficulty than the 90%–60% task. Trope and Brickman report that in this situation subjects chose to perform the tasks of greater diagnosticity rather than the tasks more intermediate in difficulty. This suggests that the preference for intermediate difficulty is attributable to the high diagnostic value of these tasks, rather than to their difficulty per se. Much more research is needed, however, that relates to the basic motivational issue of informational versus hedonic determinants of action.

2. Long-Term Goals

One oversimplification of laboratory research is that an experiment has a final outcome that ends a short-term behavioral episode. This outcome typically is divorced from the individual's long-term life goals. Outside the laboratory, however, many human activities are future oriented, with both immediate and future consequences. For example, one receives a high grade in a course and that increases one's chance for admission into medical school; or one makes a good impression at a party and that enhances the possibility of initiating new friendships. Many other affiliative activities may intervene between the first episode and the continuation of the new relationship, yet these two events remain connected. Henry Murray (1959) identified temporally separated yet psychologically interrelated events as "serials." Because motivational researchers have concentrated upon short-term behavioral episodes, such as the time it takes for a hungry rat to run down a maze for food, serials have been neglected in psychological investigations.

There have recently been some studies of "serials" within achievement-related contexts that build upon the notion of expectancy. The model of achievement motivation shown in Table 2 indicates that motivation is maximal when a task is perceived as intermediate in difficulty. One implication of this derivation is that, if, for example, a crossword puzzle has a $P_s = .50$ and a test for admission into medical school has a $P_s = .50$, then the two situations arouse identical and maximal amounts of achievement motivation. One intuitively feels, however, that this inference is incorrect. The reason is evident: in the medical test situation an individual's future career and long-term goals are involved. The performance at the test is but one "step" in the "path" to the final goal. Obtaining a good score is an instrumental activity as well as an end in itself. Thus, multiple expectancies may be implicated. There is an expectancy of success at the particular test, but also an expectancy of success at medical school and an expectancy of success as a doctor.

Recent investigations have shown that the relationship between a particular activity and long-term goals indeed influences behavior (see Atkinson & Raynor, 1974). For example, persons with high achievement needs receive higher grades in courses when the grades are perceived as highly relevant to future goals. In sum, future orientation, yet another cognitive capacity, affects motivation.

3. Expectancy Change

Inasmuch as the expectancy of goal attainment or the perceived action–outcome contingency has such an important function in human behavior, the topic of expectancy change assumes major importance. The antecedents of structural change is the focus of many other chapters in these volumes and will not be discussed in any detail here. However, I want to introduce one cognitive determinant of expectancy change: the perceived characteristics of the task being performed. This factor generally is discussed within motivational contexts and is relevant to the last section of this chapter, in which causal attributions are examined.

One characteristic of a task or an endeavor that has a major influence on expectancy shifts is whether the outcome at that endeavor is perceived as determined by chance or skill. Consider, for example, a situation in which one correctly guesses the side that is "up" on a coin toss. The perceived likelihood of success on the second toss generally is the same as it was on the first toss (.50) and at times may slightly decrease. The decrease is due to the incorrect belief that in games of luck the same outcome is not anticipated on successive occasions. In contrast, in activities perceived as determined by skill, a success indicates that one "can" and a failure conveys information that one "cannot." This information produces increments in the expectancy of success following a success and decrements in the expectancy of success after a failure. That is, the same outcome is expected on successive occasions.

Of course, to predict expectancy changes correctly the viewpoint or the phenomenology of the actor must be taken into account. Games objectively determined by chance often are perceived as having a skill component (witness the behaviors of slot-machine players). Conversely, activities determined by skill often are perceived as having a large luck component (it is said that luck accounts for the success of our enemies). In short, the perceived structure of the task influences the perceived expectancy of success, which, in turn, affects a variety of overt behaviors.

One finding of theoretical interest related to skill versus chance causal perceptions is that resistance to extinction in skill tasks has been shown to be greater given 100% than 50% reinforcement during the learning period (see Rotter, 1966). This finding is a reversal of what is known as the Partial Reinforcement Effect, that is, the consistent empirical fact that extinction of conditioned responses is slower following 50% (partial reinforcement) than 100% reinforcement during the learning period. Apparently, 100% reward imparts information to humans that they are highly skilled at the task. This self-perception takes a relatively long period of nonreward at the activity before it is altered.

V. COGNITIVE INHIBITORS

Thus far, the instigational and the directional functions of cognitions have been introduced. In addition, cognitions can inhibit goal-directed activity. Psychoanalytic theorists such as Freud (1915) were among the first to call attention to the existence of mechanisms that "turn off" or redirect motivation. These so-called "defense" mechanisms theoretically are under the control of an executive agency, the "ego." Ego functioning is guided by reality principles, including the knowledge that under certain circumstances motivational expression is likely to result in greater pain than pleasure. Thus, at times motivational tendencies must be inhibited, or delayed, or channeled into socially acceptable forms of behavior.

A. Delay of Gratification

As the reader can readily imagine, the scientific study of the delay or the "time binding" of desires presents many obstacles, but laboratory research paradigms have been devised to examine the general process of impulse control. In one paradigm, the subjects (frequently younger children) are placed in conflict between the choice of a small, immediate reward or a more attractive reward that can be received at a later time (see Mischel, 1975). The experimenter then assesses the time that the subjects are able to delay gratification and wait for the larger reward. In addition, the content of the subjects' thoughts can be manipulated or guided during the waiting period to determine the relationships between particular cognitions and the ability to postpone gratification.

In an interesting series of studies, Mischel (1975) examined the Freudian notion that volitional delay would be increased if there was a mental representation of the desired object during the delay interval. Freud had suggested that hallucinations are wish fulfilling and thus are partial goal satisfiers. Contrary to expectation, however, Mischel's data indicated that, when the desired reward was directly visible to the subjects during the delay period, their ability to postpone gratification decreased. That is, the subjects were less able to wait and receive the larger reward and opted for the immediate reception of the less preferred reward. Apparently, the physical presence of the desired goal increased frustration, thus making the delay period less tolerable. However, the consequences of directly viewing the longed-for objects also depends upon the cognitive transformations made by the subjects. For example, if the subjects thought about the consummatory properties of the reward (for example, its taste), then their ability to delay gratification was weakened. If the nonconsummatory qualities of the object were focused upon (for example, marshmallows were thought of as clouds), however, then the delay period was greatly increased. Further experimentation also revealed that the ability to delay is enhanced if the subject is cognitively distracted from thinking about the reward. Instructions to "think fun" markedly increase impulse control.

In sum, delay of reward is influenced by how the subject cognitively represents or transforms his or her environment and to what the subject is attending. Cognitions may facilitate or inhibit the capability of individuals to ward off or to control motivational impulses.

B. Threat Reduction

In the preceding section it was revealed that cognitive mechanisms can facilitate adaptation by promoting impulse control. In addition, defenses function to protect the person from anxiety and other unpleasant affects. For example, one mechanism that prevents continued exposure to aversive sensations, such as the sight of blood or the feelings that accompany the death of a significant other, is fainting.

An observer can recognize a faint, and the fainter later readily comprehends what has happened. Thus, it is not considered to be a typical defense. Psychologists tend to believe that most defenses, such as repression, operate on an unconscious level. Individuals generally are not consciously aware of defenses or of their functional significance. In addition, it is not self-evident to an observer that defenses are inhibiting behavioral expression.

Denial and Intellectualization

Two mechanisms of defense that have been the subject of investigation are denial and intellectualization. Denial refers to a refusal to accept consciously the existence of a threatening situation. The neurotic person with a compulsion to wash his or her hands every 10 min performs this act with little affective expression, although the event theoretically has significant emotional connotations. Intellectualization, or isolation, occurs when an idea and its emotional accompaniment become detached. That is, an emotional event is dealt with in an overly intellectual manner, thus neutralizing its affective significance. The doctor who must concentrate upon the medical features of an illness and ignore its emotional meaning often may be adapting to his or her continual stress with the defense of intellectualization (see Lazarus, 1975).

The existence of these defenses has been best demonstrated by examining their controlling effects on stress reactions. Lazarus (1966) has conducted a systematic program of research in which denial and intellectualization actually are manipulated in an experimental setting. The general experimental procedure is to present subjects a film that gives rise to stress reactions. Lazarus has used two films that yield similar results: a subincision movie showing a stone-age ritual in which adolescent boys have their penises cut and a safety film depicting workshop accidents. While subjects view the movie, various measures of autonomic arousal, such as heart rate and galvanic skin response, are continuously recorded.

The sound track that precedes or accompanies the film presentation evokes the psychological defenses of denial or intellectualization. The denial theme indicates that the subincision operation is not harmful, that the participants in the safety film are actors, and so forth. The intellectualization sound track presents a detached view of the situations. The subincision film is narrated by an objective anthropologist merely viewing strange customs; during the safety film the viewer is asked to take an objective look at the dynamics of the situation. Lazarus then ascertains whether the manipulations of these defensive processes, or modes of thought, influence the manner in which the individual copes with the content of the film. More specifically, he examines whether the emotional reactivity to the film is lowered when ways to cognitively transform the meaning of the stimulus are introduced.

In one typical study, the subincission film was shown, and the denial orientation was introduced either prior to or during the film presentation. Skin conductance was used to measure emotional reactivity. The data clearly revealed that in both conditions the degree of reactivity to the stressor was reduced, relative to a control group not receiving a defensive sound track. Lazarus contends that these defensive interpretations lead the viewer to a ''cognitive reappraisal'' of the film. This cognitive reappraisal intervenes between the antecedent stimulus registration and the final reaction to the stimulus, altering the individual's emotional response. However, convincing demonstrations of the other alleged mechanisms of defense, including repression, remain to be conducted.

VI. THE INFORMATION VALUE OF BEHAVIOR

Complete acceptance of the interactionist position (see Eq. 2, Section I), includes the proposal that thoughts follow behavior. Cognitivists do accept the hypothesis that behavior has informational value and at times can influence subsequent thought processes. Indeed, this hypothesis must be accepted, for it is relatively well documented in experimental studies.

Acknowledgment of evidence demonstrating an action–thought sequence does not preclude the fact that thoughts also influence behavior.

A. Extrinsic Reward and Perceived Intrinsic Interest

An observation consistent with cognitive assumptions is that man often is acting to increase stimulation. For example, during the sensory deprivation procedure reported in Section I. A, subjects repeatedly listen to the same stock market report, if given the opportunity. Animals as well as humans seek stimulation and information. Rats learn to press a light to change their level of visual stimulation; monkeys repeatedly act to receive a puzzle to manipulate; and so on.

These "intrinsically regulated" motivations may be adversely affected by extrinsic incentives, such as food rewards. For example, monkeys engage in puzzle manipulations for endless periods of time—pressing a button for a puzzle, solving it, pressing for another puzzle, and so on. Now food is introduced into this experimental situation and is given to the monkey after each puzzle is solved. If the food is later withheld following the correct puzzle solutions, the monkey stops pushing the button for the puzzles (Harlow, 1953). One can interpret this behavior as indicating that the intrinsic attractiveness of the puzzles no longer is perceived as sufficient to instigate behavior.

Experimentation with humans in which the effects of extrinsic incentives on intrinsic interests are examined has yielded similar results. For example, in one investigation children were given special materials to complete an art project. The children worked either with or without the knowledge that they would receive an extrinsic reward (a special certificate). Several days later all the children were given an opportunity to work with this attractive material again. It was found that the children originally drawing for the expected reward spent less than half the time with the material than did the other children. The extrinsic reward thus undermined their intrinsic interest in the activity (see Nisbett & Valins, 1971). One wonders if the intrinsic rewards of school learning may be squashed in a similar manner.

Note that the experiments described above are amenable to interpretation within cognitive dissonance theory. For example, it can be contended that it is more dissonant to work on the puzzles for no reward than it is to engage in this activity given a large extrinsic reward. Therefore, the puzzles in the no extrinsic reward condition come to be perceived as more attractive than they "really" are. Again, therefore, there are disparate interpretations of an empirical observation, thus arousing controversy and hopefully new experimentation to resolve the uncertainty.

Experiments in which the behavior is "overjustified" have been conducted that perhaps permit a choice between dissonance and attributional
interpretations of the intrinsic–extrinsic reward studies (see Jones & Nisbett, 1971). In these investigations a reward is given for an act perceived as
very desirable (for example, arguing in favor of a position that one holds).
Note that in such situations dissonance is not aroused. However, it has been
reported that when one is externally rewarded for such behavior, the initial
positive attitude that promoted the argument declines. Evidently, one
perceives that the argument was made *because of* the external reward.
Again, however, much more research is needed to determine the relative
adequacies of the theories under question.

B. Overt Behavior and Attitudes

A related series of studies has shown that attitudes are inferred from overt
behavior (see Bem, 1972). In a representative investigation demonstrating
this point, subjects were given a series of escapable shocks. In one condition the experiment was presented as an investigation of reaction time. The
subjects were expected to escape as fast as possible. In a second experimental condition the subjects were told that they need not escape if they did
not find the shock uncomfortable. Thus, when the subjects escaped in this
situation (which they did), the inference would be made that the shocks
must have been painful. As predicted, the subjects rated the shocks in the
escape condition as more painful than the shocks in the reaction-time
condition, although the shocks in the two conditions were of the same
intensity. Escape behavior therefore is used to infer one's attitudes or
beliefs about the shocks.

VII. GENERAL SUMMARY

Let us take stock for a moment and review the wealth of material that has
been briefly introduced in the prior pages. The cognitive approach to
motivation assumes that the mind and the body interact and that thoughts
influence action. Empirical evidence has been presented demonstrating
that: (1) there is a need for cognitive activity; (2) cognitive imbalance
instigates motivation; (3) intentions have motivational significance. In addition to this instigating function, cognitions direct behavior through the
mediation of expectancies, or structures that represent "means–ends"
relationships. Investigations have shown that: (1) tasks with an intermediate subjective expectancy of success arouse the greatest amount of
affective motivation and provide the person with the most feedback about

his or her capabilities; (2) multiple expectancies or long-term goals also influence the motivation to perform at an immediate task; (3) expectancy change is determined in part by perceptions of task performance as skill or chance determined. In addition to their instigating and directional functions, cognitions may also inhibit behavior. Cognitive transformations of the distal stimulus can increase the ability to delay gratification and influence the appraisal of, and reactions to, threat. In sum, there is an abundance of evidence firmly establishing that cognitions affect behavior. Finally, it also is accepted that at times behavior itself is another source of information that is processed and used to infer personal values and beliefs.

These data have been generated by paradigms or experimental methodologies that are consistent with, and are appropriate to, the cognitive viewpoint. Cognitive activity is restricted; inconsistent cognitions are introduced; intentions are ascertained; the subjective probability of success is manipulated and/or measured; task perceptions are altered; instructions concerning how to think about a stimulus are induced; and so on. That is, the reference experiments assume that cognitions are not epiphenomena, but are processes that can be manipulated and measured, and their influence on action can be ascertained.

The new experimental methodologies and increasing empirical knowledge have fostered cognitive theories of behavior. Cognitive theories start with a conception of humans as information-processing, stimulus-seeking organisms. The theories pertain to inconsistent cognitions, achievement striving, emotionality, and a vast domain of other behaviors. All the conceptions include cognitive variables among the determinants of action, such as cognitive fit, the subjective expectancy of success, and cognitive appraisal. The data, experimental paradigms, and theoretical advances in the cognitive psychology of motivation reveal that thought can be related to action in a scientific, reliable, and interpretable manner. Yet it also is obvious that new methodologies need to be developed, and that new and more encompassing theories need to be fostered.

VIII.   ATTRIBUTION THEORY

One of the less appealing characteristics of an introductory or a review chapter is that a great deal of information is presented in a very cursory manner. This whets the reader's appetite, but leaves an unsatisfied desire for more detailed information and a fuller depth of understanding. Therefore, in the closing pages of this chapter one specific cognitive approach to motivation, known as attribution theory, is examined in greater detail. Of course, the reader should not think that the few pages devoted to this complex topic appease my conscience, and in reality the sins of omission are again being committed.

A. Perceptions of Causality

Attribution theory primarily is concerned with causal ascriptions, or the perceived reasons "why" an event has occurred (see Heider, 1958; Jones, Kanouse, Kelley, Nisbett, Valins, & Weiner, 1972). The functional significance of causal attributions is immediately evident. Assume, for example, that while riding the subway someone steps on your toes. Your interpretation of this event, or the perceived reasons for the action, greatly influences your subsequent thoughts and behaviors. If you believe that the event was accidently caused, you might smile and exchange comments about the transportation system. On the other hand, if the action is perceived as intentionally caused, you might move to a different place, respond with hostility, or even seek help from others.

The effects of causal ascription on aggressive retaliation have been well documented in experimental studies. For example, in one investigation subjects were given electric shocks by another "subject" (a confederate) supposedly to facilitate learning (Nickel, 1974). The confederate was perceived as free to determine the level of shock administered. In one experimental condition the subjects were lead to believe that the confederate intended to administer a small amount of shock, but because the apparatus was poorly labeled, a large amount of shock was given. In a second condition no "excuse" was given for the large shock that was administered. In both these conditions the actual amount of shock received was identical. The roles then were reversed, and the subjects were allowed to shock the confederate during the learning task. As anticipated, a much greater level of shock was given in the control or "intentional" condition than in the "misinformed" condition.

B. Determinants of Causal Judgments

Inasmuch as behavior is so significantly influenced by causal ascriptions, it is of obvious functional importance to reach veridical inferences. There are many cues that might be used to determine the causes of the toe-stepping incident. For example, how many other people are having their toes stepped upon? Does this individual repeatedly step upon your toes? Does he apologize? Is your toe stepped upon when the subway car is less crowded? Surely if only your toe is being stepped upon, and if this is repeatedly done by the same person, then it is likely to be perceived as an intentional, aggressive act.

Kelley (1967) has systematically related various sources of information to causal inferences. He states that if the behaviors observed are consistent with social norms (all toes are being stepped upon), and the action is inconsistent with the usual behavior of the actor (he does not step upon your toe in other situations), then the action is likely to be ascribed to the environment (for example, the crowded subway conditions). In contrast, if the action is inconsistent with social norms (only your toe is being stepped on), and the behavior is consistent for the person (he does this even when the subway car is less crowded), then the behavior will be ascribed to the actor. In a similar manner, if one succeeds at an exam that most others fail, and also has succeeded at other past exams, then the success is ascribed to the person (he is perceived as being smart). On the other hand, if one succeeds when others also succeed, and that person typically fails, then the recent success is perceived as resulting from the ease of the task, an environmental cause.

There are a number of other interesting determinants of causal ascriptions in addition to specific informational cues. For example, some evidence suggests that one tends to ascribe the behaviors of others to personality traits ("He hit me because he is aggressive"). Conversely, there is a bent to attribute one's own behavior to situational factors ("I hit him because I was provoked"). This differential bias in causal ascription has been labeled the "actor versus observer" hypothesis (see Jones & Nisbett, 1971), and remains to be convincingly proven. Jones and Nisbett argue that the actor has knowledge about the variability of his own behavior. In addition, from the perspective of the actor one's behavioral reactions are "ground," whereas the environment in which the action occurs is "figure." Thus, personal behavior tends to be ascribed to environmental sources. On the other hand, one often has little knowledge about the behavioral variability of others, and the behavior of others is "figure" whereas the environment in which the behavior is expressed is "ground." For these reasons Jones and Nisbett (1971) contend that the behavior of others is ascribed to personal dispositions.

In addition, ego-enhancing and ego-defensive influences on causal ascriptions have been demonstrated. For example, there is a general tendency to ascribe success more than failure to oneself. One interesting manifestation of this bias is that teachers may take credit when the performance of their students is increasing, but may blame the students when the students' behaviors are deteriorating (Beckman, 1970). The extent of such hedonic biases is badly in need of investigation.

C.   The Consequences of Causal Attributions

Two very general consequences of causal ascriptions have been identified: affective reactions and expectancy change. Recall that earlier in this chapter it was noted that affect (incentive value of the goal) and expectancy are the two main determinants of behavior, according to many cognitive theorists (see Section IV). Thus, attribution theory, which is a theory of social perception, has been linked with expectancy-value theory, which is a conception for motivated behavior (see Weiner, 1974).

The relationships between causal ascriptions and affect, and between causal ascriptions and expectancy, have been demonstrated most clearly in achievement-related contexts. For example, success ascribed to personal ability or effort produces greater pride in accomplishment than attributions to the ease of the task or to good luck. In general, outcomes attributed to the self magnify affective reactions in achievement-related contexts, whereas outcomes ascribed to the environment minimize affective reactions. The so-called "locus of control," or the ascriptions of outcomes to onself versus to the environment, also has been conceived as an individual difference variable and correlates with a variety of behaviors (see Rotter, 1966). For example, individuals with a tendency to perceive the world as personally or internally controlled appear better able to cope with failure and adapt better to their environment. There also is evidence documenting a maladaptive state called "learned helplessness." Learned helplessness connotes the belief that instrumental behaviors cannot be undertaken to alleviate one of his plight, when in reality the organism can indeed engage in behaviors that are instrumental to the gaining of rewards or the avoiding of punishments (Maier, Seligman, & Solomon, 1969).

Expectancy changes are related to a "stability" dimension of causality. For example, if failure is ascribed to low ability, or to the difficulty of the task, then there is a heightened expectancy of future failure when the task is again attempted. If the failure is attributed to bad luck, or to a lack of effort, however, then the expectancy of future failure is modulated. In sum, if causes are subject to change, such as luck or effort, then the outcome is perceived as changeable. But if the causes of an event are perceived as relatively stable over time, such as one's level of ability, then the outcomes are expected to remain unchanged. Many educators have experienced the situation in which a student with a poor record wants to be admitted to a graduate program. The student ascribes the past performance to a lack of effort because of some special circumstances (for example, personal difficulties) and anticipates doing well in the future. But we, as observers, ascribe the performance to some stable disposition, such as low ability or "laziness," and refuse admission because the poor performance is expected to continue.

Inasmuch as thoughts (causal ascriptions) are presumed to influence action, it logically follows that if the attribution process can be altered, then the subsequent or contingent actions also will change. In one study demonstrating such a cognitive control of action, Weiner and Sierad (1975) induced external causal ascriptions as well as repeated failures among individuals classified as high or low in achievement needs. Subjects in one experimental condition were given a placebo pill that allegedly caused failure at a task by interfering with eye–hand coordination. Hence, failure could be ascribed externally to the pill. It was found that individuals low in achievement needs performed better in the pill attribution condition than in a condition in which their causal attributions were not manipulated. Weiner and Sierad argue that individuals low in achievement needs typically as- cribe failure to their low ability. This produces negative affect (shame) that inhibits performance. In the pill attribution condition, however, the failures could be externalized, or "rationalized," thus minimizing negative affect and relatively enhancing performance. Weiner and Sierad also report that external ascriptions for failure hinder the performance of persons highly motivated to achieve success. Apparently, these individuals perform best when taking personal responsibility for their actions.

D. Summary

In sum, an attributional model of motivation takes the following form:

causal antecedents → causal inferences →
causal dimensions → causal consequences.

That is, there are various sources of information in the world that enable one to reach causal inferences. The causal antecedents in achievement settings include social norms, the nature of the task, past performance history, and so on. The perceived causes of success and failure, which are partially determined on the basis of these cues, primarily are ability, effort, task difficulty, and luck. These causes can be placed within causal taxonomies, or dimensions of causality, such as locus of control, causal stability, and the intentionality of the cause. The dimensions, in turn, influence the affec- tive reactions (pride and shame) to success and failure, as well as the sub- jective expectancy of success. Affect and expectancy in part determine subsequent action.

Causal ascriptions thus are the cornerstone of this cognitive model. But other higher-order processes, such as information search and combination, judgment, decision making, and so on, play important roles. It is quite clear that cognitive and motivational processes form a constellation that cannot be meaningfully separated. The cognition–motivation linkage forms the foundation for future research in the field of motivation.

ACKNOWLEDGMENTS

This contribution was written while the author was supported by Grant MH25687-01 from the National Institute of Mental Health.

REFERENCES

Aronson, E., & Mills, J. The effect of severity of initiation on liking for a group. *Journal of Abnormal and Social Psychology,* 1959, **59,** 177–181.

Atkinson, J. W. *An introduction to motivation.* Princeton, New Jersey: Van Nostrand, 1964.

Atkinson, J. W., & Birch, D. *The dynamics of action.* New York: Wiley, 1970.

Atkinson, J. W., & Raynor, J. O. (Eds.) *Motivation and achievement.* Washington, D.C.: Winston, 1974.

Beckman, L. J. Effects of students' performance on teachers' and observers' attributions of causality. *Journal of Educational Psychology,* 1970, **61,** 76–82.

Bem, D. J. Self-perception theory. In L. Berkowitz (Ed.), *Advances in experimental social psychology.* Vol. 6. New York: Academic Press, 1972. Pp. 1–62.

Brehm, J. W. Motivational effects of cognitive dissonance. In M. R. Jones (Ed.), *Nebraska symposium on motivation.* Vol. 10. Lincoln, Nebraska: University of Nebraska Press, 1962. Pp. 51–77.

Festinger, L. *A theory of cognitive dissonance.* Evanston, Illinois: Row, Peterson, 1957.

Festinger, L., & Carlsmith, J. M. Cognitive consequences of forced compliance. *Journal of Abnormal and Social Psychology,* 1959, **58,** 203–210.

Freud, S. (1915) Instincts and their vicissitudes. *Collected papers of Sigmund Freud.* Vol. 4. London: Hogarth Press, 1948. Pp. 60–83.

Harlow, H. F. Motivation as a factor in new responses. In *Nebraska symposium on motivation.* Lincoln, Nebraska: University of Nebraska Press. Vol. 1. 1953. Pp. 24–48.

Heider, F. *The psychology of interpersonal relations.* New York: Wiley, 1958.

Hull, C. L. *Principles of behavior.* New York: Appleton-Century-Crofts, 1943.

Jones, E. E., Kanouse, D. E., Kelley, H. H., Nisbett, R. E., Valins, S., & Weiner, B. (Eds.) *Attribution: Perceiving the causes of behavior.* Morristown, New Jersey: General Learning Press, 1972.

Jones, E. E., & Nisbett, R. E. *The actor and the observer: Divergent perceptions of the causes of behavior.* Morristown, New Jersey: General Learning Press, 1971.

Kelley, H. H. Attribution theory in social psychology. In D. Levine (Ed.), *Nebraska symposium on motivation.* Lincoln, Nebraska: University of Nebraska Press, 1967. Pp. 192–237.

Lazarus, R. S. *Psychological stress and the coping process.* New York: McGraw-Hill, 1966.

Lazarus, R. S. Cognitive and coping processes in emotion. In B. Weiner (Ed.), *Cognitive views of human motivation.* New York: Academic Press, 1975. Pp. 21–32.

Lewin, K. *The conceptual representation and the measurement of psychological forces.* Durham, North Carolina: Duke University Press, 1938.

Locke, E. A. Toward a theory of task motivation and incentives. *Organizational Behavior and Human Performance,* 1968, **3,** 157–189.

Maier, S. F., Seligman, M. E. P., & Solomon, R. L. Pavlovian fear conditioning and learned helplessness: Effects on escape and avoidance behavior of (a) the CS–UCS contingency and (b) the independence of voluntary responding. In B. A. Campbell & R. M. Church (Eds.), *Punishment and aversive behavior.* New York: Appleton-Century-Crofts, 1969.

Meyer, W. U., Folkes, V., & Weiner, B. The perceived informational value and affective consequences of choice behavior and intermediate difficulty task selection. *Journal of Research in Personality,* in press.

Mischel, W. Cognitive appraisals and transformations in self-control. In B. Weiner (Ed.), *Cognitive views of human motivation.* New York: Academic Press, 1975. Pp. 33–50.

Murray, H. A. Preparations for the scaffold of a comprehensive system. In S. Koch (Ed.), *Psychology: A study of a science.* Vol. 3. New York: McGraw-Hill, 1959. Pp. 7–54.

Nickel, T. The attribution of intention as a critical factor in the relation between pain-frustration and aggression. *Journal of Personality,* 1974, **42,** 482–492.

Nisbett, R. E., & Valins, S. *Perceiving the causes of one's own behavior*. Morristown, New Jersey: General Learning Press, 1971.

Rotter, J. B. Generalized expectancies for internal versus external control of reinforcement. *Psychological Monographs*, 1966, **80**(1, Whole No. 609), 1–28.

Schultz, D. P. *Sensory restriction*. New York: Academic Press, 1965.

Tolman, E. C. Principles of performance. *Psychological Review*, 1952, **62**, 315–326.

Trope, Y., & Brickman, P. Difficulty and diagnosticity as determinants of choice among tasks. *Journal of Personality and Social Psychology*, 1975, **31**, 918–925.

Weiner, B. *Theories of motivation: From mechanism to cognition*. Chicago, Illinois: Rand-McNally, 1972.

Weiner, B. (Ed.) *Achievement motivation and attribution theory*. Morristown, New Jersey: General Learning Press, 1974.

Weiner, B. (Ed.) *Cognitive views of human motivation*. New York: Academic Press, 1975.

Weiner, B., & Sierad, J. Misattribution for failure and the enhancement of achievement strivings. *Journal of Personality and Social Psychology*, 1975 **31**, 415–421.

Zajonc, R. B. Cognitive theories in social psychology. In G. Lindzey & E. Aronson (Eds.), *Handbook of social psychology*. Vol. 1. (2nd ed.) Reading, Massachusetts: Addison-Wesley, 1968. Pp. 320–411.

9

Learning Theory and Behavior Therapy

Alexander M. Buchwald

Indiana University, Bloomington

I. INTRODUCTION

This chapter deals with behavior therapy. The rationale for including a chapter on this topic is the close connection between behavior therapy and the psychology of learning. Most of the founders of behavior therapy believed that clinical problems were acquired and maintained according to the principles of classical and instrumental conditioning. With some exceptions (see Buchwald & Young, 1969), their treatment procedures were based on these principles. Today a number of prominent behavior therapists do not agree that behavior therapy is, or should be, merely applied learning theory (e.g. Davison, 1969; Franks, 1969; Lazarus, 1967). However, research in learning continues to influence behavior therapy, and psychologists and laymen alike tend to identify behavior therapy with the field of learning.

Section I of this chapter presents the background in which behavior therapy developed, and a brief survey of several types of treatment techniques. Since the literature is too large and too diffuse to be discussed in the available space the remainder of the chapter will deal with treatment based on operant conditioning. Section II contains a brief history and an account of the principles of operant conditioning, a description of treatment procedures and their effects, and a discussion of the role of behavioral consequences in operant treatment. The studies cited exemplify techniques and results, and are not exhaustive. Section III deals with the concept of reinforcement, the question of what is learned in operant treatment programs, and implications for the causes of disordered behavior.

A. Background

Treatment procedures based on methods and ideas used in the study of learning began to be widely used in 1960. Important early influences included the work of Wolpe, Yates, and Ayllon and Michael. Wolpe (1958) devised a treatment procedure that he called "psychotherapy by reciprocal inhibition." His basic idea was that fear or other disabling behavior would be inhibited if a person engaged in an antagonistic response while imagining himself in situations that elicited the undesirable behavior. Yates (1958) treated a woman who suffered from tics (involuntary, repetitive movements) by having her engage in long periods of voluntary practice of the movements. Ayllon and Michael (1959) used techniques based on operant conditioning and extinction to treat various types of disturbed behavior in mental hospital patients. Their work followed Lindsley's (1956) studies of operant conditioning in chronic schizophrenic patients. Articles and case reports by early behavior therapists were presented in three edited books (Eysenck, 1960; Ullmann & Krasner, 1965a; Wolpe, Salter & Reyna, 1964) that helped popularize behavior therapy among psychologists.

Procedures derived from the psychology of learning had been used to treat disordered behavior long before. For example, Mary Cover Jones (1924) used a counterconditioning technique to overcome a child's fear of a rabbit, and Mowrer and Mowrer (1938) had developed a treatment for bed wetting based on classical conditioning. These early efforts had little effect upon clinical practice, but by 1960 the climate of opinion had changed so that many clinical workers were prepared to accept behavior therapy.

A number of factors had contributed to this change in attitude. Many practitioners had become disenchanted with the results of psychoanalysis, and of psychotherapy more generally. The idea that personal problems were signs of mental illness was under heavy attack. The fact that psychologists were now employed in clinical settings in large numbers encouraged the search for forms of treatment that were psychological and not medical. The importance of these currents is undeniable, yet it seems unlikely that behavior therapy would have won ready acceptance without the work of psychologists who had shown that clinical phenomena and concepts could be discussed in terms of the psychology of learning.

Between 1935 and 1945 a number of psychologists had made concerted efforts to discuss phenomena such as amnesia, anxiety, conflict, frustration, and neurosis, using the concepts and theories of learning. Important contributors included John Dollard, E. R. Guthrie, N. E. Miller, O. H. Mowrer, and R. R. Sears. One of the landmarks of this era, was Mowrer's (1939) analysis of anxiety in terms of stimulus, response, and reinforcement, which led to extensive research on the acquisition of fear (or anxiety) and its effects on behavior. In the years immediately after World War II, several writers published analyses of psychotherapy in terms of learning principles. The most ambitious of these efforts was the book, *Personality and Psychotherapy* by Dollard and Miller (1950), which deals with the nature and acquisition of neurosis, and the process of psychoanalytic psychotherapy. Dollard and Miller attempted to integrate Freud's ideas with those of Hull and his associates. They analyzed concepts such as unconscious impulses, repression, and the roles of conflict, anxiety, and defenses in symptom formation in terms of cue, response, drive, reinforcement, and related ideas. Another influential book was Skinner's *Science and Human Behavior* (1953), which discussed clinical problems, although it did not emphasize them. Skinner attempted to show that all behavioral phenomena could be accounted for in terms of the principles of conditioning.

The writings discussed above did not contribute to behavior therapy directly. None of them proposed innovations in treatment. However, they set the stage for behavior therapy by proposing (*a*) that psychological disorders are learned, and (*b*) that psychotherapy operates according to principles of learning.

B. A Brief Survey of Behavior Therapy

Over the years behavior therapists have developed many different procedures to deal with various kinds of problems. These procedures have several sources. Some are based on analogies with procedures used in research on animals, others come from studies of learning by human subjects, still others are based on observations made in the course of attempts to treat people with psychological problems. A brief account of some of these treatment procedures follows.

One set of procedures has been inspired by studies of operant conditioning and by the ideas of B. F. Skinner. The operant therapist selects some fairly specific overt behavior or behaviors, called *target behaviors,* and attempts to have the client make them more frequently if they are considered desirable, or make them less frequently if they are considered undesirable. The frequency of target behaviors is manipulated by making various environmental occurrences (rewards and punishments in popular parlance) contingent upon the client's behavior.

Several different treatment procedures are used to help people overcome specific fears, or general anxiety. The most widely used of these is *systematic desensitization,* which is basically Wolpe's treatment by reciprocal inhibition. Systematic desensitization consists of three parts, training in relaxation, construction of one or more anxiety hierarchies, and desensitization, per se. During the early sessions the client is taught how to relax his muscles, and the client and therapist jointly construct one or more anxiety hierarchies. Each hierarchy consists of a series of related scenes or situations graded according to the degree to which they evoke anxiety. For example, in the case of a person with a fear of heights the series might begin with a scene in which the person stands on level ground and progresses through scenes in which he stands higher and higher on a ladder until finally he is several stories above the ground. In desensitization proper, the client is instructed to relax and asked to visualize the scene that provokes the least anxiety. If he can do this several times without anxiety he is asked to visualize the next scene, and so on, until he can visualize the most frightening scene without anxiety. (In a variant form of treatment, *in vivo desensitization,* the client acts out the scenes in the hierarchy under instructions to relax.)

A basic principle of systematic desensitization is that the client must remain relaxed (nonanxious) while he visualizes himself in the various situations (Paul, 1969). If the client feels anxious while visualizing a scene, he signals the therapist and is told to visualize a scene earlier in the hierarchy. In contrast, in *implosion* or *flooding* the client is immediately asked to visualize himself in extremely frightening situations. The idea is that the experience of intense anxiety without harmful consequences will extinguish the ability of the situation to elicit anxiety. Marks (1972) indicates that therapists often use procedures that are intermediate between those of systematic desensitization and flooding.

Electric shock, chemically induced nausea, the visualization of disgusting scenes, and other forms of aversive stimulation have been used to treat appetitive conditions, such as alcoholism, deviant sexual behavior, and smoking. The desired object (for example, a cigarette) may be shown to the subject and aversive stimulation presented. Alternatively, the subject may be told to engage in the behavior, in actuality or in fantasy, and aversive stimulation applied when he does so. In other procedures, aversive stimulation (or relief from such stimulation) may depend upon looking (or not looking) at a picture of the desired object. For example in the treatment of male homosexuality the client may be shocked when he looks at slides of nude males, or he may be able to escape from shock, or to avoid it, by turning off the slides (Barlow, 1972).

Observation of the behavior of another person, a model, is another technique used in behavior therapy. Albert Bandura and his students have been pioneers in this work. Observation of models has been used to teach various skills, to increase the frequency of desirable behaviors, and to eliminate fears. For example, films showing a model engaged in play with a dog were used to help children overcome fear of dogs (Bandura, Grusec, & Menlove, 1967).

Self-instructional training is a procedure developed by Donald Meichenbaum (1974), who believes that problems such as fears and anxieties involve negative self-statements (thoughts). For example, if a person who is anxious about public speaking gives a speech and notices two members of the audience conversing, he thinks, "I'm losing their attention." This increases the speaker's anxiety. Meichenbaum also believes that other problems, for example the behavior of hyperactive, impulsive children, arise from a failure to use "cognitive and behavioral strategies," that is, from a failure to generate appropriate self-statements. He uses various techniques to train clients to make positive self-statements, or to verbalize appropriate behavioral instructions.

The preceding paragraphs do not give a complete description of behavior therapy. Space does not permit description of all the techniques that have been used. The interested reader can consult any of a number of recent books (e.g., Agras, 1972; or Rimm & Masters, 1974) for accounts of other procedures.

Even a description of all the specific procedures that have been developed would not give a complete picture of behavior therapy because different behavior therapy procedures are often combined within a single treatment program. For example, Wheeler and Sulzer (1970) used a technique that combined the use of operant conditioning with observation of a model to train a retarded child to use complete sentences to describe pictures. Behavior therapy procedures may also be used in conjunction with other procedures. For example, Birky, Chambliss, and Wasden (1971) rewarded patients in a mental hospital for self-care and supplemented this with classes in such things as dieting and grooming. With noninstitutionalized cases the therapist often spends considerable time in explorations of the client's concerns, either prior to setting up a treatment program, or as part of a treatment program. Such discussions resemble conventional psychotherapy. In addition, clients are often given theoretical accounts as to how their troubles arose and how the treatment will help. Naturally, these accounts contain strong suggestions that the treatment will work. Such nonspecific placebo factors are very likely to contribute to the effects of treatment.

In the remainder of the chapter, I will concentrate on work in which overt behavior by a subject, client, or patient is followed by observable environmental consequences produced by a therapist, an experimenter, or an agent of the therapist or experimenter. (For simplicity, the terms *subject* and *experimenter* or *agent* will be used in the subsequent discussion.)

II. TREATMENT BASED ON OPERANT CONDITIONING

A. History and Principles

The experimental study of learning has three separate traditions. These originated in Ebbinghaus's studies of memory, Pavlov's studies of "classical" conditioning, and in Thorndike's work on trial-and-error learning or instrumental learning. Operant conditioning arose within this last tradition.

Thorndike studied the way in which animals learned to solve problems. For example, a hungry cat was placed in a cage with a bit of food outside. To get the food the cat had to press a knob which opened the door of the cage. On the first trial the cat engaged in various activities until it finally pressed the knob. On subsequent trials behavior that did not open the door tended to disappear until finally the subjects pressed the button immediately after they were placed in the cage (Thorndike, 1898). On the basis of his work Thorndike formulated the *law of effect* (Thorndike, 1911): satisfying consequences (rewards or escape from punishment) strengthen connections between stimuli and responses, annoying consequences (punishment) weaken connections. Later, Thorndike (1931) dropped the second part of the law.

Among the many psychologists who have studied instrumental learning in animals the major figure has been B. F. Skinner. Skinner has emphasized certain ways of thinking about phenomena; he believes that psychologists should eschew concepts that are not strictly defined by specific observations or operations. Instead he advocates the "functional analysis of behavior," the study of how the frequency of behavior changes as a function of events in the external environment (Skinner, 1953). He introduced methods that permit the investigator to study changes in the frequency of responses in individual subjects produced by experimental manipulations. (For a more detailed but still concise account of Skinner's work, see Dinsmoor, 1974).

On the substantive side, Skinner distinguished two kinds of behavior, *respondents* and *operants*. Respondents are basically involuntary reflex activities which are elicited by stimuli that precede them. Operants are behaviors that are emitted by the subject, rather than being elicited by stimuli, and are controlled by the environmental stimuli that follow them. (See Hearst, Chapter 5, Volume 2 for a discussion of this distinction.) Skinner believes that the stimuli that follow behavior are of three types, positive reinforcers, negative reinforcers, and neutral stimuli. The presentation of a positive reinforcer (for example, delivery of food to a hungry pigeon) or the removal of a negative reinforcer (for example, turning off an electric shock) will increase the frequency of immediately preceding behavior. Neither the presentation nor the removal of a neutral stimulus will reinforce behavior. Whether a particular consequence is, or is not, a reinforcer for a given subject under particular conditions can only be determined by observation of the effects of that consequence on behavior.

Behavior can also be followed by the removal of a positive reinforcer or the presentation of a negative one. Skinner calls these operations *punishment*. He argues that punishment is an undesirable way of controlling behavior because its use often leads to undesirable side effects, anxiety, shame, or rage. Further, punishment may temporarily suppress the punished behavior but does not weaken it in a way that corresponds to the way in which reinforcement strengthens it. Instead, an operant that has been reinforced will be weakened (show a decrease in frequency in the long run) if reinforcement no longer follows instances of that behavior. The procedures and the effect are called *extinction*. Thus according to the principle of reinforcement, behavior that is reinforced will show an increase in frequency, and unless the behavior continues to be reinforced its frequency will decline, that is, reinforcement is needed to maintain the frequency of a given behavior. This principle is Skinner's restatement of the law of effect. It should be noted that the reinforcement that maintains an operant need not be the same type of reinforcement that initially strengthened it.

Thorndike and his students performed many experiments designed to demonstrate that the law of effect applied to humans as well as animals (Thorndike, 1931). Skinner's own early work and that of most of his early followers was confined to animals. Greenspoon (1955) reported one of the first attempts to apply Skinner's ideas and technology to human subjects. He had college students utter words and found certain kinds of words (for example, plural nouns) increased in frequency when he said "good" or "mm-hmm" after them. Shortly afterwards, Taffel (1955) had subjects make up sentences using one of several pronouns and found that the use of particular pronouns increased if the experimenter said "good" when those pronouns were used. Both investigators reported that the increases occurred even if the subjects were not aware of the relationship between their behavior and the experimenter's. Later work casts considerable doubt on these assertions (Spielberger, 1962). However, the Greenspoon and Taffel results led to a spate of studies of "verbal conditioning" in college students and psychiatric patients. Other investigators reported operant conditioning and extinction of nonverbal responses in children and infants (e.g., Azrin & Lindsley, 1956; Brackbill, 1958), and in chronic psychotic patients (Lindsley, 1956). The first application of operant conditioning to a severely retarded subject had been carried out earlier by Fuller (1949) but had relatively little impact at the time.

The final step in the application of operant procedures to clinical problems came with the demonstration that the procedures could alleviate problems such as stuttering (Flanagan, Goldiamond, & Azrin, 1958), tantrums (Williams, 1959), and various undesirable behaviors displayed by patients in mental hospitals (Ayllon & Michael, 1959).

B. Applications

Operant treatment programs have had wide and varied usage. Treatment has been conducted in mental hospitals and other residential institutions, in clinics and practitioners offices, in classrooms, and in the home. The subjects have been of all ages. Some of them have been basically normal except for a single restricted problem, for example, stuttering. Others have belonged to special populations—the mentally retarded, delinquent youths, severely neurotic or psychotic adults (including chronic patients in mental hospitals), and autistic children. (Autistic children have a number of problems that often include absence of language, a lack of responsiveness to others, and ritualistic behavior.) The range of target behaviors is exemplified by the following. Programs have been designed to train subjects to use language appropriately, to engage in normal social behavior, or to improve academic performance. Others have been designed to increase the frequency of compliance with rules, or of eating, or of attention to schoolwork. Still other programs have been used to decrease the frequency of thumb sucking, of disruptive behavior in the classroom, of avoidance of feared objects, of self-mutilation, or of delusional speech.

C. Evaluation of Treatment Programs

1. Issues

Are operant treatment programs effective? This is a deceptively simple question. How is effectiveness to be judged? We cannot simply ask, "do the programs produce changes in behavior?" because this question is too broad. It must be broken down into a series of narrower questions:

1. Do the treatment programs change the frequencies of target behaviors in the desired directions?
2. Are these changes maintained after treatment ends?
3. Are the changes manifest beyond the treatment setting?
4. Do the programs change the subjects' behavior more generally?

Subsequent discussion will be organized around these questions.

The practical importance of the answers to the various questions depends upon the nature of the problem, the treatment program, and the goals of treatment. Suppose a teacher begins to ignore disruptive behavior and praise orderly behavior in order to decrease the amount of disruptive behavior in the classroom. The treatment should be judged effective if it reduces disruption substantially since the goals of treatment are limited and it is feasible to continue the treatment throughout the school year. Contrast this with a treatment program in which candy and toys are used as reinforcers in special speech therapy sessions in order to eliminate stuttering. This program cannot be considered effective unless it improves speech outside of the therapy sessions and unless the gains are maintained after the treatment ends. Finally consider a treatment program established in a mental hospital. In such programs, the subjects are typically reinforced if they groom themselves appropriately, make their own beds, and work at various jobs in the hospital. An increase in the frequencies of these behaviors is enough to indicate the effectiveness of the program, if that is its aim, but not if the goal of treatment is to enable the subjects to live ordinary lives outside of the hospital.

2. Treatment Paradigms

Woods (1974) proposed a taxonomy of instrumental conditioning and punishment procedures and suggested names for them. A simplified version of this system based on the experimenter's actions will be used to classify treatment programs.

As a consequence of the subject's behavior, the experimenter may present a stimulus or remove a stimulus. The stimulus may be positive (expected to function as a positive reinforcer) or negative (expected to function as a negative reinforcer). If the stimulus is positive, its presentation defines *reward conditioning* and its removal *penalty conditioning*. If the stimulus is negative, its presentation defines *punishment conditioning* and its removal *relief conditioning*. To illustrate, a child might be given points that can be exchanged for candy for obeying instructions (reward conditioning) or might lose points for failing to do so (penalty conditioning). Or, a child might be spanked for failure to put his or her toys away (punishment conditioning) or released from her or his room when they have been put away (relief conditioning). Each of the four types of events might be contingent upn the subject making a specified response, or not making a specified response. A child might be rewarded or relieved for not whining, or punished or penalized for whining.

Several paradigms may be used simultaneously. A combination of paradigms may be used to treat the same target behavior, as when a child is rewarded for not sucking his thumb and penalized for thumbsucking. Different paradigms may also be used to treat different target behaviors simultaneously.

The extinction paradigm has also been used clinically in the attempt to eliminate undesirable behavior. Its use is based on the assumption that the behavior would not be maintained unless there were environmental consequences that reinforced it. In the laboratory, an experimenter introduces extinction by withholding a reinforcer that has been used in conditioning. In the clinic, the experimenter has not deliberately reinforced the target behavior and therefore must try to identify the stimulus events that presumably reinforce the behavior in order to withhold reinforcement. The behavior is usually assumed to be maintained by the actions of other people, for example, by expressions of solicitude, of interest, or of affection, or by any display of attention. ("Attention" is typically defined as any verbal or physical behavior directed toward the subject.) To extinguish behavior, the clinical experimenter tries to eliminate other people's reactions to it. Often extinction is combined with reward conditioning, in which alternatives to the undesirable behavior are followed by expressions of approbation, or praise, or by a display of attention to the subject. This procedure is called *differential attention.*

3. Effects on Target Behavior

a. Conditioning procedures. Operant treatment programs that embody the various conditioning paradigms, alone or in combination, have been used to treat subjects individually and in groups. Most of the large number of published accounts report increases in desirable target behaviors or decreases in undesirable ones. Beneficial results have been reported for various subject populations and for various target behaviors. As is to be expected, the programs are not uniformly effective. This can be seen in the results of group programs, in which a small proportion of the subjects are often found not to be affected by the treatment procedures (Kazdin & Bootzin, 1972).

The most frequently used paradigm is reward conditioning. Experimenters have used commodities such as cigarettes (Kale, Kaye, Whelan, & Hopkins, 1968), social events such as smiles, hugs and pats (Kazdin & Klock, 1973), and contingent privileges such as access to television (Agras, Barlow, Chapin, Abel, & Leitenberg, 1974) to increase target behaviors. Currently, the most widely used positive reinforcer is the *token,* sometimes in the form of pieces of plastic or paper, sometimes in the form of recorded points. When tokens are used they can be exchanged for various commodities or privileges (*backup reinforcers*). Tokens have been used successfully in both individual and group programs. (See Kazdin & Bootzin, 1972; O'Leary & Drabman, 1971; for reviews.)

The use of tokens has several advantages. They are easy to dispense and their delivery is less likely to interrupt ongoing behavior than the delivery of many backup reinforcers. Tokens also make it easier to treat subjects in a group, since with a variety of backup reinforcers there is more likely to be some commodity or privilege that will serve as a reinforcer for every subject.

Programs that use tokens vary widely in scope. The term *token reward system* will be used to refer to all programs that use tokens. The term *token economy* will be reserved for broad-scale programs, usually used in residential institutions, in which the subjects can earn tokens by many different behaviors and must use tokens to obtain many commodities and privileges. The backup reinforcers often include meals, desirable sleeping quarters, access to recreational activities, and permission to leave the ward.

Penalty conditioning (response cost) is most often used in connection with a token reward system. The combination usually leads to a decrease in undesirable behavior, but the independent contribution of penalty conditioning is seldom assessed. Boren and Colman (1970) introduced penalty conditioning into an ongoing token reward system and found that both the target behavior and general rebelliousness increased. In contrast, Kaufman and O'Leary (1972) compared loss of tokens for undesirable classroom behavior and token rewards for desirable behavior in separate groups of subjects and found the two procedures controlled undesirable behavior equally effectively. Whether the difference was due to the late introduction of penalties in the earlier study or to differences in the subject populations cannot be determined.

Experimenters sometimes make use of punishment conditioning. Electric shock and slaps have been used to eliminate behavior such as self-mutilation by severely retarded and autistic subjects (Lovaas & Simmons, 1969). Verbal expressions of disapproval are also occasionally used (Moore & Bailey, 1973).

The event most often used in punishment conditioning is isolation. When the subject engages in the undesirable behavior, he or she is removed from the environment and is placed alone in a barren environment, often a small room. Isolation has been used to reduce the frequency of various kinds of behavior, including tantrums, disruptive behavior in the classroom, drinking by alcoholics (Bigelow, Liebson, & Griffiths, 1974), and episodes of screaming and swearing presumed to be induced by delusions in a schizophrenic woman (Cayner & Kiland, 1974).

The use of isolation in a punishment paradigm is one of several clinical procedures usually called *time-out from positive reinforcement,* or *time-out,* in brief. The concept is in need of clarification. In research on animals, time-out periods are used during or after reward conditioning. As a consequence of the subject's behavior, the experimenter either makes it impossible for the subject to make the response being reinforced, or fails to reinforce responses when they occur. Clinically, a similar procedure is sometimes used during reward conditioning, but isolation periods are often used without reward conditioning. Isolation is considered analogous to time-out from positive reinforcement because it involves removal of "all social reinforcers for a period of time" (Wolf, Risley, & Mees, 1964, p. 306).

Removal from a social setting to a bare room is a complex event. It is not clear why it is so effective. Sherman and Baer (1969) noted four factors that might contribute to its effectiveness: (a) a loss of opportunity to obtain positive reinforcement; (b) relief conditioning (the subject is usually not released until the undesirable behavior ends); (c) extinction of the undesirable behavior that led to isolation, if the behavior was maintained by social reinforcement; (d) the aversive nature of isolation, per se. Other factors might also contribute. Isolation signals that the experimenter disapproves of the undesirable behavior and perhaps more importantly, the procedure involves the subject being publicly shamed. An experiment designed to determine which of these components contributes to the effectiveness of the procedure should not be difficult.

Relief conditioning (escape training) is usually used in combination with isolation (see above). Occasionally it is used in other contexts; for example, Lovaas, Schaeffer, and Simmons (1965) used escape from electric shock to train autistic children to come to the experimenter on command.

b. *Extinction procedures.* Two different procedures have been used clinically. Sometimes the subject is ignored when he engages in the target behavior. For example, Ayllon and Michael (1959) reported a decrease in the frequency with which a mental hospital patient entered the nurses' office when the nurses ignored her when she entered. Prior to this, they had argued with her and even pushed her out of the door because her frequent visits created a nuisance. Sometimes the subject is simply left in a room alone for an extended period of time. Lovaas and Simmons (1969) used this procedure successfully to treat self-injurious behavior in two severely retarded children. Corte, Wolf, and Locke (1971) used the same procedure with two subjects and found no decrease in self-injurious behavior. They attributed this failure to the fact that they used the procedure for a shorter period of time.

The differential attention procedure has been used more often, especially with children. Both successful and unsuccessful results have been reported. For example, Wahler (1969a) trained parents to attend to their child when he studied (during a homework period) and to ignore him when he did not and found a large increase in studying. However, the same procedure had had no effect on "oppositional behavior" (failure to comply with parents' orders) in the cases of five children with marked oppositional behavior (Wahler, 1969b). The use of differential attention by the mothers led to an increase in undesirable behavior in four of six cases studied by Herbert, Pinkston, Hayden, Sajwaj, Pinkston, Cordua, and Jackson

(1973). Additional experimental manipulations indicated that maternal attention did not function as a negative reinforcer.

Several studies have directly compared the effectiveness of extinction and punishment conditioning as ways of eliminating target behaviors. Electric shock administered contingently upon self-injurious behavior was found to be faster and more effective than extinction (Corte *et al.*, 1971; Lovaas & Simmons, 1969). Similarly, Wahler (1969b) found that a combination of reward conditioning (expressions of approbation) and isolation was effective in eliminating oppositional behavior. The undesirable side effects of punishment mentioned by Skinner have not been found in clinical work (see also Risley, 1968). For these reasons, punishment conditioning now appears to be used more often than extinction as a treatment for undesirable behavior.

c. *Research methodology.* Changes in the frequency of target behavior from a baseline (pretreatment) period to a posttreatment period are not necessarily due to the treatment program, per se. Changes may reflect the occurrence of events outside of treatment, spontaneous (unexplained) fluctuations, or nonspecific placebo factors such as the subject's knowledge that he is in treatment and the attention paid to the subject in general and to his target behavior in particular. One way to evaluate treatment programs is to use separate groups of subjects to control for these extraneous sources of change. For various reasons (see Kazdin, 1973a; Leitenberg, 1973) such designs are seldom used to evaluate operant treatment programs.

Formal evaluations of operant treatment programs tend to use one of three designs. In the *multiple-baseline* design, baseline observations are made on (*a*) the same behavior in different subjects, or (*b*) different behaviors of the same subject, or (*c*) the behavior of a subject in different settings. Treatment is introduced at different points in time for the several subjects, behaviors, or settings. This allows those that have not been treated as yet to serve as control conditions. Thus the design is only appropriate when treatment of one subject or behavior, or in one setting, will not affect the others (Kazdin, 1973a). Both the withdrawal and reversal designs begin with a baseline period followed by a period of treatment. In the *withdrawal design* treatment is alternately withdrawn and reintroduced in subsequent periods. The *reversal design* is similar except that the treatment operations are applied to some behavior that is incompatible with the target behavior during alternate periods, rather than being withdrawn. For example, if the subject is rewarded for not sucking his thumb during treatment periods, he will be rewarded for thumb sucking during reversal periods. The effectiveness of treatment is demonstrated with these designs if the target behavior changes in the desired way during treatment periods, and these changes tend to vanish during withdrawal or reversal periods.

Therefore, these designs are only appropriate when the effects of treatment are transient or easily reversed (Kazdin, 1973a).

In many studies in which withdrawal or reversal designs have been used changes that occur during treatment periods disappear during withdrawal or reversal. Occasionally they do not, and some authors have argued that in such cases the changed behavior is maintained by other consequences (Surratt, Ulrich, & Hawkins, 1969; Comments by Reviewer C, 1973). Such statements are mere affirmations of faith in the absence of experimental evidence. As an example of appropriate evidence, Agras *et al.* (1974) found that subjects with anorexia nervosa (emaciation due to failure to eat) increased their food intake during both reward conditioning and withdrawal periods. To test the hypothesis that this resulted from the subjects' desire to gain weight in order to leave the hospital, a new subject was told on admission that she must remain for a fixed number of days. She showed an increase in food consumption during reward conditioning and a decrease when reinforcement was withdrawn.

When multiple-baseline, withdrawal, or reversal designs are used to evaluate treatment programs, certain precautions are needed. To avoid taking advantage of behavioral changes due to extratreatment events or to spontaneous fluctuation, rules that specify when treatment is to be introduced, withdrawn, or reversed should be set before the experiment begins. It is more difficult to rule out nonspecific placebo effects, particularly when subjects are told what changes are desired and what the consequences of their actions will be. Experimenters should guard against the possibility that behavior will change when treatment is introduced, withdrawn, or reversed, because the instructions demand change. In multiple-baseline designs all of the desired changes should be suggested when treatment is first introduced. In withdrawal and reversal designs instructions should not suggest relapse during withdrawal or reversal periods. These precautions are not always taken. For example, Ayllon and Azrin (1965) used a withdrawal design to demonstrate that reward conditioning was responsible for mental hospital patients working on jobs in the hospital. At the start of the withdrawal period the subjects were told they would have a paid vacation. Kazdin and Bootzin (1972) pointed out that this is not mere withdrawal of rewards since it suggests to the subjects that they should not work. A better procedure was used by Kaufman and O'Leary (1972), who followed a period of treatment designed to decrease disruptive behavior in the classroom with a withdrawal period. At the start of withdrawal the subjects were told that they were expected to continue to be well behaved.

The behaviors that are treated are usually complex actions that cannot be identified or recorded by automatic equipment. This makes it necessary to have observers to carry out these tasks, and the use of observers introduces several methodological problems. Observation, itself, may lead to changes in behavior. In some cases subjects are asked to record their own behavior, a procedure that often changes the frequency of target behavior in the absence of any treatment (e.g., Maletzky, 1974). Even when other persons serve as observers, subjects sometimes behave differently in the presence of observers than they do under surreptitious observations (e.g., Surratt *et al.*, 1969).

Another problem arises from the fact that the recorded data depend upon the judgments of a particular observer as well as on the subjects' behavior. In order to minimize the contribution of the observers, many experimenters describe the behavior of interest in detail and train their observers carefully. Most experimenters also study the reliability of observers, comparing reports by several observers. High levels of agreement are usually reported, but many common practices can result in inaccurate estimates of reliability. For example, the amount of agreement is greater when observers know that agreement is to be studied than it is when they do not know, and agreement is also increased when the observers are familiar with each others' practices (Romanczyk, Kent, Diament, & O'Leary, 1973). In addition, reliability data are seldom corrected for agreement that could occur by chance. (For a more extensive discussion of these problems see Lipinski & Nelson, 1974.) The most important problem that results from the use of observers is the possibility of biased observation. Whenever observers must be used in the evaluation of treatment, the observers should be blind, that is, not aware of the conditions that are applied to particular subjects at a given point in time. Failure to use blind observers raises the possibility that the observers' reports will be affected by the results that they expect. There is evidence to indicate that experiments on operant treatments are susceptible to this kind of bias (Lipinski & Nelson, 1974). To date, most studies have not used blind observers, and this poses a major threat to conclusions about the effects of treatment.

4. Maintenance of Treatment Changes

Operant treatment programs often change the frequency of target behaviors but what happens when the treatment ends? Are the changes maintained or does behavior revert to pretreatment levels?

The available evidence from the few long-term followup studies that have been conducted and the experience of practitioners indicate that treatment gains often disappear once programs are discontinued (Baer, Wolf, & Risley, 1968; Kazdin & Bootzin, 1972; O'Leary & Drabman, 1971). The many instances in which a return to baseline conditions in a withdrawal design lead to a rapid loss in the effects of treatment also point to the transient nature of treatment effects. One of the few exceptions is self-care activities, for example, grooming, on the part of chronic mental hospital patients. Such behavior is often increased by the use of a token economy and tends to be maintained when token reinforcement is withdrawn (Gripp & Magaro, 1974).

The fact that changes in behavior often vanish when treatment ends is consistent with the principle of reinforcement. If the effective component of treatment programs is operant conditioning, extinction should occur after conditioning ends unless the changed behavior is maintained by other consequences. Nevertheless, the transitory nature of treatment effects is unsatisfactory clinically, and behavior therapists have been concerned with procedures that can be used to maintain the effects of treatment.

Three general lines of attack on the problem have been suggested (e.g., Kazdin & Bootzin, 1972). One proposal is to use intermittent reinforcement during conditioning since, in the laboratory, intermittent reinforcement delays extinction. The effects of various schedules of reinforcement have not been systematically studied in clinical work. However, intermittent reinforcement does not prevent the occurrence of extinction in the laboratory and there is no reason to believe that it would do so in clinical work. A second line of attack is to "reprogram the natural environment," that is, to train parents, teachers, and peers to use operant conditioning principles to control the subject's behavior. A considerable body of research shows that such agents can produce changes in the subject's target behavior. However, as O'Dell (1974) notes, this merely shifts the problem to one of producing permanent changes in the agent's behavior. A third approach consists of training subjects to control their own behavior. Experimenters have trained subjects to evaluate their own behavior and to reward themselves. Glynn, Thomas, and Shee (1973) found that this procedure maintained an increase in time spent in studying over a period of 45 days in a class of normal school children. However, Santogrossi, O'Leary, Romanczyk, and Kaufman (1973) found that the procedure rapidly became ineffective in a class consisting of adolescent patients in a psychiatric hospital. They suggested that the procedure might not be effective with subjects with serious problems.

It would be unduly pessimistic to conclude that a solution to the problem of maintaining behavioral change will not eventually be found. However, at present no truly effective procedure is known.

5. Transfer of Treatment Effects

a. *Stimulus generalization.*   Pavlov found that a response that had been conditioned to a particular stimulus could then be elicited by similar stimuli. He called the phenomenon *generalization*. Generalization has been widely studied, usually using stimuli that vary along a single quantitative dimension.

In clinical work more complex generalization is usually desired. A subject is typically treated by a single experimenter in a specific setting under particular conditions, yet the problem for which treatment is sought is usually manifest under a range of conditions. With a few exceptions, the effects of treatment are limited to the treatment setting. Token reward systems that are used during morning classes do not affect behavior in afternoon classes (O'Leary & Drabman, 1971). Extinction and punishment conditioning eliminated self-mutilation by severely retarded subjects only in the rooms in which treatment took place (Lovaas & Simmons, 1969). Schizophrenics, reinforced for nondelusional answers to questions, continued to speak delusionally on the ward and in psychiatric interviews (Wincze, Leitenberg, & Agras, 1972). Autistic children trained in classroom skills when alone with the experimenter failed to show these skills in small classes (Koegel & Rincover, 1974).

The failure of changes produced by operant treatment programs to generalize to other settings has been recognized for a long time and clinical workers have been advised to devise treatment programs that will overcome the problem (Baer *et al.*, 1968). One way to overcome the need for generalization is to conduct the treatment in the setting where the target behavior poses a problem, but this is not always feasible.

Suggestions as to how to produce generalization across settings resemble those for maintaining changes in behavior. One additional suggestion is that generalization is more likely to occur if the subject is treated in various settings and under various conditions. To date this has been tested only in connection with generalization over various experimenters. With severely retarded or chronic schizophrenic subjects the effects of either reward conditioning or punishment conditioning, administered by a single experimenter, do not generalize to other experimenters. After several different experimenters have administered the treatment to a subject, the behavioral changes are seen with additional experimenters (Corte *et al.*, 1971; Kale *et al.*, 1968).

b. *Response generalization.* When conditioning procedures applied to one type of behavior also produce changes in other related behaviors, the phenomenon may be called *response generalization*. In clinical work conditioning procedures are often only part of a treatment program and changes in behaviors other than the target behavior may result from other aspects of the program. Because of this the term *response generalization* should be used cautiously.

The clearest examples of response generalization have been found when severely retarded subjects were trained to use particular linguistic forms.

For example, Wheeler and Sulzer (1970) trained a subject to use a simple stereotyped sentence form, for example, "The man is smoking the pipe," when showed a picture. The subject used the same sentence form for pictures that were not used for training. Similar results have been found in other experiments, and this contrasts sharply with the lack of generalization across settings shown by similar subjects.

6. Effects on Nontarget Behavior

a. *Token economy programs in mental hospitals.* In most studies of operant treatment programs attention is confined to the target behavior. However, a number of studies have compared mental hospital patients in token economy programs with patients given other experimental treatments or routine hospital treatment on variables other than frequency of target behaviors. Token economy subjects have sometimes shown more improvement than other subjects, and seldom, if ever, show less improvement. (For a detailed review see Gripp & Magaro, 1974.) While these results suggest that token economy programs may have a general beneficial effect on mental hospital patients, most studies have suffered from methodological weaknesses.

Many studies have failed to control for nonspecific placebo factors:

1. For ease of administration, patients are often transferred to a token economy ward at the start of the study while control subjects usually remain on the wards on which they have been living. Merely moving long-term patients to new wards, with no changes in program, has been shown to produce changes in ratings of symptoms (Higgs, 1970), and in observed behavior (De Vries, 1968).

2. The token economy ward sometimes has amenities such as rugs, curtains, bedspreads, and clocks, which are not provided on other wards (Heap, Boblitt, Moore, & Hord, 1970), and which may affect the subjects' behavior.

3. The token economy ward frequently has more staff members, and staff members often pay more attention to the patients than those on control wards. Further, the personnel on the token economy ward may volunteer because they are interested in a novel program, or they may be selected because of such interests. In addition as the token program continues and target behaviors change, attendants may show an increase in morale (Lloyd & Abel, 1970).

All of these factors may be conducive to improvement on the part of the subjects.

In addition, in some studies the judges who evaluated the status of the subjects were aware of the conditions to which various subjects had been exposed. Since many of the dependent variables used require the exercise of considerable judgment, failure to use blind evaluation of subjects renders results useless as evidence.

b. Undesirable effects.   Occasional studies report an increase in other undesirable behaviors when attempts are made to control a particular target behavior (e.g., Clark, Rowbury, Baer, & Baer, 1973; Sajwaj, Twardosz, & Burke, 1972). Ordinarily the added undesirable behaviors are brought under control by extending treatment to them as well as to the original target behavior. Most studies do not report undesirable side effects from the use of operant treatments.

7. Summary

Operant treatment programs have been shown to produce changes in a number of different behaviors, in different classes of subjects, and in various settings. However, the programs are not uniformly effective, and estimates of the proportion of cases in which treatment succeeds are not available. The changes are usually confined to the specific setting in which treatment takes place and are seldom maintained after treatment ends. This limitation may be due to the techniques currently used. The fact that operant treatments do not lead to "cures" does not mean that they are not useful. Neither the use of eyeglasses nor injections of insulin are cures, but they allow individuals to function adequately. By the same token operant treatments can produce changes in behavior within particular settings that are valuable in their own right.

D. The Role of Consequences: Research Methodology

1. Conditioning

All operant treatment programs systematically manipulate the consequences of behavior. In many instances these manipulations are only part of a complex program that combines various procedures. For example, Johnston and Johnston (1972) treated severe articulation defects in children, using a token reward system. After a baseline period each child was informed of the defect being treated and given several examples. The subjects were told that a dot would be put on a display board for each correct sound and that they could play during the next play period if they received enough dots. During treatment the contingencies were frequently restated, errors were corrected and correct sounds were always reinforced with a dot and were praised intermittently. A program this complex may have been necessary to produce the desired improvement in speech. Any serious attempt to deal with people's problems must aim at maximizing effectiveness (within certain constraints imposed by cost, time, etc.) rather than at purity of procedure. However, the use of complex programs makes it impossible to know which of the components of the treatment are responsible for treatment effects. It cannot be simply assumed that improvement is due to the use of reinforcement. The situation is further complicated by the fact that experimenters do not always describe their procedures in detail (Comments by Reviewer A, 1973).

Withdrawal, reversal, and multiple-baseline designs were originally developed in order to be able to demonstrate that behavior is controlled by reinforcement contingencies. The use of these designs cannot serve this purpose when the introduction and withdrawal of reinforcement is accompanied by other changes in procedure. To illustrate this point, consider in more detail the study by Wheeler and Sulzer (1970), mentioned in the discussion of response generalization. The subject was shown pictures and asked, "What do you see?" During baseline, responses were recorded without comment. During training to use a complete sentence form, the subject received a token if he responded correctly and was immediately interrupted and the correct form illustrated, if he responded incorrectly. During reversal the same procedure was used to train the subject to omit auxiliary words and articles from his responses. The use of complete sentences increased during the original training, decreased during reversal, and increased again when training in the use of complete sentences was reinstated. As the authors concluded, the results show that the entire procedure could improve language usage. They do not show that reinforcement was responsible for the improvement in whole or in part.

An experimenter can show that reinforcement operations contribute to treatment effects by means of a within-subject design, if he introduces all of the treatment components except for reinforcement at the start of the experiment. Leitenberg, Wincze, Butz, Callahan, and Agras (1970) treated a subject who was bothered by neurotic fears and avoidance of a number of harmless activities. Several avoidance responses were studied separately. For each response, during the first phase of the study the subject was instructed to try to spend more time in the activity and told that this would be therapeutic. In subsequent phases reward conditioning was introduced, then withdrawn, then reinstated. During withdrawal periods, the subject was told to continue to try to increase the amount of time spent in the activity, and withdrawal of the token contingency used for one response was described to him as therapeutic. The length of time spent in each activity increased during conditioning and decreased during withdrawal.

Thus, reinforcement added to instructions was more effective than instructions alone.

When two procedures are combined in a treatment program neither one alone may be sufficient to change behavior, although the combination may be effective. This is illustrated by a series of experiments on cases of anorexia nervosa by Agras *et al.* (1974). The first experiments (described previously under "Research Methodology") found that when privileges were contingent on weight gain, intake of calories increased. In all phases of these experiments a complex "feedback" procedure was used. The subjects counted the number of mouthfuls they ate, were told the number of calories eaten at each meal, were informed as to their daily weight, and plotted mouthfuls and weight on a graph. In a subsequent experiment, subjects did not gain weight nor increase caloric intake during periods of reward conditioning with privileges as reinforcers unless the reward conditioning was accompanied by the feedback procedure.

To demonstrate that conditioning procedures alone can affect target behavior the experimenter must avoid introducing other procedures. An example can be found in work by Barton (1970). She used a combination of reward conditioning and punishment conditioning to train a retarded subject to give relevant and coherent answers to questions about pictures. When she reversed the contingencies, appropriate answers became less frequent. However, such results do not show that conditioning is necessary for changes in target behavior. Winkler (1970) studied the effects of a token economy on mental hospital patients. He found that some behaviors, for example, shining shoes, depended on the receipt of tokens. However, the amount of noise and violence decreased when the token economy was introduced prior to specific treatment for these behaviors. Leitenberg, Agras, Thompson, and Wright (1968) found, with the use of a withdrawal design, that phobic subjects would increase the time spent in feared activities if they were instructed to keep track of the time or if the time was reported to them after each session. Subsequently, Leitenberg, Agras, Edwards, Thompson, and Wincze (1970) found that phobic subjects increased the time spent in feared activities solely as a result of practice even though told that the practice periods were for purposes of assessment rather than treatment.

2. Extinction

To demonstrate that changes are due to extinction procedures requires the same kinds of evidence as in the case of conditioning procedures. When conditioning and extinction procedures are combined it is harder to show the role of extinction since undesirable behavior may be eliminated solely because the absence of this behavior is reinforced. An experimenter could first introduce reward conditioning for omission of the target behavior and then introduce the extinction–conditioning combination. If behavior changed more rapidly after the extinction procedure was added, it would show that the combination was more effective than reward conditioning alone. A complete study of the roles of the two components would require the use of more than one subject because prior experience on one component might change the effects of the other. Although the effectiveness of the "pure" extinction procedure has been demonstrated (e.g., Solomon & Wahler, 1973), the role of extinction in extinction–conditioning combinations has not been studied.

A different question that arises when extinction procedures are used clinically is whether the procedure merits being called "extinction." Does the procedure eliminate reinforcers that formerly maintained the undesirable behavior? To demonstrate that it does requires several kinds of evidence that are seldom offered.

An experimenter who uses an extinction procedure in a treatment program usually starts with a hypothesis as to the nature of the events that are reinforcing the target behavior. Most experimenters record and study the occurrence of these events in order to show that they follow instances of the behavior less often during treatment than during baseline. However, few experimenters have attempted to show that the events that are eliminated in treatment have actually operated as reinforcers to maintain the undesirable behavior.

The first step in such a demonstration is to collect data, prior to treatment, to show that the alleged reinforcer is contingent upon the target behavior. An environmental event is contingent upon a particular behavior if the event is more likely to occur after instances of the behavior than in the absence of the behavior. Data are sometimes presented in such a way that it is impossible to tell whether the alleged reinforcer is contingent on the target behavior. Sometimes it clearly is not. In the study by Herbert *et al*. (1973) (see Section II.C.3, Effects on Target Behavior) most of the mothers were more likely to attend to desirable behavior than to undesirable behavior. Thus, maternal attention was not the source of reinforcement for the undesirable behavior, and it is not surprising that the treatment was not effective. In many of the cases in which either extinction procedures or the differential attention procedure are ineffective the events that were eliminated were not contingent on the undesirable behavior.

Even if the alleged reinforcer is contingent upon the target behavior, it still remains to be shown that it maintained the behavior because it was a consequence of the behavior. It is not enough to show that the rate of the target behavior falls when the behavior is no longer followed by the alleged reinforcer and rises again when the alleged reinforcer is introduced. The same pattern can occur if the events in question instigate the behavior rather than reinforcing it. (See Church & Getty, 1972, for a discussion of this possibility in connection with aversive events.) For example, Pinkston, Reese, LeBlanc, and Baer (1973) used an extinction procedure to treat attacks on other children by a three-year-old. When the teachers no longer administered verbal reprimands after such behavior, the behavior became much less frequent. When the reprimands were reinstituted, the attacks increased in frequency. The reprimands may have angered the child and thus elicited the aggressive behavior. The most straightforward way to test the possibility that an event instigates behavior rather than reinforcing it is to use a control procedure that is analogous to the "truly random" procedure, proposed by Rescorla (1967) as a control procedure to demonstrate classical conditioning. The frequency of the behavior can be compared for periods in which the event is contingent upon the behavior and for periods in which the event occurs with the same frequency but on a random schedule, regardless of the subject's behavior. Unless the behavior occurs more frequently during periods in which the conditioning paradigm is applied than it does during the truly random control periods, one cannot conclude that the event reinforces the behavior in question. A test of this kind has never been applied clinically.

III. THEORETICAL IMPLICATIONS

A. Human Learning

1. Consequences and the Concept of "Reinforcement"

For some decades, the role played by consequences of behavior has been a major theoretical issue in analyses of learning. Psychologists have disagreed with each other about how the effects of past rewards and punishments on future behavior should be explained. Reinforcement theorists believe that certain consequences (reinforcers) automatically strengthen either responses, or stimulus–response associations, and thus directly increase the likelihood of responses that they have followed. Other psychologists believe that consequences affect behavior indirectly. A subject who is rewarded or punished for behaving in a certain way in the presence of a given stimulus, learns the relationship between stimuli, responses, and consequences, because they have been experienced in temporal contiguity (Estes,1969). Learning of these relationships is neither facilitated nor hindered by the consequences of behavior; past consequences affect subsequent performance and not learning. A subject who has been rewarded in a given situation for making response A, and has not been rewarded for making response B, is more likely to repeat response A than response B when that situation recurs, if the subject (a) has learned the consequences of each of these responses, and (b) prefers the reward that followed A in the past to whatever consequence followed B. In short, the consequences of past behaviors function as incentives, that is, the subject selects behaviors that he has learned lead to preferred consequences.

The distinction between these two kinds of explanation can be illustrated by reference to simple Thorndikian experiments. A list of words is read to a subject, who is required to select one of several digits as a response to each word. Immediately after each response the experimenter says "Right" or "Wrong." When the subject has gone through the entire list once, he is given a second trial on which he is asked to give correct responses. Responses that were called "Right" are more often repeated than those that were called "Wrong." Thorndike explained this by the assumption that announcements of "Right" strengthened preceding stimulus–response associations. In contrast, Buchwald (1969) explained these results by assuming that when the subject could recall both the response he had made to a stimulus and the consequence of that response, he would repeat responses that had been called "Right" and would alter responses that had been called "Wrong."

Studies of operant treatment programs show that past rewards and punishments affect subsequent behavior, but this does not tell us why they do so. While the question may not be of prime importance clinically, it is of theoretical importance for our understanding of human learning and of abnormal behavior. Accordingly, we will examine the literature on operant treatment to see if it sheds any light on the issue.

Traditionally, reinforcement theorists have argued that reinforcement strengthens behavior automatically and that its effects do not depend upon a subject's knowledge of the relationship between his behavior and its consequences. For example, the Greenspoon and Taffel experiments (see Section II.A) were interpreted as operant conditioning of verbal behavior partly because the subjects appeared unaware of the response-reinforcement contingencies. Opponents of reinforcement theory have argued that knowledge of the relationship between behavior and its consequences is necessary for rewards and punishments to alter behavior (Buchwald, 1969; Estes, 1969). In many operant treatment programs, the subjects are told what they must do in order to receive rewards or to avoid punishment or penalties. Even when verbal reinforcement is used, experimenters often specify the behavior that is being "reinforced" as part of their praise or approving remarks (Schutte & Hopkins, 1970). While these practices seem more consistent with "information-incentive" theory than with reinforcement theory, their use cannot count as evidence. But partly because of these practices, experimenters have studied the effects on behavior of instructions to behave in particular ways, and of information about the consequences of various behaviors. Examination of the resulting data may help decide between opposing theories.

Bandura (1962) described the verbal conditioning experiments as a problem solving task. He argued that the experimenters' verbalizations served to guide the subject in selecting appropriate responses and suggested that simply telling the subject what responses to make would be more effective than the "reinforcement" procedure. Merbaum and Lukens (1968) conducted an experiment of this kind with college students as subjects and found that subjects who were told to use emotional words in telling stories showed a larger increase in the frequency of usage than subjects who were given social reinforcement for the use of such words. Similar direct comparisons of instructions and consequences have not been reported for subjects from populations of interest clinically. However, several experimenters have studied the effects of instructions and the subsequent effects of rewards without explicit mention of contingencies, using subjects from several different clinical populations and various target behaviors (Agras, Leitenberg and Barlow, 1968; Ayllon & Azrin, 1964; Hopkins, 1968). Typically, the introduction of instructions led to an increase in the target behavior but as time went on either no further gains were seen, or the frequency of the behavior decreased. With the introduction of rewards the behavior again increased in frequency and usually rewards produced bigger gains than instructions. These results suggest that instructions to engage in specific behavior are apt to have only minimal effects upon clinical subjects in the absence of extrinsic consequences.

Some speculation about the reasons for the difference in results between the Merbaum–Lukens experiment and the clinical experiments may be in order. Assume that for each person preferences exist over the set of behaviors possible in a given situation. (Premack, 1965, 1971, has presented the evidence for rather similar assumptions and suggested that the values placed on various behaviors can be measured by noting their frequency of occurrence in the absence of constraints.) Suppose that the effects of instructions to engage in a certain activity depend upon the relative preference of that activity as opposed to the preferences for other activities. If the various behaviors have fairly similar values, subjects may exhibit a nonpreferred behavior much more frequently when asked to do so. If the various behaviors have quite dissimilar values, subjects asked to engage in nonpreferred behavior may show little change and the change may be short-lived unless inducements to engage in the behavior are offered. It appears unlikely that college students have a strong preference for nonemotional words rather than emotional ones, when asked to tell stories. In contrast, there are indications that the clinical subjects greatly preferred other behaviors to the target behaviors. Not only did the target behaviors almost never occur spontaneously but since the absence of these behaviors was considered to pose a clinical problem it is likely that their low rates had continued despite earlier efforts to treat the problem.

Whatever the merits of this speculation, the fact that rewards are more effective in changing the behavior of clinical subjects than mere instructions does not embarrass nonreinforcement views. It simply provides another illustration of the effects of past consequences on subsequent behavior and does not indicate the source of these effects. Behavior might have changed because the subjects had learned that they would be rewarded if they engaged in the target behavior and consequently behaved so as to obtain the rewards.

Experiments have been performed with clinical subjects to test the effects of reward conditioning alone versus the subsequent effects of reward conditioning and information about contingencies. Ayllon and Azrin (1964) worked with chronic psychiatric patients who typically failed to pick up knives, forks, and spoons before getting their food. Giving subjects candy, cigarettes, or extra coffee if they picked up the cutlery had no effect, but the rate greatly increased immediately when subjects were told that they would receive these rewards if they picked up cutlery. Similar results were found by Herman and Tramontana (1971), who used a token reward system in an attempt to increase the frequency with which children in a "headstart" program stayed on their sleeping mats during rest periods. In the Ayllon and Azrin experiment, the subjects seldom engaged in the desired behavior prior to being told of the contingencies, so that there was little opportunity for reinforcement. Rewards without information may have had a much stronger effect in both experiments, if they had been used for a longer period of time. Different results were found by Kazdin (1973b), who studied the effects of token rewards with, and without, information about the contingencies, on the disruptive behavior of children in the primary grades using a between-subjects design. Differences between the groups were not significant, although orderly behavior increased more when the subjects were informed as to the contingencies.

The effects of exposure to complex schedules of intermittent reinforcement and of information about these contingencies have been compared in experiments in which college students were awarded points for pressing a button. Subjects given misleading information about reinforcement schedules tended to show response patterns consistent with this information rather than with the schedules actually used (Kaufman, Baron, & Kopp, 1966). Subjects given no information about schedules showed erratic response patterns, whereas subjects given information produced patterns that resemble those seen in experiments with animals (Baron, Kaufman, & Stauber, 1969).

These results show that rewards without information about response–reward contingencies are relatively ineffective in changing behavior. Thus, they seem more consistent with the idea that knowledge of rewards serves to provide incentives for behavior rather than the idea that past rewards strengthen behavior automatically. Additional evidence pointing in this direction comes from studies (conducted to investigate other issues) which show that when clinical subjects are informed about the contingencies of reinforcement, behavior may change prior to the occurrence of the first reinforcement (Copeland, Brown, & Hall, 1974; Dietz & Repp, 1973; Fjellstedt & Sulzer-Azároff, 1973; Santogrossi et al., 1973). On the last day of the baseline period subjects told that they would be rewarded for specified behaviors in the next session showed marked changes in behavior during the next session, although the promised reinforcers were not dispensed until the end of that session. The finding has considerable generality since subjects in these experiments came from various clinical populations. Since the changes in behavior preceded the receipt of "reinforcers," they cannot be attributed to the effects of the reinforcement. Rather, the mere presentation of information about future contingencies was sufficient to change behavior. This suggests that the promised rewards functioned as incentives, that is, the subjects were motivated to behave differently in order to obtain the rewards. These results also suggest that the crucial aspect of conditioning is that it allows the subject to learn that certain events will occur if he behaves in a given way, and will not occur otherwise.

Reinforcement theorists will undoubtedly offer alternative explanations. For example, they might argue that the subjects had been reinforced in the past when they complied with instructions, and that compliance had generalized in the present instances. The actual reinforcement histories of the subjects is, as usual, unknown, but there is no indication that anything of this kind had occurred in the treatment settings and none of the subjects were reported to have been exposed to systematic conditioning treatments previously. While generalization of compliance across settings is possible, it remains to be demonstrated.

Clinical experimenters have seldom tried to study the reasons why rewards and punishments affect subsequent behavior. In contrast, many laboratory experiments have been addressed to this issue and the results often favor information-incentive interpretations over reinforcement interpretations. For example, Buchwald (1969) studied both the recall and the repetition of responses in a standard Thorndikian experiment and found that subjects recalled wrong responses and right responses equally well but repeated the right ones more often when asked to give correct responses. In other experiments, a modified procedure was used, so that subjects were either told whether their responses were right or wrong immediately after they responded on Trial 1, or were given this information when stimuli were presented on Trial 2. Although immediate reinforcement or punishment should have a greater effect than delayed information, the results were quite the opposite (Buchwald, 1967, 1969). Thus, performance in these experiments depended upon the information that the subject had about the relationships between stimuli, responses, and consequences rather than upon the experimenter's announcements of "Right" strengthening associations between the stimuli and responses that they followed. Additional evidence has been reviewed by Buchwald (1969) and by Estes (1969, 1971).

2. Learning and Operant Treatment Programs

In the prototypical operant conditioning experiment, the experimenter selects a single type of response, for example, the bar press or the key peck, and observes changes in its rate as a function of experimental operations. The behavior that is selected for study is one that the subject is capable of carrying out at the start of the experiment and that will occasionally occur during the baseline period. In fact, the experimenter may train the subject to press the bar or peck the key before the formal experiment begins. Skinner (e.g., 1953) has argued that the laws found in these experiments apply to all operant behavior. He has analyzed a number of behavioral phenomena in terms of the concepts and laws of operant conditioning. But these are verbal analyses based on assumption, not on experimentation. There are experimental results that indicate that even within the experimental paradigm the basic principles of operant conditioning may not apply to all behaviors (see Bolles, 1972, for a review). Accordingly, I will examine the use of operant treatment programs for various types of problems to see what the subjects learn in these various programs, and whether behavioral consequences have different functions in different programs.

A number of programs have been designed to teach autistic or severely retarded children such rudimentary language skills as the use of past tense endings (Schumaker & Sherman, 1970), or the use of plural forms of nouns (Sailor, 1971). Programs designed to teach skills usually use a reward conditioning procedure and make provisions for the subjects to engage in guided and corrected practice. In teaching language skills, subjects are given repeated illustrations of correct usage. Experimenters have not attempted to analyze the roles of these components, experimentally. From the viewpoint of reinforcement theory, procedures such as guided practice and provision of models for the subject to imitate merely serve to produce instances of behavior that can be strengthened by reinforcement. An alternative hypothesis is that the subjects actually learn by practice and by imitation of models and that rewards merely serve to keep the subjects attending to the experimenter and working at the task. An experiment that provides some support for the latter hypothesis has been done by Forehand and Yoder (1974). Both normal and mildly retarded children were trained to put blocks together to make designs. On training designs, the subjects either saw the experimenter assemble the designs (model) or not, and were either given verbal rules for making the design (concept), or not. Each of these variables was independent of the other, so that there were four groups of normal children and four groups of retardates. After training, the subjects were tested on new designs. Within each group of subjects, equal numbers were offered and given candy for each correct design, or praised for each correct design, or neither. On a series of test designs, subjects who had neither been exposed to a model nor been given concepts made more errors than other subjects but the three reinforcement conditions (candy, praise, or neither) had no effect. The quality of performance depended upon training and not upon reward. Forehand and Yoder suggested that reinforcement had no effect upon performance because the subjects were eager to please the experimenter. Alternatively, the puzzles may have been sufficiently interesting and challenging so that the subjects tried to learn how to do them without external inducements being necessary. This explanation might be tested by studying the effects of training with and without rewards on the subsequent performance of subjects who display varying degrees of interest in the task prior to the experiment.

The training given to the subjects in the Forehand and Yoder experiment resulted in better performance on designs that the subjects had not seen previously. The subjects learned a skill, how to assemble block designs, rather than learning specific responses. Treatment programs designed to teach basic linguistic skills sometimes have more limited results.

For instance, Sailor (1971) trained children to use the singular form of nouns to label single objects and the plural form to label pairs of objects. After training, the subjects were able to apply singular and plural forms appropriately to objects not seen during the course of training. However, if the subject was first trained on nouns the plural form of which was an unvoiced s, for example, *cups, hats,* subsequent training on nouns whose plural forms ended in voiced s, for example, *pens, cards,* led to a loss of the plural form that was first learned, although the singular–plural distinction was retained. What the subject learns may be even more specific. Striefel and Wetherby (1973) trained a subject to make appropriate responses to simple commands, such as "drop ball" and "blow on feather." After training, the subject would blow on the feather when told "drop feather," and would drop the ball when told "blow on ball." It seems clear that he had learned to make specific responses to specific stimuli, rather than learning to follow instructions or to comprehend language. What is actually learned in skill-training programs undoubtedly varies with the characteristics of the subjects, the nature of the task to be learned, and variations in training procedures. The influence of these several variables has not, as yet, been systematically studied.

Some treatment programs are designed to change the frequencies of various behaviors that subjects already are capable of exhibiting rather than to teach the subjects new behaviors or new skills. These will be called *motivational programs*. Examples are token reward systems used to increase the frequency of self-care behavior in chronic mental hospital patients, or to decrease the frequency of disruptive behavior in the classroom. Motivational programs seldom make use of guided practice, correction procedures, or the copious examples of the desired behavior that are typical of skill-training programs. However, experimenters sometimes use procedures designed to elicit instances of the behavior that they wish to reinforce. The systematic manipulation of the consequences of behavior very likely plays a major part in producing the changes due to motivational programs.

Although motivational programs are typically described in the language of operant conditioning, they may also be described in other terms. Basically, these programs consist of the establishment of a system of rules that specify the consequences (rewards, penalties, punishments) of various behaviors. (This description also applies to many operant conditioning experiments.) The rules that are established and enforced often increase the probability of behavior that the experimenter regards as desirable and decrease the probability of behavior that the experimenter regards as undesirable. Again, these effects can be described in terms of operant conditioning or in alternative terms. If a subject knows which consequences follow various behaviors, and if he prefers the consequences of desirable behaviors to the consequences of undesirable behaviors, he is apt to engage in desirable behaviors more frequently and in undesirable behaviors less frequently. The experimenter may arrange conditions to produce the necessary preference gradient. For instance, the preference for food can be increased by a period of deprivation. Alternatively, the experimenter may select events that he knows are differentially preferred by the subject and assign them as consequences for different behavior.

Motivational programs often use penalty conditioning or punishment conditioning procedures, and the available evidence suggests that these are as effective in changing behavior as reward conditioning. This is not surprising since presumably all that is needed to have undesirable behavior occur less often is that its consequences should be less preferred than the consequences of alternative behaviors, assuming that the subject knows the consequences of various behaviors.

In the laboratory (and occasionally in the clinic) subjects are not told what the rules (reinforcement contingencies) are. Under these circumstances the subjects must learn how to obtain the preferred consequences, and they can only do this by observing the consequences of various behaviors. It may be difficult for the subjects to learn the rules, since they may be quite complicated. The experimenter may use a complex schedule of intermittent reinforcement, the consequences of the same behavior may depend upon variations in a stimulus which are difficult for the subjects to discriminate, or the precise nature of the behavior that will be rewarded or punished may be difficult for the subjects to determine. Because of this, behavior may change slowly and erratically, and it may come to conform to a distorted version of the rules. When the subjects are explicitly told what the rules are, these problems can be avoided. Behavior may change rapidly because the subjects need not learn the rules by trial and observation. This explains why information about contingencies is more effective in changing behavior than mere exposure to these contingencies. When subjects are informed about the rules, the only thing left for them to learn is that the rules will be enforced, and that they will not be able to obtain the preferred incentives except by engaging in the required actions.

Providing subjects with explicit information about the rules may also lead to a more rapid disappearance of the behavioral changes produced by a treatment program when the treatment program is ended. A subject with clear knowledge of the rules may be better able to realize that the rules are no longer in effect than a subject who is not quite sure as to what the rules are or who has a mistaken notion as to what they are. Resick, Forehand, and Peed (1974) found that nursery school children who had been informed that they would be rewarded for putting toys away quickly on earlier trials performed more slowly on subsequent nonreward trials than subjects who had not previously been informed of the contingencies. However, the effect was not great, and there was only one instance of noncompliance on 1600 trials. Patterson and Teigen (1973) rewarded a delusional subject with tokens for nondelusional answers to questions, and then instituted a withdrawal period during which she was given the tokens before the session, and nondelusional answers were no longer rewarded. She continued to give nondelusional answers to all questions until she was told that she would receive the tokens, regardless of her answers. Following this, she gave delusional answers to all questions. The issue deserves further study.

Occasionally operant treatment programs have been used in cases in which the problem consists of states or events such as fears, depression, or delusional thinking, that although indicated by behavior are not identical with any specifiable set of overt behaviors. In such cases the target of treatment is overt behavior that indicates the underlying state. For example, there have been at least partly successful attempts to eliminate delusional talk by psychotic patients. Liberman, Teigen, Patterson, and Baker, (1973), and Wincze et al. (1972) found that operant treatment programs decreased the amount of delusional talk shown by most of their subjects. However changes were largely confined to the treatment setting and in the experiment by Wincze *et al.* tended to disappear quickly when rewards were withdrawn. The limited nature of the changes and certain incidental observations in these reports suggest that the programs changed verbalization but not belief. (One would expect changed beliefs, unlike changed behavior, to be manifest in various settings.) This indicates that the programs operated as motivational programs rather than teaching subjects realistic beliefs.

B.   Causes and Conceptions of Maladjustment

Behavior therapy arose from the idea that the phenomena traditionally called "psychopathology" or "mental illness" consist of learned responses that are produced and maintained by reinforcement, by classical conditioning, or by some combination of these. This idea was frequently expressed in early articles on behavior therapy, and has been presented in some detail by Wolpe (1958), and by Ullmann and Krasner (1965b, 1969). Davison (1969), and Buchwald and Young (1969) have presented critiques of this view. The authors of recent articles on behavior therapy generally devote more attention to the treatment of behavioral problems and less to speculation about the origins of those problems than earlier writers. Despite this, it seems appropriate to conclude with some discussion of the idea that disordered behavior is the result of conditioning that takes place in the natural environment of the individual. In keeping with the rest of this chapter, the focus will be on operant conditioning.

The belief that conditioning is responsible for disordered behavior arose initially from the view that the laws found in experiments on Pavlonian and operant conditioning applied to all behavior. Thus, it was believed that any stimulus presented contiguously with an unconditioned stimulus would acquire the power to elicit the unconditioned response (or some aspect of it) if the neutral stimulus and the unconditioned stimulus were presented in the optimal temporal sequence, and that any effective reinforcer could be used to strengthen any operant response that preceded it. Recent experiments suggest that neither of these is true (see, for example, Premack, 1965, 1971; Seligman, 1970). For example, rats learn to avoid a food substance with a distinctive taste if they become ill after ingesting the food, but not if the food is paired with electric shock. On the other hand, rats learn to avoid visual and auditory stimuli paired with shock but do not learn to avoid such stimuli if they become ill after contact with it (Garcia & Koelling, 1966). Similarly, food is often used as a reinforcer to condition key pecking in the pigeon. Yet, Williams and Williams (1969) found that pigeons would peck the response key if food was given occasionally, regardless of the subjects' behavior, and that key pecking was maintained at a high rate even if the key pecks delayed the presentation of food. That is, the behavior that led to the delay or the absence of reinforcement was maintained.

While the generality of the laws of conditioning was being undermined by research with animals, the belief that these laws could explain the origin and maintenance of disordered behavior seemed to be bolstered by work with human subjects.

1. The Implications of Successful Treatment

Many experimenters have reported successful treatment of disordered behavior by behavior therapy. With operant treatment procedures the results have largely been limited to changes in target behavior in the treatment setting, but until quite recently the successful aspects of the treatment have been emphasized. These successes have led some psychologists to believe that the disordered behavior that was treated must have been learned.

The argument has been hinted at more often than explicitly stated, but it seems to take the following form: (a) the treatment procedures are based on operant conditioning; (b) their effects on behavior result from the fact that reinforcement strengthens behavior and extinction weakens it; and (c) since the disordered behavior is changed by operant conditioning, it must have been initially produced by operant conditioning. Statement a is only partially true, since operant treatment programs often combine operant conditioning procedures with other procedures. Statement b is a theoretical proposition that actually has two parts. The first part asserts that the changes in behavior produced by operant treatment programs are due to the systematic manipulation of the consequences of behavior. We saw in discussion of the role of consequences that this has seldom been shown to be the case, and that it sometimes is not so. The second part asserts that the consequences of past behavior affect future behavior according to the principle of reinforcement. We saw in discussion of the concept of reinforcement that this is not the only interpretation of the effects of rewards and punishments, and that there is some reason to believe that it is not the best interpretation. However, regardless of the merits of statements a and b, statement c is logically faulty. The success of operant treatment procedures does not imply that the disordered behavior must have been produced and maintained by operant conditioning.

Effective treatment of physical illness or of disordered behavior must either reverse the processes responsible for the disorder or enable the subject to compensate for them. The idea that effective treatment must attack the initiating cause of the disorder presumably comes from the fact that antibiotics cure infectious diseases by killing the microorganisms that are the cause of the disorder. But even in medicine, all effective treatment does not attack the cause. Aspirin relieves headaches, but headaches are not the result of aspirin deficiency. Some aphasics, who have lost the use of language as the result of brain lesions, can be taught to speak and to comprehend language again. The behavioral defect produced by anatomical damage can be remedied by training.

At present, an adequate account cannot be given of the way in which people acquire disordered behavior, or even most normal behavior. It is known that behavior is influenced by a large number of variables. There is no reason to believe that persistent behavior can only be changed by the processes originally involved in its acquisition. If college students were trained to emit plural nouns by a verbal conditioning procedure, the effects of such training could undoubtedly be reversed by asking them to say only singular nouns. The fact that the behavior can be changed by instructions does not imply that it was produced by instructions. Similarly, the fact that a psychotic subject can be trained to speak nondelusionally by reward conditioning does not imply that his delusional speech was either produced or maintained by conditioning.

2. The Experimental Production of Disordered Behavior

One way to obtain evidence for an etiological theory is to show that the agent or process that is hypothesized to cause the disorder actually can do so. For example, an important piece of evidence for the germ theory of disease was Koch's demonstration that animals injected with the bacillus responsible for anthrax developed that disease and died of it (Wightman, 1951). Several experimenters have attempted to demonstrate that even extreme forms of disordered behavior can be produced by operant conditioning.

In an early demonstration, Haughton and Ayllon (1965) used a reward conditioning procedure, with cigarettes as reinforcers, to train a long-term patient in a mental hospital to spend much of her time holding a broom. To demonstrate that this behavior was similar to naturally occurring "symptoms" the authors asked two psychiatrists to observe and evaluate the patient. Both psychiatrists agreed that this was a psychotic symptom and interpreted it in psychoanalytic terms. Davison (1969), and Buchwald and Young (1969) independently offered similar criticisms of this demonstration. The psychiatrists had observed the subject but not talked with her. An important criterion for deciding that unusual behavior is psychotic behavior is the individual's inability to give a rational and plausible-sounding explanation for it. If the subject had been asked why she held the broom and had explained that she was given cigarettes when she did so, her behavior would not have qualified as disordered behavior despite its superficial resemblance to psychotic symptoms.

In a formal experiment, Levitz and Ullmann (1969) used a verbal conditioning procedure to train college students to give unusual responses on a word association task, and to give responses of poor quality on an ink-blot test. Both of these behaviors are sometimes taken as indicators of disturbed thinking, and disturbed thinking is commonly considered to be an important characteristic of schizophrenia. The authors did not claim to have demonstrated that schizophrenia was produced by social reinforcement, but merely argued that their data were consistent with this view.

Although Levitz and Ullmann's claim is modest, their results are too. They did not show that a conditioning procedure could produce a set of behaviors that are indistinguishable from those seen in clinical cases of schizophrenia. Even if the behavior that was produced by training is characteristic of schizophrenia, it is at most a part of the clinical picture. The authors pointed out that it would have been unethical to produce cases of clinical schizophrenia, but (ethics aside) there is no evidence that they could have done so.

Any claim that a disorder can be produced experimentally requires evidence. The type of evidence needed will vary with the nature of the disorder. In the case of schizophrenia, the claim might well be accepted if expert diagnosticians were unable to distinguish experimental cases from natural cases, under blind conditions. Suppose, however, that an experimenter used an operant conditioning procedure to train school children to emit disruptive behavior in the classroom, and claimed that the resulting cases were identical with cases that occurred naturally. Suppose further that teachers could not distinguish between natural and experimental cases by mere observation of behavior. The claim should still be rejected if, for example, admonitions to behave properly produced a permanent change in the behavior of the experimental cases, and not of the natural cases.

Even if an experimenter showed that a conditioning procedure could produce disordered behavior, this would not show that actual cases of the disorder were produced by conditioning. The point was made forcefully by Chapman (1969) in a commentary on the Levitz–Ullmann experiment. He pointed out that the mere fact that operant conditioning procedures were sufficient to produce disturbed thinking did not logically imply that disturbed thinking must necessarily be produced by conditioning procedures. Presumably, college students could be trained by operant techniques to mimic the behavior of patients with general paresis (syphilis of the central nervous system), but no one would seriously suggest that this showed that the behavior of paretics was mainly due to their reinforcement histories. Chapman also noted that a large number of conditions have been shown to produce behavior that resembles the disturbed thinking of schizophrenics. His list of conditions included drugs, sensory deprivation, sleep deprivation, hypnosis, distraction, and insufficient oxygen, among others.

Chapman concluded his discussion with the suggestion that the best way to test the hypothesis that the disturbed thinking of schizophrenics results from reinforcement would be to conduct longitudinal studies. Presumably, such studies would investigate the reinforcement of disturbed thinking in persons who later became schizophrenic and those who did not. The problem is that studies of this kind would be extremely difficult to perform.

3. Operant Treatment Studies

Does the operant treatment literature yield any evidence that bears on the idea that disordered behavior is learned? Writers have argued that the fact that extinction procedures result in a decrease in target behavior shows that the behavior was maintained by reinforcement. Evidence sufficient to support such a claim is seldom, if ever, offered. Yet the idea that disordered behavior is often maintained, at least partly because it is rewarded, is accepted by most clinical workers, regardless of their theoretical orientation. Psychoanalysts, for example, refer to such rewards as "secondary gain"—benefits that the subject receives as a result of his disorder. This serves to show that the idea that rewards maintain disordered behavior is compatible with a broad range of etiological theories, and evidence that it does occur cannot be considered to favor any particular theory.

The evidence reviewed earlier shows that changes in behavior produced by operant treatment programs tend to disappear when treatment ends and are seldom seen in settings other than the one in which treatment took place. In contrast, undesirable behavior is typically extremely persistent and often shows considerable generality over settings. These discrepancies pose an explanatory problem for adherents of the view that problem behavior occurs because it has been reinforced.

Operant theorists assume that undesirable behavior is maintained because it is reinforced by people in the subject's natural environment. This leads to the recommendation that the natural environment should be programmed in order to maintain treatment gains, but why should this be necessary? Most of the problem behaviors that are treated clinically are not seen frequently in the bulk of the population. Presumably this means that the social environment does not reinforce undesirable behavior for all people, but only for some. This idea is plausible, since different people live in different social environments, but cases that strain this explanation have been reported. For example, Wahler (1969b) treated a boy for oppositional behavior and mentioned that neither of his siblings showed the same problem. Billy's behavior was attributed to parental attention reinforcing his failure to obey instructions. Did the parents attend to Billy when he did not obey and ignore the other children under the same circumstances? Was parental attention a reinforcer for Billy but not for the other children, or were there other reasons why only one child showed the problem be-havior? Unfortunately, Wahler did not present any evidence that would allow a choice among these alternatives.

Writers who attempt to explain disordered behavior as a result of the individual's reinforcement history usually invoke the concept of *generalization,* either explicitly or implicitly. Undesirable behavior, presumed to have been acquired by reinforcement in one setting, is assumed to be exhibited in a new setting because the effects of conditioning have generalized. This explanation implies that generalization is a ubiquitous and powerful phenomenon.

Studies of operant treatment programs reveal a curious phenomenon, generalization is apparently asymmetrical. Subjects who come for treatment because their behavior constitutes a problem in a setting such as school or home show the same behavior in the treatment setting. However, the behavioral changes produced by operant treatment seldom generalize to the subjects' natural settings. An extreme example of this asymmetry can be seen in the study of self-destructive behavior in retarded children by Lovaas and Simmons (1969). The subjects had entered the research hospital shortly before the experiments began and prior to the experiments seem to have worn restraints that prevented them from engaging in the destructive behavior. If the behavior had been originally engendered and later maintained by social reinforcement, almost all of the reinforcement must have been received in other settings. Despite this, each of the subjects treated by extinction engaged in thousands of self-destructive acts during the treatment. In contrast, the decrements in rate of responding produced by extinction were seen only in the specific rooms in which the treatments took place.

What is responsible for the apparent asymmetry of generalization? According to operant theory, behavior is strengthened and maintained by reinforcement and weakened by extinction in both the treatment setting and the natural setting. Why then does behavior generalize from one setting and not from the other?

Behavior therapists are advised to "program for generalization" and not to expect it to occur otherwise (Baer *et al.*, 1968). This suggests that the asymmetry represents a technical problem. Perhaps the techniques used in treatment programs tend to hinder generalization, whereas the way reinforcement occurs in the natural environment tends to promote generalization. If so, behavior therapists need to study the natural environment in order to learn how to program for generalization.

However, the apparent asymmetry of generalization may not be due to a technical problem. It may be that operant theory is incorrect, and that the processes that affect behavior in operant treatment programs are fundamentally different from those that affect behavior in everyday life. Operant

treatment programs (except for skill-training programs) use extrinsic rewards and punishments to affect behavior. These may naturally lead to
behavior that is specific to the learning situation. Disordered behavior may
not be merely a consequence of the individual's history of extrinsic reinforcement. It may occur because it is intrinsically preferred to behavior that
is generally regarded as more desirable, and because of this it may have
considerable generality. Disorder may not consist merely of deviant behavior; deviant behavior may reflect deviant values, deviant beliefs, or
peculiar styles of thinking, and these are not necessarily the product of the
individual's reinforcement history.

As yet it is not known why disordered behavior is more persistent and
more general than the changed behavior that is produced by operant treatment programs. These are facts that need to be explained, and undoubtedly
operant theorists will be able to explain them without abandoning the view
that disordered behavior is acquired by operant conditioning. Let us hope
that those who propound these explanations will be as eager to test them by
experiment as they are to propose them.

REFERENCES

Agras, W. S. (Ed.) *Behavior modification: Principles and clinical applications.* Boston:
Little, Brown, 1972.
Agras, W. S., Barlow, D. H., Chapin, H. N., Abel, G. G., & Leitenberg, H. Behavior
modification of anorexia nervosa. *Archives of General Psychiatry,* 1974, **30,** 279–286.
Agras, W. S., Leitenberg, H., & Barlow, D. H. Social reinforcement in the modification of
agoraphobia. *Archives of General Psychiatry,* 1968, **19,** 423–427.
Ayllon, T., & Azrin, N. H. Reinforcement and instructions with mental patients. *Journal of
the Experimental Analysis of Behavior,* 1964, **7,** 327–331.
Ayllon, T., & Azrin, N. H. The measurement and reinforcement of behavior in psychotics.
Journal of the Experimental Analysis of Behavior, 1965, **8,** 357–383.
Ayllon, T., & Michael, J. The psychiatric nurse as a behavioral engineer. *Journal of the
Experimental Analysis of Behavior,* 1959, **2,** 323–334.
Azrin, N. H., & Lindsley, D. R. The reinforcement of cooperation between children. *Journal
of Abnormal and Social Psychology,* 1956, **52,** 100–102.
Baer, A. M., Rowbury, T., & Baer, D. M. The development of instructional control over
classroom activities of deviant preschool children. *Journal of Applied Behavior Analysis,*
1973, **6,** 289–298.
Baer, D. M., Wolf, M. M., & Risley, T. R. Some current dimensions of applied behavior
analysis. *Journal of Applied Behavior Analysis,* 1968, **1,** 91–97.
Bandura, A. Social learning through imitation. In M. R. Jones (Ed.), *Nebraska symposium on
motivation.* Lincoln, Nebraska: University of Nebraska Press, 1962.
Bandura, A., Grusec, J. E., & Menlove, F. L. Vicarious extinction of avoidance behavior.
Journal of Personality and Social Psychology, 1967, **5,** 16–23.
Barlow, D. H. Aversive procedures. In W. S. Agras (Ed.), *Behavior modification: Principles
and clinical applications.* Boston: Little, Brown, 1972.
Baron, A., Kaufman, A., & Stauber, K. A. Effects of instructions and reinforcement feedback
on human operant behavior maintained by fixed-interval reinforcement. *Journal of the
Experimental Analysis of Behavior,* 1969, **12,** 701–712.

Barton, E. S. Inappropriate speech in a severely retarded child: A case study in language conditioning and generalization. *Journal of Applied Behavioral Analysis*, 1970, **3**, 299–307.

Bigelow, G., Liebson, I., & Griffiths, R. Alcoholic drinking: Suppression by a brief time-out procedure. *Behaviour Research and Therapy*, 1974, **12**, 107–115.

Birky, H. J., Chambliss, J. E., & Wasden, R. A comparison of residents discharged from a token economy and two traditional psychiatric programs. *Behavior Therapy*, 1971, **2**, 46–51.

Bolles, R. C. Reinforcement, expectancy, and learning. *Psychological Review*, 1972, **79**, 394–409.

Boren, J. J., & Colman, A. D. Some experiments on reinforcement principles within a psychiatric ward for delinquent soldiers. *Journal of Applied Behavior Analysis*, 1970, **3**, 29–37.

Brackbill, Y. Extinction of the smiling response in infants as a function of reinforcement schedule. *Child Development*, 1958, **29**, 115–124.

Buchwald, A. M. The effects of immediate vs. delayed outcomes. *Journal of Verbal Learning and Verbal Behavior*, 1967, **6**, 317–320.

Buchwald, A. M. Effects of "right" and "wrong" on subsequent behavior: A new interpretation. *Psychological Review*, 1969, **76**, 132–143.

Buchwald, A. M., & Young, R. D. Some comments on the foundations of behavior therapy. In C. M. Franks (Ed.), *Behavior therapy: Appraisal and status*. New York: McGraw-Hill, 1969.

Cayner, J. J., & Kiland, J. R. Use of brief time out with three schizophrenic patients. *Journal of Behavior Therapy and Experimental Psychiatry*, 1974, **5**, 141–145.

Chapman, L. J. Schizomimetic conditions and schizophrenia. *Journal of Consulting and Clinical Psychology*, 1969, **33**, 646–650.

Church, R. M., & Getty, D. J. Some consequences of the reaction to an aversive event. *Psychological Bulletin*, 1972, **78**, 21–27.

Clark, H. B., Rowbury, T., Baer, A. M., & Baer, D. M. Timeout as a punishing stimulus in continuous and intermittent schedules. *Journal of Applied Behavior Analysis*, 1973, **6**, 443–455.

Comments by Reviewer A. Methodological and assessment considerations in applied settings: Reviewers' Comments. *Journal of Applied Behavior Analysis*, 1973, **6**, 532–539.

Comments by Reviewer C. Methodological and assessment considerations in applied settings: Reviewers' comments. *Journal of Applied Behavior Analysis*, 1973, **6**, 532–539.

Copeland, R. E., Brown, R. E., & Hall, R. V. The effects of principal-implemented techniques on the behavior of pupils. *Journal of Applied Behavior Analysis*, 1974, **7**, 77–86.

Corte, H. E., Wolf, M. M., & Locke, B. J. A comparison of procedures for eliminating self-injurious behavior of retarded adolescents. *Journal of Applied Behavior Analysis*, 1971, **4**, 201–213.

Davison, G. C. Appraisal of behavior modification techniques with adults in institutional settings. In C. M. Franks (Ed.), *Behavior therapy: Appraisal and status*. New York: McGraw-Hill, 1969.

DeVries, D. L. Effects of environmental changes and of participation on the behavior of mental patients. *Journal of Consulting and Clinical Psychology*, 1968, **32**, 532–536.

Dietz, S. M., & Repp, A. C. Decreasing classroom misbehavior through the use of DRL schedules of reinforcement. *Journal of Applied Behavior Analysis*, 1973, **6**, 457–463.

Dinsmoor, J. A. Operant conditioning. In B. B. Wolman (Ed.), *Handbook of general psychology*. Englewood Cliffs, New Jersey: Prentice-Hall, 1974.

Dollard, J., & Miller, N. E. *Personality and psychotherapy*. New York: McGraw-Hill, 1950.

Estes, W. K. Reinforcement in human learning. In J. Tapp (Ed.), *Reinforcement and behavior*. New York: Academic Press, 1969.

Estes, W. K. Reward in human learning: Theoretical issues and strategic choice points. In R. Glaser (Ed.), *The nature of reinforcement*. New York: Academic Press, 1971.

Eysenck, H. J. *Behaviour therapy and the neuroses*. New York: Pergamon, 1960.

Flanagan, B., Goldiamond, I., & Azrin, N. Operant stuttering: The control of stuttering behavior through response-contingent consequences. *Journal of the Experimental Analysis of Behavior*, 1958, **1**, 173–177.

Fjellstedt, N., & Sulzer-Azároff, B. Reducing the latency of a child's responding to instructions by means of a token system. *Journal of Applied Behavior Analysis*, 1973, **6**, 125–130.

Forehand, R., & Yoder, P. Acquisition and transfer of conceptual learning by normals and retardates: The effects of modeling, verbal cues, and reinforcement. *Behaviour Research and Therapy*, 1974, **12**, 199–204.

Franks, C. M. Introduction: Behavior therapy and its Pavlovian origins: Review and perspectives. In C. M. Franks (Ed.), *Behavior therapy: Appraisal and status*. New York: McGraw-Hill, 1969.

Fuller, P. R. Operant conditioning of a vegetative human organism. *American Journal of Psychology*, 1949, **62**, 587–590.

Garcia, J., & Koelling, R. A. Relation of cue to consequence in avoidance learning. *Psychonomic Science*, 1966, **4**, 123–124.

Glynn, E. L., Thomas, J. D., & Shee, S. M. Behavioral self-control of ontask behavior in an elementary classroom. *Journal of Applied Behavior Analysis*, 1973, **6**, 105–113.

Greenspoon, J. The reinforcing effect of two spoken sounds on the frequency of two responses. *American Journal of Psychology*, 1955, **68**, 409–416.

Gripp, R. F., & Magaro, P. A. The token economy program in the psychiatric hospital: A review and analysis. *Behaviour Research and Therapy*, 1974, **12**, 205–228.

Haughton, E., & Ayllon, T. Production and elimination of symptomatic behavior. In L. P. Ullmann & L. Krasner (Eds.), *Case studies in behavior modification*. New York: Holt, Rinehart & Winston, 1965.

Heap, R. F., Boblitt, W. E., Moore, C. H., & Hord, J. E. Behavioral-milieu therapy with chronic neuropsychiatric patients. *Journal of Abnormal Psychology*, 1970, **76**, 349–354.

Herbert, E. W., Pinkston, E. M., Hayden, M. L., Sajwaj, E. T., Pinkston, S., Cordua, G., & Jackson, C. Adverse effects of differential parental attention. *Journal of Applied Behavior Analysis*, 1973, **6**, 15–30.

Herman, S. H., & Tramontana, J. Instructions and group vs. individual reinforcement in modifying disruptive group behavior. *Journal of Applied Behavior Analysis*, 1971, **4**, 113–119.

Higgs, W. J. Effects of gross environmental change upon behavior of schizophrenics: A cautionary note. *Journal of Abnormal Psychology*, 1970, **76**, 421–422.

Hopkins, B. L. Effects of candy and social reinforcement, instructions, and reinforcement schedule leaning on the modification and maintenance of smiling. *Journal of Applied Behavior Analysis*, 1968, **1**, 121–129.

Johnston, J. M., & Johnston, G. T. Modification of consonant speech–sound articulation in young children. *Journal of Applied Behavior Analysis*, 1972, **5**, 233–246.

Jones, M. C. A laboratory study of fear: The case of Peter. *Pedagogical Seminary*, 1924, **31**, 308–315.

Kale, R. J., Kaye, J. H., Whelan, P. A., & Hopkins, B. L. The effects of reinforcement on the modification, maintenance, and generalization of social responses of mental patients. *Journal of Applied Behavior Analysis*, 1968, **1**, 307–314.

Kaufman, A., Baron, A., & Kopp, R. M. Some effects of instructions on human operant behavior. *Psychonomic Monograph Supplements*, 1966, **1**, No. 11, 243–250.

Kaufman, K. F., & O'Leary, D. K. Reward, cost, and self-evaluation procedures for disruptive adolescents in a psychiatric hospital school. *Journal of Applied Behavior Analysis*, 1972, **5**, 293–309.

Kazdin, A. E. Methodological and assessment considerations in evaluating reinforcement programs in applied settings. *Journal of Applied Behavior Analysis*, 1973, **6**, 517–531. (a)

Kazdin, A. E. Role of instructions and reinforcement in behavior changes in token reinforcement programs. *Journal of Educational Psychology*, 1973, **64**, 63–71. (b)

Kazdin, A. E., & Bootzin, R. R. The token economy: An evaluative review. *Journal of Applied Behavior Analysis*, 1972, **5**, 343–372.

Kazdin, A. E., & Klock, J. The effect of nonverbal teacher approval on student attentive behavior. *Journal of Applied Behavior Analysis*, 1973, **6**, 643–654.

Koegel, R. L., & Rincover, A. Treatment of psychotic children in a classroom environment: I. Learning in a large group. *Journal of Applied Behavior Analysis*, 1974, **7**, 45–60.

Lazarus, A. A. In support of technical eclecticism. *Psychological Reports*, 1967, **21**, 415–416.

Leitenberg, H. The use of single-case methodology in psychotherapy research. *Journal of Abnormal Psychology*, 1973, **82**, 87–101.

Leitenberg, H., Agras, W. S., Edwards, J. A., Thompson, L. E., & Wincze, J. P. Practice as a psychotherapeutic variable: An experimental analysis within single cases. *Journal of Psychiatric Research*, 1970, **7**, 215–225.

Leintenberg, H., Agras, W. S., Thompson, L. E., & Wright, D. E. Feedback in behavior modification: An experimental analysis in two phobic cases. *Journal of Applied Behavior Analysis*, 1968, **1**, 131–137.

Leitenberg, H., Wincze, J. P., Butz, R. A., Callahan, E. J., & Agras, S. W. Comparison of the effects of instructions and reinforcement in the treatment of a neurotic avoidance response: A single case experiment. *Journal of Behavior Therapy and Experimental Psychiatry*, 1970, **1**, 53–58.

Levitz, L. S., & Ullman, L. P. Manipulation of indications of disturbed thinking in normal subjects. *Journal of Consulting and Clinical Psychology*, 1969, **33**, 633–641.

Liberman, R. P., Teigen, J., Patterson, R., & Baker, V. Reducing delusional speech in chronic, paranoid schizophrenics. *Journal of Applied Behavior Analysis*, 1973, **6**, 57–64.

Lindsley, O. R. Operant conditioning methods applied to research in chronic schizophrenia. *Psychiatric Research Reports*, 1956, **5**, 118–139.

Lipinski, D., & Nelson, R. Problems in the use of naturalistic observation as a means of behavioral assessment. *Behavior Therapy*, 1974, **5**, 341–351.

Lloyd, K. E., & Abel, L. Performance on a token economy psychiatric ward: A two year summary. *Behaviour Research and Therapy*, 1970, **8**, 1–9.

Lovaas, O. I., Schaeffer, B., & Simmons, J. Building social behavior in autistic children by use of electric shock. *Journal of Experimental Research in Personality*, 1965, **1**, 99–109.

Lovaas, O. I., & Simmons, J. Q. Manipulation of self-destruction in three retarded children. *Journal of Applied Behavior Analysis*, 1969, **2**, 143–157.

Maletzky, B. M. Behavior recording as a treatment: A brief note. *Behavior Therapy*, 1974, **5**, 107–111.

Marks, I. M. Flooding (implosion) and allied techniques. In W. S. Agras (Ed.), *Behavior modification: Principles and clinical applications*. Boston: Little, Brown, 1972.

Meichenbaum, D. Clinical implications of modifying what clients say to themselves. In W. McReynolds (Ed.), *Behavior therapy in review*. New York: Jason Aronson, 1974.

Merbaum, M., & Lukens, H. C. Effects of instructions, elicitations, and reinforcements in the manipulation of affective verbal behavior. *Journal of Abnormal Psychology*, 1968, **73**, 376–380.

Moore, B. L., & Bailey, J. S. Social punishment in the modification of a pre-school child's ''autistic-like'' behavior with a mother as therapist. *Journal of Applied Behavior Analysis*, 1973, **6**, 497–507.

Mowrer, O. H. A stimulus-response analysis of anxiety and its role as a reinforcing agent. *Psychological Review*, 1939, **46**, 553–565.

Mowrer, O. H., & Mowrer, W. M. Enuresis: A method for its study and treatment. *American Journal of Orthopsychiatry*, 1938, **8**, 436–459.

O'Dell, S. Training parents in behavior modification: A review. *Psychological Bulletin*, 1974, **81**, 418–433.

O'Leary, K. D., & Drabman, R. Token reinforcement programs in the classroom: A review. *Psychological Bulletin*, 1971, **75**, 379–398.

Patterson, R. L., & Teigen, J. R. Conditioning and post-hospital generalization of nondelusional responses in a chronic psychotic patient. *Journal of Applied Behavior Analysis*, 1973, **6**, 65–70.

Paul, G. L. Outcome of systematic desensitization. I: Background, procedures, and uncontrolled reports of individual treatment. In C. M. Franks (Ed.), *Behavior therapy: Appraisal and status*. New York: McGraw-Hill, 1969.

Pinkston, E. M., Reese, N. M., LeBlanc, J. M., & Baer, D. M. Independent control of a preschool child's aggression and peer interaction by contingent teacher attention. *Journal of Applied Behavior Analysis*, 1973, **6**, 115–124.

Premack, D. Reinforcement theory. In D. Levine (Ed.), *Nebraska symposium on motivation*. Vol. XIII. Lincoln, Nebraska: University of Nebraska Press, 1965.

Premack, D. Catching up with common sense or two sides of a generalization: Reinforcement and punishment. In R. Glaser (Ed.), *The nature of reinforcement*. New York: Academic Press, 1971.

Rescorla, R. A. Pavlovian conditioning and its proper control procedures. *Psychological Review*, 1967, **74**, 71–80.

Resick, P. A, Forehand, R., & Peed, S. Prestatement of contingencies: The effects on acquisition and maintenance of behavior. *Behavior Therapy*, 1974, **5**, 642–647.

Risley, T. R. The effects and side effects of punishing the autistic behaviors of a deviant child. *Journal of Applied Behavior Analysis*, 1968, **1**, 21–34.

Rimm, D. C., & Masters, J. C. *Behavior therapy: Techniques and empirical findings*. New York: Academic Press, 1974.

Romanczyk, R. G., Kent, R. N., Diament, C., & O'Leary, D. K. Measuring the reliability of observational data: A reactive process. *Journal of Applied Behavior Analysis*, 1973, **6**, 175–184.

Sailor, W. Reinforcement and generalization of productive plural allomorphs in two retarded children. *Journal of Applied Behavior Analysis*, 1971, **4**, 305–310.

Sajwaj, T., Twardosz, S., & Burke, M. Side effects of extinction procedures in a remedial preschool. *Journal of Applied Behavior Analysis*, 1972, **5**, 163–175.

Santogrossi, D. A., O'Leary, K. D., Romanczyk, R. G., & Kaufman, K. F. Self-evaluation by adolescents in a psychiatric hospital school token program. *Journal of Applied Behavior Analysis*, 1973, **6**, 277–287.

Schumaker, J., & Sherman, J. A. Training generative verb usage by imitation and reinforcement procedures. *Journal of Applied Behavior Analysis*, 1970, **3**, 273–287.

Schutte, R. C., & Hopkins, B. L. The effects of teacher attention on following instructions in a kindergarten class. *Journal of Applied Behavior Analysis*, 1970, **3**, 117–122.

Seligman, M. E. P. On the generality of the laws of learning. *Psychological Review*, 1970, **77**, 406–418.

Sherman, J. A., & Baer, D. M. Appraisal of operant therapy techniques with children and adults. In C. M. Franks (Ed.), *Behavior therapy: Appraisal and status*. New York: McGraw-Hill, 1969.

Skinner, B. F. *Science and human behavior*. New York: Macmillan, 1953.

Solomon, R. W., & Wahler, R. G. Peer reinforcement control of classroom problem behavior. *Journal of Applied Behavior Analysis*, 1973, **6**, 49–56.

Spielberger, C. D. The role of awareness in verbal conditioning. In C. W. Eriksen (Ed.), *Behavior and awareness*. Durham, North Carolina: Duke University Press, 1962.

Striefel, S., & Wetherby, B. Instruction-following behavior of a retarded child and its controlling stimuli. *Journal of Applied Behavior Analysis*, 1973, **6**, 663–670.

Surratt, P. R., Ulrich, R. E., & Hawkins, R. P. An elementary student as a behavioral engineer. *Journal of Applied Behavior Analysis*, 1969, **2**, 85–92.

Taffel, C. Anxiety and the conditioning of verbal behavior. *Journal of Abnormal and Social Psychology*, 1955, **51**, 496–501.

Thorndike, E. L. Animal intelligence: an experimental study of the associative processes in animals. *Psychological Review Monograph Supplement*, 1898, 2(Whole No. 8).

Thorndike, E. L. *Animal intelligence, experimental studies*. New York: Macmillan, 1911.

Thorndike, E. L. *Human learning*. New York: Century, 1931.

Ullmann, L. P., & Krasner, L. *Case studies in behavior modification*. New York: Holt, Rinehart & Winston, 1965.   (a)

Ullmann, L. P., & Krasner, L. Introduction. In L. P. Ullmann & L. Krasner (Eds.), *Case studies in behavior modification*. New York: Holt, Rinehart & Winston, 1965.   (b)

Ullmann, L. P., & Krasner, L. *A psychological approach to abnormal behavior*. Englewood Cliffs, New Jersey: Prentice-Hall, 1969.

Wahler, R. G. Setting generality: Some specific and general effects of child behavior therapy. *Journal of Applied Behavior Analysis*, 1969, **2**, 239–246.   (a)

Wahler, R. G. Oppositional children: A quest for parental reinforcement control. *Journal of Applied Behavior Analysis*, 1969, **2**, 159–170.   (b)

Wheeler, A. J., & Sulzer, B. Operant training and generalization of a verbal response form in a speech-deficient child. *Journal of Applied Behavior Analysis*, 1970, **3**, 139–147.

Wightman, W. P. D. *The growth of scientific ideas*. New Haven: Yale University Press, 1953.

Williams, C. D. The elimination of tantrum behavior by extinction procedures. *Journal of Abnormal and Social Psychology*, 1959, **59**, 269.

Williams, D. R., & Williams, H. Auto-maintenance in the pigeon: Sustained pecking despite contingent non-reinforcement. *Journal of the Experimental Analysis of Behavior*, 1969, **12**, 511–520.

Wincze, J. P., Leitenberg, H., & Agras, W. S. The effects of token reinforcement and feedback on the delusional verbal behavior of chronic paranoid schizophrenics. *Journal of Applied Behavior Analysis*, 1972, **5**, 247–262.

Winkler, R. C. Management of chronic psychiatric patients by a token reinforcement system. *Journal of Applied Behavior Analysis*, 1970, **3**, 47–55.

Wolf, M., Risley, T., & Mees, H. Application of operant conditioning procedures to the behavior problems of an autistic child. *Behaviour Research and Therapy*, 1964, **1**, 305–312.

Wolpe, J. *Psychotherapy by reciprocal inhibition*. Stanford, California: Stanford University Press, 1958.

Wolpe, J., Salter, A., & Reyna, L. J. *The conditioning therapies*. New York: Holt, Rinehart & Winston, 1964.

Woods, P. J. A taxonomy of instrumental conditioning. *American Psychologist*, 1974, **29**, 584–597.

Yates, A. J. The application of learning theory to the treatment of tics. *Journal of Abnormal and Social Psychology*, 1958, **56**, 175–182.

Author Index

Subject Index

A

Acquired distinctiveness of cues, 151–152
Acquisition,
  performance and, 12
  retention and, 11–13
Actor versus observer hypothesis, 304
Adaptation model, 149
Affect versus information in task
  preferences, 294–295
Afferent neural interaction, 142
Aggression, 303
All-or-none learning, 135–137, 143
  of binary patterns, 194, 195, 196
Analyzers, *see* Stimulus analyzers
Anticipatory errors in sequence predictions,
  188, 189, 192
Arousal, memory and, 264–265
Association, 2
Association model for binary patterns,
  193–196
Associative loss, 22–23
Associative mediation, 43
Associative unlearning, 21, 23
Attending responses, 163
  changes in, 153–154
Attention
  activity and, 263
  differential, 320
  identifiability and, 270
  memory and, 264, 265–266
  selective, 7, 152, 263
Attention model, *see* Attention theory

Attention theory, 149, 151–157, 164
  modified, 160–162
  multiple-look, 161
  two-stage, 152, 153–157
Attitudes, 301
Attributes of stimuli, 28, 53
  encoding of, 28–30
Attribution theory, 8, 302–308,
    see also Causal ascription
Autonomic conditioning, 106
  multiple response phenomena in, 109
Awareness
  autonomic conditioning and, 107
  as cognitive factor, 104
  of contingencies, 107, 333–336, 339
  effect on classical conditioning of, 106,
    107, 108
  functional, 107
  masking tasks and, 107–108
  verbal conditioning and, 315, 332

B

Backup reinforcer, 318
Behavior, dimensions of, 292
Behavior therapy, conditioning in, 309
Behaviorism, 134
Binary prediction, 195–197
Brightness discrimination, 135

C

Causal ascription, 303–304, 306
Choice behavior, 163–164
Choice models, 149–150